Phoenix, Arizona
Jan. 12, 1991

For Drothy and Earl Zarbin
in appreciation of a warm
friendship.
    Julian DeVries

Arizona Medicine Historical Essays

Published by

Heritage Publishers, Inc.
3104 East Camelback Road, #540
Phoenix, Arizona 85016
(602) 468-9143

Copyright © 1990
All rights reserved including those of translation, dramatization, serialization, reprinting, abstraction and international use. This book in its entirety nor any portion or portions thereof may not be reproduced in any quantity whatsoever by any means whether manually, mechanically or electronically or any other method without the express written permission of the copyright holder, The Academy of Medical Science of Maricopa County, Phoenix, Arizona.

Library of Congress Catalog Number: 90-80759
ISBN 0-929690-09-5

Printed in the United States of America

Gilbert S. Reed, M. D., in his Phoenix office shortly after 1900 when he moved to Phoenix from Snowflake, Arizona. The decor is said to be somewhat typical of the times. Note the spittoon in the foreground and the white mice in the cage on the stool under the wall calendar.

Dr. Reed graduated from Hahnemann Medical School in Philadelphia, 1878. His Phoenix office in March, 1914 was at First Avenue and Washington Street. He held Arizona license #35.

Photo courtesy of the Arizona Historical Society, Phoenix, Arizona.

Dedication

This book is lovingly and humbly dedicated to the memory of my late wife
Willa R. Hinkle Kennedy, R.N.

Contents

Table of Photographs	iii
Preface	vii
Foreword	ix
Acknowledgements	xi
The Authors	xiii
Introduction	xiv

I.	Medicine and the American Revolution (1775-1783)	1
II.	Military Medicine	
	Introduction	3
	Army Medicine	4
	Military Medicine on the Arizona Frontier (circa 1870-1880)	5
	Physician Medal of Honor Winners in the Arizona Territory	9
	Arivaca Revisited	10
	Fort Bowie Hospital	13
III.	Early Use of X-Ray by the Military	16
	Portable Military Radiology	19
	No Cathode Rays in Nogales	21
	Early X-Ray Tube Collection	22
IV.	Arizona Mental Health	24
	Introduction	24
	Arizona Mental Health in Territorial Days	25
	Report of the Medical Superintendent of the Insane Asylum of Arizona	33
	Insane Board (Poem)	40
V.	Territorial Doctors—Lawyers of Arizona	41
VI.	Squaw Peak Sketches of Pithy Pioneer Physicians	43
	Four Peaks, Fort McDowell and Wassaja	
VII.	The Summerhayes Trek	47
VIII.	Leonard Wood, M.D.—Some Arizona Territory Influences	52
IX.	Alexander Tuthill, M.D.—Another Pithy Pioneer Physician of Territorial Arizona	60
X.	Public Health	64
	Introduction	64
	The Perils of Public Health	65
	The Public Health and Related Problems Early in the Territory and State	68
	Flying Chlamydospores	76
	"Ditch Fever" in the Salt River Valley	79
	Coccidioidal Infection in Phoenix	81
	"Father of a Disease"	82
	The Balmie Expedition	83
	Smallpox	85
	Goats of Arizona	86
	Skunk Boats—1	88
	Skunk Boats—2	90
	Hansen's Disease (Leprosy)	91
	Hansen's Disease Today	93
	Records of Demise	95
	A Commissioner of Public Health	96
	A Non-Arizona Note on the Search for the Yellow Fever Virus (Hara Kiri by Virus)	98

XI.	The California—Arizona Maneuver Area, World War II	99
	Part I	99
	Part II	107
	Part III	111
XII.	Arizona Physicians	123
	Introduction	123
	Orville Harry Brown, M.D.	124
	Trevor G. Browne, M.D.	126
	Lewis W. Claypool, M.D.	130
	Palmer Dysart, M.D.	132
	Stanford F. Farnsworth, M.D.	138
	Robert S. Flinn, M.D.	141
	R. Lee Foster, M.D.	146
	Ben "Pat" Frissell, M.D.	148
	Francis Henry Goodwin, M.D.	150
	Peter Hayward-Butt, M.D.	151
	Louis Kossuth, M.D., M.P.H.	153
	Robert N. Looney, M.D.	155
	George G. McKhann, M.D.	156
	Ancil E. Martin, M.D.	158
	Frank J. Milloy, M.D.	160
	James R. Moore, M.D.	164
	Adolphus Henry Noon, M.D.	166
	E. Payne Palmer, M.D.	168
	Clarence G. Salsbury, M.D.	174
	W. O. Sweek, M.D.	177
	George C. Truman, M.D.	178
	W. Warner Watkins, M.D.	182
	W. V. Whitmore, M.D.	185
XIII.	Vignettes of Prescott Physicians by Dry Gulch Jake	189
	John B. McNally, M.D.	189
	John W. Flinn, M.D.	189
	Charles Robert Niberg, M.D.	191
	Walter B. Purcell, M.D.	191
XIV.	The First University Chancellor—John C. Handy, M.D.	192
XV.	Origin and Organization of the Arizona Medical Association	196
XVI.	Odds and Ends	204
	Introduction	204
	The Winslow Incident	205
	Not So Ancient History, Oxygen—Tucson 1932	207
	Case of the Century	207
	The Return of the Wapiti to Arizona: A Salute to Robert N. Looney, Pioneer Arizona Physician	208
	Florence Nightingale—Mission Impossible	213
	Florence Nightingale—The Revolting Revisionist Historian Perspective	216
	Blood Banking History in Arizona	218
XVII.	Arizona Medical History Quiz	219
XVIII.	Willa (Billie) Kennedy, R.N.	222
XIX.	Billie—Squaw Peak Notes	224
XX.	Postscript	244

Table of Photographs

John W. Kennedy, M. D.	Back Jacket
Robert E. Kravetz, M. D.	Inside Back Jacket
Mr. Julian DeVries	Inside Back Jacket

Photograph · Page

Photograph	Page
Office of Gilbert S. Reed, M.D.	
Captain John W. Kennedy, M.D.	viii
Second Lieutenant Willa R. Hinkle, ANC	viii
Dry Gulch Jake and Squaw Peak Billie	x
Jake's Cabin	xi
B Troop, 4th U.S. Cavalry	4
Geronimo, Chief of the Chiricahua Apaches	5
Dr. Leonard Wood	6
Dr. B. J. D. Irwin	9
Surgeons' Quarters at Arivaca, World War I	11
A Street in Arivaca, 1975	11
Adobe Ruins at Arivaca	11
The Old School House and Bell at Arivaca	12
Fort Bowie, late 1874	13
Commanding Officer's Quarters, Fort Bowie, 1884-1885	14
Fort Bowie fire damage	14
Fort Bowie fire damage	14
Fort Bowie as it appeared in 1893-1894	15
Fort Bowie in 1894, shortly before it was abandoned	15
Physicist William Konrad Roentgen	16
John Gretzer, Jr., X-ray	17
Private John Gretzer, Jr., after recovery from his head wound	17
X-Ray Apparatus, 1898	18
Marie Curie at the wheel of the famous converted Renault, circa 1914	19
W. Warner Watkins, M.D.	22
Early X-Ray tube collection	23
Non-shockproof X-Ray tubes	23
Arizona Insane Asylum, circa 1890	30
Arizona Territorial Insane Asylum, 1896	32
Patient receiving hydrotherapy at Arizona State Insane Asylum, circa 1920	35
Sleeping accommodations for patients at Arizona State Hospital	35
Nurse preparing treatment equipment at Arizona State Hospital	36
Patients' lavatory at Arizona State Hospital, 1969	36
Patients milking cows at Arizona State Hospital dairy farm	36
Insane Asylum, Phoenix, Arizona, circa 1920	37
Arizona State Hospital office building converted to employees' quarters/canteen	38
Building "A" Arizona State Hospital	38
Aerial view of the Arizona State Hospital farm, 1953	39
Professional staff, Arizona State Hospital, Phoenix, Arizona, 1925	39
Medical staff, Arizona State Hospital, 1963	39
Patients working in field, Arizona State Hospital farm	39
Win Wylie, M.D., J.D.	41
John Taber Alsap, M.D.	42
Fort McDowell—Hospital stewards' quarters	43
Ruins of the headquarters building at Fort McDowell, circa 1965	44
Remains of medical quarters at Fort McDowell	45
Wassaja's grave at Fort McDowell	46
Martha Summerhayes	47
Barney's store at Ehrenberg, 1875	49

Fort Yuma, Arizona, and railroad bridge over the great Colorado, 1877 49
Summerhayes' Quarters at Ehrenberg, 1875 50
Artist Frederic Remington and Lieutenant Jack Summerhayes in Mexico 50
Native dress of the Cocopah and Yuma Indian women in 1875 51
Summerhayes' Quarters at old Camp McDowell, 1877 51
Hospital building, Fort Whipple, 1878 52
Troops from Fort Huachuca near the Mexican border, in 1881 53
Muster of 6th U. S. Cavalry Company at Fort Huachuca, Arizona, 1882 53
Fort Whipple, Arizona Territory, circa 1880 53
5th Memorial Cavalry on Parade Fort Huachuca, 1973 54
Rough Riders 1898 54
The Rough Rider statue, Prescott, Arizona 55
Guard House—Fort Whipple, Arizona, circa 1970 55
Apache Scouts—U. S. Service 1860s 56
Party of packers and Indian guides detailed by General Miles 57
Postoperative sketch, skull 58
Joseph Madison Greer, M.D., of Phoenix 58
Alexander M. Tuthill, M.D. 61
Editorial page cartoon by Pulitzer Prize Winner, Reg Manning 61
Bullet Proof Hotel, Naco, Arizona, undergoing demolition August 1973 62
Allied officers during inspection of 40th Sunshine Division, March, 1919 62
Entrance to Fort Tuthill near Flagstaff, Arizona 63
Lt. Gen. Louis B. Hershey & Maj. Gen. A. M. Tuthill at Selective Services HQ 63
El Paso and Southern Railroad Depot, Douglas, Arizona Territory 67
West Main Street in Benson, Arizona 68
Robert Nelson Looney, M.D. 69
United Eastern Mine in Oatman, Arizona 69
William Duffield, M.D. 71
Thomas Peyton Manning, M.D. 71
Arizona State Teachers' College 72
Library of Arizona State Teachers' College 73
X-ray of lungs, showing "coin-like shadow" on right lung 77
The "Flying Chlamydospore" 78
"Big C" (Chlamydospore) 78
The home of E. W. Phillips, M.D. 80
Nelson Charles Bledsoe, M.D. 85
Goats on the Apache Indian Reservation 86
"Gadabout" striped skunk 89
Indian Camp Plantation in Louisiana in 1894 92
Aerial view of Carville, Louisiana hospital 92
Louis Kossuth, M.D. 96
Flight Surgeon Colonel Louis Kossuth, M.D. 97
Flight Surgeon Major Louis Kossuth, M.D. 97
Albert Perkins Batchelder 98
General McNair and General Patton 99
General Patton, 1943 100
General Patton with the troops 101
Map of main areas of Desert Training Center 102
C-AMA Installations 102
Camp Coxcomb, California, 1982 104
Site of a mess kitchen at Camp Hyder, Arizona 109
80th Division Medics "Digging In," Camp Laguna, Arizona, 1943 109
Headquarters POW Camp, Florence, Arizona 112
POWs arrive at Florence, Arizona, WW II 112
Camp Bouse, Arizona, today from the air 116
150th Station Hospital, Camp Bouse, Arizona, 1943 116
Rock monument, Butler Valley, Camp Bouse, Arizona, May 21, 1981 117
Chow Line, Field Problem, 3rd Armored Division, Iron Mountain, California 119

Medical Detachment 315 Engineers, 90th Division Desert, 1943	119
Orville H. Brown, M.D.	125
Trevor G. Browne, M.D.	127
Dr. Browne with a Teddy Bear	128
Lewis B. Claypool, M.D.	131
Palmer Dysart, M.D.	133
Palmer Dysart, M.D., U. S. Army Air Force, 1944	135
Stanford F. Farnsworth, M.D.	139
Robert S. Flinn, M.D., 1937	142
Dedication of the Robert S. Flinn Library, Maricopa County Medical Society	143
Doctors R. S. Flinn, E. A. Born, and D. W. Melick, early 1980s	144
Airman Robert S. Flinn, Royal Canadian Air Force, WW I, 1916	145
R. Lee Foster, M.D.	147
Ben "Pat" Frissell, M.D.	149
Francis H. Goodwin, M.D.	150
Peter Hayward-Butt, M.D.	152
Colonel Louis Kossuth, M.C., U.S.A.F.	154
Doctor Looney at his desk shortly after announcing his retirement, circa 1950	155
George G. McKhann, M.D.	157
Ancil E. Martin, M.D.	159
Frank J. Milloy, M.D.	161
James Russell Moore, M.D.	165
Adolphus H. Noon, M.D.	167
E. Payne Palmer, Sr., M.D.	169
Clarence G. Salsbury, M.D.	175
Dr. John Kennedy presents a M. C. M. S. plaque to Dr. Clarence G. Salsbury	175
Navajo People present Dr. Salsbury a retirement plaque, 1961	176
Clarence G. Salsbury, M.D. and "Dry Gulch Jake," 1969	176
George C. Truman, M.D.	179
W. Warner Watkins, M.D.	183
St. Luke's Home at Phoenix in 1907	183
St. Luke's Chest Conference, circa 1940	186
William V. Whitmore, M.D.	186
John B. McNally, M.D.	189
John W. Flinn, M.D.	189
The Flinn Sanatorium laboratory in Prescott, 1987	190
The Flinn residence at Willow and Guerney Streets in Prescott, 1987	191
John C. Handy, M.D.	192
Dr. George E. Goodfellow and Dr. John C. Handy	195
Old grave sites at Canyon Diablo	205
Remains of trading post at Canyon Diablo	205
Site of the Canyon Diablo Station on the Santa Fe railroad	206
Santa Fe railroad tracks and cemetery at Canyon Diablo	206
Sans pinnae (without ears)	207
Robert N. Looney, M.D., Arizona Commissioner of Health, 1912	208
An Elegant Elk, a descendent of the Looney transplant program, 1914	208
George Wiley Paul Hunt, Governor of Arizona	209
Letter from Governor Hunt to Dr. Looney	209
Letter from Dr. Looney to Governor Hunt	210
Letter from Governor Hunt to Dr. Looney	211
Remnants of a wagon used to haul elk from Winslow to the Chevron Creek, 1912	212
Florence Nightingale	213
St. Thomas' Hospital, built in London in 1868-71	214
First Lieutenant Willa R. Hinkle, ANC	223
First Lieutenant Willa R. Hinkle, ANC	224
Drill Uniform, circa 1942	226
Lieutenant Hinkle in England, WW II	226
Lieutenant Hinkle in England, WW II	227

The Nurses' Limo: "The Good Old Army 6 x 6 Truck"..227
U. S. Army nurses of the 39th Evacuation Hospital..227
39th Evacuation Hospital..234
First Lieutenant Willa R. Hinkle, ANC, being awarded the Legion of Merit 241
Finis..244

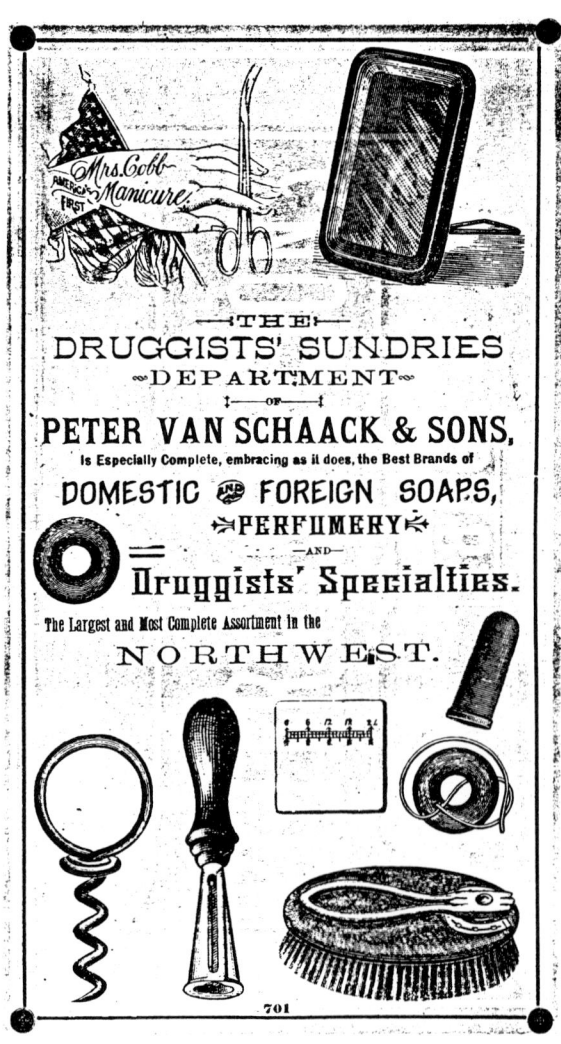

Preface

What you will read in the pages that follow this brief introduction is a history of medicine in Arizona. But it is not a history in the academic sense of the word—a neatly ordered chronology of places, events and people—but rather an informal and often whimsical and humorous retrospective glance along dusty desert trails, treacherous mountain passes, lonely military outposts, ranches, cow towns and mining communities that was territorial, and for a time, post-territorial Arizona.

Most of the material presented herewith was written by John W. Kennedy, M.D. and his wife, Willa Kennedy, R.N., respectively self-identified in these pages as Dry Gulch Jake and Squaw Peak Billie. I will leave to Doctor Kennedy an explanation of those appellations elsewhere in this book.

A portion of this volume, incidentally, has nothing to do with the history of medicine in Arizona. Written by Mrs. Kennedy (Squaw Peak Billie) it relates instead, with wry humor and penetrating insight, the adventures of an American army nurse in Europe during World War II, in which Doctor Kennedy also served with distinction.

Much of the material by both Kennedys originally appeared in *Roundup*, the official publication of the Maricopa County Medical Society in Phoenix and with whose gracious permission it is reproduced here. As the reader will quickly discern, no attempt except in its very broadest sense, has been made to divide the book chronologically, geographically or topically. To do so, in the opinion of the editors, would detract from its unique flavor, spirit and originality.

Admittedly, there may be gaps in some of the material recorded herein by Doctor Kennedy, but research shows that the substances with which to fill them are lost in the mists of time. These few hiatuses, however, in no way detract from the charm, wit and overall readability and worth of the book. Much remains of the spirit, resourcefulness and aura of pioneer medicine in Arizona. The story of Carlos Montezuma, M.D. (Wassaja) is especially intriguing.

The list of Arizona physicians who have left their marks on the scrolls of the state's medical history is a long and distinguished one. The reader will encounter many of these pioneers in the pages that follow, their exploits chronicled therein by retired Phoenix radiologist John W. Kennedy, M.D. Other than some minor corrections in spelling, punctuation, syntax and sundry other quibbles, the editor has not disturbed Doctor Kennedy's prose. That has been left pretty much as he wrote it to preserve the originality and flavor of a man who could have made his mark in literature had he not opted for a career in medicine.

Like Doctor Kennedy, Orville Harry Brown, M.D. of whom you will read herein, was a prolific writer and could have been a crusading journalist had he not decided to become a physician. His home was at 2025 North Central Ave. in Phoenix. With some periodic remodeling, the structure later became the headquarters of the Maricopa County Medical Society with the redoubtable Fred Mitten serving as executive secretary. The edifice served as the county society's home until near the close of 1986 when the society moved into its much needed new and larger quarters at 326 E. Coronado Road.

Together with the late W. Warner Watkins, M.D., Brown, like Kennedy, collected data on early day Arizona physicians. The material, well organized and permanently bound, reposes in the special history section in the library of the College of Medicine at the University of Arizona in Tucson. Other materials, such as newspaper clippings subsequently have been added in bound form to the collection so that now it is a multi-volume set of memorabilia.

J. DeV.

Captain John W. Kennedy, M.C.
Consultant in Radiology to General George Patton's Third Army, European Theater of Operations, World War II

Second Lieutenant Willa R. Hinkle, ANC
Army Nurse Corps, 1942

Foreword

I arrived in Phoenix, Arizona in 1949 to practice radiology with W. Warner Watkins, M.D. His knowledge of the state's medical history was little short of phenomenal. Arizona was still a Territory when Doctor Watkins settled in Morenci, a mining community, as a mining company physician. Among his contemporaries were E. Payne Palmer, Sr., M.D. who arrived in 1900 and was known as the dean of Phoenix surgeons. Others were Joseph Madison Greer, M.D., a veteran of both World Wars and a co-founder of Mesa Southside Hospital, General Alexander M. Tuthill, M.D., the most accomplished soldier-physician in Arizona, and a host of others.

The trials and triumphs of the practice of medicine in the state as these men lived and related it was like experiencing the closing of a medical era. Later, when electronic recorders became portable, I began interviewing some of these medical pioneers. It was, at best, a feeble effort. Many had already passed away. But I wrote what I could about them and the *Journal of the Arizona Medical Association* and *Roundup*, the official publication of the Maricopa County Medical Society were kind enough to publish them. Most of them, in part re-edited, form the contents of this book. While most of this book related to Arizona's medical history, the reader will note that some of it deals with important medical events elsewhere.

J. W. K.

Dry Gulch Jake and Squaw Peak Billie

Acknowledgements

It would be less than candid not to acknowledge the major role in the production of this book played by Robert Kravetz, M.D., a Phoenix gastroenterologist who envisioned, nurtured and encouraged this project to fruition.

Himself a history buff in that he is a collector of medical and pharmaceutical memorabilia, Doctor Kravetz embodies that rare combination of human traits being both a visionary and a doer as the emergence of this book from a morass of material amply attests.

I wish also to express my sincere thanks to Julian DeVries, confidant and long-time medical editor (now retired) of *The Arizona Republic* for his advice, editorial guidance and introductions to the book and its chapters.

My deep appreciation also goes to Delbert Hensley for his photographic expertise and to Judi Cook, long-time friend and typist who lovingly prepared the manuscript.

And last, but by no means least, I am most indebted to the Robert S. Flinn Foundation of Phoenix and the Maricopa County Medical Society for their staunch support without which this volume would never have seen the light of day.

Finally, any errors of fact, historical or otherwise, are the sole responsibility of the author.

J. W. K.

Jake's Cabin

The Authors

JOHN W. KENNEDY, M.D.

Twenty-mile hikes as a first lieutenant in the U.S. army medical corps during World War II prompted Doctor Kennedy to become a board certified specialist in radiology. But it didn't work. He still had to take the hikes.

After earning his M.D. degree at Harvard University School of Medicine in 1933, Doctor Kennedy was commissioned as an assistant surgeon in the U.S. Public Health Service, a rank equivalent to first lieutenant in the army. His interest in radiology was kindled by an assignment to the X-ray department of the U. S. Marine Hospital on Staten Island in New York.

Resigning from the public health service in 1939, Doctor Kennedy entered the private practice of general medicine in West New York, New Jersey until World War II, a first lieutenant's commission and assignment as consultant in radiology to the surgeon of General George S. Patton's Third Army in Europe.

After the war he returned to the private practice of medicine in West New York, but greener pastures called and in 1949 joined the Veterans Administration in Denver, Colorado. There he married Willa R. Hinkle, R.N., whom he had met during his tour of duty in Europe.

By the end of that year, the couple moved to Phoenix, Arizona where Doctor Kennedy practiced radiology until his retirement in 1973.

In Phoenix, the Kennedys joined the army reserves from which he retired in 1969 with the rank of colonel and she with the rank of lieutenant colonel. Mrs. Kennedy passed away in 1984.

WILLA R. (HINKLE) KENNEDY, R.N. (1910-1984)

If an exception proves the rule, then a law of physics that opposites attract each other is correct. The exceptions are John and Willa Kennedy. Each was born on a Missouri farm, although at opposite ends of the state. Each suffered financial hardships during their early years and both chose medicine as their careers.

In addition, they shared a sense of humor and the ability to express it that was a source of never ending delight to all who knew them. That humor illuminates the accounts herein of Mrs. Kennedy's (Squaw Peak Billie) experiences as an army nurse in Europe during World War II and enlivens the writings of Doctor Kennedy under the pseudonym of Dry Gulch Jake.

Doctor Kennedy explains the origin of those names thus: "Early on we acquired a very tired World War II cast-off army jeep. Since Billie and I both were enamored of desert trails and washes, many hours were spent rescuing the jeep from dry washes and desert sand. Billie thought my efforts in those directions were less than effective and dubbed me Dry Gulch Jake. We lived at that time in a two-by-four house just to the west of Squaw Peak. So I, in turn, dubbed her Squaw Peak Billie."

Willa R. Hinkle, the youngest of seven children, was five years old when their father died, leaving his brood in dire financial straits. Economic necessity broke up the family, but Willa remained with her mother. After graduation from high school, she supported herself and her parent by working in a factory but labor unrest and the Depression showed her the handwriting on the wall. With no small sacrifice on her part, she became a nurse.

Pearl Harbor brought an end to her first nursing job as office manager, nurse assistant and surgical nurse to a Flint, Michigan eye, ear, nose and throat specialist. She entered the Army Nurse Corps in 1942 as a second lieutenant and, after many assignments, was detailed to General George S. Patton's Third Army in Europe, where she met Doctor Kennedy.

They were married in 1949 in Denver, Colorado following her resignation from the army. But that did not end her military career. Moving to Phoenix in 1950, the couple joined the army reserves and were assigned to an army hospital where Willa Kennedy became chief nurse and the only woman reservist in Arizona to achieve the rank of lieutenant colonel.

J. DeV.

Introduction

I would like to share with you the story of how and why this book came to be published. While doing research on the subject of Arizona Territorial Medicine for a medical museum exhibit, I came across Dr. Kennedy's excellent article on the subject. It was then that I recalled the many other articles that had been written by him that had appeared in *Arizona Medicine* and the Maricopa County Medical Society bulletin—*Roundup*. With the able assistance of the Society's librarian, Sue Newell, I was able to obtain a bibliography of his writings and copies of the nearly 100 articles, brief biographies and other items that he had penned.

It became apparent to me that this material would be lost forever and remain buried in dust-covered journals and bulletins never to be read or appreciated by future generations. As a medical historian, I felt obliged to attempt to preserve these writings by collecting them into a single published volume.

An application was made to the Flinn Foundation for funding to underwrite the publication of this material and it was approved. It is of interest to note that Dr. Robert Flinn, the founder of the foundation, was a good friend of Dr. Kennedy and would have very likely heartily endorsed this project. Additional support from the Maricopa Medical Society Foundation was necessary, and tzheir generous grant brought funding to a level suitable for publication. Without this broad-based support, the project never would have been completed.

This material is a potpourri of medical articles, biographical sketches and short stories as they relate mainly to Arizona medicine and those early physicians and practitioners who made it all possible. This is in no way a complete history of Arizona medicine but rather a brief glance into the Territory's and state's medical history. Some of the material does not relate to Arizona at all, but is included because it is part of Dr. Kennedy's writings and makes for interesting reading. Each section should be read and enjoyed on its own merits.

Dr. Kennedy wished that his wife's World War II nursing experience be preserved also and presented here for our reader's pleasure. It serves as a fitting tribute to a dedicated member of the nursing profession who so eloquently shared her military experiences with us.

My role has been that of a facilitator to ensure that these writings be preserved for Arizona physicians, researchers, and the general public. It was undertaken as a labor of love, and I hope that I have brought some pleasure into the lives of two delightful elderly gentlemen who have been friends for many years—John Kennedy and Julian DeVries.

R. E. K.

I.

Medicine and the American Revolution 1775-1783

In the 18th century, Occidental medicine had been rescued from the barber surgeons, but just barely. Things were no better than when Ambrose Pare "dressed the wounds and God healed them." What American physicians may have lacked in effective medical and surgical methods they did not lack in their acceptance of active participation in all matters of public office and public duties.

D. S. Sabine has summarized for Massachusetts that the provincial Congress of 1774-1775 had twenty-three doctors. Four physicians were signers of the Declaration of Independence, Doctors Josiah Bartlett and Matthew Thornton of New Hampshire, Benjamin Rush of Pennsylvania and Doctor Lyman Hall of Georgia. Two physicians commanded troops. They were John Warren at Bunker Hill and Hugh Mercer who was killed in action at Princeton. (1)

In 1775 there was but one medical society—New Jersey, organized in 1766. Massachusetts became organized before the close of the war.

Variolation or inoculation for smallpox was the only preventive disease measure used. Jenner and his milkmaid-cowpox vaccination did not appear until 1798.

In a barrel of books to be discarded from a hospital library in Norfolk, Virginia in 1933, I rescued what is still the most definitive description of the physicians of the Revolution and their time. (2)

Doctor James Tilton of Delaware, a hospital surgeon, later surgeon general, 1812-1814, ticked it off this way: "The French make greater hospitals than the English, the English than the Germans; yet the French lose more men from camp diseases than the English, and the English more than the Germans and I may add the Americans have outdone all their predecessors in the pomp and extravagance of their hospital arrangements, and have surpassed all other nations in the havoc thereby committed on their fellow citizens."

As elsewhere—in all the world—smallpox was endemic in America. In 1776 John Adams called it "this distemper—the King of Terrors of America this year." The natural disease killed one-sixth of its victims and variolation, using the virulent virus from a patient, killed about one in three hundred. So the proponents of this variolation had a rough going. Inoculation smallpox was spread to many more people and the total number of deaths was greater but the percentage of people involved was less.

With the threat of the presence of epidemics in the crude army camps, inoculation became necessary and it was so directed by the authorities. The recruits were usually inoculated in the spring and fall when it was thought that they were less likely to succumb. Later, Congress ordered, February 12, 1777, General Washington "to consult on the propriety of causing all troops in his Army, who have not had smallpox, to be inoculated." (2)

It was never entirely clear why inoculated smallpox was much less fatal than the natural disease. The virus was taken from young and healthy individuals, on the 12th to the 13th day of their disease, and it possibly was taken from milder cases.

The hospitals were makeshift and seldom more than a place for troops to acquire camp diseases. For an army in the field, a fixed general hospital was started in any available building. Each regiment had a smaller hospital and these were many times built with logs and canvas or anything that happened to be readily available.

One observer noted: "The regimental hospitals were always full, yet usually well conducted. Acute disease rarely exceeds a fortnight in duration; from general hospitals few returned in less than three months." A high percentage never returned. Washington, always plagued by inefficient and inexperienced officers and troops, fared little better with his medical department. In the very beginning, Doctor John Warren of Boston was considered for the post of director and chief physician but he refused but fought at Bunker Hill serving as a major general of the line of the Massachusetts militia. The choice then fell to Benjamin Church. He was suspected of giving aid and information to the British. He is said to have tipped off British General Gage where John Hancock and Sam Adams could be captured but was foiled at Concord and Lexington. He was arrested and jailed but allowed to leave the country.

Congress then appointed Doctor John Morgan of Philadelphia, but he was given no support and dismissed, and succeeded eventually by Doctor William Shippen, Jr., a schoolmate and friend who had opposed Morgan's methods. Shippen met the same fate and was replaced by Doctor Benjamin Rush. Rush was suspected of participation in the "Conway Cabal," a fruitless plot to relieve Washington of his command, stemming from a letter written by General Thomas Conway to General Horatio Gates, and Washington let his opinion be known. Rush then rushed back to civilian life.

Finally, Doctor J. Cochran of Philadelphia was appointed and served until the Treaty of Paris ended the war. Casualties of the Revolution are difficult to establish in numbers. One estimate is 250,000 men served, 4,000 were killed, 6,000 wounded with 60,000 deaths from disease, for a total of 70,000 casualties. Six from disease to one from battle wounds—that seemed to be the going rate.(2)

Probably, Doctor James Thatcher spoke for all who serve the sick and wounded in war: "This day (January 1, 1783) I close my military career and quit forever the toils and vicissitudes incident to the storms of war." But there are still those who believe that "war is the greatest adventure of life, if you survive it physically intact."

References:

1. Sabine, D. S., *American History*, Illustrated. Vol. VII, pp. 36-44, 1973.
2. Duncan, Louis C., *Medical Men in the American Revolution*, Army Medical Bulletin, Number 25, 1931, 414 pps.

II.

Military Medicine

Introduction

Military medicine in early Arizona left much to be desired by doctors and patients alike. Food and medical supplies more often than not were inadequate; buildings and tents used as hospitals were ramshackle at best and woefully lacking both as to space and sanitation. It was indeed a hardy breed of soldiers and the doctors who treated them who garrisoned the makeshift camps and forts scattered across the deadly Arizona desert, made even more so by marauding bands of Indians.

It was no secret among the world's military powers that disease and infection claimed more lives than did the flesh and blood enemy and the military campaigns in Arizona were no exception. Indian arrows, of course, took their toll, compounded by the infections that followed arrows, as well as gunshot wounds. But it was the diseases, against many of which in those days doctors had no defense, as well as the bites and stings of desert predators that weighed heavily on the debit side.

Dysentery, malaria, smallpox, syphilis were common as was malnutrition. The latter owed its presence not only to inadequate food supplies, but even more to lack of refrigeration, sanitation and the generally poor quality of the army mess, which made an adequate diet impossible.

Napoleon is credited with having said that an army travels on its stomach and history is replete with mess hall gripes. Such gripes in early day Arizona were more than justified. They are almost completely unwarranted today even though as late as World War II the following Biblical criticism of military cuisine appeared on signs posted in many mess halls from coast to coast.

The quotation is from Hebrews, 13:8 and reads: "Jesus Christ the same yesterday, and today and forever." In some installations, only the Biblical reference appeared on the sign, prompting the more inquisitive to do a little research to learn of the quotation's applicability to the monotony of the army's mess. Also aptly descriptive of the military menu, according to many who had no alternative but to partake of it, was the last word in the preceding sentence.

Although many Arizona physicians have served and continue to serve their country well and honorably, perhaps the most colorful of them all was Major General Alexander Tuthill, M.D. who served with General John Joseph "Black Jack" Pershing on the U.S.-Mexican border in 1916 during a fruitless search for the Mexican bandit and revolutionary, Pancho Villa who earlier had invaded American territory in New Mexico.

Two years later, "Tut" again was with Pershing, this time as a member of the American Expeditionary Force in France during World War I. In both campaigns, Doctor Tuthill functioned as a military commander rather than as a physician. He continued his military role after the first World War and during World War II in the Arizona National Guard.

While not directly concerned with the status of military medicine in Arizona, a small booklet entitled "Patton's Desert Training Center," co-authored by Doctor Kennedy who holds the rank of Colonel in the army reserves, with then (World War II) Lieutenant Colonel John Lynch and civilian military historian Robert L. Wooley, holds much that may be of interest.

Excerpts from its pages are reprinted herein with permission from its publishers, the Council on America's Military Posts of Fort Myer, Virginia. The booklet details the history of the ill-fated Desert Training Area, later re-named the California-Arizona Maneuver Area, briefly commanded by General George S. Patton. Its mission was to train American troops, especially tank units for battle in North Africa.

One aspect of that training involved a highly secret development called the Canal Defense Light Project, first proposed by a British naval officer during World War I but never utilized. Resurrected for use in the African campaign of World War II, the project was developed at Camp Bouse, Arizona, a remote, desolate region in Butler Valley in western Arizona. It consisted of intensely bright white and colored lights flashed from tank turrets to blind and confuse the enemy. It worked for a little while but then the Germans equipped their tanks with light filters to render the development useless.

But while it lasted, the secrecy surrounding what was going on at Camp Bouse was on a par with that cloaking the Manhattan Project of atomic bomb fame.

J. DeV.

Army Medicine

Army medicine on the Arizona Frontier was, for the time and place, quite rudimentary: The Fort Bowie Hospital in southern Arizona, Fort McDowell, 15 miles to the east of Phoenix, the classic description by Martha Summmerhayes, who accompanied her husband to Arizona Territory in 1870s-80s, Leonard Wood, M.D. who accompanied Captain Lawton into the Sierra Madre Mountains of northern Mexico on the last Geronimo campaign in 1885, Arivaca occupied by cavalry on the border WW I and the account of Doctor Prentiss Hyder who was assigned as physician to the post.

Alexander M. Tuthill, M.D. was probably the most colorful Arizona soldier physician—on the border and with Pershing and the American Expeditionary Force, World War I. Some medical and non-medical notes about the California-Arizona Desert Training Center World War II 1942-44. At least four army training camps were on the Arizona side, Laguna near Yuma, Camps Horn and Hyder between Yuma and Phoenix, and Camp Bouse—a secret camp near Bouse, Arizona.

It was during WW II that the widespread evidence of coccidioidomycosis, Valley Fever, was really elucidated. One outbreak occurred at Florence, Arizona where a prisoner of war (POW) camp, principally German POWs, was located. Another outbreak was at Sacaton, Arizona where Japanese civilians were detained. But it was the diseases, infections, inadequate nutrition, poor

B Troop, 4th U. S. Cavalry, led by Capt. Henry W. Lawton, left Ft. Huachuca, May, 1886 in a last, desperate attempt to capture Geronimo. Indian scouts led the way in what was to be a harrowing ordeal before the elusive Geronimo finally surrendered many months later. History records that as the troops left, the army band played the then popular tune, "The Girl I Left Behind Me." The reason for that selection is not explained.

housing and a total lack of adequate sanitation on the Arizona frontier which concerns us here.

Deplorable and intolerable though such conditions were, with their high morbidity, mortality, considering the circumstances, was surprising low. These statistics bear ample testimony not only to the heartiness of the military personnel of that era, they speak eloquently of the skill and dedication of the army physicians who took care of them. With little more than the most primitive medical and surgical facilities at their command, they fulfilled their missions in the best traditions of Aesculapian medicine. We salute them.

Military Medicine on Arizona Frontier (circa 1870-1880)

Following the close of the Civil War, miners, prospectors and ranchers resumed the trek into the Southwest. The frontier army posts had been abandoned or severely depleted of troops by the needs of the war effort in the east. With the influx of miners, settlers, and travelers there began again the depredations by the Indian raiders. This brought the troops back.

The Arizona Apaches, fighting for home and game land, met their match in one General George Crook. He ran no garrison campaign, but one of continuous field pursuit and destroy missions. He became a scourge to the Indian desperadoes. While Crook defeated them, he always kept his promise to the Indians and for this they respected and trusted him. Unfortunately, the same cannot be said for many Indian agents and other troop commanders who were sent to the area.

The number of active military posts in the Arizona Territory varied. One of the last to be established, in 1877, was Fort Huachucha. It has remained continuously an active post, with a short hiatus after World War II and with a modern mission; it still retains the barracks, warehouses, quarters and parade grounds as they were in the Geronimo campaign days.

If you would care to test your location knowledge of Arizona Territory forts and camps— give these place names a try. Fort Yuma—well, that was easy, but it was really on the California side, the warehouses were on the Arizona side; Fort Mohave, one time terminus of the Colorado River steamboats and of the Mohave Trail, a land supply route for the army across California; Camp Beale Springs noted for its clear spring water and

Geronimo, chief of the Chiricahua Apaches
Photo courtesy of the National Archives.

named for Lt. Edward F. Beale, of the Army Camel Corps fame; Fort Whipple, now a veteran's facility; Camp Verde, Fort Apache, Camp Reno, Fort McDowell, Camp Crittenden, Fort Grant, Camp Stephen D. Little and Fort Bowie. If you are still with us, try Fort Lowell, Fort Defiance, Camp Hualapai, Camp Lincoln, Camp Supply and Camp Thomas. There are others but this gives you an idea of the widespread troop activity between 1851 when the First Dragoons arrived at Fort Defiance and 1899 when the 25th Infantry served at Fort Huachuca.

Medical officers who accompanied these troops were a varied lot. A few were regular army doctors, such as Leonard Wood who arrived in 1885 and made the last Geronimo campaign with Captain Henry W. Lawton based at Fort Huachuca. His later career was distinguished and varied, such as physician to President McKinley; commander of the Rough Riders, Teddy Roosevelt was the executive officer; military governor of Santiago and Havana, Cuba, army chief of staff, and later governor general of the Philippine Islands. Walter Reed served at Fort Apache

(1876) long before his yellow fever exploits in Cuba.

But, the greater proportion were contract surgeons. Acting assistant surgeons signed for a stipulated period of service. John Charles Handy came to Arizona as a contract army surgeon; he later entered private practice in Tucson, and became the first chancellor of the University of Arizona. He met an untimely death from wounds sustained in a gun fight on the streets of Tucson. Doctor George Emory Goodfellow, of Tombstone, made an emergency trip to consult, and perform surgery, but the patient succumbed of multiple abdominal wounds. More is known of some of the hospital facilities at the army forts than of the physicians who manned them in these remote areas with meager knowledge, supplies, or for that matter, hospital facilities of any consequence.

A trove of data on the physical characteristics of posts and stations of this era is contained in Circular No. 4 from the Surgeon General's Office dated 1870 by John S. Billings, assistant surgeon, U.S. Army. This covered all of the active posts in the continental United States.

And least you forget who Billings was and what a prominent part he played in medicine during his time, you should be reminded that he served as a combat surgeon during the Civil War and thereafter for thirty years in the surgeon general's office. He began the Index Medicus, which was later the Quarterly Cumulative Index of Medical Literature; designed the Johns Hopkins Hospital; chaired a committee that modernized the sanitation system of Memphis, Tennessee after a yellow fever epidemic; organized and served in various official capacities of the American Public Health Association and designed the Peter Brigham Hospital in Boston, Massachusetts; and the city hospital in Sydney, Australia. This gives you a glimpse of the widespread talent and interest of John Billings. This Circular No. 4 was derived from material which he compiled from reports of the medical officers on field duty at the various posts.

So what were the conditions, medically speaking, in these areas? For the most part, abysmal even by standards of that day.

A report on Camp Lowell, Tucson, Arizona Territory, reads in part: "The Post is on the eastern outskirts of the old Mexican town of Tucson." Then followed a description of the terrain and climate. The report continues, "The Camp consists of two hospital tents, roughly fitted together, with tables and benches. The hospital is an old adobe building on the main street of the town, at a distance of about one thousand yards from the camp. Even if this building was in good condition, its position in the center of the town, its proximity to the irrigated fields in the river bottom, its distance from camp, and the smallness of its rooms, render it undesirable as a hospital; but when, in addition to this, its leaky roof, worn out floor, and rain washed walls are taken into consideration, and the series of old sinks that are covered up in its enclosure, it is found to be totally unfitted for such a use." The report goes on to say that all of this was appreciated by the post commander and medical officer and that they had applied for permission to build an adobe hospital

Dr. Leonard Wood at the time of the last Geronimo campaign.
Photo Source Unknown.

of twelve beds but this was not favorably considered. "There is no well attached to the building; all of the water used in the hospital has to be carried from the well about four hundred yards distant. Water could readily be found in the hospital enclosure but the presence of sinks forbids the sinking of a well in this place. Medical supplies are obtained from San Francisco, a year's supply being required at one time. There are about two thousand inhabitants consisting of American and Mexican people in the town."

In 1869 the average military strength was 103, there were 227 cases of illness, 114 of malarial fever, six of scurvy, six of venereal disease and two deaths. At Camp Grant, Arizona Territory, the information was furnished by the assistant surgeon, Charles Smart, United States Army. He reported "The hospital at first consisted of a building 30 by 16 feet which is the ward; but recently a wing was added to it, 18 by 18 feet, as a dispensary, storehouse and surgeon's office. The ward is furnished with eight iron bedsteads, and has an average occupation of eight, giving per man 650 feet. Often there are more patients admitted than the hospital can accommodate and in this case hospital tents are pitched adjoining and furnished with iron bedsteads." He goes on to describe something of the food. He said that vegetables were obtained from the subsistence department preserved in cans, but the main supply was from the company gardens in the river bottoms. Onions and potatoes were sometimes brought from Sonora via Tombstone, at 25 cents per pound. Chickens and eggs were scarce, having to be brought from Tucson or Maricopa Wells, while butter was almost unknown.

"The diseases are all malarial, (malarial was a generic term still used for fever as a group) true malaria that is recurrent fever, was from an organism that had not yet been recognized but the clinical types were recognized. Anyway this is how the original read and prevailed to such an extent during the autumn and winter months as to unfit the garrison for any active service.

In 1868, fevers were so general that the affected troops had to be moved from the post to a temporary convalescent camp, 28 miles south, on the road to Tucson. In 1868 the post reported a main strength of 214, that means that the average number of personnel on duty was 214, but they also reported that there were 2,096 cases of illness, this seems outlandish, but it is so reported. Of these, 1,735 were malarial fever, (this was not a specific term in those days, as the organism had not yet been identified), 266 diarrhea and dysentery, 5 venereal disease, 27 scurvy, with a total of 2 deaths during the year, the cause of which is not listed.

Camp Mohave over on the Colorado River was reported by Acting Assistant Surgeon F. S. Stirling and he described the hospital, "The hospital is an old, dilapidated stockade building, not worth repairs, with a dirt roof and floor. A new building is much needed, and will be commenced as soon as possible, the work to be done by the troops. The present hospital is warmed by means of fireplaces, lighted by windows. The ventilation is deficient. The ward contains six beds. There are no bath or washrooms; a bathing tub is used in the ward.

"The supply of water is afforded by water carts at the river, and that used for drinking purposes is cooled in the oyers (olliers) or earthen jars covered with matting. The water of the Colorado, although muddy, does not produce diarrhea or other unpleasant effects.

"Subsistence and other stores are received by light draught steamboats on the river. Vegetables are scarce. Potatoes and onions are brought 250 miles from California. Milk costs $1.50 per gallon, butter $1.00 per pound, eggs $1.00 per dozen, potatoes 12 to 15 cents per pound. In 1868 there were 263 cases of illness reported with 26 malarials, 35 diarrhea (frequent, liquid stools), and dysentery (intestinal inflammation, pain and frequent bloody, mucus containing stools), 61 venereal disease, 11 of scurvy and 3 deaths.

Assistant Surgeon Charles Smart reported from Camp Verde and he described the hospital as "A small log house, 15 by 13 feet containing three beds." He further stated, "There was no mess room, the men eating their rations in quarters. The officers quarters, miserable hovels; that of the commanding officer being formed of rough boards with gaping seams. Its size was 12 by 13 feet." The log hospital was soon abandoned and he states, "The sick were then placed in a ward of hospital tents, with an adobe fireplace and chimney built at one end. The average occupation of this was seven men." He reported that in 1869 there were 146 cases of illness with the main strength of 69 men. There were 51 cases of malarial fever, 21 of dysentery, 2 of venereal disease and no deaths reported.

Camp Whipple was reported by Assistant Surgeon P. Middleton. It was one of the oldest posts and was the headquarters of the Military District of Arizona. He noted that the building used as a hospital was originally erected in 1864, as the quarters for the commanding officer, District of Arizona. "It is a strong structure of hewn pine, floored, ceiled and plastered, well lighted, with ridge ventilation, and warmed by open fireplaces and stoves. It can accommodate 24 patients. It has a kitchen, a dispensary, and a storeroom with furnishings complete and in excellent condition. The bath and washroom has the water supplied from tanks and the waste water carried out by lead pipes. It is situated on an elevated ridge about midway between the post and the town, with some shade trees around it."

He continues, "One great objection to this hospital is its distance from the post, and among other things, the consequent labor required to keep the tanks supplied by the water wagons. There is no ambulance at the post." He noted that the market price of vegetables is 20 cents a pound. The cavalry companies have suffered considerably from sickness due to lack of fresh vegetables, their frequent absences from the post, placing them on a poor ration, the hard riding, want of sleep, exposure while scouting, and the poor quarters to which, until recently, they have had to return to for rest. In addition to scurvy, and its frequent accompaniment, diarrhea, intermittent and remittent fevers are the only diseases present at the post and its vicinity."

The mean strength was reported at 206, the number of illnesses was 188, 33 with malaria, 36 with dysentery, 18 with venereal disease with other scattered cases of rheumatism and phthisis (tuberculosis) but no deaths reported that year. From this brief account it is quite evident that at the time of this report, 1870, the hospital facilities, the sanitary facilities, and the rations at these camps and posts left a good deal to be desired. The troops seemed to suffer from scurvy, and it is rather strange that there was little, or not enough, communication with the Indians to learn how they managed to survive without its incidence. There must have been some native "greens" which the Indians used in their diet to prevent this disease. In my reading of accounts on conditions among the Indians, I have not read anything about scurvy being an indigenous disease among the native Americans.

The physicians who served with the army in this period and in this Territory had very primitive hospital facilities, the medical and surgical equipment was sparse, malaria was endemic and so was scurvy.

The 1871 Circular No. 3 from the surgeon general's office consisted of a rather complete report of surgical cases treated in the Army of the United States and there is a section devoted to "Arrow Wounds."

A private, Robert Nix of the 14th Infantry, was wounded near Camp Lincoln, Arizona Territory in October 1868 and died the next day, suffering multiple arrow wounds. A private, Andrew Snowden of the 14th Infantry, while stationed at Fort McDowell, on March 22, 1866, was struck on the back of the head by an arrow which penetrated his skull. It was said that he was nine days traveling to Maricopa Wells from the place where he was wounded. He lived for about three weeks and postmortem showed a brain abscess.

Some other casualties were more fortunate. Private William Drum was wounded in a fight with the Apache Indians on November 11, 1867, and was admitted to the post hospital at Fort Whipple the following day. His face wound healed by first intention (without secondary infection) and on December 3, 1867, he returned to duty. Private Thomas Dutton had an arrow wound of the neck, and was admitted the day after his injury to the post hospital at Camp Crittenden. He recovered and returned to duty a week later. Private George Dugan of the 8th Cavalry was wounded near Camp Willow Grove, Arizona Territory on November 8, 1867, by an arrow which penetrated the posterior side of his chest. He died December 17, 1867. At autopsy the arrow was found to have penetrated the chest a little above the diaphragm, and the head of the arrow was lying in contact. There was also an abscess at the same site.

Private Conrad Tragesor, of the 8th Cavalry, was wounded by the Apache Indians, at Sunflower Valley, on March 9, 1870. The arrow entered the left side about four inches from the spine above the crest of the ilium (hip bone) and from below upward. The kidney was evidently injured as the patient passed bloody urine in small quantities. He was conveyed by ambulance to Camp McDowell a distance of thirty miles, over a rough, stony and hilly road and died the next day. In discussing these cases the following quote may surprise you. "The force with which arrows are projected by the Indians is so great that it has been estimated that the initial velocity of the missile nearly equals that of a musket ball. At a short distance, an arrow will perforate the larger bones without comminuting (fragmenting) them, or causing a slight fissure only, resembling the effect of a pistol ball fired through a pane of glass a few yards off.

"I have frequently been informed, by officers who served on the Plains, that it was not infrequent for an Indian to send an arrow fairly through the body of a horse or buffalo, provided the missile entered one of the intercostal spaces (between ribs) and did not impinge on bone on the opposite side."

So as we go about our hospital duties, and grouse about the nursing service, and the paper work; stop and reflect for a moment, or at least five seconds, about the problems which faced our predecessors who came with the army to Arizona Territory so very many years ago.

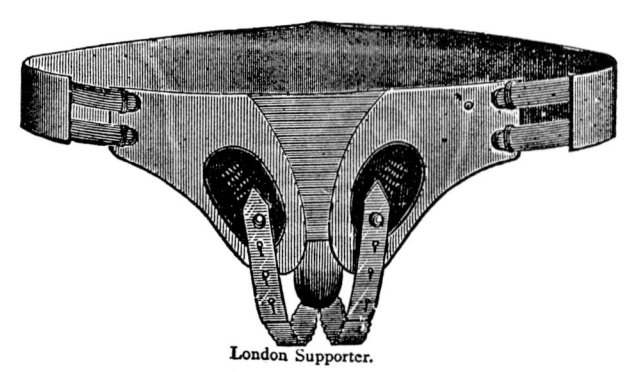

London Supporter.

Physician Medal of Honor Winners in the Arizona Territory

The medal of honor has a long, varied, and distinguished history. The bill authorizing the Navy Medal was passed by Congress and approved by President Abraham Lincoln on December 21, 1861. This was soon followed by a similar action which authorized the Army Medal and was signed into law July 12, 1862.

On March 25, 1863, the first army medals were awarded, "In the name of the Congress of the United States." A few days later on April 3, 1863, the first navy medals were awarded to sailors and marines.

As time wore on, and after the close of the Civil War, there was some dispute about the propriety of some of the awards so that by October 16, 1916, a board was authorized by Congress to gather all of the Medal of Honor records, prepare statistics, classify cases and organize the evidence which was to be reviewed. By January 1917, all of the 2,625 Medals of Honor which had been awarded up to that time had been considered by the board and 911 names were stricken from the list.

One curious incident came up—of these 911 names 864 involved were in one group, a case in which the medal had been given to members of a single regiment. The regiment's 27th Maine Volunteer Infantry enlistment was to have expired in June, 1863. As an inducement to keep the regiment on active duty during a critical period, President Lincoln authorized Medals of Honor to any of its members who volunteered for another tour of duty. The 309 men who volunteered for extended duty, in the face of more action and possible death, certainly were demonstrating "soldier like" qualities and as such were entitled to the medal under one provision of the original law. But their act in no way measured up to 1916 standards. A clerical error compounded the abuse. Not only did 309 volunteers receive the medal, but the balance of the regiment, which had gone home in spite of the president's offer, were also awarded the medal. There were 47 other scattered cases in which the board felt the medal had not been properly awarded and two of these were William F. Cody, better known as Buffalo Bill, and Mary Walker, a Civil War surgeon, and the only woman ever to receive the honor. Now to get back to Arizona Territory.

During the Indian campaigns in the far west, the first physician awarded the Medal of Honor was Assistant Surgeon Bernard J. D. Irwin. The award stated, "Place and Date: Apache Pass, Arizona, February 13-14, 1861. Entered service at New York. Birth Place: Ireland. Date of Issue: January 24, 1894. Citation: Voluntarily took command of troops and attacked and defeated hostile Indians he met on the way." (Please note that the citation in those days was succinct and to the point and not belabored as it is these days.)

The only other physician to receive the medal while on duty with the army in the Arizona

Dr. B. J. D. Irwin
Photo courtesy of the Arizona Historical Society, Tucson, Arizona.

Territory was Assistant Surgeon Leonard Wood. He entered the service from Massachusetts and the citation read: "Voluntarily carried dispatches through a region infested with hostile Indians, making a journey of 70 miles in one night and walking 30 miles the next day. Also for several weeks, while in close pursuit of Geronimo's band and constantly expecting an encounter, commanded a detachment of infantry, which was without an officer and to the command of which he was assigned upon his own request." The place and date was "An Apache campaign," summer of 1886. However, this award, recommended by his commanding officer, Captain Henry W. Lawton, was to hang around Wood's neck like an albatross.

It was a good many years before it was finally awarded, not until after the turn of the century when his good friend Theodore Roosevelt was president. By this time Wood had become a general officer and was commanding troops of the line. He later was to be chief of staff, but he lost out to Pershing for the command of the expeditionary force in France in World War I.

The Indian Campaign Medals of Honor were awarded in operations which took place between March 25, 1865 and December 30, 1891.

We can find records of only two other physicians who received this award during these Indian campaigns, but they were not awarded for action in Arizona. John O. Skinner, contract surgeon for the army, was awarded the medal for action at Lava Beds, Oregon when he "Rescued a wounded soldier who lay under a close and heavy fire during the assault on the Modock stronghold after two soldiers had unsuccessfully attempted to make the rescue and both had been wounded." The second physician, Henry R. Tilton, major and surgeon, U. S. Army at Bear Paw Mountain, Montana, was awarded the medal when he "Fearlessly risked his life and displayed great gallantry in rescuing and protecting the wounded men." The army gave nearly 200 awards of this medal during the Indian campaigns. The navy wasn't exactly negligent in its awards during this time; it appeared that any man who rescued a shipmate who had fallen overboard, was awarded a Medal of Honor.

But after review by the board in 1916, the standards for awarding the medal became far more stringent. Prior to this period it was unusual for a man to lose his life in the performance of his duties for which he was awarded the medal. From 1916 about 30 percent of the awards were given posthumously.

From the inception of the award of this medal in 1861 until 1968, only nine recipients are listed from the State of Arizona. Doctors Irwin and Wood were the only physicians to be awarded the medal for service in Arizona Territory.

Reference:

Medal of Honor 1863-1968. U. S. Government Printing Office, Washington, D.C., 1968.

Arivaca Revisited

Before and during WWI, U.S. army troops were stationed all along the Mexican border, from Texas to California. It was Pancho Villa and his irregulars who captured the attention of the Anglos along the border. Pancho's raid on Columbus, New Mexico where he shot up the town and let the life out of a few of the Anglos finally caught the attention of President Wilson. The reluctant Presbyterian dispatched Black Jack Pershing sashaying into the Mexican interior. It proved one thing, our national military preparedness was not an instrument of precision. True, Lt. George Patton brought in a couple of Villistas, quite dead, across the hood of a Dodge touring car, after a private patrol of his own. Perhaps that was Patton's first demonstration of one of his battle axioms "Let the goddam enemy worry about his flanks, I never worry about mine." Anyway we squandered what few planes the Signal Corps had acquired, the forerunner of the Army Air Corps, and the embryonic motorized transportation corps consisting of Dodge and Ford trucks didn't fare much better but the infantry and cavalry marched and countermarched across arid, rugged, north central Mexico and finally withdrew.

About this time units of the Arizona National Guard were on the border at Naco, under the command of Col. A. M. Tuthill. Tuthill was an industrial physician and surgeon, at that time practicing in Morenci. He was later to command troops in France, and was one of the few state guard officers from any state, to attain general officer rank and hold it under Pershing in WWI. Tuthill served in the armed forces forty years or more, never as a physician, but as an officer of the line and attained the rank of lieutenant general. In fact the old landmark, the Bullet Proof Hotel in Naco, served as his headquarters at that time, and has recently been demolished.

The Germans then came along and kept the Mexican pot boiling so that even during the course of the United States' intervention in WWI, troops were still stationed along the border; in Arizona they were principally detailed from Fort Huachuca. Details were sent to Nogales and later this became Camp Little, and a detachment from Nogales was sent further west to Arivaca, a detachment of the 10th Cavalry.

Doctor Prentiss L. Hyder, a mighty Texan from Corpus Christi, attended grade school in Arivaca during 1917 and 1918, when his father Doctor D. C. Hyder of Commerce, Texas, was stationed in Arivaca with the 10th Cavalry troops, 1916-1919. The senior Doctor Hyder was a graduate of the University of the South Medical

A Street in Arivaca, 1975
Photo by author.

Surgeons' Quarters at Arivaca, World War I
Photo by author.

There were army pyramidal tents on Arivaca's street (circa 1917). Other landmarks noted by the junior Doctor Hyder included the "Cavalry Saddle Shop where I got leather things and pocket for a sling," and "Smooth gravel area where I caught Eileen and kissed her each recess," Ah! These Texans, they begin early. There is "The village blacksmith shop were father boiled cow horns and made handles for a 45" and "Where I found a frog as big as a dinner plate." That is really Texas for you! "Walking cane cactus used

College, Sewanee, Tennessee and was awarded the first honor in his class of 1909.

Since Arivaca is not on the Butterfield Stage Route, some may not have encountered this population center. Kit Peak afficionados will have no problem. Turn off US 89, south of Tucson, at the Arivaca junction and wander out through the Cero Colorado Mountains south by west 20 miles or so to the village. Or you can take the Pena Blanca road five miles north of Nogales out across some wonderful winding mountainous and unpaved roads, and there are not many of these left in Arizona, this brings you close to the abandoned Ruby mine and on to Arivaca.

Adobe Ruins at Arivaca of Officers' Quarters in Use During World War I
Photo courtesy of the Arizona Historical Society, Tucson, Arizona.

The Old School House and Bell at Arivaca
Photo by author.

for making ribs for a canoe by father for hunting ducks." Then there is a poignant story about "The spot where I decided to kill the cat father told me to get rid of" and "The mesquite tree where I tried to kill the cat by hanging it with wire, failed and got a whippin'." These are memories that would befit Huck Finn.

    Well, Doctor Hyder, a good many of your landmarks have remained. Harvey and Mary Riggs restored what I believe was the building that your family occupied as quarters during your sojourn in Arivaca. About four other adobe buildings on the south side of the street have also been restored. Others are falling into disrepair. The cottonwoods south of town are mighty and a trickle of water still runs past your old swimming hole and an antique filling station occupies the extreme west end of the main street. The schoolhouse, a "ragged beggar sunning," is slowly disintegrating and the silent bell hangs over the front door, a lone fire plug up the street from the schoolhouse and close to the cemetery seems to be of 1917 vintage. Then there are the grave markers of Teresa Celaya and Romona Montano who lived to be 102 and 95 years respectively.

    Prentiss and I were medical school classmates on Longwood Avenue in Boston, a long time ago. And little did I suspect that as we scurried around the Brigham avoiding the junior residents, who always had a new patient who required a twenty page history and physical a la Henry Christian, the awesome Hersey professor of the Theory and Practise of Physic, little did I realize this Texan almost lost his heart in Arizona, lo these many moons ago.

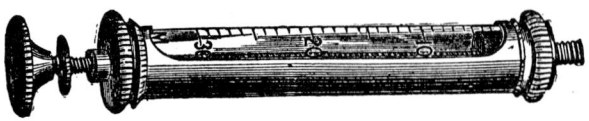

Fort Bowie Hospital

There has recently been published a very complete review of the history of this fort together with rather explicit army records or portions thereof, concerning the hospital. (l)

This account goes, in part, something like this: "Fort Bowie consisted of two distinct posts, the first of which lasted from 1862 until 1869, when it was succeeded by a new and larger fort, built one hundred yards away from the earlier site. Both posts, and especially the first, were erected at commanding positions about three miles east of the summit of Apache Pass in the northern part of the Chiricahua Mountains. Despite its growing notoriety as a place of Indian ambush, plunder, and murder, Apache Pass with its bountiful springs continued to be a landmark for travelers. In 1857 a mail route from San Antonio to San Diego was traced through the pass and a year later the Butterfield Overland Mail Company selected it for the location of one of its stations. But the Civil War forced the closure of the Butterfield route and the mail station at Apache Pass was abandoned. It assumed importance a bit later when, in July 1862, volunteer troops from California fought a desperate battle with Cochise's warriors for control of the central springs. So important did Brigadier General James H. Carleton consider this watering place on his supply line between Tucson and El Paso that he ordered the erection of a permanent garrison facility. Thus began the turbulent history of Fort Bowie, guardian of Apache Pass for the next thirty years. Descriptions of the original hospital are meager but it has been described like this: "Probably the large structure built of logs and located near the corral was the Post Hospital, as suggested in the verbal description—a log house and a cellar like room containing three or four beds."

In 1869, the first fort was superseded. The first hospital there was described as follows: "The hospital at Fort Bowie for most of the post's existence was in this building, an adobe structure of one large and two small rooms with a flat mud roof erected late in 1868 as a quartermaster

Fort Bowie, Late 1874 Photo courtesy of the United States National Park Service.

storehouse. It served various functions at times, and was the guardhouse, at other times the adjutant's office. The rooms, north to south, consisted of a storeroom, a wardroom, a combination dispensary, office and storage room. Doors were located on the east side of the building for each room except the ward which was reached through the dispensary. Capacity of the ward was eight beds. Four to five windows were situated along the west or rear side, and a fireplace and

Commanding Officer's Quarters, Fort Bowie, 1884-1885
Photo courtesy of the United States National Park Service.

chimney stood at the south end of the structure. The earthen roof of the hospital was covered with a coat of lime cement."

The hospital was damaged by the heavy rains of early 1874 and its condition was deemed "untenable," although repairs were evidently made toward the end of the year. A needed addition was erected at approximately this time, a wing off to the north rear of the structure and at right angles to it.

All of the fort buildings were made of adobe and the roofs were always leaking. The account continues: "Every measure was taken to prevent the roof of the hospital from leaking. In 1876 an adobe roof was placed on the new addition. Two years later the post surgeon reported that the roofs of the hospital and out building required repairs." All this time the post surgeons were requesting that a new hospital be erected. "This hospital," wrote an inspector in the summer of 1880, "I consider the poorest in the department in regard to adaptability of the building."

Sanitation was as primitive as the hospital and the following is a description: "Privy. This large hip roofed outhouse was erected at the north east corner of the corrals in about 1886. Apparently at the time, the back of the enclosures was being altered. Probably built of adobe, the structure served as an earth closet, or sink, until 1889 when a pipe drainage system was installed at Fort Bowie. Thereafter it functioned as a water closet for the enlisted men and was frequently flushed out when water can be spared."

In May 1887, drawings and estimates for a new hospital building to replace the old were prepared and submitted for approval by the War Department. The account continues: "Construction on the new building actually got under way in late 1888 or early 1889. The site selected for it was on a rise of ground off the southwest corner of the post and away from the potential garrison noises. Thirty thousand adobe bricks were furnished under contract by laborers employed by the post trader at Fort Bowie. Toward the end of March 1889, an officer reported that, 'A foundation for a new hospital has been laid' and the adobes and woodwork for the building are nearly ready."

There were some starts and stops due to lack of funds, and due to rumors that the post would be abandoned, but finally it was completed and in addition a hospital's stewards' quarters were built in 1889. The fort was finally closed in 1892 and it soon fell into disarray and little remains except some molding adobe walls.

Fires were a constant menace at the old Territorial military posts. This one damaged the post canteen at Fort Bowie in October, 1893. Note the pipes protruding from the top of the building. They were used to drain water from the flat roof when it rained.
Photos courtesy of the United States National Park Service.

*The first Fort Bowie as it appeared in 1893-1894.
Photo courtesy of the National Archives.*

*Fort Bowie in 1894, shortly before it was abandoned by the Federal Government.
Photo courtesy of the United States National Park Service.*

Reference:

Historical Structural Report, Fort Bowie 1862-1894. Fort Bowie Historical Site, Jerome. Greene A. (editor), Park Service, Department of the Interior, 1980.

III.

Early Use of X-Ray by the Military

As ponderous as the military may be in the design and implementation of new methods the army did catch on rather quickly about the use of X-ray and used it to advantage during the Spanish-American War in 1898.

Roentgen had first observed the phenomenon in December 1895, and by January 1896, had published his findings.

"In all, 17 machines were available during the war, of which 5 were static and 12 were coil machines. These proved to be not only invaluable aides in military medicine, but the use of the two types, coil and static, gave an opportunity for comparison of these two methods for producing the Roentgen ray as adapted to the needs and environments of military hospitals." (1)

The length of exposure was a definite disadvantage and this report of the army concerning their Spanish-American War experiences recommends:

Forearm and hand—1 to 2 minutes
Shoulder and chest—10 minutes
Knee—9 minutes
Hip joint, head and pelvis—20 minutes

Now these 1 to 20 minute times are exposure times and when the modern technologist shudders at anything as long as a one second exposure, I suppose he would indeed faint and fall in it if you told him it would take from 1 to 20 minutes for an exposure.

So the apparatus was primitive but very simple by present day standards. The emulsion was more or less made on the spot and applied to glass plates and the author of this report to the surgeon general dwells on this quite a bit and states that you have to make the emulsion very thick in relation to what was usually accustomed to be used in the usual photographic work. Thick emulsion was his plea.

Physicist William Konrad Roentgen, discoverer of X-rays
Photo courtesy of the New York Academy of Medicine.

This report also gives some reproductions of the original roentgenograms and considering the time and place, they show good detail. These cases were reported along with clinical findings and, in instances, photographs of the patient himself, for instance John Gretzer, Jr., Private, Company D, First Nebraska Volunteers. Photograph 22 shows a lateral view of his skull. Private John was not operated for this and it states that, "afterwards the patient entered the mail service and returned to Manilla on duty." This apparently was within a year after his original injury.

The principal use of the early X-ray plates was to find foreign bodies and to assess bone damage.

It was also recognized that Roentgen ray burns could be produced by prolonged exposure with tubes which "were not working properly."

This report describes two Roentgen ray burns that had been reported as a result of the use of the Roentgen ray apparatus during the Spanish-American War. One burn was produced by coil and one by static machine. In each case exposure was prolonged and frequently repeated, when the apparatus was not working in its maximum capacity.

The first case, Thomas McKenna, discharged soldier, formerly private, Company C, 6th U.S. Infantry had received a gunshot fracture of the upper third of the right humerus (upper arm bone) during the Santiago campaign for which an excision of the upper part of the humerus was made.

"December 5, 1898 an attempt was made to radiograph the shoulder in order to ascertain the condition of the bone. An exposure of 20 minutes was made, with the tube 10 inches from the shoulder. The result was so unsuccessful that a second and third trial on successive days was made, but the tube was working so poorly that no satisfactory radiograph was obtained. Six days after the last exposure slight redness of the skin appeared in the front of the chest and shoulder. These broke into ulcers, there was tissue necrosis (death), treatments of various kinds were tried without benefit, but healing was not complete even 11 months after the appearance of the first injury."

There is a considerable comparison of Civil War and Spanish-American War casualties, for instance the mortality from head wounds was about the same, 28% Civil War; 26%, Spanish-American War; chest, Civil War 27.85%; Spanish-American War 11.6% a reduction there. But on the whole things went along about the same, rather dismally.

So with the apparatus available, and only three years after the announcement of Roentgen's discovery, and of course what he really discovered was what was going on with a Crooke's tube that wasn't revealed readily to the eye, simply because he left some photographic film around in the way and developed it and sure enough something had happened.

There is a note which came across my desk

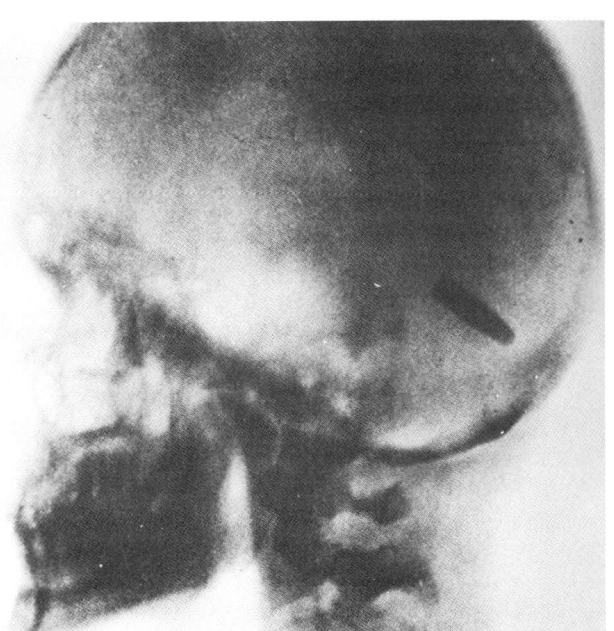

John Gretzer, Jr., Private, Company D, First Nebraska Volunteers. Radiograph of head viewed from the left side, showing Mauser bullet lodged in the brain.
Photo courtesy of the United States Army.

Private John Gretzer, Jr., after recovery from his head wound.
Photo courtesy of the United States Army.

several years ago describing another worker who was searching for bullets during the Spanish-American War and it reads as follows: "It was a surprise in 1896 when Elizabeth Fleischman Ascheim gave up her comfortable job as a bookkeeper. But her brother-in-law's enthusiasm for the newly discovered Roentgen rays had so inspired her, that she insisted on taking a six-month's course in electrical science. Upon graduation she helped to set up the first privately owned X-ray laboratory in California.

"During the Spanish-American War, countless war casualties were brought to this small laboratory, where Elizabeth Ascheim localized bullets and even determined the extent of bone injuries. Her work was so successful that it convinced medical men of the value of X-ray in military surgery. In spite of repeated warnings she had early radiation dermatitis and carcinoma which led to her death in 1905." Now it doesn't say just where this laboratory was and perhaps it is a little over-enthusiastic in saying that this was the only place in which X-ray was demonstrated to be useful to the military. The military apparently had something of their own going and the British military had used it before in Turkey.

Reference:

The Use of the Roentgen Ray by the Medical Department, U.S. Army in the War with Spain. Document #729, 1900.

X-Ray Apparatus, 1898
Photo courtesy of the United States Army.

Portable Military Radiology

We have remarked upon the energies quickly displayed by the U.S. army in the use of X-ray in the Spanish-American War. X-ray had been used in the Russo-Turkish War by the British certainly who had some primitive apparatus available. But none of the accounts which we have come across make any mention about a truly portable apparatus and I would therefore suggest that this first, along with many others, be awarded to the late illustrious and serene Madame Curie.

Her impetus in this field is vividly related by her daughter, Eve Curie, in the biography of her mother. These excerpts are straight out of Eve's sympathetic description of her mother's wartime work.

On August 6, 1914 Madame Curie wrote to her daughters who were summering in Brittany, "The Germans are crossing Belgium and fighting their way. Poland is occupied by the Germans. I know nothing about my family." (1)

And later she urged her daughters to take good care of themselves and behave properly while their mother stayed in Paris to contribute what she might. Professor Curie had been killed some years before, leaving Madame with two children.

"The discovery of X-rays by Roentgen in 1895 had made it possible to explore without surgical aid the interior of the human body and in 1914 only a limited number of Roentgen machines existed in France and were used by radiographic doctors. The wartime Military Health Service had provided equipment in certain big centers, but this was all." (1)

"Madame Curie quickly saw how this could be applied in widespread areas; she had delivered lectures on the physics of X-ray to her students at the University of Paris and she quickly set about to supply X-ray material. She found there was very little of it. Volunteer operators she recruited from amongst professors, engineers and scientists. But even if she got this material together what could she do with it?"

Well her solution as related by her daughter was, "She created with funds from the Union Of Women Of France the first 'Radiological Car.' It was an ordinary automobile in which she put a Roentgen apparatus and a dynamo which, driven by the motor of the car, furnished the necessary current. This complete mobile post circulated from hospital to hospital from August, 1914 onward. It was the only one to take care of the examination of the wounded evacuated toward Paris during the Battle of the Marne."

All during August she continued to send encouraging letters to her daughter and stated that she could not then abandon Paris. Photograph 25 is a picture of the famous radiological unit which Madame Curie drove herself and circulated from hospital to hospital. (1)

"To further raise the funds that were necessary for these cars which were nicknamed 'Little Curies' in the army zones, these were equipped by Marie and the laboratory, one by one, regardless of the indifference or the dull hostility of the Bureaucrats."

Her daughter continues, "Our timid woman had suddenly became an exacting authoritative person. She nagged at the lazy officials, demanded passes from them, visas and requisitions. They made difficulties—brandished the regulations at her—'Civilians mustn't bother us.' Such was the spirit that animated many amongst them. But Marie hung on, argued and won.

"She held up individual citizens mercilessly. At her request such generous women as the Marquise de Ganay and Princess Murat gave or lent her their limousines which she immediately transformed into radiological stations. 'I shall give you back your motor car after the war' she would promise with slightly mocking assurance. 'Truthfully if it is not useless by then I shall give it back to you.'

"Of the twenty cars which she put into service Marie kept one for her personal use: a flat nosed Renault with a body like that of a lorry. Aboard this chariot of the regulation gray, ornamented by a Red Cross and a French flag painted on its plates, she led the life of an adventurer, of a great captain."

It is further related, "Aside from the twenty motor cars she equipped, Marie thus installed two-hundred radiological rooms. The total number of wounded men examined by these two hundred and twenty posts, fixed and mobile, posts created and started going by Madame Curie personally, went above a million."

While billeted in the Midlands of England in 1944, awaiting the unpleasantness in Normandy, I became acquainted with a Doctor O'Neal who had served with the British forces in a radiological unit in World War I in France. I was curious about whether or not they had any mobile units such as were envisioned by the late Doctor K. D. K. Allen of Denver, who was then the consultant in radiology for the European Theater. But Doctor O'Neal states that while he fluoroscoped from morning until night, and he must have used some protection because he had no visible effects on his hands twenty years later, they did not have any mobile units as such, and all of the work or the principal amount of work was done fluoroscopically, not with the glass plates which were scarcely available in the army field installations in those days. These units were with their clearing stations—roughly equivalent to our forward field hospitals and collecting companies.

As those ancient survivors of WW II, of the medical department will recall, the Picker Mobile Unit was almost as indestructible as a German 88. Just as no conscious GI would ever admit his wounds were dealt by anything less than an 88, so radiographs of note were produced in the field and evacuation hospitals overseas with nothing less than a Picker portable.

These were powered by a gasoline motor generator, the army item number was 96060, and this shall be indelible upon my cerebral cortex until everything gets wiped out. This was absolutely worthless, it could be used principally to power a movie projector but hardly anything more than that. We operated the apparatus at 5 to 15 MA (milliamperes), not more than that because we simply didn't have the electrical power. After getting into Normandy, we were able to get some 15 kilowatt diesel generators which were captured from the Germans and these indeed gave enough power.

In the meantime, still World War II, the British had perfected what was truly a mobile unit. All of this apparatus was housed in a truck, a lorry if you will, about the size of the secret weapon used by the U.S. forces known as the 6 x 6. In the truck then would be a table, the X-ray unit, a darkroom with wet tanks, and it was supplied with the greatest current generator this side of heaven. It was provided to the British forces by way of lend-lease and manufactured in the United States but not a one of these generators was ever available to the U.S. Army, as far as I am aware.

To return to World War I, "Madame Curie continued to apply herself diligently to this X-ray work, and she herself traveled with her little portable unit all over the French front." She didn't stay fixed in one place but traveled wherever the casualties were thick.

She conducted classes for the Americans to train some of their people in field wartime radiology.

As we view the modern "portable" X-ray apparatus designed for field use by the army in 1942, it was indeed in some respects superior to a lot of the civilian apparatus which was available at the time of World War II. Surely the next step will be to rid ourselves of the necessity to use X-ray film as we know it now and the image will no doubt come up displayed before the eye of the operating surgeon in living red, white and blue colors with arrows pointing to all of the bullet fragments and fractures.

Reference:

Curie, Eve, *Madame Curie—A Biography*, Doubleday, Doran & Company, 1938 pp.289-307.

No Cathode Rays in Nogales

In March, 1896—the month in which the reporter for the *Arizona Gazette* wrote his astute article—Doctor Edward Davis, in Philadelphia, used an x-ray exposure of one-and-one-half hours in order to try to demonstrate a fetus in a pregnant woman. Not only might Rufino Mavante have died from indecision if the x-ray had been employed on him; but if he had survived he might have been the victim of an x-ray burn.

We hope that Doctor Kennedy, who has uncovered a fascinating contribution to Arizona roentgeonology, will now explore the possibility of Rufino Mavante's still being alive. If so, one of the most historically interesting roentgenograms is in the offing.

Surgeons and reporters of today may be more elegant in their work and description thereof but hardly more effective than this report. This is the title of an interesting medical experience related in the *Arizona Gazette* (Phoenix) March 13, 1896. (1)

It reads in part: "Among the persons indicted by the grand jury yesterday was Juan Cota, of Nogales, for assault with intent to murder. That the indictment was not for murder will always be a wonder to the physicians who remodeled this victim after the encounter was over. The victim, a boy named Rufino Mavante, was a witness before the jury, and though it was only a couple of months since he received a wound from which not one man in 10,000 recovers, he was apparently none the worse. He had been shot in the abdomen. The ball entered on one side and cut obliquely through the intestines. When he didn't die at once, doctors went to work, not with the hope of saving him, but because they thought the bystanders were expecting them to do something. So they merely engaged in that time-destroying occupation known as 'soldering,' and they felt that it would be a relief to the boy and to them when he was dead.

"The abdomen was cut open, the mangled intestines were taken out and washed and the gaps and holes were sewed up. The abdominal cavity was washed out, and as nothing else could be done, the intestines were put back and the abdomen sewed up. At least one thing had resulted from the operation—the boy was cleaner inside than he had been before. With nothing else to do, they stood around waiting for Mavante to die. Today he is in rather better health than he was before Cota pulled the trigger of his 45. But then Cota is not given credit for his victim's improved condition and probably will get a long term in the penitentiary.

"All of this happened a month before the x-ray was discovered. If that recent accession to surgical science had been employed, Mavante would probably have died while they were trying to get a negative of his insides. The Nogales doctors went straight to the root of the trouble, pistol ball, and they followed it like a boy does a ground-hog—by the hole it made in the joint."

The reporter who wrote this interesting account must surely have been doing his homework. This was written in March, 1896, and it was in December, 1895 that Professor Roentgen had made his preliminary communication to the Wurtzburg Physico-Medical Society announcing the description of this "striking new phenomenon." He must have also known something about the time of exposure which was necessary to produce these fascinating x-ray plates.

The medical department of the United States Army reported on the use of the roentgen ray in the war with Spain, 1898. (2) Some interesting technical data is included. There are several reproductions of x-ray plates, and these are diagnostic even by present standards showing bullets in various parts of the anatomy. It is recorded that the exposure time necessary to produce those of the forearm and hand was one to two minutes, of the shoulder and chest ten minutes, of the knee nine minutes, the hip joint, head and pelvis, twenty minutes.

The reporter's statement that "Mavante would probably have died while they were trying to get a negative" is well taken, it would probably have been in the nature of 10 to 20 minutes.

It is probable that "cathode rays did not come to Arizona" before 1898 when Doctor Ancil Martin, of Phoenix, began searching for foreign bodies with a Crookes tube and a static machine which he brought to Phoenix. (3)

Doctor Martin reported in 1926 on "Magnetic Foreign Bodies in the Eye," describing 136 cases which he studied. He records "the first radiographs in this country were probably recorded by Professor Musterberg of Boston on January 31, 1896. The first removal of a foreign body was by Doctor James Bury, February 11, 1896." (3)

The first eye localization was probably by Doctor Francis Williams of Boston, June 5, 1896. William M. Sweet, M.D., professor of ophthalmology at Jefferson Medical College, Philadelphia, reported localization by his own method, eye cases, November 27, 1898. Doctor Martin continues: "My case number 7 of October 20, 1901, was my first attempt to localize a foreign body within the globe, a fluoroscope was used. Extraction was made by a magnet using the posterior route. Incidentally, I will say I brought the first Crookes tube to Arizona, and with the assistance of an electrician, hooked it up to an old static machine but it was of little service. The localizations done prior to 1910 were performed with a static machine brought to Phoenix in 1898."

Doctor Martin stated his first observations on intra-occular foreign bodies was in 1896, and as stated above, he did his first localization with the aid of x-ray on October 20, 1901. These few hundred words notwithstanding, there were "no cathode rays in Nogales" when Juan Cota fired his 45 at Ruffino Mavante.

References:

1. Library and Archives, Capitol Building. Phoenix, Arizona.
2. Borden, W. C., *The Use of Roentgen Ray in the War with Spain, (1898)*. Document No. 729, Government Printing Office, 1900.
3. Martin, Ancil, *Magnetic Foreign Bodies of the Eye*, Southwest Medicine X, No. 4, pp. 151-161, 1926.

Early X-Ray Tube Collection

This collection of six X-ray tubes that date back to 1930 and earlier has been placed on loan to the Maricopa County Medical Society library by Mrs. Nelle Foster, widow of R. Lee Foster, M.D.

W. Warner Watkins, M.D. 1883-1956
This pioneer Phoenix radiologist established the first clinical laboratory at St. Luke's Home (Now St. Luke's Hospital and Medical Center) and the Pathological Laboratory at 15 East Monroe Street in Phoenix.

Photo courtesy of Roundup.

All but one of the tubes are the gas type and were used at the Pathological Laboratory, 15 E. Monroe St., Phoenix, Arizona, from 1915 to 1930. These antedate the vacuum or Coolidge tubes that are used now. Doctor Foster practiced radiology in Phoenix and succeeded Warner Watkins, M.D., as director of the Pathological Laboratory. Looking at the collection with Mrs. Foster are (left to right): J. W. Kennedy, M.D., MacDonald Wood, M.D. and Alan Gordon, M.D.

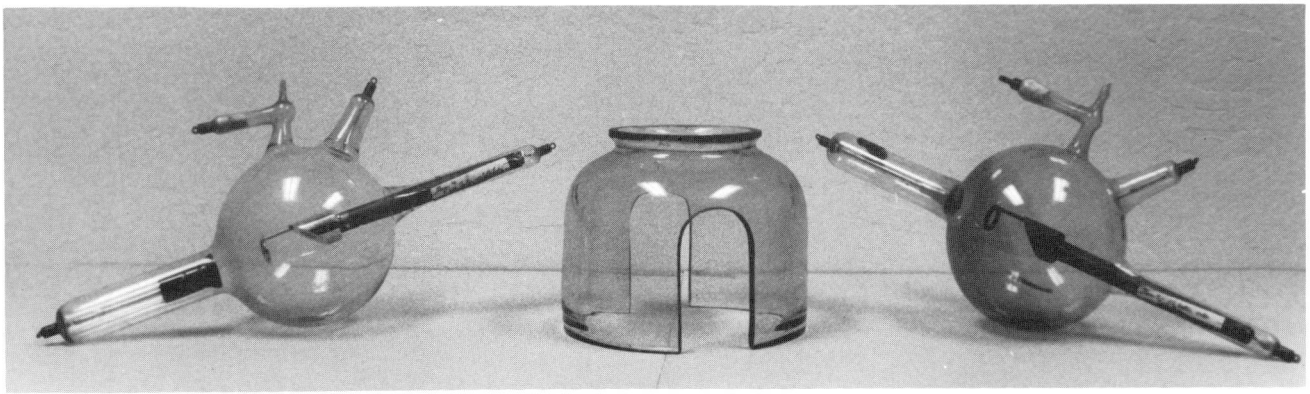

Non-shockproof X-Ray tubes and the lead glass bowl shield (center) in which they were placed. This type of air cooled tube was used in the 1920s.
Photo from the Foster-Watkins Collections.
Courtesy the Maricopa County Medical Society.

IV.

Arizona Mental Health

Introduction

Until the founding in 1794 of the Quaker Retreat in York, England by British coffee and tea merchant William Tuke, mentally ill patients were treated (but not in the clinical sense) with indescribable brutality. It was the widely held belief then that such sadism would make the unfortunate victims "come to their senses." Four years later, French psychiatrist Phillipe Pinel, warned that his own life would be at stake if the experiment failed, persuaded the city authorities of Paris to allow him to free 49 mentally ill patients at Bicetre Hospital from their chains. Both experiments, centering on the more humane treatment of the mentally ill, were successful. Many were able to function, albeit minimally, in society. Others continued to be "warehoused" but under much more humane conditions. A history of the Quaker (or York) Retreat is the subject of a book by Anne Digby, published in 1985 by Cambridge University Press. It is part of the Cambridge History of Medicine series edited by C. Webster and C. Rosenberg. Steven S. Sharfstein, M.D. of the American Psychiatric Association in Washington, D.C., who reviewed the book in the August 15, 1986 *Journal of the American Medical Association,* calls it "a superb historical study of one of the most significant experiments in the treatment of mental illness." Tuke's grandson continued his grandfather's interest in the mentally ill and his great-grandson became a physician with a special interest in mental illness. Pinal, however, who also was an early adherent of William Jenner of "cowpox vaccination" fame, soon attracted others to his humane handling of the mentally ill. But while that aspect of the mentally ill patient's plight improved, clinical treatment failed to keep pace until the advent of the tranquilizers and other psychotropic drugs. In the pages that follow, Doctor Kennedy provides a revealing insight to the status of mental illness during the early days of Arizona medicine and the physicians who tried to bring order out of the political and medical chaos of that time.

J. DeV.

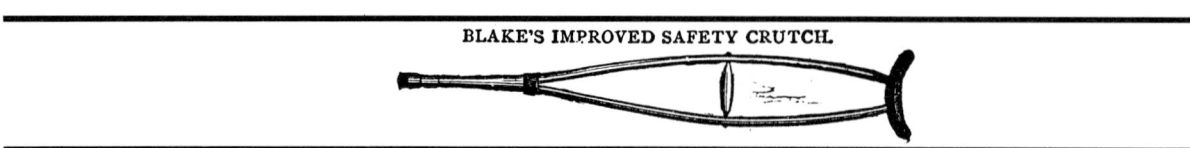
BLAKE'S IMPROVED SAFETY CRUTCH.

References:

1. F. H. Garrison, M.D., *History of Medicine*, Saunders, 1969.
2. Silvano Arieti, M.D., *American Handbook of Psychiatry*, Vol. 1, Basic Books, Inc., 1959.
3. *Columbia Encyclopedia*, Columbia University Press, 1942.
4. *Journal of the American Medical Association,* August 15, 1986, pg. 931

Arizona Mental Health in Territorial Days

EDITOR'S NOTE: The following factual historical review of the beginnings of mental health in Territorial days is the first definitive account that we have found. We are indebted to the Palo Verde Foundation for Mental Health, Tucson, for permission to reproduce their legislative history.

The first few assemblies in 1864, 1865, 1866, and 1867 made no recognition of any problems of mental illness in the Territory. Message for Governor Richard G. McCormick: "Let it here be determined that social progress shall keep pace with material prosperity and that as rapidly as possible institutions which are the strength and glory of the States and older Territories, shall be established and maintained."

First the problem of mental illness had become too obvious to be ignored. This is some 30 years after Dorothea Dix's famous memorial to the legislature of Massachusetts. Message for Governor A. P. K. Safford: No provision has been made for the care and maintenance of this unfortunate class of our people, and speedy action should be had in their behalf. It will probably be some time before the Territory will be in a condition to incur the expense of erecting buildings suitable for an asylum; and, knowing that the State of Nevada had contracted with California for the care of her insane, I addressed a letter to the Governor of California inquiring upon what terms the insane were received from Nevada and also if similar arrangements could be effected for the care of those of Arizona. The Governor in reply informed me that he was not advised of the particulars, but had addressed a letter to the Superintendent at Stockton, asking him to forward me the desired information at as early a day as possible. As soon as I receive the information I will lay it before you."

First official recognition of the state's obligation for the care of the sick, came during this legislative assembly as a result of Gov. Safford's plea.

1873—7th Assembly—Message from Governor A. P. K. Safford: "I again call your attention to the insane of this Territory. Under the present statute, the care and maintenance of this unfortunate class of our people are left to the boards of supervisors of the several counties, and the only place available for their safe keeping is a common felon's cell. Such confinement is against the dictates of humanity, and the treatment is not calculated to restore to reason the poor lunatic; besides, the shrieks of the insane often become almost intolerable to all within hearing of them. The evil became so annoying that I addressed a letter to Governor Booth, of California, by the Honorable C. A. Tweed, upon the subject, and chiefly through Judge Tweed's exertions and influence an arrangement was effected for the reception of a limited number of lunatics from this Territory at Stockton. This arrangement was only temporary, and does not meet the public necessities in this respect. A practical system should be adopted at this session for the care and maintenance of the insane, at the expense of the Territory." Governor Safford again showed remarkable insight in preconceiving the idea of the advantages of caring for the patient in his own community.

1875—8th Assembly Message from Governor A. P. K. Safford: "The last Legislature passed a law authorizing me to enter into contract for the maintenance of the insane, with such parties as I might deem advisable outside of the Territory. In pursuance of said duty I entered into contract with Doctors Langdon and Clark of Stockton, California, for the care of such insane as might be sent from this Territory, at a cost of $10.00 each per week, in gold. But two patients have thus far been sent; one of whom has died, and the other sufficiently recovered his reason to be discharged. So far as I have been able to ascertain, Doctors Langdon and Clark have faithfully performed their duty; but if arrangements can be made whereby the insane can be properly cared for within the Territory, it would save considerable expense in carrying them to California, and would doubtless be better for the unfortunates. The total cost for patients at the Asylum has been $998.86."

Governor Safford, known as the father of the public school system in Arizona, seems to have lost hope in establishing a treatment facility in the Territory as only two patients were being cared for.

1877—9th Assembly—Message for Governor A. P. K. Safford: "Under a contract made by me, in behalf of the Territory, with Doctors Langdon and Clark, of Stockton, California, the insane of the Territory are maintained and cared for. There are at the present time but two patients in the asylum. The total expense for their maintenance to June 30, 1876, was $468.75. In a report to me, dated October 29, 1876, the physicians in charge give but little encouragement of the restoration to reason of either of the patients. Under all the circumstances, the contract we have with Messrs. Langdon and Clark, is probably the most economical and humane plan that can be adopted for maintaining our insane, but, as the asylum is located so far away, I would suggest the propriety of authorizing the Governor to appoint some competent person, living at Stockton, to visit the asylum at least quarterly, to examine and report the condition of the patients, their treatment, etc. While I believe that these physicians have faithfully performed their duty to the patients who have been intrusted to their care, still it seems but justice to these unfortunate people that a disinterested individual shall visit them at least once in three months.

1879—10th Assembly. 1881—11th Assembly. Governor John C. Fremont and his assemblies took no notice of the problem of mental illness.

1883—12th Assembly. By this date the population of the Territory had increased to approximately 83,000 from 42,000 in 1880. Message from Governor F. A. Tritle: (Asylum at Stockton) The grounds consist of forty acres, a part of which is used to grow all kinds of vegetables for their use. Fresh vegetables go daily from the garden to the kitchen, and this, too, throughout the year. Recreation grounds are ample and have all conveniences. Baths with hot and cold water are at convenient places in the buildings, and there is abundant ventilation in all parts. The beds are kept clean and comfortably furnished. Every part of the building is kept perfectly clean, and nothing seems wanting for the comfort and health of the patients. The climate is equable; water good and plentiful, and all surroundings unexceptionable. I would respectfully suggest that as the number of our insane is so small, thirty-seven, that it would be an exceedingly expensive matter per capita for our territory to provide an asylum and care for their patients at this time, and that our contract be renewed by Doctor Asa Clark for the next two years. It is made the duty of your executive by act of the legislature, to appoint some person residing at Stockton, to visit the insane patients of the Territory at least once in three months, and report their condition. For this, the sum of $40.00 per annum is appropriated. I have been unable to employ any person for such salary, and suggest an increase of sum to $100.00 per annum, or the act repealed. The number of patients had grown considerably in these two years and the prognosis was gloomy. Doctor Ainsworth was also President of the legislative council in 1885. And obviously thought little of the treatment program at the Pacific Asylum. Doctor F. K. Ainsworth: "My dear Sir—If possible, I desire that you visit the Private Insane Asylum of Doctor Asa Clark, at Stockton, and ascertain, by personal observation and examination as fully as your time will permit, the physical and mental condition of the patients under Doctor Clark's care from the Territory of Arizona—with a view of reporting the result of your investigation for my information. F. A. Tritle, Governor." "And I respectfully report that in compliance with the above, on October 25, 1884, I visited the Pacific Asylum of Stockton, the designated Asylum for the insane of Arizona, and as thoroughly acquainted myself with the sanitary arrangements of an asylum in one inspection, and approximately ascertain the physical condition of a patient at one visit, it is nearly impossible, in many cases, to reach an accurate diagnosis of his mental condition, or give a prognosis of much value. For this reason I have depended largely upon the statements of Doctor Clark in assigning the patients to their respective classes. A careful inspection of the Asylum and its surroundings clearly demonstrated that there is little to be desired in the line of sanitary improvements. There are at present few, if any inmates, other than those from this Territory and consequently no overcrowding of wards as is but too frequently the case in such institutions. The general diet of the patients is far better than that I have known to be furnished in several State Asylums, and I am assured by Doctor Clark that a special diet is always ordered for any individual case requiring it. At the date of my visit there were fifty-eight (58) patients from the Territory of Arizona. The several counties were represented as follows.

TABLE 1

County	No. of Patients
Apache	1
Cochise	9
Gila	3
Graham	0
Maricopa	13
Mohave	4
Pima	10
Pinal	5
Yavapai	8
Yuma	5
Total	58

"For convenience I have classified the patients under four general heads: Dementia, Mania, Melancholia, and Paresis, and find them represented as follows: Melancholia 1; Dementia, 21; Mania, 34; Paresis, 2. Total, 58.

"I regret that I am not able to state that Doctor Clark's asylum supplies an exception to the almost universal rule, that asylums for the insane furnish only more or less complete means of restraining them from doing injury to themselves, and the persons and property of others; while the nobler department of the science of medicine, aiming at the ultimate recovery and restoration to physical and mental health of these unfortunate human beings, receives but indifferent attention. If our insane are to be sent out of the Territory to an asylum so remote that they may never be visited by relatives and friends, I am of the opinion that it will not be possible to do better than to send them to the Pacific Asylum." Respectfully submitted. Your obedient Servant, F. K. Ainsworth, M.D., Prescott, Arizona, October 8, 1884.

During this assembly the legislature passed the bill which established the state hospital, even though Governor Tritle did not ask for it. Reprinted with permission of the Palo Verde Foundation for Mental Health, from Arizona Psychiatry, "Arizona Mental Health in Territorial Days and After, Part I," Vol. 1, No. 1, May 1970, page 12.

Editor's Note: The Territorial Assembly authorized the sale of $100,000.00 in bonds to build the "asylum" in Phoenix. Also stipulated that the land and building costs were to be limited to $75,000 and not less than 80 acres of land included! Someone should search out the true acreage acquired; superficial inquiry suggests 160 acres with 40 acres later acquired. In the late 60s Brigham Young University bought 40 acres for $1,550,000.00 to build a university. In 1972 sold it back to the state of Arizona for $2,267,250.00. So for an initial investment of slightly less than $100,000.00 and most of that for a poorly constructed building, the steady march of the inflation of land value—seems almost incredible.

1885—13th Assembly "Though variously known as the 'Bloody Thirteenth' or the 'Thieving Thirteenth' because of its extravagant expenditures this legislature inaugurated and parceled out several institutions that are still a credit to Arizona. When the shouting was over and the smoke-filled rooms were aired out, the capitol was still at Prescott and the prison at Yuma. Phoenix captured the coveted insane asylum with an appropriation of $100,000, though critics argue that it would have been cheaper to continue sending patients to Stockton, California, where a charge of six dollars per week each was made for their care. Tempe was given the teacher's college and an appropriation of $5,000. Tucson had to be content with the university and a $25,000 grant, or one-fourth of the amount provided for the asylum. Other spoils were also voted to placate different sections of the Territory. Yuma was promised a new levee along the Colorado, and Florence was to receive a $12,000 bridge over the Gila. The latter project turned out to be a complete waste of money since the then water-filled river went on one of its famous rampages and cut a new channel, leaving the bridge 'high and dry' in the desert." History, University of Arizona Press, 1970. Pages 208-209. Wagoner, J. J. Arizona Territory 1863-1912.

Governor Tritle didn't ask for it, but this legislature passed the following bill to establish the Insane Asylum of Arizona. No. 58, An Act. To establish, maintain and provide for the Government of an Insane Asylum. Be it enacted by the Legislative Assembly of the Territory of Arizona: Section 1. There shall be established within and for the Territory of Arizona an asylum for the insane, which shall be known by the name of the Insane Asylum of Arizona, and all buildings used therefor shall be erected upon the lands to be hereafter obtained by the Directors hereinafter provided for, at or near the City of Phoenix, in the County of Maricopa, Territory of Arizona, and said insane asylum shall be constructed by and be, and remain under the control of said Directors of said Asylum, to be hereafter appointed in accordance with the provisions of this Act; provided, however, that said County of Maricopa, or said City of Phoenix or some private person or persons, on or before the 1st day of January, 1886, shall first have conveyed, or cause to be conveyed to the said Board of Directors, as hereinafter provided for their successors in office, for the use and benefit of the Territory of Arizona and for said Asylum, not less than eighty acres of land, with sufficient water to irrigate the same, available for the purposes of such Asylum, and free from all incumbencies; and, if such land be not so donated on or before the 1st day of January, 1886, this Act shall be void and of no further force or effect. Sec. 4. The said Board of Directors shall have full power and authority to manage the affairs of the said asylum. Said Board shall as soon as practicable receive not less than eighty acres, as heretofore provided, for the use of said asylum at or near the City of Phoenix, County of Maricopa, Territory of Arizona, and cause a draft of plans and specifications of such buildings, as said Board shall deem necessary and proper to be erected for the use of said asylum, on said lands to be prepared, and to advertise for and receive sealed proposals for furnishing the necessary material and for the erection of such buildings, and the contract shall be given to the lowest responsible bidder; provided, that the cost shall not exceed, when completed, the sum of seventy-five thousand dollars, including the purchase price of said lands, which shall have been purchased by said Board, and all furniture and improvements necessary for use of said asylum Sec. 21. The resident physician, who shall also be the superintendent, shall be the chief executive officer of the Asylum; he shall have the general superintendency of the buildings, grounds, and property, and the direction and control of all persons therein, subject to the laws and regulations established by the said Board of Directors; he shall daily ascertain the condition of the patients and prescribe their treatment; he shall appoint, with the approval of said Board, so many assistants and attendants as he may think proper and necessary for the economical and efficient performance of the business for the Asylum, prescribe their several duties and places, fix, with the approval of said Board, their compensation, and discharge any of them at his sole direction; but in every case of discharge he shall forthwith record the same with the reasons, under an appropriate head, in one of the books of the Asylum. The management of the asylum obviously had come upon a good thing. At last the Territory had its own asylum but it was unusable. The patients were still in Stockton.

1887—14th Assembly Message from Governor C. Meyer Zulick: "The last Legislature passed 'an act to establish, maintain and provide for the government of the Insane Asylum in the Territory of Arizona.' By its provisions a Board of Directors composed of three members, viz: Oscar Lincoln, Madison W. Stewart and Frank C. Hatch, who were nominated by ex-Governor Tritle and duly confirmed, assumed the powers delegated to them. Section 25 of the act provides for an honorary Board of Directors, whose duty it is to inspect said asylum, to investigate the books, accounts and doings of the Board of Directors and of all officers of said asylum, and to make a report thereof, together with such suggestions as they may deem proper, to the Governor. The honorary Board of Directors met at Prescott April 22, 1886, at 10:30 A.M. at the office of the Governor; due notice having been given each of the Directors, and the Secretary and Treasurer of their offices. Director Stewart did not attend. Directors Lincoln and Hatch were present, but had directed, as they admitted, their Secretary and Treasurer to refuse to be present with the minutes, books, papers, etc. It was under these adverse circumstances that the honorary Board attempted the discharge of their duties. Questions were propounded to Directors Lincoln and Hatch, some of which they answered and many of which they declined to answer. Sufficient information, however, was gathered to establish such facts as warranted a report of the honorary Board to the Governor that Messrs. Lincoln, Stewart, and Hatch 'had been guilty of neglect of duty and official misconduct, and that by openly violating the law under which they were created, and by extravagantly disbursing, carelessly guarding, and reckless jeopardizing the security of the public money under their control,' made it their duty to recommend, as they did, their removal from office. A full copy of this report, accompanied with the testimony and exhibits, the proceedings on hearing before me, and the executive order of removal is submitted for your consideration. At the time these officials were removed, in conformity with statutory provisions, the balance sheet of William Christy, Treasurer, showed a balance on hand of $63,441.50. They refused to recognize the executive order of removal and declined to surrender the building, books, papers or money in their hands to their legally constituted successors who were regularly appointed to fill the vacancies occasioned by their removal, thereby compelling their successors to resort to the courts for relief from their usurpations of office. A competent court in September declared them "usurpers of office," and rendered judgment of ouster, from which they appealed, and which appeal has been dismissed. Demands were again made on them and their officers for the surrender of the books, papers and property of the Territory under their control, which were denied. Writs of mandate were applied for, and on the 23rd of November, 1886, after a writ had been served on Oscar Lincoln and Madison W. Stewart, and after they had expended all the money in their hand except $7,000, which was paid into the Territorial Treasury, the asylum building, books, papers, etc. were turned over by them to the new Board, who on the 6th day of December, ultimo, appointed experts to examine the building, plumbing, gas-fittings, roofing, furniture, bedding, books and accounts. The report of the new Board and the reports of their experts are herewith submitted. By reference to the accompanying reports of the honorary Board and Board of Asylum Directors, it will be seen that Messrs. Lincoln, Hatch and Stewart constituting the old Board of the Asylum Directors, sold the bonds of the Territory appropriated for the construction of the asylum, $10,000, at 95 cents, less three months interest; and $90,000 to their own Treasurer at 95 cents, less three months interest and one percent commission; realizing for the first ten bonds 93 1/4 per cent, and for ninety bonds 92 1/4 per cent, when the law forbid them to be sold for less than 95 per cent of their face value. That all the bonds were sold at private sale, when the law required they should be sold after advertisement to the highest bidder. It is asserted that the bulk of these bonds were resold for the account of William Christy in New York in March last, at par and accrued interest, which was the price offered the Board for the entire issue, provided they would wait until Congress approved the law. The reports will also show that after adopting plans and specifications, the old Board concluded a contract with Carl, Crowly & Abernaty, the lowest bidders for the erection of a building in accordance therewith for the sum of $42,999, and that without authority of law they subsequently made additional contracts with these parties, which increased the cost of building to $70,100.92. A noted architect at Phoenix certifies that $8,500 would have been a liberal price for the work done under these additional contracts. The reports of the experts who examined the building, show that its construction was not in accordance with plans and specifications adopted, but that the mason, carpenter and plumbing work was all done in a slip-shod manner, and the material used was in every instance of the cheapest and poorest quality. So that now the Territory has a building which will require repairs amounting to $2,500 before it can be of permanent use. That on account of its faulty construction it can never be made such a building as the people had a right to expect for the money expended upon it. The building and grounds are in a state of incompleteness which will require the expenditure of several thousand dollars to make it suitable for the accommodation of the insane of the Territory. It will be seen that whereas the law limited the compensation of the local Director to $500, and non-resident Directors to $1,000 each during the year or portion of the same engaged in the construction of the buildings. Oscar Lincoln drew from the fund $1,831, M. W. Stewart $1,491.40 and F. C. Hatch, the resident Director, $2,285.53. It is also shown that furniture was placed in the building at a cost of $3,999.90, which competent experts appraise at $2,806.75. The law limited the cost of the Asylum, including buildings, grounds, furniture and all things necessary to make it a suitable receptacle for the insane, to $75,000; the Board expended $88,575, and it will require large additional sums to make it what the law contemplated. The disgraceful history of the entire transaction is a record of jobbery in wanton disregard of official propriety, decency and honor. Owing to the action of these recalcitrant officials, the Territory has been subjected to the expense of keeping the insane patients at Stockton for several months after the asylum should have been in successful operation in Phoenix. By their contumacious conduct in resisting executive and legal authority to remove them, they have proven an extravagant luxury to the taxpayers of Arizona. The patients were brought back to the Territory and the Asylum was finally functioning well, under the guidance of Doctor I. S. Titus.

1889—15th Assembly Message from Governor C. Meyer Zulick: "The administration of the Insane Asylum, under the direction of the present Board of Commissioners and Doctor I. S. Titus, the Medical Superintendent, is most efficient and praiseworthy, the expenses of maintaining the institution being $4,754.42 less than last year. I desire to especially direct your attention to the necessary repairs of the Insane Asylum Building, the importance of a good system of sewage and more perfect method of lighting, greater precaution against fire, and the fencing of the grounds as recommended by the Board, and for which a suitable appropriation should be made. Reprinted with permission of the Palo Verde Foundation for Mental Health from Arizona Psychiatry, "Arizona Mental Health in Territorial Days and After." Part II, Vol 1, No. 2, August, 1970, pg. 15.

Arizona Insane Asylum, Phoenix, Arizona Territory, circa 1890
Photo courtesy of the Arizona Historical Society, Phoenix, Arizona.

1891—16th Assembly Message from Governor Louis Wolfley: I submit herewith the reports of the Board of Directors and the Superintendent of the Insane Asylum, which set forth fully the condition of the institution. I recommend that an investigating committee be appointed to examine and report upon the condition of the building and grounds, and for the purpose of making suggestions for Legislative action. A hint of further trouble, this time with the physical plant. No action was taken on this recommendation during the 17th Assembly. The Board of Directors did not mention this in its report to the Governor. Report from Superintendent J. Miller, M.D. to the Board of Directors of the Insane Asylum—Feb. 10, 1893. I would respectfully request your Honorable Board to ask for some legislation prohibiting the committing of non-insane persons to the Asylum. During the past year several cases have occurred where petty criminals or other objectionable characters, not insane, have been committed here by Probate Courts, apparently for the sole reason of getting rid of them. The result of this practice if permitted, must be bad. It lays the Superintendent liable to suits for damages and gives the individuals so committed a license to commit crimes under the plea of insanity. A statutory limit should be fixed in which the sanity or insanity of an individual committed to the Asylum may be determined, thus relieving the Superintendent of the liability of damage suits. I suggest thirty days as such a period. A report to the Board by architect W. A. McGinnis, suggested inferior construction brought about the dilapidated condition of the asylum building. The board did include the architect's report in its recommendations, and supported the recommendations for building repairs. I would suggest that your Honorable Board recommend to his Excellency the Governor of Arizona and the Legislature, appropriations for the following purpose, viz: A foundation of stone should be put under the entire Asylum building with an area and retaining wall. Iron ceilings should be put in the five remaining wards. Steam should be utilized for heating the building on the ground of safety, economy and comfort to the patients. The roof of the entire building leaks, destroying the plastering in nearly all the upper rooms and halls, and requires attention. The entire building is dilapidated and calls for repairs. A new steam boiler is required. The one now in use is worn out, full of scale, and unsafe. The sewage system of this hospital remains an unsolved problem. The present system consists in running the sewage into a cesspool and then pumping it out again upon the land, where in the hot sun it develops disease germs and a stench that at times is almost intolerable. In case of an accident to our pump, which has occurred several times, the back flow deluges our kitchen with a combination of all the filth of the House. I most earnestly hope your Honorable Board will secure an appropriation sufficient to build a sewer to the river and thus end the expense and annoyance of this much vexed problem. The Governor concurred, and supported the Board's recommendations.

1893—17th Assembly Message from Governor N. O. Murphy. From personal observation, as well as from reports of the officers, I am convinced that in order to protect and preserve Territorial property, it is clearly in the interest of wise economy that provision be at once made by you to improve the foundation of the asylum building, repair ceilings, and for proper sewerage, and lighting and watering the institution, and I earnestly approve the recommendations of the Board of Directors in this respect. The Board of Directors asked for $24,600 for improvements. The Legislature, on the recommendation of Governor Louis C. Hughes was also cognizant of fiscal necessities. Was it also an election year?

1895—18th Assembly Message from Governor Louis C. Hughes: All political parties are pledged to retrenchment and economy in the administration of public affairs, and in the reduction of taxation. You have now the opportunity to make good this pledge. You are no doubt willing to keep good faith with your constituents. How can this be accomplished? Abolish all offices not absolutely necessary. Remove, as far as possible, the cost of maintaining our penitentiary, insane asylum, our criminal courts and jails by abolishing, curtailing or restraining the chief cause of crime—strong drink. In the interest of retrenchment and economy in the public service, I recommend the abolishment of the Territorial Boards of Prison, Insane Asylum and Reform School, and in lieu thereof the creation of a non-partisan board of control, the majority composed of Territorial officers who are required to give their entire time to the public service. Under the present system the Territory is fortunate in having exceptionally efficient and honorable men constituting these commissions—men of business affairs, who, in the performance of their official trusts, have sacrificed their personal business interests. These duties call them together monthly or quarterly, as fixed by law. As a rule, when they meet, they are greatly hurried or rushed; they do not devote sufficient of their time to the institutions or interests in their official keeping, hence they depend almost entirely upon the suggestions of the superintendents. Fortunately the present superintendents are men of high character and especial fitness for the duties assigned them, so that no harm results; but, by the Legislature creating a board of control, such as I suggest, expensive commissions could be dispensed with, thus saving the Territory annually about $12,000. The deficit of the Territory aggregates about a like sum. Your attention is called to these facts. This recommendation was put into effect and the insane asylum was directed by the Board of Control much later, when the Legislature, reinstated a Board of Directors for the state hospital. Superintendent Miller left and was replaced by Doctor Ira B. Hamblin, who remained with the asylum for 18 months and made no report to the Board of Control or to the Governor. He, in turn, was replaced by H. A. Hughes, who made a report directly to the Governor, indicating his displeasure at the conditions found at the asylum. Excerpts from a Report of the Superintendent of the Insane Asylum, dated December 31, 1896:

In compliance with legal requirements I have the honor to present your Excellency the Fifth Biennial Report of the Arizona Insane Asylum, which I have deemed best to divide into two sections, the first section covering the first eighteen months of the period under the superintendency of Doctor Ira B. Hamblin, which I think is complete and intelligent as far as the business records are concerned. Regarding the history and statistical records of the institution during that period, it is very incomplete, but the best that could possibly be done with the material left by my predecessor. A fact you will understand when you are informed that this is not an entry made in the daily report book from October 31st, 1894, to November 1st, 1895. By the commitment papers covering that period and the few imperfect notes I have been able to find there are ten males and one female patient entirely unaccounted for. There are no records of the death of patients who are known to have died, and others who are known to have escaped are reported discharged. For information I therefore consider the Asylum records of that part of this biennial period as worthless, as a part of the history of this institution. This condition of affairs will doubtless suggest to you the necessity of a law compelling a retiring Superintendent to make a report in full to the Governor of the condition of the institution up to the date of his retirement. The per capita cost of maintenance during the last six months is four cents less than the preceding six months and eleven cents less than for the first half of this biennial period. This too, notwithstanding we come to an empty larder and the supply of clothing so meagre that after taking careful invoice, one of our leading clothiers estimated the value of the entire lot at fifty dollars. I have endeavored to use economy in the management of the Asylum, but the comfort and welfare of the unfortunates who are under my charge must not be lost sight of or even take a second place in my consideration. Since assuming charge of the institution the first day of July last, we have instituted several important changes with a view of benefit and add to the comfort of our patients. The greatest amount of liberty possible consistent with safety to themselves and others had been granted the patients and they have been encouraged to do light work about the premises and spend as much time outside the wards as possible. The unsafe foundation walls, sewerage, and a better plant for heating and cooling had been installed, but much repair work previously mentioned in the Superintendent's report in 1893 was still left undone, including new ceilings, cement floors, and extensive re-plastering. The steam heaters, which had been such a failure that stoves had to replace them in the wards, have been replaced by competent workmen, and the entire work done over, so that they are now giving entire satisfaction, heating the wards comfortably, and are much safer and better in every way. Today we find the following improvements are absolute necessities for the accommodation of our increasing population, and for the protection of the property. We now have one hundred and fifty patients housed in four wards intended for one hundred persons, some of the rooms ten by fifteen feet have six beds in them. This is incompatible with the rules of hygiene and should not be. The two basement wards can be put in order for occupancy by cementing the floors and plastering the walls. Estimate cost of same, $1,200. The door casings were never properly put in and are not safe and should be replaced by new casings throughout the six wards.

1897—19th Assembly Message from Governor B. J. Franklin: While by strict economy and careful management it is probable that the present revenues would meet the current expenses, yet the margin is small and no provision is made to create a sinking fund to pay Asylum and other bonds as they fall due. $20,000 of Insane Asylum Bonds are now subject to call and they mature at the rate of $10,000 per annum until 1905. Reprinted with permission of the Palo Verde Foundation for Mental Health from Arizona Psychiatry, "Arizona Mental Health in Territorial days" Part III, Vol. 1, Number 3, 1971, pg. 11-14.

Arizona Territorial Insane Asylum, Phoenix, Arizona, 1896
Photo courtesy of the Arizona Historical Society, Tucson, Arizona.

Report of the Medical Superintendent of the Insane Asylum of Arizona

Phoenix, Arizona, October 1, 1900. To His Excellency, Governor N. O. Murphy. Sir: I have the honor to submit the seventh biennial report of the affairs of this institution. In accordance with the act of the Twenty-first Legislature establishing the fiscal year, this report covers a period of eighteen months extending from January 1, 1900, with which date the period covered by the previous report closes, to June 30, 1900. In the tables covering my report this period of eighteen months is divided in accordance with the fiscal year into two periods, vis: January 1, 1899, to June 30, 1900. As a preliminary to the compilation of these tables, a record of all patients admitted to the institution since its opening was constructed from the commitments and other records of the institution. Careful discussion of discrepancies and comparison of all available data have eliminated many of the grosser errors and filled many of the glaring omissions which previously existed in the records of the institution. In course of the preparation of this register the disposal of all but three of the seventeen patients noted as missing in my report for 1897-1898 was found to have been recorded, though in an obscure manner. All those patients carried on the records as visiting by the preceding administration, none of whom have since communicated with the asylum, are considered in these tables as discharged from the date of parole. There were admitted during the period, 73 men and 10 women, a total of 93,* the ratio being approximately seven males to two females, the same ratio obtains substantially since the opening of the asylum and is only a little larger than the ratio of males to females in the present population of the asylum (June 30, 1900), which is in accord with the observed fact that the female insane are longer lived than the male. The percentage of recoveries, calculated on Table 1 shows the number of insane admitted from each county and the ratio of insane persons to population in each county. It will be noted that the number of insane persons credited to certain counties, particularly Maricopa, is out of proportion to the population.

The disproportion may be assigned to three causes: First, citizens of other counties come to the asylum for treatment and are committed here; second, in counties conveniently near the asylum, mildly insane persons and persons perhaps not insane, but objectionable on account of their deficient mental condition are committed to the asylum for lack of a more appropriate place; third perhaps the most potent factor in creating the disproportion noted is to be found in the fact that the peculiarities of eccentric and mildly insane persons are more likely to be overlooked in sparsely-settled communities. In substantiation of this it may be observed that the average number of insane per hundred thousand of population in this Territory, which is 143.19, is much lower than the average for the United States, which in 1890 was 170.0 and still less than the average for the group of Western states and territories of which Arizona is a member, which in 1890 was 194.1. From which we may infer that the average insanity in the more popular counties is probably but little greater than the true average for the Territory. Tables 2 and 3 exhibit statistics of the cause and form of insanity of patients admitted. The data for Table 2 is taken from the commitments which accompany patients. It is necessarily inaccurate on account of the inability of the examining physician to determine the usually obscure causes of insanity in a short interview with the afflicted person.

Having discussed the statistical account of the operations of the institution, I may now speak in a more general way of the details of its history, which merit particular attention. Casualties have been few. One male patient, a Mexican, swallowed a small quantity of concentrated lye, which he surreptitiously obtained while the attention of the attendant who was supervising its use was momentarily attracted in another direction. Every effort was made to save his life, but unsuccessfully. Another patient, while at the Agua Caliente Hot Springs in care of the attendant, was bitten by a rattlesnake and died. One patient managed to crawl over the top of one of the short screens in the upper ward and dropped to the ground, fortunately sustaining no more serious injury than a sprained ankle. Attention has been called to these short screens and their replacement recommended a number of times, but this is the first practical demonstration of their danger that we have had. At another time two patients escaped at night from the upper ward by wrenching the screen from its insecure fastening on the old and frail window casing. These patients lowered themselves to the ground, a distance of nearly thirty feet, by means of an old piece of sash cord, and at the imminent risk of falling.

(*Editor's note: Either a typographical mistake or the superintendent couldn't do simple arithmetic.)

TABLE 2

CAUSE OF INSANITY

As assigned in commitments of patients by examining physicians.

	6 Month 1899 M. F. T.	1899-1900 M. F. T.
Alcoholism	3 1 4	7 0 7
Apoplexy	2 0 2	0 0 0
Brain Disease	0 0 0	0 1 1
Confinement	0 0 0	2 0 2
Domestic Trouble	0 0 0	1 2 3
Epilepsy	1 1 2	0 0 0
Exposure	1 0 1	2 0 2
Fright	0 0 0	0 1 1
Heredity	0 1 1	0 0 0
Immorality	1 0 1	0 0 0
Injury to Head	2 0 2	2 0 2
Insomnia	1 0 1	0 0 0
La Grippe	1 0 1	1 0 1
Lightning Stroke	0 0 0	1 0 1
Masturbation	1 0 1	4 0 4
Meningitis	1 0 1	0 0 0
Menopause	0 0 0	0 1 1
Menstrual Trouble	0 1 1	0 1 1
Narcotism	1 0 1	3 1 4
Nephritis	0 0 0	0 1 1
Overwork	0 0 0	1 0 1
Religion	0 1 1	3 3 6
Solitary life	1 0 1	0 0 0
Syphilis	4 0 4	4 0 4
Tuberculosis	0 0 0	1 0 1
Uraemia	0 0 0	1 0 1
Uterine disease	0 0 0	0 1 1
Want of work	1 0 1	1 0 1
Worry	0 0 0	1 0 1
Not stated	4 4 8	14 0 14

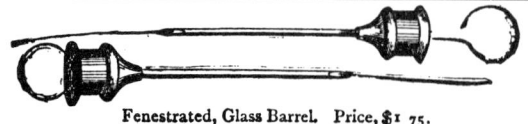

Fenestrated, Glass Barrel. Price, $1 75.

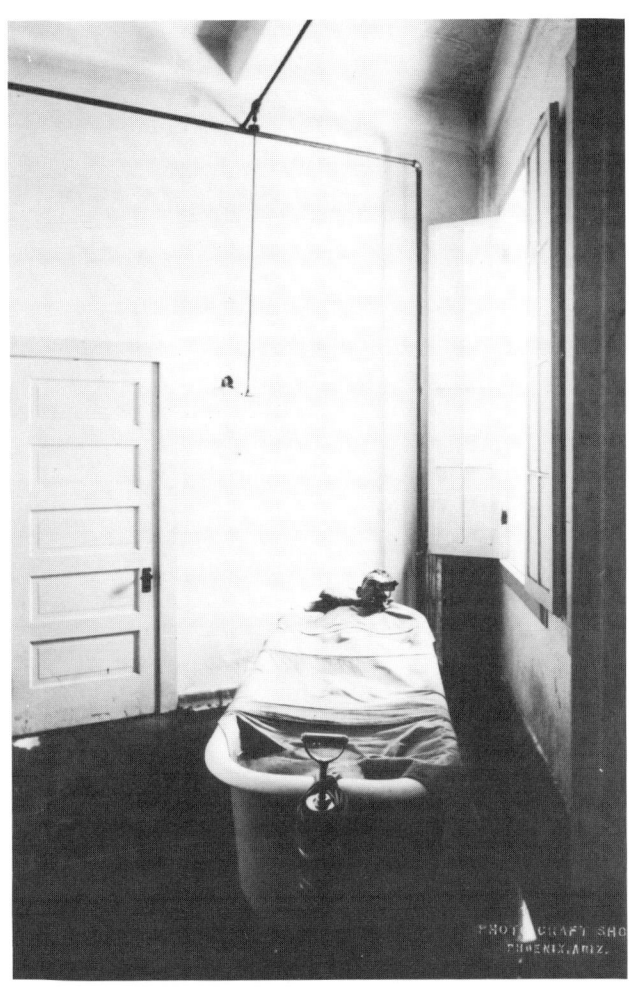

*Patient receiving hydrotherapy at Arizona State Insane Asylum, circa 1920
Photo courtesy of the Arizona State Department of Library and Archives, Phoenix, Arizona.*

As regards the treatment of insanity in this hospital little can be said. Medical treatment is given in such cases as are amenable to it; the epileptics in particular have been found to be benefited by treatment. A number of cases of narcotism have been treated. These patients are discharged entirely relieved and always in much better health than on admission, but I regret to state that they have generally found themselves unable to resist temptation. Complete mental rest and mild physical employment have been found most efficacious in relieving cases of temporary insanity. Employment and amusement are the principal means of diverting the patients and are used as extensively as possible. I must call attention to the existence of a number of cases in which surgical interference would probably be followed by recovery. This institution has absolutely no facilities of the necessary operation nor for the care of patients after the operation. The purchase of the necessary instruments and apparatus would be a paying investment in view of the relatively greater cost of the continued maintenance of this dangerous class of patients even if we lay aside the consideration of their reputation to reason. Insanity in women is commonly caused by pelvic diseases which may be remedied by surgical means. This hospital is not at present provided with the necessary appliances for the diagnosis of such cases much less their operative correction.

During the spring of 1900 I attended the annual convention of the California State Medical Association and while in that state visited three of

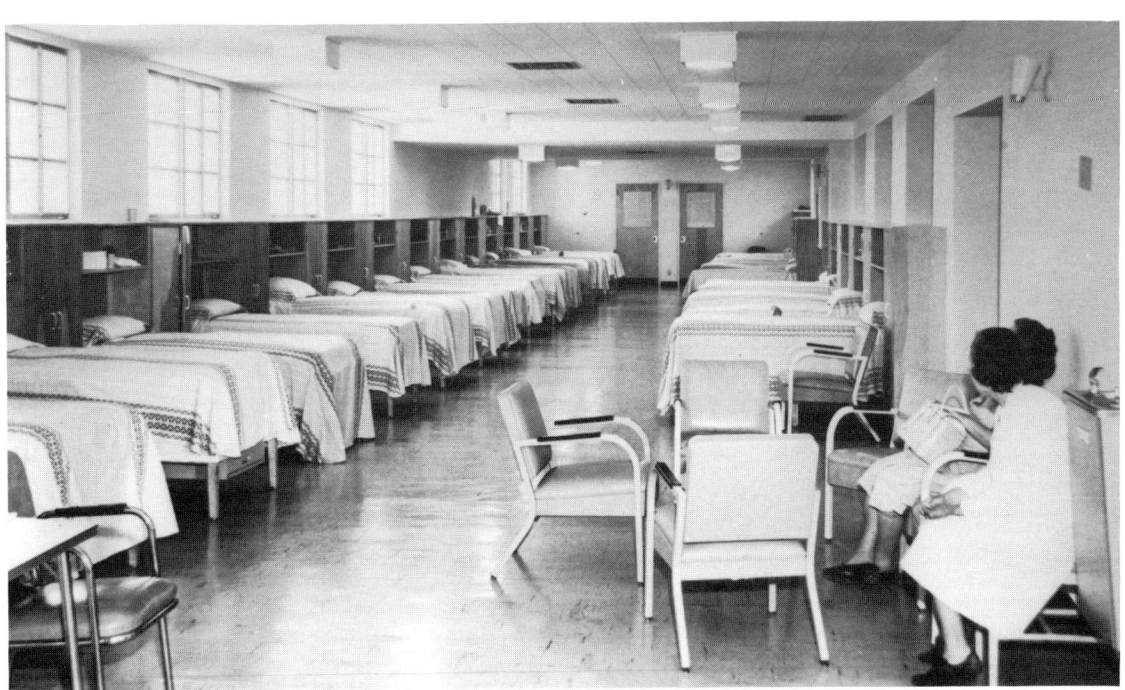

Sleeping accomodations for patients at Arizona State Hospital

Photo courtesy of Arizona State Hospital, Phoenix, Arizona.

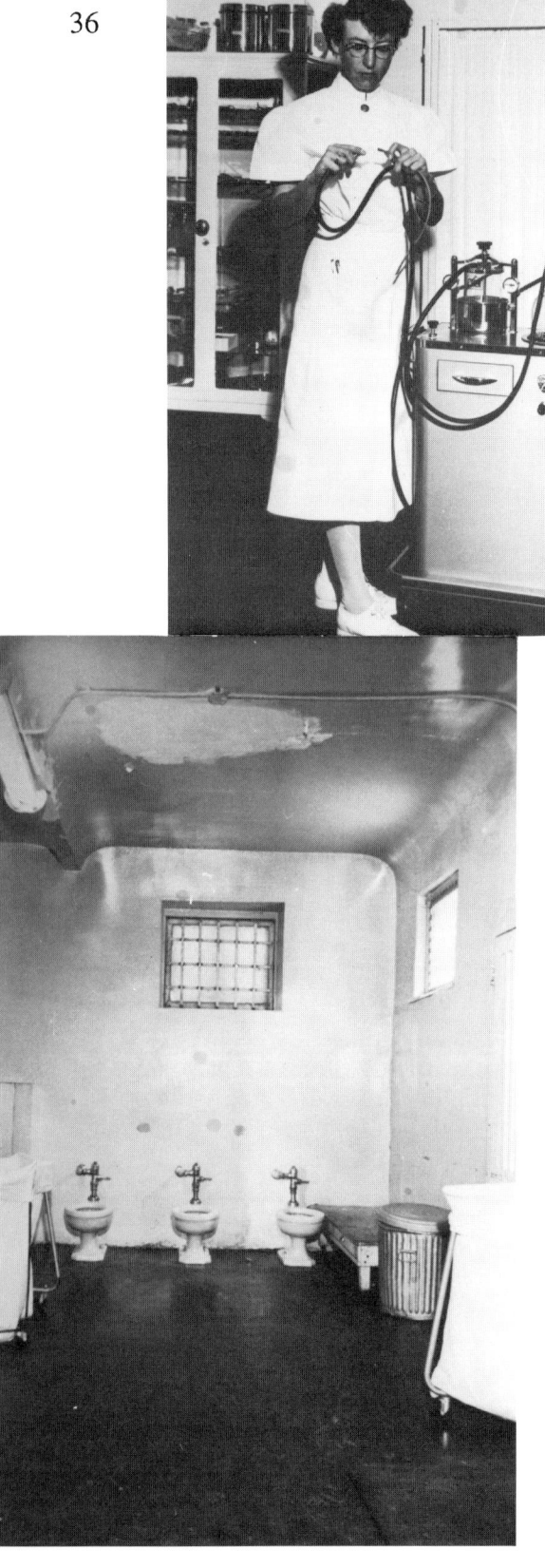

Nurse preparing treatment equipment at Arizona State Hospital.
Photo courtesy of Arizona State Hospital, Phoenix, Arizona.

the principal institutions for the insane. While I saw many details which could be imitated with benefit to this institution, in general the comparison which I was enabled to make is on the whole creditable to this institution, particularly as regards methods of treatment and administration. The sum of $12,000 appropriated by the last Legislature made it possible to make the extensive repairs and improvements which have long been needed. The new buildings constructed include a large adobe building for carpenter shop and paint shop, a building of eight rooms underneath and tank to accommodate the dairy, potato room, tool room and bedrooms for four employees. A new bake oven has been built. A large part of the appropriated sum was spent on new work in the asylum building. In particular may be mentioned the cement floor throughout the basement and the wooden floor throughout all of the upper wards. To a great extent entirely new ceilings were put in the sleeping rooms in the wards and in the basement hall in the central building. A completely new system of steam heating has been installed throughout the asylum building and the general dining hall. The plumbing system was almost entirely renewed. The cracks throughout the

Patients were taught the art of milking at Arizona State Hospital dairy farm. Their faces are masked to avoid identification.
Photo courtesy of Arizona State Hospital, Phoenix, Arizona.

Patients' lavatory, dubbed the "Encanto Bathroom" at Arizona State Hospital, 1969
Photo courtesy of Arizona State Hospital, Phoenix, Arizona.

building, the result of improper construction had increased in size and number to such an alarming extent that it was deemed necessary to secure the walls by means of stayrods. The building is now considered to be safe. My recommendations for the future are of two classes: First, needed legislation, second, needed improvements. A law excluding from the asylum such ineligible classes

Fig. 529.—Curved Hand Gouge. $1.50.

Insane Asylum, Phoenix, Arizona, circa 1920
Photo courtesy of the Arizona State Department of Library and Archives, Phoenix, Arizona.

TABLE 3

FORM OF INSANITY

	6 Months 1899 M. F. T.	1899-90 M. F. T.
Mania	10 2 12	21 3 24
Religious Mania	1 1 2	1 0 1
Acute Mania	2 0 2	1 1 2
Chronic Mania	1 1 2	1 0 1
Dipsomania	0 0 0	5 0 5
Narcomania	1 0 1	4 1 5
Melancholia	7 3 10	6 6 12
Dementia	0 0 0	3 0 3
Epilepsy	1 1 2	0 0 0
Imbecility	0 0 0	1 0 1
Paresis	0 0 0	1 0 1
Not insane	1 1 2	1 0 1
Unascertained	0 0 0	4 0 4

as inebriates, idiots and imbeciles, is desirable. The former is not insane ordinarily and the loss of mental equilibrium is generally of such short duration as to make confinement in the asylum a needless expense; the second class is not amenable to treatment and we have no facilities for their education, nor are they dangerous to be at large, so why should the burden of their support be thrown upon this Institution? Several patients in a dying condition have been sent to the asylum, their delirium being mistaken for insanity. A number of cases have occurred in which wholly ineligible *(sic)* persons have been sent to the asylum, possibly through deception practiced by interested persons. I would advise the establishment by law of a probationary period for the detention of insane persons for the determination of their sanity. The establishment of such a term of probation would relieve the superintendent of the asylum of liability for damage on account of the detention of persons who are really sane during the period necessary to determine this point. In view of an unfortunate accident which has occurred after the close of the period covered by this report, I would earnestly advise the asylum to lay aside all firearms and other weapons while in charge of such insane persons. (This rather cryptic note is not explained but it would appear that a patient confiscated the gun of a law officer. Editor.)

A legal provision requiring at least partial support of patients not without means to do so is needed. Owing to the crowded condition of the asylum and the rapid increase of patients a new wing with the following accommodations will soon be a necessity: Two or more wards for patients. An infirmary or sick ward. A class room for training school. Dispensary. Operating room. Examination room. Laboratory. Morgue. Such a building, if created at the rear of the center of the present building, would afford a covered way for the patient to reach the dining hall, a great desideratum in wet weather. In time it will also be necessary to construct cottages for convalescent patients. In conclusion I wish to thank all who

An early Arizona State Hospital office building and later converted to use as employees' quarters and a canteen.
Photo courtesy of Arizona State Hospital, Phoenix, Arizona.

Building "A" Arizona State Hospital, Phoenix, Arizona
Photo courtesy of Arizona State Hospital, Phoenix, Arizona.

Aerial view of the Arizona State Hospital farm as it appeared in 1953
Photo courtesy of Arizona State Hospital, Phoenix, Arizona.

Professional staff, Arizona State Hospital, Phoenix, Arizona, 1925
Photo courtesy of Arizona State Hospital, Phoenix, Arizona.

Medical staff, Arizona State Hospital, Phoenix, Arizona, 1963
Psychiatrist Samuel Wick, M.D. (front row, second from the left) was hospital administrator.
Photo courtesy of Arizona State Hospital, Phoenix, Arizona.

*Patients function as field workers on the Arizona State Hospital farm.
A silo is seen in the center background.
Photo courtesy of Arizona State Hospital, Phoenix, Arizona.*

have contributed to the comfort or amusement of the patients, particularly the Phoenix Stationery and News Co., for the donation of a large number of magazines; also to the Sells, Main and Gentry Circus Companies for complimentary tickets for the use of patients. I wish to thank the Board of Control and the officers and employees of this institution, for their co-operation and for numerous courtesies.

Respectfully submitted

J. Miller, M.D.
Medical Superintendent—an account of the investigation by the legislature into the misappropriation of funds by the Arizona Asylum for the Insane Board.

Insane Board (Poem)

A reader has kindly sent us the following poem dedicated to the "Insane Board," which appeared on June 14, 1886 in the *Prescott Morning Courier:* Insane Board. (Dedicated to Messrs. Stewart, Lincoln and Hatch)

>Appointed to a trusty place
>Which should be filled with zeal and
>   grace—
>Who squandered funds at rapid pace?
>"Insane Board"
>Who when removed, attempted "bluff?"
>Avowed they hadn't had enough?
>"The courts will not treat us so rough"
>"Insane Board"
>Who swore that by no hook or crook
>Upon the coin should Zulick look,
>Or see the secretary's book? —
>"Insane Board"
>Who said they thought the question rash,
>When asked what place they kept their cash?
>Whose sole defense was "cheek" and "brash?"
>"Insane Board"
>Who, when the matter came to court,
>Knowing their time was growing short
>Vamoosed the country, quick as thought?
>"Insane Board"
>And who, with his respect for law,
>Wish not to feel the hatter draw?
>"Insane Board"

Phoenix Gazette. It appears to be a reprint from the *Phoenix Gazette.* Reprinted with permission of the Palo Verde Foundation for Mental Health from *Arizona Psychiatry*, "Arizona Mental Health in Territorial Days" Vol. 4, No. 1 & 2, 1971, pp. 11-14.

V.

Territorial Doctors—Lawyers of Arizona

The renewed interest by physicians in legal training has led several to acquire law degrees. During most of the Territorial Days, prior to 1900, there were probably not more than fifteen or twenty physicians practicing in the Territory, this excludes military.

The first lawyer physician of note was John Alsap 1832-1886. Born in Frankfort, Kentucky he obtained his law and medical degrees from New York College. He practiced for a few years in the east before following the gold-fever parade to California in 1854. By 1864 he was in the Prescott area mining and practicing medicine. He acted as surgeon with the King Woolsey party on their expedition against the Apaches in 1865. Doctor Alsap, it is said, established the first saloon in Prescott on Goose Creek Flats. Well the first saloon was opened with a wagon as the storage area with a canvas lean-to and this housed this first "hard drinkin'-likker emporium." There are no known records of the quality or the source of the spirits sold therein. Soon the law and business activities supplanted Doctor Alsap's medical practice and under Governor R. C. McCormick he became the first territorial treasurer. In 1868 he was elected to the territorial legislature. In 1869 he moved to Phoenix and began ranching and farming about a mile out of Phoenix in the vicinity of the present intersection of Seventh Street and Thomas Road. By 1870 he returned to the territorial legislature representing Maricopa County and served on the first board of supervisors when Maricopa County was organized from the southern portion of Yavapai County. He was appointed probate judge in Maricopa County in 1871 and thereafter he was known as Judge Alsap. He served as one of the first mayors of Phoenix and in 1872 was re-elected to the legislature. Doctor Alsap never followed his medical avocation in the Valley but practiced law—this interspersed between his ranching and public office duties.

Win Wylie, M.D., J.D.
1855-1939

Another prominent physician lawyer was Doctor Win Wylie 1855-1939. He practiced medicine and surgery in Phoenix for many years. Born in Wisconsin, both his father and mother were physicians. His father had graduated from Long Island Medical College Hospital, Brooklyn, New York, and the mother Harriet Amesbury Wylie graduated from Womens Medical College, Philadelphia, Pennsylvania, 1866. Doctor Wylie graduated from Rush Medical College, Chicago, 1877, and first did general practice in Warsaw, Wisconsin. But he soon yearned for the law and graduated from the Atlanta, Georgia Law School in 1895 and established practice in Phoenix in 1896. He became active in politics and medicine and was appointed surgeon-general of Arizona in 1897 and reappointed in 1898 and served with the rank of colonel. (Now this political plum carries with it the stars of a major general.) On March 15, 1927 a group of one hundred and fifty physicians, their families and friends gathered to celebrate the fiftieth anniversary of Doctor Wylie's entering upon the practice of medicine. It was served at the

Arizona Club, Doctor J. M. Greer was at that time president of the Maricopa County Medical Society and he introduced Doctor D. F. Harbridge who served as toastmaster. The doctor-lawyer training was completed by at least two early territorial physicians.

John Taber Alsap, M.D.

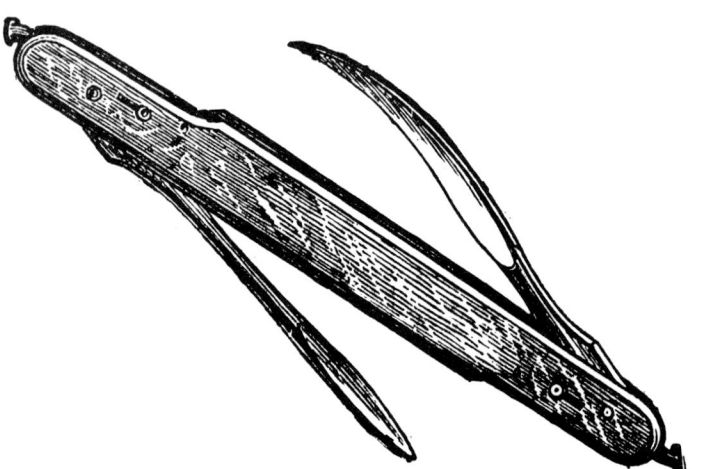

Double Shell Handle Knife. Slide catch. $2 50

VI.
Squaw Peak Sketches of Pithy Pioneer Physicians
Four Peaks, Fort McDowell and Wassaja

Some inquiries have been made following a previous note on Carlos Montezuma, the Apache physician. The inquiries were about the activities of Fort McDowell in the Apache days. Well, would you believe one inquiry? Brandes (1) in his succinct summary of Arizona military posts lists fifty camps, posts and stations which were active at one time or another in the Arizona Military Department. The earliest establishment was Camp Calhoun (later Camp Yna) 1849 and the last to be established was Fort Huachuca 1887 which has now turned to electronics and is continually expanding its facilities; the last active Arizona "Frontier Post." Camp McDowell (2) was most clearly described by army physicians, Smart, De Witt and Reagles in 1875. The following is from their account: "This post is situated on the west bank of the Rio Verde about eight miles above its junction with the Salt River—forty five miles north of the Maricopa and Pima Indian villages. It is reached by steamer from San Francisco to San Diego, California, thence by stage via Yuma to Maricopa Wells, thence by weekly mail to the post. Floods on the Gila and the Salt frequently delay mail three to four weeks. Letters usually reach San Francisco in fifteen days and Washington twenty-five days." The post was established in 1865 (2) by: "five companies of

Fort McDowell—Hospital steward's quarters. The hospital has long since disappeared. Photo by author.

Ruins of the headquarters building at Fort McDowell, circa 1965

California volunteers, as a point from which to operate against, or treat with, the Indians of the neighboring mountains. An accurate plot and minute description of the post buildings, including the hospital is given. The hospital, recently completed (1875) has a principal ward 33 x 12 feet in height contains eight beds." The consolidated sick-report for Camp McDowell 1870-74 lists the mean strength as 5-10 officers and 111-221 enlisted men. Three cases of typhoid fever were recorded, nine of remittent fever, thirty-five cases of syphilis, two hundred thirteen cases of dysentery, and under the classification of violent diseases and deaths, six gunshot wounds and an arrow wound. Leonard Wood, Assistant Surgeon, U.S.A. was stationed at Fort McDowell following his exploits at Fort Huachuca during the Geronimo campaign. He recorded in his diary Oct. 11, 1888 (3) "This is the hottest place in the world where white troops are stationed, . . .* ground temperature in the summer 170 degrees. The shade temperature is 120 degrees and above. The water in the bath tubs is so hot it cannot be used when drawn, as the pipe lies near the surface, where the heat is from 150 degrees to 170 degrees . . . so we draw it the night before." Martha Summerhayes (4) in her classic description of her life with a soldier husband, in the Arizona Territory four years beginning 1874, with adventures at Camp Apache and Camp McDowell related her saga. "We occupied quarters at the end of the row, and a large bay window looked out over a rather desolate plain and across to the large and well kept hospital. I had nothing but some shades on the windows. The walls and floor were adobe, and some men from the Company came and laid down old canvas, then the carpet and drove great spikes around the edge to hold it. In the front of our quarters was a ramada supported by two rude poles and a cottonwood tree. Then came the sidewalk, and the acequia (ditch) then a row of young cottonwood trees, then the parade ground. Through the acequia ran the clear water that supplied the post, and under the shade of the ramadas hung the large ollas (clay jars) from which we dipped the drinking water. . . ice was not dreamed of in the far plains of McDowell. With summer heat, sleep inside the house was impossible and we soon followed the example of the cavalrymen who had their beds out on the parade ground. The Sunday inspection of men and barracks, performed with precision and formality, often in full dress uniform, gave us something to mark the weeks by. Another bright winter found us gazing at the Four Peaks . . . the only landmark on the horizon."

This formality which Mrs. Summerhayes noted was not the usual custom at all posts and Brandes puts it very well: "There was always some spit and polish among the officers but even such men as George Crook realized the need for dressing in a manner which would permit him to best move around in comfort. His pith helmet, civilian jacket with large pockets, (paratroopers please note) and rough trousers reminded one of anything but an army general."

Fort McDowell on April 10, 1890, became a reservation for the Mohave-Apache (Yavapai) and some Pima Indians. Over 25,000 acres were then set aside for the Indians, and in 1903 additional acreage was allocated. (l) So indeed it was to the "homeland" of his people that Wassaja returned to spin out his short bit of time in the winter of 1922. Wassaja was a Mohave-Apache!

*These temperatures have been rechecked and this is what Wood wrote.

Remains of medical quarters, the last vestige of any structure at Fort McDowell. The ruins were purposely burned to the ground in 1989 to make room for a church building. Photo reprinted with permission of Phoenix Newspapers, Inc.

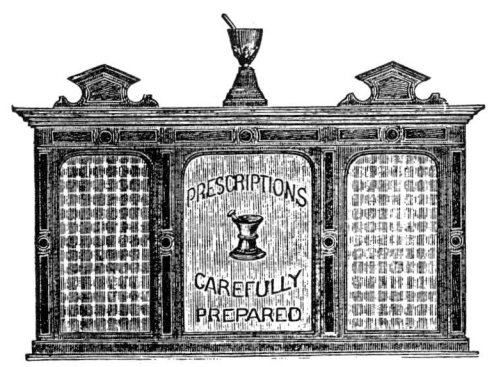

*Wassaja's (Carlos Montezuma) grave at Fort McDowell
Photo by author.*

Wassaja—Carlos Montezuma

Doctor Montezuma, who died in 1923 at the age of 56, probably, according to Doctor Kennedy's notes, was the first native American Indian (Mohave-Apache) to become a fully qualified physician.

After eight years of service as a physician with what then was called the Indian Bureau, a federal agency, Doctor Montezuma began his lifelong battle to free his fellow Indians from what Doctor Kennedy refers to as "the tentacles of the Indian Bureau and their (enforced) servitude on the reservations."

The correspondence by the late Phoenix thoracic surgeon, Dermont W. Melick, M.D., appended to Wassaja's story, is an interesting sidelight to the trials and tribulations which dogged Doctor Montezuma throughout his relatively short life.

J. DeV.

References:

1. Brandes, Ray: *Frontier Military Posts of Arizona,* Dale Stuart King Publisher, Six Shooter Canyon, Globe, Arizona, 1960 pp. 53-55.
2. Circular No. 8, War Department, Surgeon-General's Office, Washington, May 1, 1875. *A report on the Hygiene of the United States Army, with descriptions of Military Posts*, Washington Printing Office, pp. 545-546.
3. Hagerdorn, Hermann, *Leonard Wood, A Biography*, Harper & Bros. 1931, Vol. 1 pp. 113-114.
4. Summerhayes, Martha, *Vanished Arizona,* J. B. Lippincott Co., Philadelphia 1908, reprinted 1963, pp. 184-195.

VII.

The Summerhayes Trek

Martha Summerhayes with her army husband, Lt. Jack Summerhayes left San Francisco by ocean steamer about 15 July 1874 bound for the Arizona Territory. A hundred years later, the Council on Abandoned Military Posts, led by their national commander, barrister Robert Yount of Scottsdale, and Doctor Clarence Yount, Jr. of Prescott as surgeon, chief scout and woodcutter, about 25 trekkers took up Martha's trail at Fort Yuma and through the ensuing week walked and rode and sweated over much of the same trail reaching Fort Apache a week later. Other army wives and laundresses, soldiers' wives, made this journey before and many were to follow their soldier husbands into Arizona Territory through the sixties, seventies and eighties.

But none left such a poignant account of their journeys as did Martha, in her book, "Vanished Arizona, Recollections of my Army Life" first published in 1908. It has since undergone six re-printings and is a classic description of army life in those early days in the Territory. The first limited edition of one thousand copies was quickly exhausted, Martha set about editing a second edition which was published in 1911. Within two months of its publication, her husband, John, died and two months later Martha's life closed and both are now serenely settled in the Arlington National Cemetery.

W. T. Jackson, in an introduction to the 1962 edition, points out the unique factors in Martha's account. "Few pioneer women recorded their stories and observations for posterity. Those, like Martha Summerhayes, who did so, wrote for the enjoyment and edification of relatives and friends rather than for the historian or the general public. 'Vanished Arizona' is exceptional because its author was a woman, an Army wife, and a sensitive, acute observer blessed with literary talent."

The 8th Infantry had been ordered to Arizona Territory. The Summerhayes left San Francisco in mid-August 1874 and after seven days aboard the steamer Newburn, they had rounded Cape San Lucas, touched at Mazatlan with thirteen more days in the searing heat to the mouth of the Colorado. Here the wind and seas were so disturbing that it was seven more days before they could transfer to the river steamer Gila, a Colorado sternwheeler, and finally after twenty six days out of San Francisco they were to arrive at Fort Yuma. The quarters where she spent two days in comparative comfort are still in use. The remnants of Fort Yuma on the west bank of the Colorado at Yuma is one of the few structures still in existence, one hundred years later, that were visited by Martha in her Arizona days. Fourteen more days of river heat, and remember this is the last of July, first of August, and as she described it "more heat and worse food" brought them past Ehrenberg to Fort Mohave. As they passed Ehrenberg she thought this was "a most wretched place." Little did she dream that in less than a year later she and her husband would be back at this station on assignment. It was to break her health and after about a year at this dismal place she was forced to go back east to regain her health.

But now back to Fort Mohave. It was established in April, 1859 as Camp Colorado and in the same month the name changed to Fort Mohave. During the Civil War, when federal troops were recalled for duty back east, it was manned by California volunteers. Nothing remains now of the original buildings and the site is now desolate of all buildings; they were demolished for salvage in 1934. All that remains is the imagination which you bring with you, some slabs of cement, former building sites and scattered rusty nails. The fort itself was closed in 1890 and afterwards the Bureau of Indian Affairs established a school for Indian children which was closed in 1934. You can gaze across the river at the sloping hills on the California side. This was the termination of the Mohave Trail over which rolled hundreds of tons of army supplies from San Pedro, California, supplying troops in Arizona Territory. Fort Mohave was then an important supply post.

The Colorado River steamboats were to be busy for about ten years, but they faded and in the meantime were superseded by the Mohave Trail from California and then later by railroads. On the 8th of September the Summerhayes had reached Camp Mohave, eleven days from Fort Yuma and two days later were to begin the hazardous overland trip to Fort Apache. Martha described it this way: "At last the command moved out. It was to me a novel sight. The wagons and schooners were drawn by teams of six heavy mules, while a team of six lighter mules was put to each ambulance and carriage. The main body of troops marched in advance, then came the ambulances, followed by baggage wagons and a small rear guard. When the troops were halted, once an hour for rest, the officer, who marched with the soldiers, would come to the ambulances and chat a while until the bugle call for 'Assembly' sounded, then they would join their commands again and then would fall in and the call 'Forward' was sounded and the small sized Army train moved on.

"The day's march, from then on was gauged by overnight camps where water could be found. These campsites are still discernible, nothing remains in the way of a permanent structure, sometimes a rock wall or a rock foundation or a grove of trees is all that marks the site one hundred years later through which these army trains passed. The first day out of Fort Mohave they were overnight at Hardyville, then to Packwood Ranch and then to Beals Springs. This is on the north outskirts of Kingman and at one time the water from these springs was used as a source of supply for the city. But Martha's train pushed steadily on, there was not a city at the site of Kingman in those days. The next camp site was Freeze Wash, this was a short march of only 14 miles. The next day it was 28 miles to Willow Grove Springs, then to Fort Rock and Anvil Rock. This rock still sits there, shaped like the fabulous anvil, thence to Camp Hualapai. By now you are entering the green grass and pine country and Martha stated that this revived her spirits. The next and last stop on the road was at American Ranch, 10 miles or so north of Fort Whipple and it is now being encroached upon by Prescott suburban homes. After seven weeks of continuous travel, Fort Whipple seemed like a paradise to Martha, but her journey was far from over. After a day's rest they marched on to Camp Verde taking two days. Another company left their ranks and remained at Camp Verde."

Martha noted "The Command was now getting deplorably small, I thought, to enter an Indian country for we were now to start for Camp Apache." She continues, "Several routes were discussed, but, it being quite early in Autumn, and the Apache Indians being just then comparatively quiet, they decided to march the troops over

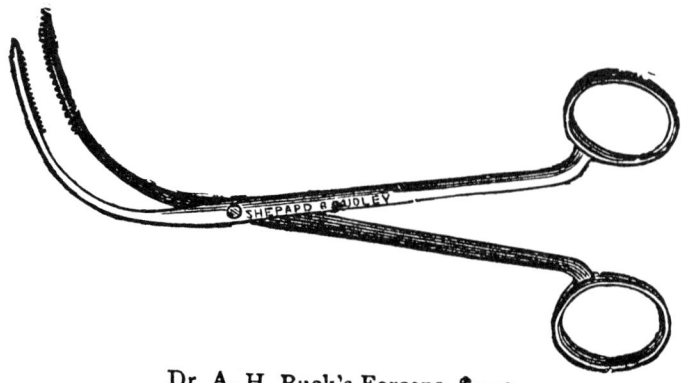

Dr. A. H. Buck's Forceps, $3.00.

Crook's Trail, which crossed the Mogollon Rim range and was considered to be shorter than any other." The final leg of the journey she describes in detail for Crook's Trail was little more than that and not by any stretch of the imagination designed for army wagons. The teamsters reported that a six mule train had rolled down the steep side of the mountain on one occasion, Martha didn't inquire as to what had happened to the mules, and neither did she learn until later that this wagon held most of her precious clothing and household supplies which she had brought with her from the east. This part of Martha's journey into Arizona Territory was completed on the 4th of October and as she describes it: "We had crossed the range and begun to see something which looked like roads. Our animals were fagged to a state of exhaustion, but the traveling was now much easier and there was good grazing, and after three more long days' march we arrived at Camp Apache." There, too, ended the sentimental "Trek" of a score or so of history buffs under the banner of C A M P, in August 1974. Martha Summerhayes was to spend nearly four years at various posts beginning with Fort Apache and Ehrenberg, Fort McDowell and Fort Lowell.

Four years later when the Eight Foot (the army infantry unit to which her husband was assigned) left Arizona, Martha observed: "We took supper in Phoenix, at a place known as 'Devine's.' I was hearing a good deal about Phoenix; for even then, its gardens, its orchards and its climate were becoming famous, but the season of the year was unpropitious to form a favorable opinion of that thriving place, even if my opinions of Arizona, with its parched up soil and insufferable heat, had not been formed already. We crossed the Gila somewhere below there, and stopped at our old camping places, but the entire valley was seething hot. We joined Captain Corliss and the company at Antelope Station, and in two more days were at Yuma City   By this

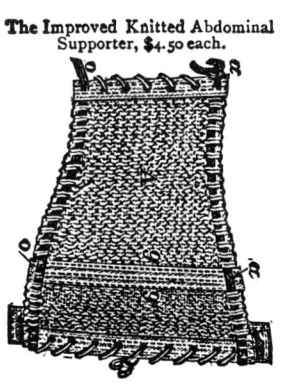

Summerhayes' Quarters at Ehrenberg, 1875

Artist Frederic Remington and Martha's husband, Lieutenant Jack Summerhayes, on a shooting trip in Mexico, pose with an army "ambulance."

time, the Southern Pacific Railroad had been built as far as Yuma, and a bridge thrown across the Colorado at this point. It seemed an incongruity. And how burning hot the cars looked, standing there in the Arizona sun. After four years in the Territory, and remembering the days, weeks and even months spent in traveling on the river, or marching through the deserts, I could not make the Pullman cars seem a reality."

Native dress of the Cocopah and Yuma Indian women in 1875

Summerhayes' Quarters at old Camp McDowell, 1877.

VIII.

Leonard Wood, M.D. Some Arizona Territory Influences

The first seeding of my interest in this soldier physician, who later was to become an eccentricity, came while browsing in a corner of the Boston City Hospital in September, 1931. Those of you who have not traversed this maze of corridors and tunnels at the BCH have missed a most enlightening experience. Medical students, in ancient days, have been known to wander there undetected for their last two years of clinical clerkship, before surfacing for graduation, all the time sought by professors who inhabited the multiple institutes and the wards. The latter always seethed with patients. There is a plaque, which we came across while AWOL from Doctor George Richards Minot's mighty dolorous lectures. (Doctor Minot was professor of clinical medicine and with Doctor William Parry Murphy had received the Nobel Prize in Medicine for the discovery of a cure for pernicious anemia—a disabling and usually fatal disease.) The plaque stated that Leonard Wood interned at Boston City Hospital. What it doesn't say is that he was dismissed before his year of servitude was completed. The hospital director took a dim view of house officers who showed signs of transgressing on the rigid hospital rules. In this instance, no surgical treatment could be rendered without a senior staff physician's consent. One charge was proven false and another partially so. In spite of the fact that his senior attending physician testified on Wood's behalf, it was to no avail. He was dismissed

September, 1884. (1) He took up rooms in a private dwelling close by to establish a private practice. This languished. At the suggestion of a physician friend he took the Army Medical Corps entrance examinations, thought nothing much about it and a few months later was told that his regular commission could not be rendered until funds became available but he was offered a position in the civil service as an acting assistant surgeon with the troops in the west. Within a fortnight he had closed his office, bade goodbye to his family and boarded the train for Arizona Territory. (1) Already the decisive character of the man was evident. He was not dismayed by his dismissal from the hospital, and he quickly accepted the challenge of serving with troops in the far west. He reported in at Fort Whipple on a June evening in 1885, and met Doctor Fred Crayton Ainsworth, who gave him advice and counsel. Ainsworth was the post physician, a regular of the medical corps, but was later to become the chief of the Record and Pension Office, now termed the adjutant general of the army. He was on duty in Washington, when some years later, Wood

reported there as chief of staff; both these men had entered the service as physicians, both outran their West Point colleagues in obtaining positions of high command, not in the medical corps but in the line. (2) This was never to occur again and it created almost as much hubbub as when George Marshall became chief of staff as a non-West Pointer four decades later. Three days later he was on his way from Fort Whipple, on orders from General Crook, directing him "not to stop at Fort Bowie as originally ordered but to go straight to Fort Huachuca." He spent a night at Maricopa, took the Southern Pacific eastward to Benson, then a spur line over to Huachuca. (1) The spur line still exists. A clerk entered in the medical record; "Act. Asst. Surgeon 'Leoander' Wood, U. S. Army arrived at Post, July 4, 1885." (3) He was ordered to report immediately to Henry W. Lawton, captain of B Troop Fourth Cavalry. (3) Lawton was a six-foot-five, hundred and eighty pound professional soldier who had been a law student at Harvard when Fort Sumter fell, and four days later he was in the army. He participated in twenty battles, and came out with a temporary commission as Lt. Colonel at twenty-two. (It may come as a surprise to learn that promotion in the army in Civil War times was almost as rapid as promotion in the Army Air Corps in World War II). Wood and Lawton became fast friends. They were both great horsemen, both New Englanders, loved the outdoors, and didn't give up any task assigned to them. Two days later, on July 6, Wood was in the field and rode "45 miles in the last 30 hours," he recorded in his diary. (4) With alternate journeys into the field, and duty on the post he was respected, but not especially popular; he was respected by the troopers because they

Troops from Fort Huachuca, Arizona Territory, waiting for orders to "hit the trail" near the Mexican border, in 1881. Photo courtesy of the Arizona Historical Society

Muster of 6th U. S. Cavalry Company at Fort Huachuca, Arizona, 1882 Photo courtesy Arizona Historical Society, Phoenix, Arizona.

Fort Whipple, Arizona Territory, circa 1880 Photo courtesy Sharlot Hall Museum, Prescott, Arizona.

5th Memorial Cavalry on Parade Fort Huachuca, 1973

found that he could take whatever mustang they gave him to ride and he could ride further and longer than anybody else. After my preliminary brush with the plaque about General Wood at Boston City Hospital, it was twenty-odd years before I heard or thought any more about this incident. Then soon after my arrival in Arizona in 1949, we took ourselves to high country to gaze upon the fair city of Prescott, the first Territorial capital. In the foreground of the court house, there is this great equestrian statue, by Solon Borglum, to the Rough Riders, albeit all true natives of Prescott say this is Buckey O'Neill, killed in action at San Juan Hill, in Cuba during the Spanish-American War, nonetheless I find nothing on the bronze plaque to indicate that it is specifically the deceased hero. It does carry a plaque listing Colonel Wood as the commanding officer and Lt. Colonel Theodore Roosevelt as the executive officer of the First United States Volunteer Cavalry. Well my interest was kindled again.*

The preceding and what follows, is not exactly new about Wood in Arizona Territory. His diary that he carefully kept during the field campaign remains a classic. Lane's *The Journal of Leonard Wood*, May-September 1886 places it in perspective. (5) The Gatewood evidence is fully presented by Faulk (6) and Thrapp. (7) Depending on their taste, partisans may now align themselves claiming sainthood for Crook, Miles, Crawford, Lawton, Wood or Gatewood for the final Geronimo defeat. To some of us, it simply exemplifies the usual train of human history and progress. Scarcely anything originates de novo, but all accomplishment is a composite of all contributors, "some are just more equal than others." The burden of my study is simply to describe Wood's character, his motivation to complete any mission to which he was assigned, and to make a few observations about his physical illness which would have stopped the ordinary mortal dead in his tracks early in his career, but this illness appears only to have spurred him on to greater endeavors. His illness was a form of brain tumor, meningioma, for which he was operated on three times.

Rough Riders 1898. Left to right: Colonel Leonard Wood, Commanding Officer; First Lt. John Greenway; Orderly Charles Siper; Colonel Theodore Roosevelt, Executive Officer, First United States Cavalry. Photo courtesy of the Arizona Historical Society Library.

When Miles asked Wood to determine if the best soldiers "could equal in activity and endurance the Apache warriors," he further continued, "I would like to have you accompany Captain Lawton's command," Miles told Wood, "As you are probably in as good condition as anyone to endure what they endure, you could make a careful study of the Indians—and discover wherein lies the superiority, if it does exist. (General Crook had been relieved and General Miles assumed command of the campaign.)

The Rough Rider statue, Prescott, Arizona

Certainly, Wood was overly optimistic when he told General Miles, "I believed the right sort of white man could eventually break these Indians up and compel them to surrender" May 4, 1886. (8) By continually moving in on the Indians and keeping them on the move, even in the roughest terrain, the troopers very nearly pulled it off. Later, Miles suspected that it wasn't to be so and reverted to a tactic devised earlier by General Crook, palaver, and to try it he selected one of Crook's most trusted lieutenants. Charles B. Gatewood had nine years service in the region, the last three in charge of the Fort Apache Agency. (9) Lt. Gatewood was to contact Lawton's command and then Geronimo and his hiding hostiles. Reluctantly, he succeeded, but was denied complete official and public recognition and died early in life in the year 1896, a bitter man, broken in health and retired from the service. (10) Lt. Gatewood's widow's pension was a paltry $24 per month. Wood, with Lawton's detachment, had traveled 1,800 miles during the latter part of the Geronimo campaign and was cited by Lawton for the Medal of Honor. It was finally awarded in 1898 by President McKinley. Wood, by that time,

Guard House—Fort Whipple, Arizona, now a canteen of the Veterans Administration facility, one of two original buildings which remain.
Photo courtesy Sharlot Hall Museum, Prescott, Arizona.

was stationed in Washington, D.C., and was the President's personal physician. This was to hang like "an albatross about his neck," and was always a fair target for all of his service non-friends, as he climbed the promotion list, as an officer of the line, who began his career as a lowly medical officer. He rolled over the West Point graduates like a pack mule down a Sierra Madre Canyon. Even his critics admitted his superior performance. Some stated that he had never heard a shot fired in anger. Well, at least on two occasions, shots were fired possibly in anger. Wood's diary, July 2 1886, you will note that this is about one year after his assignment to Huachuca: "Infantry still without an officer and greatly in need of someone to take charge of them, I volunteered and was placed in command today. The men are pretty badly demoralized."

July 13, 1886, while closing in on what they believed to be the Indian encampment: "About this time heavy firing began on the up river side. We then advanced pretty rapidly and finally were in the bottom land near the camp, and were then fired into a body of our own Scouts (Brown

Apache Scouts—U. S. Service 1860s

Scouts), who were advancing towards us having found no Indians in the camp." (12) On August 11, 1886, he recorded: "We were working up a canyon, when suddenly a couple of bullets struck so near us that we were both covered with dirt. My mouth and face were full of it. Horn was well covered. We dropped under cover of the nearest rocks without waiting to ask any questions. We kept under cover for some time and finally worked back carefully under cover over the ridge. The people who fired at us must have undoubtedly been Indians on the opposite side of the canyon." (13) Thus Wood faced fire on two occasions—once mistakenly by army scouts, and another by hostiles. It simply depends on whose barn is burning down—as to whether the bullets "were fired in anger."

The field experience in Arizona Territory and the Sierra Madre terrain of Sonora, Northern Mexico, his own bouts of fever—probably malaria, and probable knowledge gained about yellow fever in the area, served him well as governor of Cuba. Yellow fever was rampant along the coastal areas of Sonora, Mexico, and the last severe epidemic of yellow fever in that community was thought to have occurred about 1885-90. (14) All of this stood him in good stead in the Cuban campaign and prepared him for his assignment as military occupation commander of Santiago, and by 1900 he was military governor of Cuba. Yellow fever, Cuban apathy, bad sanitation, and local corruption all demanded and got his attention and by the end of 1899, he was a major general. This was a short fourteen years after his army career began. Then to the Philippines as governor of Moro Province, followed by a four-year stint as military administrator of all of the Philippines, and then was appointed chief of staff, U.S. Army, 1910. (15)

Perhaps his medical history is not of great general interest, but I do believe that it exemplifies the tenacious character of the man. (16-18) In 1904, his lameness of the left leg became obvious. It had first occurred in 1901 following an attack of typhoid fever. There was a growing numbness of his left hand. He simply pushed his exercises and physical fitness program to overcome and compensate for this disability. One physician noted a small, hard protuberance on the right side of the skull, and this was thought to be the result of an accident Wood suffered in Santiago in 1898.

Later in the year, back in Boston, he was persuaded to have surgery. Doctor Arthur Cabot

Party of packers and Indian guides detailed by General Miles to round up lost livestock after close of Geronimo campaign 1887.
Left to right: Groves, Steves, Chino, Funston, unknown, Tony Ferguson, and Leonard Wood.
Photo Courtesy of the National Archives.

performed it, and found what was described as a benign bony tumor of the skull, a psammoma. The bone was scraped and replaced, (1904). By 1910, "local seizures" occurred in his left leg and arm, with weakness, awkward gait, and unsteadiness. He consulted Doctor Harvey Cushing, then developing a new branch of medicine, neurosurgery, at Johns Hopkins in Baltimore. Cushing did a two-stage brain operation, each session about four hours duration, under local anesthesia. He found the tumor, removed it, and again replaced the bone flap. This ultimately proved to be a fatal mistake, for it was not realized at the time that the bone overlying the tumor (meningioma) must also be removed or it will recur.

A few days later, much to Cushing's chagrin, but characteristic of Wood, the general attended Doctor Welch's 60th birthday anniversary. There were 400 to 500 guests present and "Wood, much to my embarrassment, and astonishment of others, insisted on coming to the dinner with his head closely capped." (19)

Wood returned to duty, became chief of staff of the army 1912-14. but failed to obtain command of the American Expeditionary Force in 1917. The command was awarded to Pershing.

Doctor Joseph Madison Greer, a longtime physician of Phoenix, was a young medical officer stationed at Walter Reed Army Hospital, Washington, D.C. at the outbreak of World War I. He recalled that General Wood was sent over twice for a rigorous physical examination to determine whether "He was fit for field duty." He hopped "funny," but was passed each time as "fit for field duty" the third time, as Doctor Greer recalled, before Wood was ordered to the hospital, word came down "from upstairs" that the findings were not acceptable. By whom, and for what reason, Doctor Greer was not clear. (20) But Wood's brilliant career was quietly derailed by the regulars; his forthright call for preparedness some years before had incurred the displeasure of President Wilson. He was sent to the field to train troops, but never commanded troops in the A.E.F.

He lost a bid for the Republican nomination for president in 1920 when he and Frank Orren Lowden reached a stalemate in convention votes. The back room politicians rewarded the nation by giving them Warren G. Harding. "Biting the bullet" of disappointment, he accepted the appointment as governor general of the Philippines, where he served from 1921 to 1927. Slowly and relentlessly, his old malady recurred. Lameness, partial paralysis and speech slurring forced him to consult Cushing again. By this time the natural history of meningiomas was clearly understood. It had been carefully delineated by Cushing, and the tumor had locally recurred from the skull bone flap which had been replaced at each of his previous surgeries, the last one by Cushing.

Wood died a few hours after surgery due to an undetected intracranial hemorrhage. Cushing was distraught and refused to operate for two weeks. Never before had his house staff noted any break in the iron self-control for which Cushing was noted. Now the leading performers in the last Geronimo campaign were finally off stage, Gatewood, Crook, Miles, Lawton, Wood and all the others. Who, today associates them with Geronimo? Perhaps very few, except those with special interest in that era of our national times. Some say, and not without reason, that with his limited resources Geronimo outgeneraled and out-fought them all. "A victory has many fathers, but defeat is an orphan." (21)

* Solon Hannibal Borglum (1868-1922) was the older brother of Gutzon Borglum (1871-1941) of Mount rushmore fame. Unlike his brother, Solon specialized in Western outdoor sculpture. He named his statue at Prescott "The Bucking Broncho" (his spelling). It has nothing to do with Buckey O'Neill, Teddy Roosevelt or the Rough Riders.—Ed.

Reference: The New Funk & Wagnalls Encyclopedia, 1949.

Joseph Madison Greer, M.D., of Phoenix. An army veteran of WW I and a navy veteran of WW II Doctor Greer served on the medical board of Walter Reed Army Hospital in Washington, D.C. when General Leonard Wood, M.D. was rejected for overseas duty in WW I.

The original postoperative sketch to show A) manner of exposing the tumor, and B) its estimated position "in situ" drawn to scale. Cushing's first surgery February 1910.
Photo Courtesy Charles C. Thomas Publishing Company.

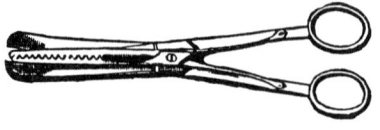

References:

1. Hagerdorn, H., *Leonard Wood—A Biography*. Harper & Brothers, New York, Vol. 1 page 23-47, 1931.
2. Ibid, Vol. 2, page 95.
3. Ibid, Vol. 1, page 54.
4. Ibid, Vol. 1, page 56.
5. Lane, J C., *Chasing Geronimo. The Journal of Leonard Wood*, May-September, 1886. University of New Mexico Press, 1970.
6. Faulk O. B., *The Geronimo Campaign.*, Oxford University Press, 1969.
7. Thrapp, D L., *The Conquest of Apacheria*. University of Oklahoma Press, 1967.
8. Lane, page 25.
9. Faulk, page 112.
10. Lane, page 118.
11. Lane, page 64.
12. Lane, page 71.
13. Lane, page 94.
14. Quebbeman, F., *Medicine in Territorial Arizona*. Arizona Historical Foundation, page 171, 1966.
15. Holme, J. G., *The Life of Leonard Wood*. Doubleday, Page & Co., New York, pp. 150-153, 1970.
16. Fulton, J. F., *Harvey Cushing, A Biography*. Charles C. Thomas, pp. 306-312, 1946.
17. Hagerdorn, Vol II, pp 60-62 and pp 83-89.
18. Cushing, H., et al: *Meningiomas*. Charles C. Thomas, 1938.
19. Fulton, J. F., page 312.
20. Greer, J., *Personal Communication*, 1967.
21. Carell, P., *Quoting Count Cinano's Diary in The Foxes of the Desert*. Dutton & Co. 1958, Bantam Edition, page 293.

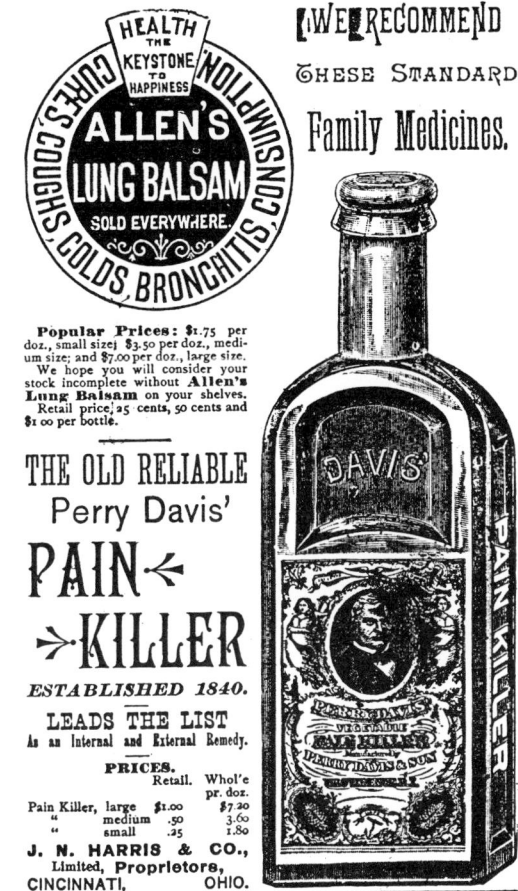

IX.

Alexander M. Tuthill, M.D. Another Pithy Pioneer Physician of Territorial Arizona

Not a few famous physician soldiers came through Arizona with the army, but Arizona can claim as its very own, or almost so, Doctor Tuthill who became, at least in this writer's opinion, the most famous of the soldier-physicians of early Arizona. These columns have already commented to some degree upon this colorful character, but there may now be some newcomers in our state who would be curious about some of the men who contended with medical problems before the advent of SMA-12 (a sophisticated laboratory blood test) and other exotic aids. The *Arizona Republic* in January 27, 1952, commented, "Arizona's most distinguished Doctor General has decided to give up his medical practice, after 56 years of administering to the ill and afflicted. He will retire February 1 and close his office in the Professional Building. He was one of the first tenants in the building when it was completed two decades ago." Now, not a physician's office remains in the Professional Building. It is filled with computers, bankers, and clerks. Tut was born in New York in 1871, moved to California in 1877, and enlisted in the cavalry, Troop D of the California National Guard in 1896. At a review of the California guard by the governor, Tut broke up the whole show by losing control of his horse which ran through the governor's party.

In 1898 after finishing medical school he left the California clime to take a position as surgeon at the mines in Morenci, Arizona. He first became assistant surgeon for the Detroit Copper Company and the Arizona Copper Company at Morenci. Two years later the two companies separated their medical staffs and Doctor Tuthill remained with the Arizona company and in 1903 he became chief surgeon of the Detroit company, a subsidiary of the Phelps Dodge Corporation. His patients were largely miners and their families in the hilly country around Morenci and Clifton, and frequently he couldn't even use a buggy to make his rounds, but usually went on horseback. Delivery of babies in huts with dirt floors was a matter of daily occurrence. When the miners went on strike they were very careful when violence broke out to protect El Doctor for they didn't know when his services would be necessary to mend their injuries which might be incurred in the fracas. At Morenci in 1903 he helped to organize a National Guard cavalry troop and his comrades unanimously elected him to the captaincy. (You will recall that this was still the day when officers were elected by the volunteer troops.) Tut was known for some of his rather curt phrases and actions, and perhaps one of the earliest that is recorded ran something like this.

In 1910 the first Arizona infantry commanded by Col. Tuthill was sent to Atascadero, California for training. On arrival it was raining so he ordered the Pullman moved to the sidetrack and kept his men in their berths, at some expense to the government. Explanations were asked for and received, "Until at about the Fortieth Endorsement of the War Department asked, 'by whose authority were these Pullman cars held over night?'" They got the following reply, "Mine. Tuthill." And that was the end of the exchange of endearments. At another time in 1916 at a dance held by the officers in Naco, Arizona, probably in the Bullet Proof Hotel, Col. Tuthill was informed that the orchestra was composed of union men and that playing would cease at midnight. "I am a union man myself, play on" and they did. At another time in 1917 when he commanded the 79th Brigade, 40th Division; during the maneuvers at Camp Kearney, California, when all the officers were assembled for the critique, after a very disappointing day, General Tuthill made the following critique, "You embryo Napoleons, I wouldn't trade the entire

Alexander M. Tuthill, M.D.
1871-1958

Editorial page cartoon in The Arizona Republic by Pulitzer Prize winner, Reg Manning

officer personnel of this brigade for the froth of one cold bottle of beer. The critique is over, you are excused."

In France in 1918, he was about the only National Guard general officer to retain his command. When his brigade was in the rear area training, General Tuthill became inquisitive as to how matters were being handled at the front. Without permission or excuse he drove to Verdon to inspect the front line and see what was going on. A high explosive shell landed near him. The general's pipe fell on the ground, struck a rock and broke. "Every time I tell that story," General Tuthill mused, "the shell strikes closer to me, and if I don't stop telling it, I fear that some day it will land too near and I shall become a casualty."

In 1919 returning from France, the general was greeted by reporters in New York. "What decorations did you receive overseas?" A reporter asked. "I received the Pomme-de-Terre," the straight faced brigadier informed the reporter who wrote down the information in all good faith and was only prevented from printing it by less gullible brothers of the Fourth Estate. In 1928 as brigade commander of the 45th Division, he received an order to report for examination to re-enter the guard. General Tuthill dropped the telegraphic order in his customary file, the waterbasket, and three days later he received a wire that his examination had been held and his appointment would be immediately forthcoming although he never even answered the wire let alone any

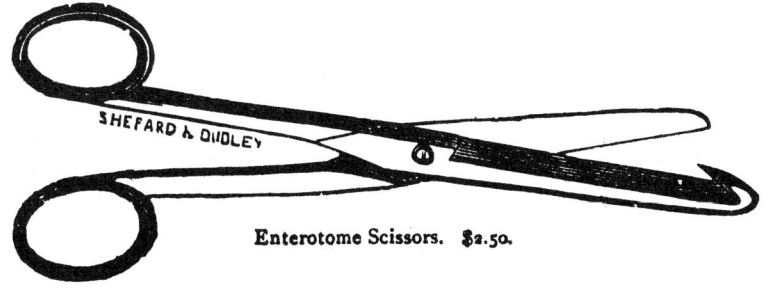

Enterotome Scissors. $2.50.

questions. After World War I he returned to Phoenix, took up the practice of medicine again and also returned to duty with the national guard, then as adjutant general. He served in this capacity through both Democratic and Republican administrations and he always served notice on the oncoming governor that when he was reappointed, that if they wanted his resignation, "They could just name one captain of the National Guard," and they would have his resignation immediately. Another officer recalled that at a summer encampment outside of Flagstaff the general was especially displeased with the way the exercises had been conducted. He pointed out not only the errors in command, and errors in carrying out directives but he also cited many errors that he had personally observed on the field.

At the critique, without further adieu, the general stormed, "This is so low in training index that we have established here through the years that I expect to have the resignations of three and perhaps four officers on my desk when I return to Phoenix, Monday next." Three of them did resign, but one of those he particularly referred to did not. This officer received one of Tuthill's famous terse telegrams. "Your resignation accepted," signed, Tuthill.

Bullet Proof Hotel, Naco, Arizona, undergoing demolition August 1973 Photo by author.

In 1940 a local paper mentioned Tuthill's name as a possible candidate for governor. He was later approached by some of his fellow Arizonans to run for governor, and he declared that he "would not take the job if elected, because of the 10,000 undesirable acquaintances I would have to make in order to be elected. Furthermore, I'd have every unemployable bum in the State of Arizona seeking a job, I simply won't run."

During WW II while Tuthill was still adjutant general of the state, there was great

Allied officers during inspection of 40th Sunshine Division, March, 1919 near Bordeaux, France. Standing in front row are (from left to right) Generals Tuthill, Pershing, and Walsh. Photo courtesy of U. S. Army.

difficulty with the large number of troops which arrived in Phoenix each weekend on pass. There were numerous training areas in the vicinity, especially the air force bases. He placed undesirable areas in Phoenix off limits, and then doubled the shore patrol and the military police patrols. With all of these precautions there was still a bit of hell raised every weekend. One devout religionist approached him and asked him if there wasn't something the general could do to stop this den of iniquity which was developing in Phoenix. The general asked this man of the cloth if there were any suggestions, to which he replied, "Yes, order all of these men to church on Sunday and that will keep them out of the hands of the Devil." To this the general replied, "Well, neither the President of the United States nor I, nor any of the men's commanding officers can order them to attend church; we can order them into battle to be killed, but not to church." Well, this somewhat incensed the man of religion who mumbled something about the military had never tried religion, and the general asked his visitor if he thought religion had ever been tried in the world. The delegate replied, "No," and to this the general rejoined, "Well, we spent a hell of a lot of money on some damn poor religious salesmen then."

Lt. Gen. Louis B. Hershey, formerly director of the Selective Service System, had on the wall of his den a reminder to keep his directives clear and simple. A telegram sent to him on December 17, 1941, by General A. M. Tuthill, Arizona draft director; "Just received instructions as to screening examinations. Stop. My God. Repeat. My God. (signed) Tuthill." They were fast friends and continued so until Tut's death in 1958.

Entrance to Fort Tuthill near Flagstaff, Arizona Photo by author.

General Hershey wrote, "In a recital of his many accomplishments and his eminent success each fails to give an adequate description of 'King Tut' as he was affectionately called. He somehow reflected a ruggedness of the state which he did so much to build. There was never any doubt about what he stood for, even less doubt about what he would stand for. He was forthright and let the chips fall where they may. His integrity like the mountains of his state, stood high and as immovable." This is a very fitting epitaph to Arizona's most famous soldier physician.

Photo courtesy of the Arizona National Guard.

X.

Public Health

Introduction

If you have read J. B. Priestly's novel "The Citadel" you will have an inkling of what is in store for you in the pages that follow.

In the novel we see a small Welsh mining town in Great Britain. The town sewer system was a disaster but even a greater disaster for the community citizenry. But the mining company which owned the town refused to correct the situation despite pleas and warnings of the company's young doctor. Finally in desperation the doctor enlisted the aid of a physician friend. Together they blew up the antiquated sewer system forcing the mining company to install a new one.

Adequate sanitation also was a problem in many of the small towns and some larger ones in early day Arizona. A handful of courageous pioneer physicians strove mightily to remedy the deplorable conditions which existed and managed, after many struggles and disappointments, to win some measure of success but without the explosive solution described by Priestly who, incidentally, was a physician himself.

Reading the accounts of public health measures, or the lack of them in territorial Arizona and even after 1912 when the territory became a state, one cannot help but wonder what kept the sparse population of the area from being wiped out by disease.

Tuberculosis was rife in the territory and continued into statehood. Smallpox was a common and open gateway to the hereafter and animal-borne diseases (zoonoses) even in the cities were no rarities because farm animals were allowed to be quartered in residential areas. A 1915 outbreak of Malta fever in Phoenix was traced by the U.S. Public Health Service to herds of goats kept by several Phoenix families. Other zoonoses traced to chickens, horses, cows and sheep living in close proximity to urban dwellings also were reported.

It was not until some time after the close of World War II that physicians, led by the redoubtable Clarence Salsbury, M.D., were able to bring about much needed public health reforms. Until then, municipal, county, territorial and state law making bodies had consistently turned deaf ears to all efforts by the medical profession and some public spirited citizens to clean up the cesspool that was Arizona.

In the pages that follow, the reader will see that public health problems at the turn of the century in Arizona related principally to infectious diseases. They included but were not limited to smallpox, dysentery of various types and, of course, Malta fever (brucellosis), also called undulant fever, previously mentioned, and tularemia, popularly called rabbit fever. The two names of the latter disease stem from the fact that the first cases were traced to infected rabbits in Tulare County, California. Public concern at that time to the contrary, however, early day Arizonans were spared the specter of leprosy or Hansen's disease. (See Introduction to Odds and Ends in Chapter XVI.)

The unfolding drama of tracking down the then so-called "Flying Chlamydospore" as the casuative agent of San Joaquin Valley (California) fever, later to be more scientifically identified as Coccidioidomycosis, is a credit to the persevering pioneer Arizona physicians who led the battle against the disease, which, despite its geographic name, was not limited to California.

Although not directly associated with public health in early Arizona, The Balmie Expedition and Hara Kiri by Virus are included in these pages because of their obvious historical interest, which reflects back to Arizona.

Smallpox, with which the Balmie Expedition treats, was a worldwide scourge which bade fair to seriously decimate the Indian population of the Territory (and later state) of Arizona as well as that of the hardy pioneers who settled the wilderness that later was to become the nation's 48th state.

Hara Kiri by Virus (a brief sketch concerning yellow fever) may be of interest to medical historians and particularly to those Arizona physicians who, like Dr. Kennedy, graduated from Harvard's Medical School.

J. DeV.

The Perils of Public Health

Public health problems at the turn of the century in Arizona related principally to infectious diseases; smallpox, dysentery of various types, Malta fever—then later the recognition of "rabbit fever" transmissible to humans and the recognition of widespread Coccidioidomycosis in the desert areas. (Reprinted with permission from the August 1974 issue of *Arizona Medicine*)

"Yes, Marion Sprague, your carefully collected collection of historical data relating to the development of the Public Health Department together with the early letters and records of the Arizona Department of Health, and the state health officers; yes, Marion, these have been preserved and they are attended by Mildred Rambaugh of the Vital Records Department of the new Department of Health Services. Marion came to the department when there were only five other employees in 1931 and closed her desk in 1964." *Arizona Public Health News*, an intramural publication, devoted a considerable portion of the 1964 number to appreciation of Marion's service to the state.

It was Mrs. Sprague, to whom the then commissioner of health, Doctor Clarence Salsbury, referred my inquiring eye when I wondered if there was any historical material in the state health department archives from the early days. Indeed there was. Mrs. Sprague was most helpful in demonstrating it to me, it has been added to and is a tribute to her early guardianship. Doctor Louis C. Kossuth, who was the last commissioner of health for the state before the latest reorganization, had been over to a planning section. Doctor Kossuth was also mindful of the value of historical treasure and kindly lent his support and assistance in further care and collection for these departmental archives. Then a new director of the department of health services assumed the hot seat and it is none other than flying doctor bioengineer, James L. Schamadan, M.D. The names change, but there is a fair possibility that some of the problems will remain the same.

The original territorial board of health was created March 19, 1903 by the 22nd Territorial Assembly. John R. Whiteside, a member of the council and representing Mohave County, introduced the bill which began the establishment of the Territorial Board of Health, county and city boards of health and regulating the record of vital statistics. The Territorial Board of Health made the governor president, the attorney general, vice president and a practicing physician of the territory was chosen to be the secretary. Many of the letters written to Doctor R. N. Looney, secretary, board of health 1912-15, are preserved. Unfortunately, almost all the answers, usually sent from his office in Prescott where he enjoyed a busy private practice, were destroyed. When Doctor R. N. Looney (Arizona license #15, 1903) of Prescott was the state superintendent of health, he received some fascinating letters by Doctor L. L. Miner (Arizona license #316) county superintendent of health, practicing in Bisbee, Arizona Territory. These letters are fascinating because they delineate the epidemiology of an outbreak of smallpox, his attempts to control it and largely defeated by public opinion apparently egged on by some competitive physicians in the adjacent city of Douglas.

The first letter was dated March 9, 1912 and parts of it read as follows: "Unintentionally I have been guilty of neglecting some of the duties of my office, i.e. in reports to you of vital statistics in contagious diseases. It was some days after my appointment before I was notified to proceed, my predecessor passed his duties to another, who in turn deputized another, and the last officer can give me no books for recording statistics—hence, with apologies for delay, I must appeal to you and request the necessary books." (It appears Doctor

Miner got "booked" on that one.) "In accordance with my telegram I shall try to acquaint you with information about smallpox at Douglas (which I am advised you have received from Doctor Green, Deputy Health Officer Protem) but also with the general pulse of public sentiment. January 17th, the proprietor of the Mission House, also a truant officer and a Salvation Army Officer (holding weekly services at the County Hospital) displayed an eruption of smallpox. Case reported to the Health Department at Douglas, January 20th. During the interval he was visited by many people including the two Salvation Army girls. He was removed to the Detention Hospital, his house quarantined, fumigated, guests vaccinated and observed fourteen days. No other cases. Quarantine raised. At this time a dress-maker who had been visited by Salvation Army girls, had a light case of smallpox and was quarantined in residence with her husband. No case from this time until February 26th, when other cases appeared which I am informed you are aware of in their sequence.

"One case, on account of public criticism, should be presented to you. February 14, the traveling man developed, at the hotel, an eruption resembling smallpox and was removed to the Detention Hospital. He gave a history of receiving 606 January 6th. (this was a form of arsenical used in the treatment of syphilis) three days after detention eruption appeared apparently syphilitic and was so pronounced by four able physicians. Clothes were fumigated, and he was dressed in sterile gowns and was removed to the County Hospital, dead two days later. His undertaker, Marty, developed smallpox seven days later. Of three undertakers who developed smallpox, one died. On account of the removal of this patient, and the published information, the public at once accepted this as the source of the disease and severe public criticism resulted.

"The above facts were dictated to me by Doctor Greene. Should this case have been smallpox as suspected on account of the undertaker contracting smallpox, possibly 606 may have had some influence in masking its symptoms. Immediately after taking this office I went to Douglas, to request the closure of the schools. Bitter resistance was encountered from some of the school board and among the bitterest was Doctor Wright. Their chief argument against this measure was that it would hurt the town as it would then admit that there was smallpox prevalent and it had been present in the most dangerous places, namely laundry wrappers, drivers, butchers, and three undertakers, and other citizens, including boarding house proprietors, all totaled eleven Americans and two Mexicans.

Bitter criticism was rife then, yet they were loath to take even the first protective measures. The following night the District Attorney and myself thought best to close theaters and churches. It would require too much space to attempt to acquaint you with the apparent and unnecessary jealousy between these two towns, mutually dependent upon one another, but jealousy evidently exists. Whether or not the fact that this office has fallen to Bisbee for the first time has been the cause of any increased jealousy to Douglas, I am unable to state, but I can state that the suggestion of the ordinary protective measures, ordinarily instituted by the average incorporated town on its own initiative, have invariably met with resistance.

"The epidemic originated in dangerous sources, laundry for one and they permitted laundry to be shipped to outside towns after the outbreak of the epidemic. Until last night that is for the past three days, conditions seemed hopeful. Three cases and one death is a history of yesterday. The driver of a coal and wood wagon is one of the cases and while not certain I think the other is a driver also. The third developed in the hospital."

He then goes on to further state that in spite of his best efforts there is still a continued resistance on the part of the people in Douglas to accept full quarantine measures. Doctor Miner felt so alarmed about the possibility of further spread of the disease in each city that he requested, "If quarantine is necessary we would be in a stronger position to do so with less damage to already strained relations, by having your advise or even your presence. The results of the next few days may decide the matter on which course to consider best." On March 15th, only four days later Doctor Miner wrote to Doctor Looney "last night Douglas reported one dead, a driver ill for six days, another case not expected to live but tonight he was reported better. Today a new case developed in a Negro woman, released from the County Hospital fourteen days ago. Since then she has been circulating at liberty." He reported "For two days the Douglas Postmaster has sent mail in a pouch against advice and request of the Health Board. In view of reports, requests and telegrams and a fresh case at large in Douglas, I can see no other recourse but to declare against their mail until the postmaster shows willingness to assist rather than resist protective measures along with disobeying postal orders." (Further on he delineates that it was the custom in those days to fumigate mail by making holes in the envelopes and I presumed fumigating with formaldehyde fumes, although it isn't stated just what fumigant was used.)

There is a copy of a letter signed by F. B.

King, superintendent, Western Division EP & SW Railroad, to the agent at Douglas, Arizona and it is interesting in that it goes into more detail about the method of fumigating. "Pursuant instructions from the County Superintendent of Health effective at once, all freight other than perishables originating at Douglas, must be fumigated before being forwarded; and in order to do this, a solution of 10 ounces of formaldehyde and 5 ounces of potassium permanganate will be used for each car of merchandise loaded at Douglas. This mixture in the above proportions, is to be placed in a porcelain, stone or tin receptacle and placed in the car merchandise after it is loaded and the doors up the town quite tight if there was any resistance from the local authorities at Douglas.

Well when they were eyeball to eyeball, that is, when Doctor Looney and Doctor Miner were eyeball to eyeball with the city authorities in Douglas, the latter were convinced that whether they agreed or not there were going to be quarantine measures instituted and so it was.

Later correspondence from Doctor Miner indicated that the epidemic began to simmer off, but as late as May 19, 1912 he reported that another case of smallpox appeared, a pressman for the newspaper became ill on May 9th, and in consultation with three other physicians it was

Depot of the El Paso and Southern Railroad in Douglas, Arizona Territory, 1910
Photo courtesy of the Arizona Historical Foundation, Tempe, Arizona.

immediately closed and sealed." He further gives explicit direction about how the baggage room, the waiting room and the entire station is to be fumigated on the close of each day.

Doctor Looney apparently had concern about the necessity of absolute quarantine measures in Douglas so he did go to visit the area, but he had, in the meantime prepared himself with authority from Governor Hunt, which would make it possible for him to declare martial law and shut agreed he had typical smallpox, so that quarantine measures were strictly invoked and enforced again. As you leaf through these old records it is evident that smallpox was present almost every year in some portion of the state in those early days, together with typhoid fever, scarlet fever and diphtheria. But it was due to the alertness, and the clinical competence of these practicing physicians that these diseases were kept under control.

The Public Health and Related Problems Early in the Territory and State

Doctor Looney of Prescott, Arizona was one of the colorful public health commissioners of early Arizona. His finesse in closing of a "Joy-House" in Prescott was unsurpassable. Some may recall the "Quarreling and Quarantine" episode in Douglas at the time of a smallpox epidemic. (1) About 15 cases and 4 deaths occurred before it was controlled. Doctor L. L. Miner of the adjacent metropolis of Bisbee was then county superintendent of health for Cochise County. He had been rebuffed when he asked for closure of certain business establishments in Douglas in which the cases seemed to originate, a laundry was one, and an undertaking parlor was another! He then asked for help from Doctor R. N. Looney, the state health commissioner, who conducted the business of the state while continuing his practice in Prescott. After discussions with state officials and more especially with Governor George W. P. Hunt, Doctor Looney went down to Douglas with full authority to "declare martial law" if there was any further resistance by the citizenry of Douglas.

Some spirited articles in the *Douglas Daily Dispatch* in March, 1912 were quite vociferous in their condemnation of the interference of Doctor Looney but when presented with the alternative of "martial law, to prevent any intercourse by citizens of Douglas either through the mail, by train or any other means with any other part of the country," there was conversation but also cooperation and no martial law was invoked. The smallpox epidemic soon died out.

The quarantine maneuver by Doctor Looney in his home town of Prescott was a bit more delicate and subtle, and it has recently been recounted by Budge Ruffner in his collection of Arizona anecdotes. (2) This is what he had to say under the title of "Public Health." "It was a very delicate situation and the old doctor knew it. This was the type of thing that made him regret he had ever agreed to serve as county health officer. It was a fact, however, and he had to deal with it. If it were handled too openly, if too much were made of it, there would be severe economic implications

West Main Street in Benson, Arizona as it looked circa 1914. Photo courtesy of the Arizona Historical Foundation, Tempe, Arizona.

Robert Nelson Looney, M.D.
1870-1962
Superintendent of the Territorial and later state board of health 1912-1915
Photo courtesy of Sharlot Hall Museum, Prescott, Arizona.

for the town. Then, too, there would be that segment of the community which would find it offensive; the health of the town, however, had to be maintained. At any cost, outright panic must be averted, he thought.

"It would be a mistake to make a public announcement, but the menace itself had to be contained. He knew this type of health problem should not become common knowledge; it would embarrass the county attorney and the sheriff, the city administration and, oh, so many who pretended the impossibility of such a development. The unsuspecting public must be protected. 'The girls' themselves were no problem. They eagerly sought the medical attention which would return them to, at least, an economically fruitful life. A garish red quarantine sign on the front door was bound to look bad; it would be blunt and frightening and have an impact on the Prescott public which could not be quickly erased. A diplomatic, even euphemistic, type of poster was the only answer, the doctor concluded; worded to discourage a prospective patron, yet with no implication of hazard to health or morals. The old man sat down at his roll-top desk, moistened his cigar, and, in his Tennessee pace, methodically printed the sign with a black crayon. When he finished he carried it down Gurley Street, one block west of the Plaza, to the brothel and tacked it to the front door of the old brick building. Only three words but it told the story: CLOSED FOR REPAIRS."

Bibliography

1. "Quarreling and Quarantine," *Arizona Medicine*, #1 Volume 19, pp 65-66, 1962.
2. *All Hell Needs is Water*, by Budge Ruffner, University of Arizona Press, 1972, pp 53-54, by permission of the author.

The United Eastern Mine in Oatman, Arizona
Photo courtesy of the Arizona Historical Foundation, Tempe, Arizona.

ITEM: In response to an inquiry about Gila monster bites, Doctor William V. Whitmore of Tucson wrote on May 14, 1906, to the health officer: "The only case of Gila monster bite that has come under my observation occurred thirteen years ago when I was an assistant to Doctor George Goodfellow here. The doctor had two or three of these pets in his yard. One noon while he was holding one of them in his left hand and was teasing it with his right hand, it grabbed him by the index finger of his right hand. I was at lunch. He rushed to the drug store, had the wound opened and cauterized. The symptoms were wholly local, the finger giving him some trouble for a few weeks—as I now recall.

"Some eight or ten years ago I saw, several times, with Doctor Henry N. Matas, a case of hydrophobia caused by the bite of a skunk. The patient died in about a week or ten days. The cases of rattlesnake poisoning that I have treated have been either so mild or so long after the reception of the poison that very little was required in the way of treatment. I have not known a patient to die of rattlesnake poisoning."

ITEM: Another reply received by Doctor William Duffield in response to his query about bites came from Doctor P. A. Melick from Williams, Arizona, May 1, 1905. "Replying to your favor of the seventeenth inst., I regret to say that it has not yet been my fortune to see any living creature bitten by the Gila monster, rattle-snake, nor hydrophobia skunk, therefore, I can give you no data upon the subject. Doctor Dennis J. Bramen in Flagstaff may be able to furnish you with some data upon the symptoms produced by the bite of a hydrophobia skunk, as I have been informed that a man died in Flagstaff some years ago from the bite of a skunk."

ITEM: A letter from Kingman, Arizona relates some of the problems encountered by the health officer there, this is dated Feb. 21, 1916. "Dear Doctor Looney: Nearly all of us over here have been run to death and I find I have to get away for a while to prevent a break-down. I think the affairs at Oatman are in a way to a satisfactory solution. The garbage question is to be settled by their Chamber of Commerce. The Supervisors will appoint the man getting the contract a deputyship, so that the red tape will be eliminated. The County will build four public toilets, each one accommodating about 25, that is 20 places on the men's compartment and 5 or 6 for the women. The question of a disinfectant is a serious one. The prices quoted for chlorinated lime FOB Chicago is 14 cents per pound, this would mean something like 25 cents a pound in Oatman." He goes on to say that "the digging of the holes over in Oatman requires dynamite and about $50 to the hole, so that it is not a popular pastime." This would suggest the relative proportion between the male and female population or does it really indicate that there was a disproportion of diarrhea amongst the male population? In any event I think the writer put it quite succinctly when he said that digging a hole in Oatman was not a popular pastime in 1916.

ITEM: Minutes of the meeting of the state board of health, Sept. 7, 1917. Doctor J. B. Nelson, state superintendent of health reported on the matter of a well at Florence being used by Doctor F. W. Randall (county superintendent of health), as a cesspool, thereby contaminating other wells in the vicinity, and a satisfactory adjustment of the matter by Doctor Randall who discontinued the use of the well. Report of Doctor J. B. Nelson on his trip to Flagstaff to investigate an unsanitary cesspool used there by laundries, and the establishment of a new system to take the place of the unsanitary cesspools. Doctor Nelson also reported his inspection of the Northern Normal School, their unsanitary method of taking care of sewage and read correspondence addressed to Doctor George Felix Manning, county health officer, suggesting that this method be replaced by septic tanks, and insisting that all diseases occurring in the dormitories be promptly reported.

After discussion by the board, it was recommended that the secretary write to Doctor Manning, that if feasible to connect the sewage system of the Normal with that of Flagstaff at an early date, the septic tanks would not be considered as a substitute. Doctor Meserve's request for leave of absence, without pay from his position as director of the state laboratory, to enable him to serve in the army, was granted without objection. The appointment of Miss Jane Rider as director of the Arizona State Laboratory, at the University of Arizona, with full pay, said appointment taking effect September 1, 1917 was made without objection, and the secretary ordered to duly advise the president and the chancellor of the university and Miss Rider of this appointment.

ITEM: A report on some of the work carried out by the Arizona State Laboratory is contained in a letter addressed to Doctor Looney, Superintendent of Health, August 24, 1916. "Referring to my letter of August 11, Doctor Meserve was only in Tucson a week before returning to Douglas and in that time it was necessary for him to go to Nogales to inspect dairies at that place. He expects to be stationed in Tucson in about three weeks, for a couple of weeks and at that time I will go to Prescott and other towns in the Northern part of the State. We are working on a method for the microscopical analysis of milk advocated by the New York Agricultural Experimental Station and if our results are good I will be able to analyze the milk at the time of collection thus doing away with the necessity of shipping it to laboratory at this time. We have just finished a very complete examination of the milk supply of Tucson and Nogales. The former has most of the dairymen producing a good grade of milk, but the latter without an exception were all bad. Doctor Albert L. Gustetter, the local Health Officer, is working with the dairymen now to help them improve their dairies and method of milk production." Signed: Jane Rider, Assistant

William Duffield, M.D.
Commissioner of Public Health, Arizona Territory, 1905-1907

Those of you who have toiled in the public health gardens will at once enjoy this report of Doctor L. Miner, city health officer, Bisbee, Arizona 1914. Doctor Miner wrote wonderful letters and reports—one series concerning his duel with a smallpox epidemic is classic. In the "Bulletin of the Arizona State Board of Health" Vol. III, January 1914, his report on "How to Keep a City Clean," is stimulating, stinging and staunch in delineating his stratagem to get a mining town to implement simple hygienic measures. This is how he reported it:

BULLETIN OF ARIZONA BOARD OF HEALTH

How to Keep a City Clean:

Doctor L. L. Miner city health officer, Bisbee, Arizona. One who has visited the Warren

Thomas Peyton Manning, M.D. 1889-1980 He and his brother, George Felix Manning, Jr., M.D. were sons of George Felix Manning, Sr., M.D., all of whom practiced in Flagstaff, Arizona.

District may remember how the houses of Bisbee were built, during the early days of the mining camp, one above the other on the hills, without any semblance of order or regularity. The suburbs, however, have been built in more regular order. Some are located in flat and some in hilly districts. Six town sites, close to Bisbee, have been a source of constant trouble from a health standpoint. The sewage of a town, Jiggerville, for years led into an arroyo, which arroyo had been flushed by a constant volume of water from a mine. While far from a perfect sewage system, the town was fairly clean and sanitary as there was a small percentage of copper in the water—enough to act as a mild germicide. Without warning the arroyo became suddenly dry. It was like a Niagara Falls suddenly diverted. Mining conditions had made it necessary to change the output of the water to another channel. The arroyo was dry for but a brief period as, while lacking the accustomed flow of copper water from the mine, it soon filled with slops and sewage. The stench and filth can be readily imagined. Some citizens like it, as it afforded an opportunity for dumping filth, unobserved, into the ditch, and to thus escape the small fee of a garbage service. The majority of citizens demanded immediate relief of the situation. Immediate relief was out of the question, as to return the water to the arroyo was impossible. The only solution was as follows: An order was issued that each person convert his outhouse into a dry toilet and that it be made fly proof.

Experiments were made with barrels placed at the outlets of drainage pipes, the pipes leading into the barrels, which were filled with rocks, sand and lime, for the purpose of filtering the water that must necessarily occupy the arroyo. The results from this were indifferent. The free use of lime about all premises was urged. Circulars were printed and placed in every house, describing the danger of the situation, outlining advice and urging precautions. A club existed known as the Lowell Improvement Club. A special meeting was advertised, and women and children were urged to come and lantern slides were exhibited, showing views taken about the town, illustrating the dangers of such conditions, which pictures were intermixed with the usual ones relative to the typhoid bearing fly. At the conclusion of the lecture, a committee was appointed, composed of

An early photo of Arizona State Teachers' College at Flagstaff
Photo courtesy of the Department of Library and Archives, Phoenix, Arizona

An early day view of the library at Arizona State Teachers' College in Flagstaff
Photo courtesy of the Department of Library and Archives, Phoenix, Arizona

six of the most prominent men of the town, who were appointed as representatives of the Board of Health with sufficient power to assist in keeping their town clean. A report was heard from but one member of this committee, and some of the other five barely escaped arrest later for carelessness and filth in connection with their own premises.

At this time there was trouble with the Southern Pacific Railroad at Benson. The toilet at their station caused a foul and stinking cesspool. A correspondence had been started with the Division Superintendent relative to this nuisance, and an early remedy was promised. The correspondence continued for three months, consisting of requests, orders and demands for abatement of the nuisance. Replies were prompt, courteous and promising immediate relief. I wish to quote a paragraph of a letter from the Superintendent, written three months after his original promise to immediately correct the one and only nuisance under discussion. Nothing had been done by the Railroad Company, during the three months after the promise for immediate action. The last paragraph of Mr. Dwyer's letter is as follows: "If there is any further complaint on the part of the inhabitants of Benson, would be pleased to have advice thereof. We will be glad to cooperate at any time, as I can assure you that we have considerable interest in the welfare of communities situated along our railroad."

"After an interval of two more months, even with such interest and promising assurances on the part of the Railroad Company—and yet nothing done, the County Attorney was asked to help. He did. The last paragraph of his brief letter to the Superintendent is as follows: If this nuisance remains unabated within two weeks from date, I shall send the sheriff up there to abate it, with instructions to arrest any individual who interferes with his actions, and a warrant will be sworn out against those who are guilty of maintaining this nuisance, including the Southern Pacific Railroad Company."

"Eight days later the County Attorney wrote me as follows: I have the pleasure of notifying you that the nuisance at Benson has been corrected. The Railroad Company has been very prompt in complying with our demands, and I find with that Company, nothing appeals to it like force. Experience has proved that but meager results have been accomplished from individuals who have needed attention by mere explanations and requests. This experience includes months of trials with slaughter houses, butcher shops, bakeries, boarding houses, restaurants and residences. A final attempt was made with a statement to them that unless conditions were improved and premises cleaned and made sanitary, arrests and closure of their places would follow. The results were nothing.

"The steps next taken were the arrest of several individuals, the closure of several saloons, a restaurant, a candy shop, and a limited time allowed for some other places to clean up or close. The experience of the County Attorney in dealing with the Southern Pacific coincided exactly with my experience with individuals. The results of the arrests and closures were widespread. Places were cleaned, garbage removed and conditions sanitary,—but only for a brief period of time. A repetition of the brute force principle and the idea of permanent closure of second offenders has proven the only method of dealing with those who must be forced to remain clean and sanitary. The photographs of a slaughter house—one doing a large business—are a vivid illustration. The offal thrown within fifty feet of the buildings, and reeking with maggots and flies. Hogs which eat the offal, dying of disease are permitted to lie where they die, within less than a hundred feet of the slaughter house—their bodies swollen and ruptured, and covered with swarms of green flies. The slaughter house unscreened and the flies having free access from the diseased hogs to the freshly killed beef. The delivery wagon, bringing two barrels of refuse, covered with a filthy tarpaulin, which is the only one to cover the beef taken to market the following day. Another photograph of a restaurant. A litter of dogs in the rear of the kitchen. Indescribable filth present, which a photograph could not show. This same restaurant received a written notice relative to its filthy conditions, and especially a warning against a dog kennel in connection with its kitchen.

"A month later this picture was taken in the rear of the restaurant. A view, not possible to photograph, consisted of two large slabs of beef, within ten feet of the dog kennel, covered with a swarm of blow flies. The proprietor had been warned repeatedly in person and by letter about his place and his dog kennel had been forbidden. The following conversation showed the necessity of forcible cleanliness: 'You received a letter about dogs in the kitchen? Yes. What is in the corner? Dogs. What are you going to do with those two slabs of meat? I was intending to use them. What is on them? Flies. What kind of flies? Green flies.' The place now is sanitary—but not from choice.

"Another phase of butcher shops and restaurants, and an important one learned by accident, is this. Old and discarded and decaying fragments of meat are not thrown away. They are made into sausages. This is done by the use of a powder called "freezum." It kills odor and causes foul meat to appear fresh and black meat to look red. In most states the presence of this powder entails a fine of $50.00. In many restaurants, salads are mixed in a large dish in which the spoon remains, and the green verdigris may be scraped off in a considerable mass. Few restaurants voluntarily remove contents of canned things to proper receptacles, even though it be milk, and they are kept thus for days. Explanations and requests do no good and produce no results in such places. Fear and force have been the only means of keeping such places safe for public use.

"Another phase of the disposal of filth is by those who are genuinely anxious to be sanitary, but who have maintained a nuisance overlooked by those in charge. The Warren Ranch is a large concern, furnishing vast quantities of vegetables and milk to thousands of homes. It is irrigated by water conveyed by a flume from the Superior mine. The flume itself cost over $10,000.00. The owners of the mine, furnishing the water, are interested in the ranch. This flume extends several miles. Along its course five outhouses had been built over the flume, thus carrying refuse to the gardens and the dairies of the ranch, and in one residence, owning an outhouse over the flume, there was a severe case of illness. The worst feature was an outhouse at the Superior mine itself, used daily by hundreds of men, which made the flume a veritable sewer. A notice from the health board to the company resulted in the destruction of the outhouses within a few hours. They had been present for some time, and through custom, had been overlooked.

"The battle of Naco left its problems. (The battle of Naco was between the followers of Pancho Vila and U.S. Army and National Guard troops protecting the border. The Guard troops on the American side were under the command of Col. A. M. Tuthill—a surgeon from Morenci, AZ.) Half of Naco is on the American side of the line and half in Mexico. The exact number killed during the fight will never be known as many were buried early during the fight in the Mexican part of the town and three were executed at the same site after the battle, and the bodies thrown into the arroyo. This arroyo leads into the watershed of the Bisbee-Naco Water Company, which furnishes water for the entire district, i.e.—Bisbee, Warren, Lowell and other towns. The bodies were unburied. Some of those killed came from districts in Mexico where typhus fever exists. The condition promised to infect the water supply of the entire Warren District of over twenty thousand inhabitants.

"A visit to Colonel Brachamonte, in charge of the state troops, resulted in a promise to dispose of the bodies by burning them. The colonel left the following day, and nothing was done. Colonel Callies, next in charge, was interviewed, who promised to cremate the bodies, but the promise failed. The Board of Directors of the water company were then informed of the situation. They promised to do everything in their power and stand every expense that might be incurred. The situation approached acute danger to thousands of families, and the State Superintendent of Health was nearly asked to take charge. Major Reed, in charge of the U. S. troops, was consulted. He stated that while he was ordered from Washington to keep his troops upon this side of the line in case of a crisis, he considered this a crisis more serious than bullets, and he offered the use of every member of the regiment to cross the line to clean up conditions and make American residents safe from a possible epidemic. With such a possibility as a last recourse, every effort was put forth to avoid this necessity. It was easily arranged with the Mexican officials that American citizens take charge of the cremation of the bodies of men, and many horses and cattle that had been killed. Yaqui soldiers were placed under American orders. Stretchers were made of doors, the bodies covered with lime, which made it possible to handle them. Iron bars were placed through the base of a small adobe house, a fire started beneath, and with the use of wood and kerosene each body was consumed in about thirty minutes time. The results of burning the many bodies were a few bones, which crumbled upon a slight touch. The watershed was cleared of all debris within forty-eight hours.

"Warren is a beautiful residence site located three miles from Bisbee. It is unincorporated and under county control, but needs little observation because of its perfect sewerage system and its cleanliness. It has needed protection itself from the city of Bisbee, because of the outlet of the sewer of Bisbee emptying within fifteen hundred feet of Warren, and garbage site of Bisbee within an equal distance. The city was asked by the County Board of Health to change its garbage site. The City Council was seen repeatedly, and nothing gained but promises. The County Superintendent of Health was compelled to select a garbage site, condemn the old one, and order it destroyed. The city was repeatedly asked to prolong the sewer. Nothing was gained but promise. After a lapse of months, the city was told that the County would build the sewer and collect all expenses from the city. Only force brought even the city to action. It has been the purpose or the custom to institute legal proceedings only where absolutely necessary and essential for protection of public health. It has been the desire and the aim to protect public health and business and the general welfare of the community and to request the aid of every individual along such lines, explaining by pictures, by press and through circulars the reasons for precautions and thereby create a wholesome public sentiment in behalf of proper sanitary environment. Experience has proved, however, that force through fear of publicity, arrest or expense, has been the only means of obtaining results. A request, often repeated, has always preceded the use of the big stick, but the use of the big stick has been the only cause of any action or results. A peculiar phase of this final method, and a surprising one, is that the majority of those who have been necessarily arrested, have later shown signs of warm friendship. Not one engaged a lawyer for a defense—all have plead guilty and all were fined, and some have called me professionally to treat them or their families. Brute force, properly used, has never failed, in my brief experience, to be the best method for results and it has brought respect and even friendship of those upon whom it was necessarily used."

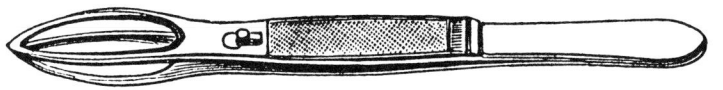

Artery Forceps, fenestrated, with catch. $2 00.

Flying Chlamydospores
Coccidioidomycosis

Coccidioidomycosis, (as noted in the title of this dissertation, is the cause of Valley fever) was thus described by the illustrious late Doctor C. E. Smith of the University of California, world authority on this disease. He listed 18 other synonyms for the disease and the last one as he stated, "with the ultimate in brevity, is simply (C)." So through this little historical rambling we'll simply refer to this Valley fever disease as "C" and for those of you who are late comers to the Salt River Valley please take note that Valley fever does not relate to this part of the desert but it does relate to the San Joaquin Valley of California.

Well when did this "Flying Chlamydospore" come into the Valley of the Salt? It is a common misapprehension amongst physicians to attribute the appearance of a disease, geographically, and the recognition of it clinically to occur simultaneously. Well such is not usually the case. But the Big "C" was one of the later diseases, infectious diseases, to be recognized as endemic here in the Salt River Valley. So let's take a short tour down through time and mention some of the highlights of the history of this fascinating disease.

Many of the contributions stemmed from the group in California based at Berkeley. In 1894 a California surgeon, Doctor E. Rixford, reported a case. From this first case he injected some of the pus into a dog. The dog developed an ulcer on his leg which failed to heal so Rixford excised it and the dog lived happily ever after. As we now know, this dog was indeed lucky for naturally acquired infection of the Big "C" by our canine friends is almost invariably fatal. Rixford correctly proposed that the disease might be infectious but not contagious, a wise and astute deduction. 1900: W. Ophuls and H. C. Moffitt cultivated the organism and demonstrated it to be a fungus. 1931: R. A. Carter published the first satisfactory analysis of osseous cocci. 1932: R. A. Stewart and K. F. Myer recovered the fungus from the soil from under a bunkhouse on a ranch where a number of Filipino grape pickers had developed the disease (California). 1936: This was a big year. It was Doctor E. C. Dickson who followed up the suggestion that the cocci granuloma might be preceded by a pneumonia and he went out to Kern County, California where Valley fever was endemic. There Doctor Myrnee Gifford, one of Doctor Dickson's Stanford graduates told him that she had observed that in San Joaquin Valley fever, the pneumonia was usually followed by a spectacular rash, erythema nodosum and she was searching for an intestinal parasite but always ended up finding coccidioides in the sputum! 1938: The joint paper by Dickson and Gifford correctly tied up all the loose ends about this famous disease and the Flying Chlamydospore was officially launched and now C. E. Smith was embroiled in the study of the disease, skin testing every suspect who could be located. 1938: C. E. Smith, et. al, had established that the coccidioidin skin test was reliable but "No syringe previously used for tuberculin testing should be used." It is impossible to get all the tuberculin out and the same thing applies to the coccidioidin syringes; they cannot be used alternately for one test and then the other because it is impossible to "destroy all the material in the syringes."

This is a practical note in this otherwise historical account. In 1938 R. W. Phillips, a Phoenix physician, read a paper before the Maricopa County Medical Society on "The Presence of Cocci in Phoenix." He had been able to secure some of the coccidioidin skin testing material from Doctor Smith and he had found some cases which he properly attributed to this famous disease. The "Flying Chlamydospore," probably already in the area for centuries, was thus given medical recognition in the Valley of the Sun. In 1938 Joe Farness of Tucson described coccidioidal cavitation and in 1940 Doctor Farness also reported the first canine case of Coccidioidomycosis in dogs in Arizona. This led Doctor C. E. Smith, the pioneer in the study of this disease, to say that, "Cocci went to the dogs in Arizona." So the Salt River Valley and Old Pueblo became aware of the Big "C" about the same time. In 1942 Doctor Chester Emmons clinched the hypothesis first enunciated by Doctor Joseph D. Aronson, a public health service worker who traveled extensively and studied the disease in the Southwest. He clinched the hypothesis that was first elucidated by Aronson that there probably was an animal reservoir. He recovered the fungus from trapped rodents and from the soil. And Doctor J. D. Aronson had also proposed that "In the Salt River Valley the widespread pulmonary calcification amongst nonreactors to tuberculosis is probably Coccidioidomycosis."

1950: Doctor C. E. Smith described methods of serological testing for the diagnosis and prognosis of the Big "C." 1954: Birsner, J. W. of the San Joaquin Hospital published a critical review of the roentgen aspects of the disease, this is the first one of importance from the X-ray point of view. 1956: Doctor C. E. Smith reported on the pattern of 39,500 serological tests in Coccidioidomycosis, a prodigious definitive study of the disease—mainly amongst army air corps recruits and other residents of endemic areas. 1958: The late Doctor D. W. Melick, a renowned surgeon of Phoenix, reported his experience in the surgery of Coccidioidomycosis which has remained a classic. 1958: Doctor K. T. Maddy gave a clear exposition of the geographical distribution of coccidioides immitis, the lower Sonora life zone. (It is a semi-arid, alkaline soil, free from severe frost, a long dry season of several months followed by some rain.) Endemic areas also exist in Mexico, Paraguay, Argentina and Venezuela. 1965: Doctor Maddy traced the spore of the cocci to its lair origin in the soil. It is usually in or near a rodent burrow, the ground squirrel, where the temperature, moisture and protein (animal droppings) is just right and that is where the spores do their thing. This is usually at the base of a creosote bush.

1965: Doctors C. J. Prachal and Gilbert Crecelius described cases in a swine herd in Tucson. They weren't the first to describe the suis infection, it had previously been noted in 1916 by Lt. Giltner and 1954 by E. E. Jones. They were the first to show it had gone to the 'hogs as well as the dogs' in Arizona! So you see the "Flying Chlamydospore" has arrived in a wide desert area and we might close this little session by a note of wisdom from Doctor Clarence Salsbury, medical missionary, master surgeon, and trusted medical advisor to the Navajos. He writes that he had observed no primary cases amongst the Navajos and he further states, "Cocci does not occur where the creosote bush does not grow," and that is a good rule in deciding whether or not you are in an endemic area of the "Flying Chlamydospore," and the lower Sonora life zone!.

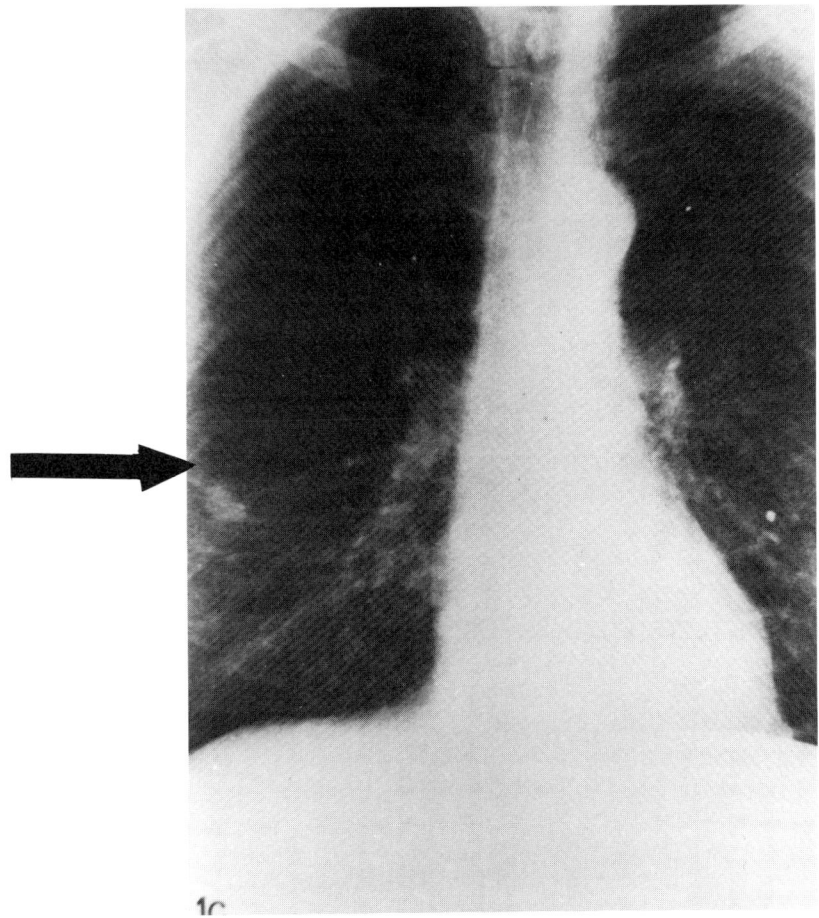

X-ray of lungs, showing "coin-like shadow" on right lung. It is a frequent finding in patients with Valley fever (coccidiodomycosis).
Photo courtesy from Seidenfeld, et.al. Arizona Medicine, Vol. 39, #6. 1982.)

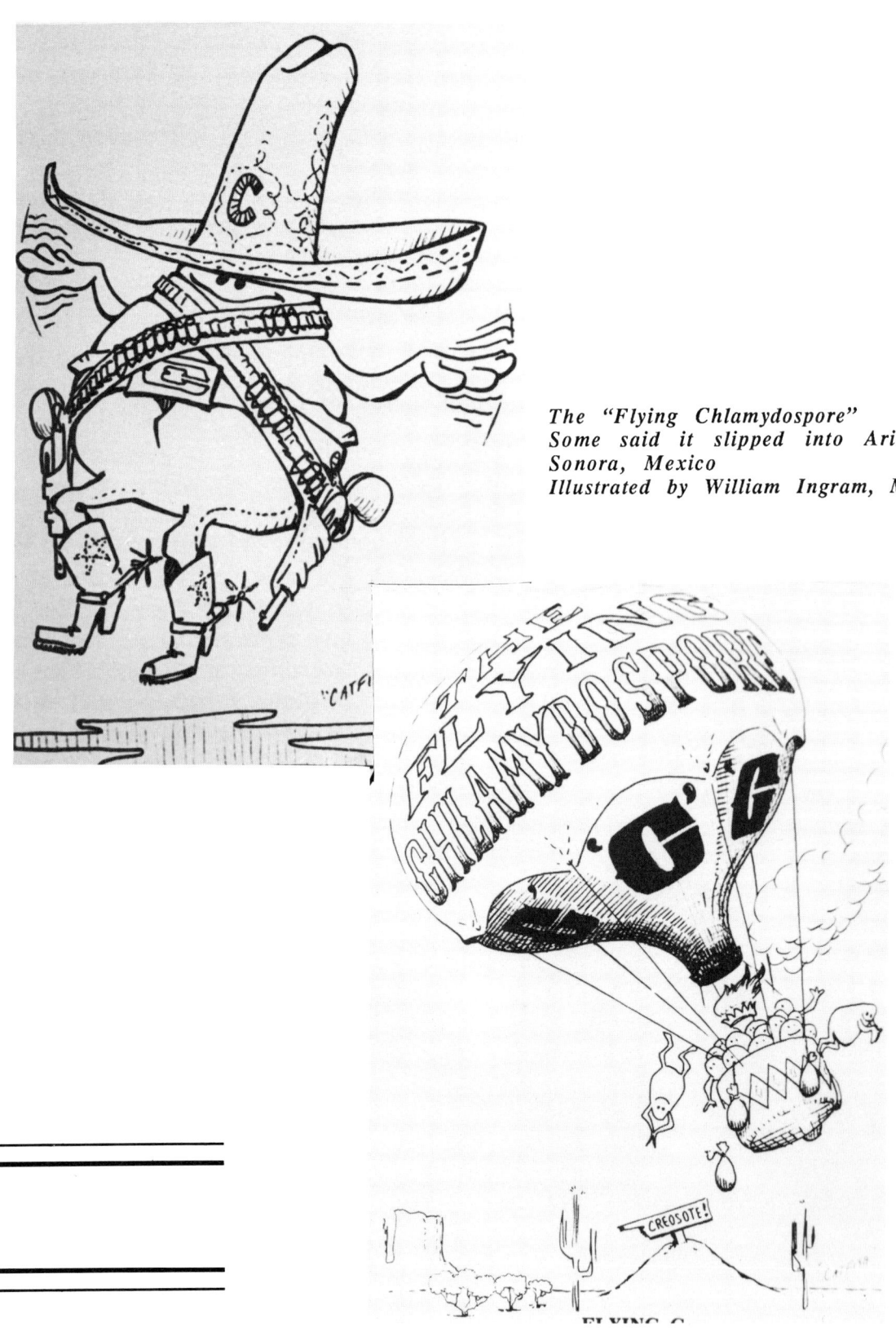

The "Flying Chlamydospore"
Some said it slipped into Arizona from Sonora, Mexico
Illustrated by William Ingram, M.D.

Others made it clear that the "Big C" arrived in style, on a hot air balloon from
Bakersfield, California.
Illustrated by William Ingram, M.D.

"Ditch Fever" in the Salt River Valley

We have commented at a previous time concerning the recognition of Coccidioidomycosis in Arizona. So far as we can tell it may have been from Doctor Earle Wood Phillips (1883-1966) Arizona license No. 715, a graduate of Cornell University Medical School. Doctor Phillips first documented his cases in a paper read before the Maricopa County Medical Society Nov. 7, 1938 and this was published in the February number of *Southwest Medicine* in 1939.

Doctor Phillips came first to Humbolt, Arizona as a physician to the mining community. Doctor Ben "Pat" Frissell, who came to Phoenix about this time by way of Tucson, cautioned me that Doctor Joseph Farness in 1936 and 1937 was studying Valley fever in Tucson and that it was known in the Safford valley as "ditch fever." Through the courtesy of Doctor Frank Tolone, who acquired the adobe home of the late Doctor Phillips, and restored it, we now have the original file of Doctor Phillips, it contains his correspondence with Doctor C. E. Smith of Stanford University at San Francisco. We have been so bold as to project that the Flying Chlamydospore conveying Valley fever, may have come on a hot air balloon from Bakersfield, pardon the expression, California. Well, as it turns out, this was not so far fetched, but the balloon was launched by Doctor Smith on August 8, 1938, in a letter to Doctor Phillips, and it reads in part as follows: "Our department is engaged in a study of fungus coccidioides. During the field work in the San Joaquin Valley I did discover a woman, who according to her history, must have developed an acute infection while working in the cotton fields near Mesa, Arizona. We know, from communications with the staff of the Desert Sanatorium at Tucson, that acute coccidioides infections occur in that region and have wondered whether they occur around Phoenix. (This refers to the work of Doctor Farness at the Desert Sanatorium at Tucson.) In a conversation with Doctor Paul Hoagland, a recent graduate, I mentioned this matter, and knowing that he came from Phoenix, asked him if he knew anyone to whom we could write.

He said that "with your special interest in tuberculosis and allergy you might well be interested. Accordingly, I am taking the liberty of communicating with you. If you yourself are not interested, if you would be so kind as to refer me to a colleague who is, I would be extremely grateful."

Then Doctor Smith gives a short resume of the present knowledge, at that time, concerning "Valley Fever," "San Joaquin Valley Fever," "Desert Fever," "Desert Rheumatism" and went on to say, "we now feel that Valley Fever is merely the way some people react to their primary infection with coccidioides fungus. On the other hand, just as with tuberculosis, very many more people have an unrecognized primary infection and clear up completely, merely by having a positive coccidioidin test subsequently. Two-thirds to three-quarters of the old residents of the San Joaquin Valley a have positive coccidioidin test; all of us who have worked with the fungus over long periods have positive tests."

He goes on to query Doctor Phillips as to whether or not he may have observed similar cases in his experience in the Salt River Valley and then suggests that he use some of the coccidioidin skin testing material which he, Doctor Smith, is forwarding to him. Doctor Phillips replied August 15, 1938. "I cannot recall having encountered an exact or similar condition, clinical picture, in the Phoenix population, but I have seen from time to time many typical lung infections with considerable X-ray change that were certainly not tuberculosis, in fact the etiologic agent remained undetected."

Between the first letter which Doctor Smith wrote in August 1938 and December 8, 1938 Doctor Phillips was able to report the results of his preliminary use of the testing material. He wrote to Doctor Smith, "A few weeks ago I read a brief article for the Maricopa County Medical Society entitled 'Coccidioidal Infection. Is it present in the Phoenix district?' Briefly reviewing the work done by your group of investigators and reporting the results of my own tests so far as they then had gone. A copy of this paper will be sent to you as soon as it is published. What will interest you is that the earlier tests, together with those since made, show about ten percent of the old residents of the Salt River Valley to be sensitive to coccidioidin. I have used all of the mold derivatives as controls, together with the control of Long's medium which you furnished. So far, the reaction appears to be specific, but, oddly enough, we have been unable in repeated attempts, to culture the fungus from the sputum of those who not only showed the strongest reactions but got the most marked therapeutic result.

"And here we come to, so far as I have seen in the literature, something new. My tests, which have now reached a considerable number, all have been made either on people with chronic bronchial disease or, usually, people who are definitely allergic. In this latter group there are to be found a number of chronic asthmatics, some of whom obtained incomplete relief by the withdrawal of known atopens (antigenics responsible for clinical hypersensitivity) or by hyposensitization with these proteins; on others no definite etiologic factor could be determined. Prompt relief, at times dramatic in its suddenness, has followed the intradermal exhibition of coccidioidin, and this at doses much less than the 0.10 cc. of the 1:110 dilution.

"So there you have it, the first definitive testing so far as I have been able to ascertain, searching for the presence of Coccidioidomycosis, San Joaquin Valley Fever, or if you prefer the Safford Valley connotation 'Ditch Fever' to be undertaken in the Salt River Valley. By the way, Frank and Ingrid Tolone, who are restoring the original adobe dwelling of Doctor Phillips, have not been able to determine the exact time at which it was built. Doctor Trevor Browne states that it was built before he arrived in Phoenix, forty-two years ago. If you have any precise information about Doctor Phillips' residence on what is now Palo Cristi, please communicate it to Frank, he would be most obliged to you."

The home of E. W. Phillips, M.D. in Paradise Valley, Arizona before its restoration. Camelback Mountain looms in the background.
Photo by author.

Coccidioidal Infection in Phoenix

(1) With this title, Doctor R. W. Phillips presented before the Maricopa County Medical Society on November 7, 1938, his experience in skin testing for this disease. He was using the newly developed coccidioidin sent to him by Doctor C. E. Smith of Stanford, soon to become the world renowned authority on the disease and its epidemiology. Doctor Phillips described five cases which he thought fit into this type of case, which was well recognized in California as San Joaquin Valley Fever, desert fever, or summer flu and was known to frequently be accompanied by a rash or "desert sore." Some of Doctor Phillips' cases had traveled or lived in California but he strongly suspected that Phoenix and the desert here in Arizona was an endemic area.

A short search of the literature does not reveal any earlier reports from Arizona. No doubt some of the senior local practitioners can point out earlier observations. In 1941, Doctor O. J. Farness (2) of Tucson reported five cases from that city, and of these three were fatal. Skin testing had been recorded on patients in the Pinal County General Hospital and thirty percent of them had a positive skin test. Doctor Farness had also observed two dogs with the infection and this was another first for Arizona.

Doctor W. Warner Watkins, a pioneer pathologist-radiologist of Phoenix, related that the Public Health Service warned the Army Air Force not to place air fields on the desert, as recruits were certain to acquire the "desert fever" or "Valley fever" which was endemic here. But the army ignored the warning and the recruits acquired the disease and spread the fame of Valley fever far and wide.

Some years later Doctor Keith T. Maddy (3) of the United States Public Health Service made quite an extended study of the habitat of the organism here in the Salt River Valley and he literally chased it under the creosote bush. He found that the organism could be recovered from the desert soil and "over a period of years positive sites remain positive, other sites that were negative remained negative. Even in areas highly infective for man, the fungus was only isolated in noncultivated and nonirrigated soils." More specifically, he found that you could frequently recover it around the burrows of the denizens of the desert, the little striped squirrel, where apparently the moisture, the temperature, and the protein content of the soil were just right for preservation of the organism.

A few years ago, the late Doctor Joe Bank sparked a committee on climatology in the county society. Arizona physicians, like others in the health resort areas, have suffered from the "dumping syndrome," the result of advice by their ever loving practitioners back east who sent patients west for "the cure." This syndrome has many variations, some subtle, others quite blatant. In years gone by, it was "the lunger" who usually suffered from tuberculosis or some other chronic lung condition and was advised to seek the "dry warm climate of the southwest desert." Many were terminal, and Sunnyslope, in the Phoenix area, was the favorite spot for the less affluent patients. One woman said she was always annoyed several times a week or month when a neighbor in a tent or cabin next door departed by way of the hearse.

Doctor Louis Baldwin, writing a section in "Radiation And Climate Therapy," (1944), edited by Doctor Edgar Mayer, made some pertinent observations about climate treatment: "A series of 100 cases of asthma under a change of climate have been collected, only 62 included in this study, many were discarded as not in the southwest long enough for conclusions, others had an allergic asthma in which infection and consequently climate did not play a part." He continues: "Of this series 27 have been entirely free of asthma at least two years; before coming to the southwest all were moderately severe or very severe asthmatics over a period of years. Twenty-one more have been improved but have periodic mild attacks of asthma. Eleven in the series have had absolutely no improvement. Thus 77% got marked or moderate relief. A good medicine, the climate, for these 'short of breath sufferers'."

Doctor Baldwin was also among those who recognized that coccidioides, Valley fever, was present here in this state. In this same book (1944), Doctor Baldwin described two cases, one in Phoenix and the other in Tucson. He also alluded to the army experience: "With the advent of large numbers of troops training under dusty conditions, more cases of the disease are being discovered in Arizona." The Public Health Service prediction was becoming a reality. It would be great if some of the practitioners of that generation who are still quite active would give us the benefit of their experience in the early recognition of this disease which indeed is endemic in the state. When queried about the incidence of cocci on the Navajo Reservation, where he founded the Ganado Mission and labored those twenty odd years, Doctor Clarence Salsbury makes this succinct epidemiological observation: "No cases were found above the creosote bush level." And this, as you may know, roughly outlines the Sonora life zone.

REFERENCES:

1 "Presence of Coccidioidal Infection in Phoenix," E. W. Philips, M.D., *South West. Medicine*, 23: 48-51, Feb., 1939.
2 "Coccidioidomycosis," O. J. Farness, M.D., *Journal of the American Medican Association*, 116: 1749-1752, April 19, 1941.
3 "Geographic Distribution of Coccidioides immitis," Keith Maddy, D.V.M., M.P.H., *Arizona Medicine*, 15: 178-188, 1958..

"Father of a Disease"

Now that the medical school in Tucson has gathered a discerning, and hopefully, a distinguished staff, let them not fallaciously believe that medical progress was never before wrought here in the "out back." Graduate training with residency programs have long been a part of the repertoire of medicine in Phoenix and Tucson. Perusal of medical practice by territorial physicians and careful clinical observations led to some original conclusions. One such pithy pioneer practitioner was Ancil Martin, M.D, 1861-1926. Doctor Martin graduated from Rush Medical College in 1885, took special training in eye, ear, nose and throat in New York, practiced for a time in Iowa and arrived Phoenix in 1891. He was a "doer." A charter member of the Maricopa County Medical Society and the Arizona Medical Association he was the first secretary of each and later president of each. He helped draft the first Medical Practice Act of the Territory and was assigned License #1, May 23, 1903. He brought the first x-ray tube to Arizona in 1898. Just a few months before his death, he delivered a paper on "Magnetic Foreign Bodies in the Eye," November, 1925, wherein he described 136 cases along with the x-ray methods of localization and extraction with the use of a "giant magnet." This magnet was still in use in 1949 when I came to the Professional Building in Phoenix.

Another paper read in Globe at the annual meeting of the state association recounts his contribution to early recognition of tularemia. "My first cases were seen in 1907, one possibly in 1902; they were not, of course, called tularemia because the term was not coined until 1911 when Frances Francis worked out the true etiology of the disease. My cases of 1907 have recently been classified by Francis as 'tularemia' and were proven to have been such by finding that one of them after a lapse of nineteen years, still has agglutinates for the organism." In 1907 Doctor Martin wrote to Doctor Frederick G. Novy, Ann Arbor, Michigan, in part as follows: "There have been during the summer months several individuals in this locality who have suffered from an infection as a result of skinning and dressing rabbits. Three persons have had their primary lesion in or about the eye. Small abscesses formed in the lids and on the bulbar conjunctiva as well. The preauricular glands were involved as well as the anterior cervical chain and the submaxillary. Onset with chills, profuse sweating with temperature elevations two to five degrees. There were no deaths; in fact the illness was not profound." This was four years before Edward Francis, working at the Hygienic Laboratory, predecessor of the National Institutes of Health, tied together the bacterium Tularense, discovered by George W. McCoy and Charles W. Chapin in 1910 in a case of rodent disease in Tulare County, California, and the clinical disease in the human. In a personal letter received by Doctor Martin, April, 1925, Doctor Francis wrote, "your cases reported to Doctor Novy in 1907 places you in the position of being 'Father of Tularemia.'" So whether under the umbrella of university academic medicine or engaged in the private sector—to all is the challenge from a "Territorial Physician" to "Father of a Disease."

The Balmie Expedition

The Balmie expedition was probably the first concerted worldwide drive against a killer disease—smallpox. One of every four of us would now be dead and one in twenty permanently disfigured were it not for smallpox vaccination. (3) Smallpox, a disease of antiquity, like typhus has changed the course of military campaigns and decimated cities. As early as 930 A.D. the Japanese had houses of isolation for the disease. The term variola was first used by Marius, Bishop of Avenches in 570 A.D., describing an epidemic of the disease. Gilbertus Angelicus, died 1250 A.D., a physician from Normandy practicing in London was probably the first to describe the contagiousness of the disease. (2) A pandemic swept Europe in 1614, England in 1666 to 1675 and New England all through the seventeenth century; Philadelphia 1661, Charleston, S.C. 1699. Edward Jenner, a student of John Hunter, recognized the importance of a countryside tradition in Gloucestershire, that milkmaids who contracted cowpox through milking, did not take smallpox. (2) Jenner asked Hunter's advice about trying this on a grand scale. "Don't think, try; be patient, be accurate," was Hunter's response. By 1798, Jenner had twenty-three cases to report and by 1800, six thousand people had been vaccinated with cowpox. Inoculation had been practiced both on the continent and in the colonies, but it carried with it a definite mortality and a threat of hanging against those who practiced it (if the patient died). Inoculation had long been practiced in the Near and Far East. It was introduced into England by Lady Mary Wortley Montagu. A woman of independent and persevering intellect, while traveling in Turkey as the first English woman ambassadress, she visited prominent Turkish ladies in their palaces and learned of the custom of inoculation. Pockmarked girls were of little value on the harem market! In 1730, on her return to England, she had her son inoculated and encouraged her family and friends to follow her example.

With the development of vaccination, inoculation became obsolete but **it was a great** advance over previous measures and was **more or** less widely practiced in the Western world.

Now finally what was this **Balmie** Expedition? During the conquest of Mexico smallpox was introduced by a Negro slave and three million Indians died, far more than were killed by the Conquistadors. (4) You might say that the cross, the sword, and smallpox traveled together with the conquering Spanish. Little credit has been given to the policy of the Spanish government to bring vaccination to its widespread colonial empire. It was the first government to recognize the validity of Jenner's work (1805). It did so while the president of Yale University was denouncing the new practice as a criminal act. (More recently a Yale president has complained about the lack of criminal justice.) The expedition and the formation of it are described in part as follows: "The recognition of the Spanish government was as energetic and well organized as it was prompt. Realizing a moral obligation to its far flung colonies where the aborigines had been decimated by the horrible and fatal disease introduced by the Conquistadores, it was considered only just to speed the great preventive to all of the crown possessions around the globe, one of the greatest empires the world had ever known, and immediately it organized a scientific expedition for that purpose. In less than six months after the first royal inquiries into the subject, despite the scarcity of shipping and the absolute lack of money except for armies and munitions, the expedition put out. At its head was appointed Francisco J. de Balmie Berenger, one of the first, most enthusiastic and most learned of Spanish proponents of vaccination. Balmie was fifty years of age, spirited, vigorous, a doctor of medicine, a military surgeon, a scientist in botany and experienced traveler in the Americas. On the third of November 1803 when all Europe was reverberating to the Napoleonic cannon, the Balmie expedition took to sea in the tiny brig Maria Pita."

On her with Balmie sailed two other doctors, Salveny and Pastor, a selected group of hospital corpsmen and nurses, and the magic culture tubes of the expedition, twenty small children in the care of a saintly lady of rank, benevolent directress of an asylum for foundlings. The need of speed and stress on this projected route precluded the use of animals. Adult or even adolescent persons could not be depended upon for there was no way of foreseeing whether or not the person had been immunized by previous, unrecognized smallpox. Therefore the only scientific method of long distance transmission of fresh virus was to use only incontestably sensitive culture media, in other words, children. This indeed was a new Children's Crusade. A new child had to be inoculated at proper intervals from the waning pustule to keep the virus going all during the weeks of peril and hardships at sea. From Coruna in Spain to the Canaries, to Puerto Rico, and then to Caracas in Venezuela. Every port they touched became a focus for spread of their divine fire. "At Caracas the mission was divided; Salvany taking to his account the great continent of South America while Balmie and Pastor, after stopping in Havana, proceeded to Yucatan. Here Pastor took to himself Yucatan, Tabasco, Guatemala and all of the southern half of New Spain. Balmie in person struck out for the north in a triumphal march to the very limits of New Spain, even to the Gila boundary of distant and savage Sonora. Undoubtedly he honored our own venerable missions of the Santa Cruz and San Pedro Valleys." The account further details the trials and tribulations of the southern part of their crusade in what is now South America. They were nearly two years there before rejoining their northern counterparts and continuing on from Acapulco on the west coast of Mexico, with twenty-six new infant recruits to be successfully vaccinated enroute on the long voyage to the Pacific.

"With entire success they reached the Philippines, propagated the vaccine there then to other portions of the Far East and finally homeward bound to Spain, around the Cape of Good Hope, stopping at St. Helena, there convincing the English who till then had rejected the blessing offered from Europe.

"In September 1806, Balmie made his modest re-entry into Madrid worn by three years of incalculable and unremitting toil but undoubtedly recompensed by his sense of duty well done and of glorious services to his country and to humanity." In these years, during the absence of Balmie, the artillery of Europe had not ceased to thunder. Later lessons learned about the value of smallpox vaccination in the Philippine Islands should convince even the most skeptical. In 1898, when the United States took over, the population in and about Manilla was about ten million. There had been an average of six thousand smallpox deaths annually. Under the superb direction of General Leonard Wood, nearly everyone was vaccinated, and, as a result, from 1906 to 1912 there was not a single smallpox death. But it was neglected again and in 1918 the worst epidemic of smallpox in modern times ensued. In three years there were 130,000 cases with 75,000 deaths. Of the 500 vaccinated soldiers stationed on the island, there were but six cases without fatality, in spite of daily intimate exposure to the disease. (4)

More recent outbreaks in Moscow, when nine million persons were immunized during one week and previously in 1957, in an outbreak in New York City should alert even the most complacent that vaccination and re-vaccination is the only method of control. It seems ironic indeed, that the medical literature now is replete with arguments about what age the child should be vaccinated, whether vaccination is indicated, or indeed whether it is necessary to vaccinate whole segments of the population. And so the crusade for vaccination against smallpox must never cease, and, "the Children's Crusade with Balmie must stand as an inspiration in applied scientific objectivity and tenacity." In 1971 when this was originally composed, the World Health Organization had completed a worldwide eradication of smallpox, and have so declared May 8, 1980 their success. The last cases reported were: Kenya 1977, Ethiopa 1976, Bangladesh 1975, Brazil, S.A. 1971. The "Balmie Expedition" remains a classic in disease control for its time, 1799, and place in the new world.

References:

1. A manuscript in the Library and Archives, Capitol Building, Phoenix, Arizona. No author given—subscript stated. "Adapted; Doctor A. Giomone El Siglo Medico," Vol. 71 Madrid (no date).
2. Garrison, F. H. *History of Medicine,* Fourth Edition, W. B. Saunders 1914, pps. 77, 125, 372-375.
3. Stiles, W. H., *Individual and Community Health*, 1953 McGraw Hill Co. p. 76.
4. Halsband, Robert, *Lady Wortley Montagu,* History Today, Feb. 1966, p. 95.
5. Riley, H. D., Jr. *Pediatric Clinics of North America*, Vol. 13 #1, Feb. 1966, p. 90.

Self-Registering Fever Thermometer. Plain, $1 75.

Smallpox

N. C. Bledsoe, M.D. Doctor Bledsoe gives an intimate firsthand account of a smallpox outbreak and the primitive care and disease control at the turn of the century in the Territory. "Smallpox, which had been the scourge of the world before the discovery of vaccination by Jenner, was still a dreaded disease in the early 1900s. Compulsory vaccination had not reached its maximum benefits. Along the Mexican border smallpox was still quite prevalent. In 1906 I was appointed assistant health officer of the Bisbee district, and at this time the so-called 'Pest House' was located on the edge of the garbage dump. It consisted of a one room shack where the inmates cooked, ate and slept. Some individual who had had the disease was installed as nurse. It was isolated. The laity believed that whiskey was the medicine of choice and the saloon keepers kept the inmates plentifully supplied. Later on an adequate and comfortable hospital was provided with a trained nurse in charge. In 1906 an epidemic of smallpox broke out in Tin Town, most of the houses in that section being made from flattened five gallon oil tins. There were six or eight cases of smallpox and about 20 people had been in actual contact with the six. These latter were placed in isolation in a barbed wire enclosure and guards stationed around the camp. Tents were provided as well as food and medicines. Relatives did the nursing. Rounds were made every day, and on entering the camp I donned an old fashioned ulster, close fitting and hot, and cotton gloves, all of which were kept in a suitcase doused in formaldehyde between wearings, and stashed under a mesquite until some thieving rascal stole the entire outfit. One night one of the internees escaped, and I searched for him through every house in Tin Town and was about to give up the search when an old Mexican woman called: 'Senor, aqui esta un viruela!' (There is one with smallpox here) and pointed to an abandoned frame shack. Looking in I saw a cot, unoccupied, and behind it a man crouching. It was my escapee. I called the deputy sheriff to come and get him. He came, and as he was too lazy to send for a spring wagon (we had no ambulance) he told the fellow to get up on the horse behind him and in this fashion he was taken back to the camp. The deputy was loaded with spirits so he allowed he was immune from all ills. There was one case

Nelson Charles Bledsoe, M.D.
1876-1974
His long association with the Arizona Medical Association, starting in 1904, earned him the honorary title as "dean" of that organization.
Photo courtesy of the Arizona Historical Foundation, Tempe, Arizona, 1966.

which stands out in my mind very vividly.

"One of the young lads about 14 years of age came down with the disease and in 12 hours he was bleeding from the nose, mouth, bladder and rectum. It was a very fulminating case of 'Black Smallpox.' This one really scared me as I had never had the disease and I was to be married the following week, so I decided that I had better stay away from the smallpox victims. I explained my fears to my employers and while they laughed at me, they readily took over my task. No one can foretell how a given case may develop; some are mild and others virulent, and I was taking no chances. The following week the quarantine was lifted. No one can doubt the efficiency of successful vaccination as the following case will demonstrate. An itinerant family consisting of a mother and three children, ages 19, six, and an infant, drove into Bisbee. The mother had smallpox. I immediately vaccinated the children, the only 'take' was in the 19-year old girl. She got off with only a few lesions, but the two younger children had severe cases and died. The mother lived but was terribly disfigured. Thank God for vaccination."

Goats of Arizona

To those who collect improbable statistics you might add this one. In 1913 Doctor Robert Looney, of fair Prescott, then secretary of the Arizona Board of Health reported that of the five states having over 100,000 goats, Arizona ranked third. The 1900 census gave it in this fashion: Texas 1,135,244; New Mexico 412,050; Arizona 246,617; Oregon 185,411 and California 138,413 goats. The same census gave the number of people in Arizona as 204,354, a few more goats than there were people. Now you can travel almost from border to border in any direction, except in Navajo land, and never does a goat cross the road. In the early part of 1912 Doctors Clarence Yount and Robert Looney demonstrated conclusively that Malta fever existed in Arizona.

Amongst a group of cases presenting fever as a main symptom they found eight who proved to be positive in their blood reaction. These patients were engaged in the goat raising industry in Yavapai County and bacteriological findings were positive for Malta fever. I imagine that it scarcely enters into the differential diagnosis these days, but perhaps we should resharpen our attention to this disease as it still lingers around. Packing plant employees are now amongst the most vulnerable together with veterinarians and stockmen. Some of the high points in the history of the recognition of this disease runs something as follows: In 1814 it was recognized on the shores of the Mediterranean as "the bilious remittent fever of the Mediterranean." In 1886 R. Bruce, an Englishman isolated from the spleen of a human case in Malta an organism which was later termed B melitensis. In 1895 B. Bang demonstrated B. abortus as a causative organism of infectious abortion in cattle, sometimes called Bang's disease.

Possibly the first cases reported in the United States were noted in 1911, by First Lt. Thomas L. Ferenbaugh, MC, U.S. Army while stationed with troops at Del Rio, Texas. He reported these five cases from individuals who had been engaged in the goat industry in the Pecos River country, and seven other cases of Malta fever as well as having made bacteriologic investigations of the goat herds, which was the probable source of the infection. This careful

Goats, goats and more goats. These Angora goats are grazing on the Apache Indian Reservation at Emigrant Springs in Apache County, Arizona.
Photo courtesy of the Arizona Historical Foundation, Tempe, Arizona.

scientific work enabled Lt. Ferenbaugh to announce the ultimate conclusion that Malta fever existed in Texas. This focused the attention of other medical men in the states having a high goat population on the possibility of the presence of the disease in their own communities. Doctors Clarence Yount and Harry Southworth were thus alerted and deserve credit for making the first positive diagnoses in this state. They reported this in 1913 in the bulletin of the Arizona State Board of Health.

So far it was recognized that these diseases then existed in cattle and goats especially but it remained for Alice C. Evans, in 1918, to point out that the organisms from the goat and from the cow were closely related seriologically and this test could be used, agglutination, a blood test, to detect the presence of present or past disease. Experimental abortion in a cow was produced by Evans by inoculating the pregnant animal with Brucella melitensis, the caprine goat strain. Other investigators isolated Brucella abortus from a human fetus, and this confirmed an earlier suggestion by another observer that there might be a rare relationship between abortion in women and cattle. In 1924 C. S. Keefer proved a case of human infection from Brucella abortus in man and this confirmed the suggestion which was earlier made by Evans on the basis of her serological study of human serum that cattle might be a source of Malta fever in this country. Now the whole thing was tied together and later work has shown that there are several associated organisms; bovine, caprine, and porcine strains.

In later times most of the attention has been devoted to the bovine reservoir of the disease since this seemed to be the source of most of the cases in the middle west and east. A positive agglutination in a 1:80 or higher dilution of the patient's serum is strong evidence of past or existing infection with an organism of this group. L. A. Busch and R. L. Parker reviewing the status of this disease in the United States in 1972 stated: "In the United States, effective control of Brucellosis in animal populations, primarily cattle, has resulted in the reduction of the number of human infections from 6,321 cases in 1947 to 231 cases in 1969. Employees in packing houses accounted for 68% of the human cases in 1969 and most of these were related to swine." They continue, "It is a preventable disease, and dependent upon the control of the disease in animals, since Brucella organisms are readily transmitted to man from natural reservoirs in domestic animals." Arizona reported four cases in 1965-69, Texas eighty-four and Iowa the leader, with two hundred twenty six cases. Veterinarians are still high on the list of victims, 35 cases or 3% of those reported cases for a total of 1,085 in the 1965-69 study.

The Jones-Connally Act established the State Federal Co-operative Brucellosis Eradication Program and it was directed primarily at cattle. This was based simply upon the test and slaughter method. The farmers were indemnified for the infected cattle at a certain nominal rate. Between 1947 and 1961 it was estimated that the loss in the cattle industry was reduced from fifty million to twenty-five millions of dollars annually by the control program. There may be a few of you who observed the workings of this in the middle west on the farms in the thirties and forties at which time cattle were all tested by securing a sample of of blood from the jugular veins then sending it to a central testing laboratory. During my college and early medical school days I worked in a laboratory where these tests were conducted, and also was the diener (a general assistant in a laboratory) for some veterinarians who were studying the disease in swine. Along with another pre-med student, it was my great privilege to carefully observe farrowing sows and to get a sample of blood from the piglets before they nursed and then soon afterwards. This study determined that apparently the organism didn't cross the placenta because these piglets, newborn and not having nursed were immunologically negative when tested but soon became positive as they nursed the first two or three days.

The illustrious Alice Evans, who devoted so much of her time to unravelling the interrelation of the various sub-species of this organism and its relation to this disease in man, was hospitalized in an institution where I served as a house officer. Like so many laboratory workers of that era, she had acquired the disease. An astute medical officer thought that she might have a focus of infection since her disease had been of some years duration and had never abated, at that time there was no specific treatment available. After a test and treatment for chronic cervicitis her health improved rather markedly and her blood titer as I recall, in the succeeding months began to fall. I understand that with tetracycline and streptomycin the morbidity and mortality from the disease, if properly diagnosed, is sharply reduced. The disease is worldwide and the Russian publications especially devote a great deal of attention to it even these days.

So even though you may scarcely run across a goat crossing the road, there was a time when many of them were wandering over the range in Arizona and at that time Malta fever was very common. We are indebted to these early Arizona physicians, Doctors Yount and Looney who demonstrated conclusively that Malta fever existed in Arizona as early as 1912.

References:

1. Bulletin of the Arizona State Board of Health, Vol. III, Oct. 1913 No. 3, *Malta Fever in Arizona*, R. M. Looney, M.D. Textbook of Bacteriology, Zinsser & Bayne-Jones, 8th Edition 1928. The Brucella Group, p. 566-573.

2. Evans, Alice C., "Further Studies on Bacterium Abortus and Related Bacteria."*Journal of Infectious Disease,* Vol. XXII 1918, p. 576-580.

3. Busch, L. A. and Parker, R. L., "Brucellosis in the United States." *Journal of Infectious Diseases*, Vol. 125, No. 3 March 1972, p. 289-294.

Skunk Boats—1

These romantic remarks gained no inspiration from perusal of "The Papyra of Thebes;" no emendation from Vesalius, "De Fabrica Humanis Corpis," but are prompted by an article on "Skunk Hydrophobia" which appeared in the Prescott, Arizona, *Miner Journal*, 1908. "In the throes of unutterable agonies, J. W. Scantlin, the trapper who Saturday was brought to the county hospital a victim of hydrophobia, died at midnight Sunday. A month and ten days passed after the skunk bite, and before the victim noted anything wrong. Three days later—he was a corpse."

Doctor C. E. Yount, a pioneer Prescott physician, reported on "Skunk Hydrophobia" at the annual meeting of the Arizona Medical Society, May 10-20, 1909. "After careful investigation, I am of the opinion, that the skunk is not more the cause of hydrophobia than the dog. It seems that while it is possible for one to have hydrophobia after being bitten by a skunk, the idea has gained ground, to such an extent in the southwest, that all skunks are called 'hydrophobia skunks.'" (1)

Yount reported, (2) two fatal human cases of his own, with four fatal cases from other counties in Arizona. Eighteen cases of skunk bite were reported between 1907 and 1909, the period of his study. Five of these developed rabies and all died. At that time the Pasteur treatment for rabies was given only at special Pasteur institutes. The nearest, or at least the one most frequently used by patients from Arizona, was located in Chicago. Yount further noted, "From the record of the Chicago Pasteur Institute for the past eighteen years, New Mexico has sent them only four cases for treatment as against thirty-three from Arizona. The Pasteur Institute at Austin, Texas from 1904 to 1908 received five cases from New Mexico and four from Arizona." (2) Doctor Yount reports that in 1875, Janeway, (2) while on duty with the army, reported ten fatal cases of rabies from skunk bite on the then Kansas frontier, "Fort Hayes." The skunk was a well recognized cause of the source of rabies and, for Arizona at least, the skunk was the most prolific source of infection; in fact, almost the only cause of rabies, quite reversing the order of frequency given by several authorities for other parts of the United States. Yount further deduced "In the absence of experimental proof, we believe that there is no such thing as a 'hydrophobia skunk' per se, that all skunks are, like other animals, susceptible to rabies. When a skunk, an animal of nocturnal habits, generally timid, attacks man or other animals, accept this as evidence of rabies and have the victim receive Pasteur treatment."

Newspaper accounts of the dangers of hydrophobia skunk bite were not uncommon, Joseph Miller, a local authority on early news accounts in the territory and state, has several such accounts in his files. (3) (4) (5) The fear of hydrophobia skunks became so great that the department of the interior sent Prof. H. L. Simmons to the desert areas of California and Arizona to find out the exact species of hydrophobia skunks (6). He stopped over in Flagstaff to see about the extermination of the skunk population. This same authority reported that seven persons died on the Arizona frontier in a six weeks period from the bite of hydrophobia skunks (1910). The learned professor also stated these skunks have a white stripe across the back and spots on the sides. To this country boy it seems the professor was confused about whether

"Gadabout" striped skunk, a purveyor of rabies.
Photo courtesy of the Arizona Game and Fish Department

he was dealing with a broad stripe, narrow stripe or spotted civet cat (spigole) (7) species of the chemical warfare quadruped.

The account of the site of the bite usually related was the nose or face, rarely a toe. The skunk is usually a slow, pedantic character, unafraid of Homo sapiens but not prone to attack. Therefore arose the great fear of the hydrophobia skunk and the belief that it must be a separate and distinct species of skunk. Well informed students, as Doctor Yount, were not so deluded. A decade later the Salt River Valley was reported by Nelson (2), "The last record shows twenty-two cases of rabies (dogs) in a three month period in the Salt River Valley." (1917).

(8) A plea was made for the control of dogs and no mention was made of skunk bites. He advised sending the brain of all dogs suspected of rabies to "The Warner Watkins Laboratory" in Phoenix for examination before treatment was started. All writers of this period classified anti-rabies vaccine inoculations as treatment and commented upon the "cures."

By this time the material was available to private physicians and the trip to the Pasteur Institutes no longer was necessary. Now fifty years later careful epizootological work indicts the bat as a principle animal reservoir with epizootics waxing and waning amongst the desert dwellers such as the bats, coyotes, dogs, foxes, ground squirrels, skunks and wolves.

"Hydrophobia skunks," were real enough to the Arizona cowhands. As late as the "roaring twenties" skunk boats were made to order by a local tent and awning purveyor (9). These "boats" were made of heavy canvas, about six by three by two feet high. This could be folded and carried in a bed roll, opened it could be staked out, held by a stick at each corner with the bed roll thrown in it for sleeping at night. One cow puncher put it this way, "I wasn't much put out by rattlers, but to be bitten by a hydrophobia skunk, man that would be fatal." The skunk boat has joined the prairie schooner in limbo. The schooner has suffered, of late, rediscovery by television. Now "home on the range," hardly a pick-up cowpoke has ever heard of a skunk boat!

REFERENCES

1. Yount, C. E., "Arizona Report," *Journal American Medical Association*, 53, No. 3, July 1909, p. 228.
2. Yount, C. E., "Rabies, With Report of Cases from Skunk Bites," *Southern California Practitioner*, 25, March 1910, pp. 105-116.
3. Miller, Joseph, *Personal communication.*
4. *Journal Miner*, Prescott, Arizona, 1908.
5. *Arizona Bulletin*, Solomonville, Arizona, 8, No. 1, March 31, 1899.
6. *The Coconino Sun*, 27, No. 35, July 29, 1910, p. 6.
7. *Colliers Encyclopedia*, 17, p. 630.
8. Drance, V. E., *Hydrophobia, Bulletin*, Arizona State Board of Health, 16, No. 3, July 1917, pp. 5-6.
9. Manning, Everett, Personal Communication.

Skunk Boats—2

Some years ago we noted in these aberrant notes, that in early times the cowpokes here about carried skunk boats. This was questioned by some local historians. Albeit our informant was for many years associated with the Phoenix Tent and Awning Company and had taken orders for and made these desert boats for the locals.

To my surprise and delight Doctor Ralph F. Palmer, 1875-1954, Arizona license No. 53, dated June 23rd, 1903, gave a delightful account of a camping trip with his wife from Camp Verde circa 1903. They had reached Fossil Creek about dark the first day out on horseback and his account continues, "We laid out our canvas tarp and put our bedroll on it, thinking to have a good sleep (1). This was the time of year that grub beetles came out of the ground, climbed the sycamore trees, clenched their claws into the bark and the back splits open letting the matured beetles come out. Shortly thereafter the wings are developed and the beetles take flight. The noise of the beetles becomes terrific when several hundred are buzzing around, and sleep was impossible. After an hour or so of this, Mame (his wife) was also dubious about a rattlesnake getting in bed with us or that possibly one of the little black hydrophobia skunks might come along and bite our noses. I never saw one of these skunks, but had heard plenty of stories about them. At any rate she insisted and I had to get up and get a fire going for light and rig up our 'skunk boat.'

"The skunk boat which they had fixed up at the store and advised us to take along was a 24 foot strip of muslin, 36 inches wide, sewed together at the ends. It also had loops at the corners through which stakes were driven into the ground, making a pen about six feet long, four feet wide and with sidewalls about two feet high. The bottom edge was staked to the ground and the canvas and the bedroll covered the edges, as the walls slanted in, neither a snake nor a small skunk could, theoretically, climb over it or get under it. I never heard of one trying to, but I have seen rattlesnakes go over higher obstacles and I imagine an agile skunk could hop over it; but, at any rate, the psychology was good and we finally got used to the beetles, we had some sleep." (1) So much for skunk boats, please note also that he refers to hydrophobia skunks. Doctor Yount of Prescott, soon put the record straight on that and wrote an article which informed his fellow practitioners that hydrophobia skunks were not a separate species, as indeed the department of agriculture suggested, but were simply rabid skunks and that the Pasteur treatment was the only possible means of warding off the disease. Trappers, hunters and cowhands who frequently slept in the open, were frequent victims all through the southwest at the turn of the century.

To return to Doctor Palmer and his early experiences, *Doctor on Horseback* has recently been published by his daughter, Harriett Palmer McArder in association with the Mesa Historical and Archaeological Society. His experiences in Territorial Arizona are sometimes hilarious and always informative.

REFERENCE
1. Palmer, R. F., *Doctor on Horseback*, Mesa Historical and Archaeological Society, Mesa, Arizona, p. 60-61, 1979.

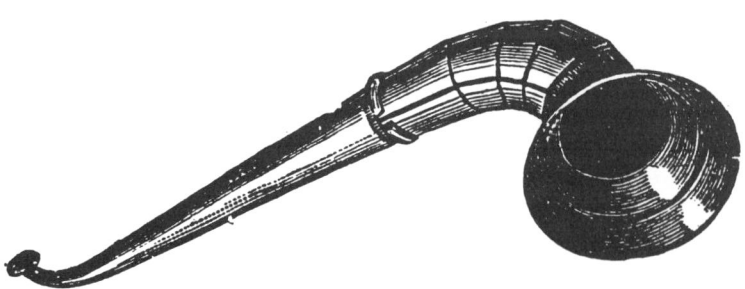

Japanned Ear Trumpet. $4 ∞ to $8 ∞.

Hansen's Disease (Leprosy)

Introduction

Not even syphilis or cancer, to the average freeway driver, brings the specter of dissolution that the word "leprosy" connotes. There is now a determined movement by leprosy patients and physicians to banish the dread word and settle for "Hansen's disease." Those of us not emotionally involved may view this with mild enthusiasm, but there is the hope that it may ease the repugnance with which the disease and its victims are generally viewed. It is a hundred years since Doctor Gerhard Henrik Armauer Hansen, a Norwegian, then thirty-two years old, announced his discovery in Bergen, Norway of the microorganism of the disease now named after him.

Doctor Bob Collings, erstwhile naval person, musician, and medical practitioner diagnosed a case in his Casa Grande office by searching for the bacilli. The patient presented a nasal septum necrosis. There may have been other cases that were diagnosed by solo practitioners here in late years in Arizona but only two cases with which I am familiar were finally tracked down by an army of sleuths on a hospital scene.

There are a few new things about Hansen's disease besides its 100th anniversary, in fact plenty, the Hansenologists proclaim. Some of you who knew Doctor Guy Faget, under whose direction the sulfone, promin, was proven effective at the USPHS Hospital in Carville, La., may recall what a great leap forward over chalmoogra oil, isolation and voodoo this treatment advance represented. Doctor Faget, a gentle Cajun from New Orleans and a career PHS officer, later committed suicide when forced into retirement by the bureaucracy which he had served for nearly thirty years. Very soon sulfone-resistant strains of M leprae appeared. Doctor Stanley Browne found that lamprene, or clofazimine, had a place in the treatment of the drug-resistant disease.

Mass treatment still depends on the sulfones in the developing countries. A new drug, rifampin, may even be more effective than the sulfones, but it is too costly for widespread use. (1).

An animal susceptible to the disease, found after a wide search, is the armadillo. It is probably the best animal prototype. It has been demonstrated that the nine-banded species have individuals who are both resistant and non-resistant to Hansen's disease. If only the individuals who have resistance and non-resistance can be separated out before infecting them with the disease!

To return to Doctor Hansen. Seven hundred years ago, the first Jorgen Hospital was built in Bergen for leprosy patients. The disease was prevalent, one in fifty of the population was said to have it. By 1883, two additional hospitals for segregation of leprosy patients were built, and in 1873 Hansen reported the discovery of Mycobacterium lepra. In 1909 the Second International Leprosy Congress was held in Bergen under the presidency of Doctor Hansen himself. Now there is another new kink about the disease since it is felt that insects may be the vector spreading it from patient to patient, with armadillos an agreeable host for investigation purposes, and there is still need for a great deal of work. So if we as individuals can't wipe out the dread disease maybe we can help to wipe out the dread name of leprosy and simply switch to euphonious Hansen's Disease.

Reference

(1) The Star, Vol. 32, No. 5, May-June, 1973 (Carville, La.) pp. 1-16.

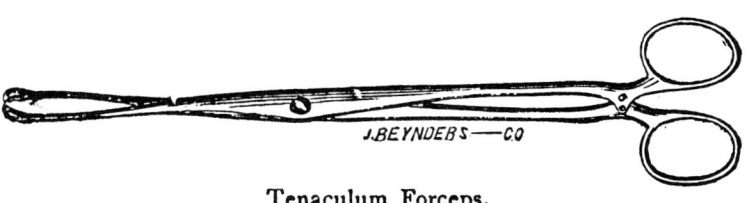

Tenaculum Forceps.

The first victims of leprosy in the United States to be cared for under an organized medical plan were sent to Indian Camp Plantation in Louisiana in 1894. Two years later, the Daughters of Charity of Saint Vincent de Paul accepted the responsibility for their care. The federal government acquired the property in 1921.
Photo courtesy of The Star, a camp publication, 1980, Carville Louisiana.

Aerial view of the Carville, Louisiana hospital now known as the National Hansen's Disease Center, as it appeared in 1980 Photo courtesy of The Star.

Hansen's Disease Today

Elsewhere we have commented about the 100th anniversary of Hansen's discovery of the causative organism of the ancient and now would-be abandoned name for it, leprosy. (1) You will recall that in Hansen's home town, Bergen, Norway, one in ten of the inhabitants were infected with the disease at the time of his definitive study.

Now certainly all of the patients and most of the forward looking investigators ask us to name the disease for Hansen and abandon the old term. Be that as it may, it still hangs around and Jerri Davis at the Acute Disease Control Division of the Department of Health Services in Phoenix has come up with some interesting findings. She says that the records are far from complete but a recent review shows that between 1938 and 1952 five cases of leprosy came from this state and were sent to the leprosarium in Carville, La., maintained by U.S. Public Health Service. From 1952 to 1963, three of these were still in the hospital. From 1963 to 1972 there were nine new cases referred to Carville all from Pima and Maricopa counties, except one from Yuma in 1966. The average stay of these cases has been one year at Carville, some of them have been in and out of the hospital as many as four times and one is AWOL.

When they are returned to their home community, they are supposedly kept under surveillance by the local county health department. It is further noted that most of these cases are of the local, nodular skin type and most apparently are diagnosed on the basis of biopsy of the skin.

Dr. Onie Williams a long time pathologist at the Grunow Clinic and St. Joseph's Hospital in Phoenix has made the diagnosis several times on biopsy material referred by local dermatologists. At one time he was urged by the public health service to publish a record of the cases but demurred. The cases are widespread through the southwest, although few in number, but the stigma of the name of the disease itself is so intense that any publicity for the area about the local incidence was thought to be adverse.

Dr. Robert Collings, erstwhile naval person, musician, linguist and practitioner of the art, diagnosed a case in his Casa Grande office. A smear from the nasal septum was positive. Perception par excellence.

Jerri Davis reports that within the year two new cases were discovered in Tucson, a mother and daughter both of whom were born in Sonora, Mexico were sent to Carville, remained there one month and have been discharged back to Pima County for therapy to be continued. The daughter was age 14 with a neurological form of leprosy, the mother had an ulcer of the leg which healed under local therapy and the sulfones during the month she was in Carville.

There have been a few cases occur in service men who served in the south Pacific, especially during WW II. I have not been able to find out the exact number, you see it alluded to occasionally, and that is about all.

Leonard Wood, the physician, who began his medical career with the army in 1895 at Fort Huachuca, later to become commanding officer of the Rough Riders with Teddy Roosevelt as his executive officer, then military governor of Santiago, Cuba and then of the entire Cuban occupational forces. He was sent to the Philippines where he subdued the remnant rebel forces on Mindanao returned to the states and served as chief of staff of the army, and lost out as commander of the American Expeditionary Force in World War I. The command went to General John J. Pershing for various and sundry political reasons. Wood lost out again as a candidate for nomination as president at the Republican convention in 1920. The backroom politicos gave us Harding instead, probably one of our greatest non-entity presidents.

Wood was asked to become president of the University of Pennsylvania but took the position as governor-general of the Philippines for a period of one year but eventually stayed on until 1927. During his tenure in the Philippines leprosy was and apparently still is quite prevalent and he did his utmost to further the humane care of these people. The main leper segregation colony at that time was on Culion which lies about 200 miles south of Manila.

There is a rather moving description of this leprosarium given by Perry Burgess in his description of an American named Ned Langford, a Spanish-American War veteran who elected to return to the Philippines as an exile when it became evident that he had acquired the disease as a soldier in the Philippines. It was recognized only after he had returned to his home in Missouri, three years later. He felt the stigma of the disease so keenly that he arranged for his death to be called a suicide. He changed his name and went to the Philippines to this leprosarium with none of his family aware that he was still living, except a younger brother who was later killed in World War II.

There is a very vivid description of Wood's inspection trip to this island and how Ned Langford tried to avoid meeting General Wood. But, he was searched out and they had a long conversation and even made plans about how certain things could be rectified and changed, improving the lot of of these lepers, many of whom were never to regain a place in society.

In spite of Wood's long service in various capacities to his country, I am not aware of any memorial to him, or any special note about him here in the states. He lost his life at the time of the third operation for meningioma by Harvey Cushing in Boston in 1927. Cushing endeavored to get Congress to give Wood's widow a pension but she received nothing. By that time he had long since retired from the army and had spent several years in the Philippines as governor-general. However, in the the Philippines, on Culion, friends of Wood did perpetuate his memory by contributing to a laboratory and research building at the leper colony and there is also a statue in his honor. It is very impressive. This Leonard Wood Memorial is the only organization devoting its entire efforts, on an international basis, to scientific studies dealing with the problem of Hansen's disease. Its purpose is to seek, through scientific investigations, the means to eradicate the disease.

Epilogue

Ned Langford, the Spanish-American War veteran who spent 25 years on the island of Culion as a leper, at last gained permission to return to the United States and to resume hospitalization at Carville. The following note has been gleaned from a New Orleans news item of the day:

"The body of Ned Langford, a veteran of the Spanish-American War, who contracted leprosy while serving in the Philippines, was taken from a compartment of the express when it arrived in the city last night. Langford was being transferred from Culion, the Leper island of the Philippines to the federal leprosarium at Carville. The ex-soldier had been isolated during the entire journey, for the protection of the passengers. The federal health officer who accompanied him stated that his patient had died shortly after the train entered Louisiana. Langford seemed reasonably well the previous day except that he was greatly excited because the train had passed through his hometown and he had seen the house in which he was born."

The saga of Hansen's disease is never less than a searing sorrow.

References:

1. *Round-Up,* Maricopa County Medical Society, November, 1972, p. 10.
2. *Who Walk Along,* Perry Burgess, New York 1940, pp.299-307.

Records of Demise

For these demise notes of one time Arizona citizens, we are indebted to the late Doctor Louis Kossuth. Doctor Kossuth had a long list with which some of you may not be too familiar. He was a flight surgeon in the United States Army Air Corps, World War II, and specialized in public health when the air force became a separate service. He was one of the principal founders of the American Board of Public Health and a founder of the American College of Preventive Medicine. After retirement from the air force, he was commissioner of health for this fair state. We are indebted to him for rescuing some copies of early death certificates, some of which are rather unique.

Edith E. of Fort Apache was given the following cause of death: "Accidental scalding for which no person was to blame directly. This baby was playing near the camp fire and was scalded from boiling water overturning, missing the observation of parents." A Walapi squaw "burned to death in cabin by dress catching fire from stove." An Apache from Ganado "burned foot while asleep and died of shock." Not all of the deaths were violent. This patient from Bisbee died from "croupous laryngitis following smallpox." An Indian, name unknown, was reported from Tuba City about July 15, 1911, and the cause of death "was said to have been bitten by a snake." Christian C. on May 15, 1983 died of arsenic poisoning some place in Cochise County and the certificate was signed by James F. Duncan, J. P. Charles M. of Hackberry in Mohave County October 28, 1887, was reported to have died from an "overdose of morphine." (The more things change the more they remain the same.) George O. of Cochise County met his end in 1894 from alcoholism. A mining accident took Phillip H. In 1897, William P. lost out "being caved on in Mohawk Mine." This mine was located in Pinal County.

Now come some accidents and some not so accidental causes of demise. A citizen of Polacca on the Navajo reservation: "accident—fell from cliff." It doesn't say whether he was pushed or fell. Then there follow instances like "fractured skull from fall from hammock." The vicissitudes of a hammock swing were indeed fatal at Sacaton on that October 10, 1912.

Violent death was apparently the order of the day and some of the causes listed are as follows: "Leg crushed by falling rail accident contributory amputation of leg," Morenci, 1924. Gunshot wounds were in abundance, for instance 1887 "gunshot wound in the abdomen, accidentally inflicted by himself." Then there was "perforating gunshot wound of abdomen and pelvis. Homicidal. A cavalry man from Fort Huachuca, July 12, 1917. Septic infection following gunshot wound. Homicidal—at San Carlos in 1910. Now we get a little more specific. How do you like this one? "Gunshot wound inflicted by Edward Robertson at Lone Star Ranch near Fort Huachuca." (Nothing is said about whether they tried the shooter or not). A little more succinct was the cause of death as "gunshot wound." With a little more anatomy another one reads: "Gunshot wound of the abdomen." This one had "multiple wounds." But by 1916 "general septicemia following gunshot wound." But Edward W. of Winslow in 1894 got this short cause: "Shot." Another soldier from Fort Huachuca. "ruptured lower lobe right lung and contusion of colon due to being run over by a wagon. In 1895 another character, "he was freighting." In coupling up his loaded wagon he hit his head against a bolt under the wagon bed. He thought little of it, but later on it turned to cancer which terminated in his death." And there you have it. In 1910 a Navajo brave "fell from housetop, immediate death."

On the Pima reservation "injury to spine, result of kicked by horse." In Mammoth in Pinal County this fatality was from "wounds received by horse falling on him." Injuries of unknown origin, or at least not stated, were such as "laceration of the bladder," "fracture of the base of the skull and other injuries." But the strangest cause of death, probably in recorded history, was given on January 29, 1916 concerning Rosa V. who died at San Xavier follows: "Doctor Thomas, he wouldn't come--too busy," and there follows, the information that Doctor Thomas stated that, "he was too busy to come when requested by father on telephone," so an aunt of Valdez said.

Well, there must have been a few of the early settlers who died quietly in bed, but some others met perplexing situations they could not tolerate.

A Commissioner of Public Health

Prior to his tenure as health commissioner of Arizona, Dr. Louis Kossuth was a retired career flight surgeon first in the army air force and its successor, the U. S Air Force. During this time poliomyelitis was endemic and at times epidemic throughout the country. The Salk and Sabin vaccines had not arrived for prevention. Patients not infrequently suffered respiratory failure, especially in "bulbar paralysis." The Drinker respirator to aid such patients was developed by Philip Drinker and Louis A. Shaw of Harvard's School of Public Health in 1928. Doctor Kossuth aided in the development of this transportable respirator, weighing less than one-tenth of the massive hospital "Iron Lung." The air force flew many missions transporting both civilian and service patients to special treatment centers where these patients could be placed in the Drinker respirator.

Louis Kossuth, M.D.
1913-1989
Arizona Commissioner of Health, 1970-1974
Photo courtesy of Mrs. Louis Kossuth.

*Flight Surgeon Major Louis Kossuth, M.D. (far left) with the 340th Bomb Group,
12th Air Force, in Italy, March 1945, before taking off on a bombing run to the Brenner Pass railroad station and other enemy marshalling areas in World War II.
Photo courtesy of Mrs. Louis Kossuth.*

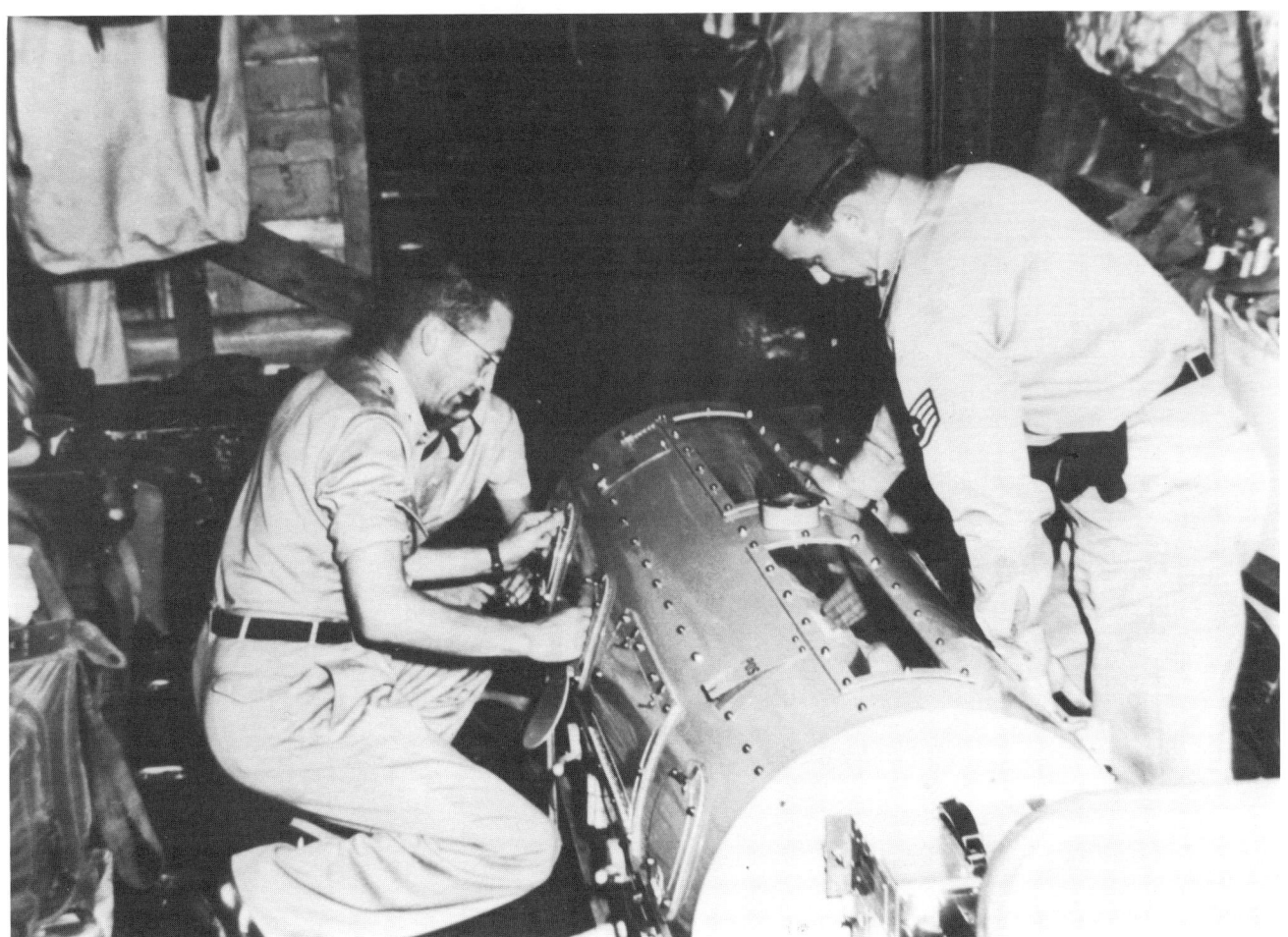

*Flight Surgeon Colonel Louis Kossuth, M.D. and an areonedical technician attend a patient placed in a transportable respirator.
Photo courtesy the U. S. Air Force.*

A Non-Arizona Note on the Search for the Yellow Fever Virus (Hara Kiri by Virus)

Albert Perkins Batchelder
1894-1932
Author's collection of photos.

Yellow fever doesn't occupy much of our scientific time these days especially not in this hemisphere. But it has some interesting historical facets. It is said by historians to have been a contribution of the new world. Syphilis probably came as well as an added bonus for the cross-bearing Spaniards and the many Europeans who followed them. But measles, smallpox and tuberculosis were brought along in exchange, and that more than evened it up.

Doctor Byron Stinson has given a very excellent resume of some of the early knowledge about yellow fever but the origin of the term itself is especially intriguing. This is how he put it: "The virus reached Barbados aboard the French brigantine Oriflamme (The Golden Flame) which put ashore at Martinique in 1664. This ship had come from Siam via Brazil. When the ensuing epidemic erupted it was called the Oriflamme and the illness was referred to as the Siamese fever. Griffin Hughes combined the terms (1750) and called it yellow fever. The Spanish called it "The Black Vomit." So in this very unique way it ended up with the proper clinical description, if you will, yellow fever, but it got it from a "yellow boat." (1)

Later there followed the epidemics on the east coast, Philadelphia 1793, 4,041 of the population of 25,000 died; in 1823 it was reigning in New Orleans, in 1839 in Galveston and the last great epidemic was in 1878 in Memphis. It began when the steamer Golden Crown (note how this word golden keeps following it around) disembarked three sick ladies from New Orleans on the fifth of August. Of the Memphis population then 37,000, 15,000 became ill and 6,000 died by the time the epidemic burned itself out about two months later (2) in October of the same year.

Doctor Carlos Finlay of Havana, in 1881, published his finding indicating that the mosquito, stegomyia calopus, now named stegomyia aegypti, was the patient to patient vector. Finlay was appointed to the Walter Reed Yellow Fever Commission, at the close of the Spanish-American War, and, as you know, this entirely vindicated Finlay's findings and nailed the female stegomyia to the vector cross once and for all.

Hideyo Noguchi, a long-time investigator in the Rockerfeller Institute, working in South Africa, discovered what he considered the cause of yellow fever, a bacterium. This work was completed between 1918 and 1921. But this didn't hold up and Noguchi later died of yellow fever in South Africa although he had taken the vaccine which he had developed.

Some suspected the disease may not have been accidentally acquired, but may have been purposely acquired, a viral hara kiri committed in 1928. This story was bruited around medical circles for a time, but I think the best evidence for it came from a medical student who was admitted to my medical class of 1933, and his name was Albert Batchelder, a long-time research bacteriologist in Noguchi's laboratory. Batchelder on entrance into medical school was then 35 years of age and as I scan casually through the class year book it seemed that most of us were about 21, 22 and one or two old men of 25. Batchelder was a special case. It was because of his long association with Noguchi that he was accepted as a member of the class. But the gods had other plans for Batchelder. He died in 1932 of cancer of the stomach and never made the graduation of 1933.

References:

1. Stinson, Bryon: *Yellow Fever*, American History Illustrated, May, 1967, pp. 42 to 51.
2. Rountree, Leonard G.: *Master of Twentieth Century Medicine*, Charles C. Thomas, 1958, p. 20, 433 & 669.

XI.

The California—Arizona Maneuver Area, World War II

Some Medical and Non-Medical Notes About this Desert Training Center, 1942—1944

Part 1

Those of you who are history buffs World War II type, must have been somewhat amazed at the lack of reference to the medical experiences encountered in the widespread army maneuvers of that era. Unit histories have very little about it, and perhaps rightfully so, dwelling upon the heroism and bravery exhibited by the members of their unit in closing in on the dreaded enemy in the European and Pacific theaters.

The California-Arizona Maneuver Area (C-AMA) was located up and down the Colorado River on both the Arizona and California sides. We have abbreviated some of the findings noted in the official history of the area published by the Army Ground Forces Historical Section, supplemented by corresponding with over a hundred surviving veterans of that place and time. (1)

The War Plans Division of the War Department, General Staff, believed that the campaign in North Africa, like those that had taken place in Norway, Albania, and Crete had proved conclusively the necessity for troops especially organized, trained and equipped to operate on difficult terrain. The war plans division therefore recommended that the troops be trained in desert warfare and this was approved by Lt. Gen. Wesley J. McNair, Chief of Staff, General Headquarters, on February 5, 1942. (1)

On March 7, 1942, General George S. Patton, Jr. arrived by airplane at March Field, California, with a staff to reconnoiter the area from the ground and air. General Patton thought this the greatest area possible and foresaw that the numerous mountain chains, the very nature of the soil, the presence of considerable vegetation in

General Patton explains maneuvers to his troops
Photo courtesy U. S. Army.

General McNair and General Patton (in helmet) at the Desert Training Center, July, 1942 Photo courtesy U. S. Army.

some sections, all of this rendered the area suitable not only for the armored combat service, but also practically all forms of combat exercise. Patton grew up in California and was no stranger to the terrain. The site varied from desert floor to mountains 7,000 feet high, the desert was hot in summer, but in winter was cold; it suffered from sandstorms and cloudbursts although the total rainfall was seldom over five inches a year. The area supported no great center of population, and some army camps had already been established in this area of California, viz: A field artillery range south of Indio, an ordinance section at Camp Seeley, and the Engineer Board Desert Test Section at Yuma and later at Thermal. Also, an army air base at Victorville, the San Bernardino Air Depot at San Bernardino, Camp Haan at Riverside, an army air base at March Field, Camp Irwin at Barstow, a holding and reconsigning depot at Yermo and an army air base at Las Vegas, Nevada.

General Patton was instructed to train under realistic conditions, without frills and this

General Patton addressing troops, 1943
Photo courtesy U. S. Army.

included special features of hygiene, sanitation, and first aid. (1) The eventual land mass area was subsequently known as areas A, B, and C, these were tremendous in extent. Area A was the largest and principally on the California side. It began at Yuma, followed the Colorado River at its eastern border until it reached just above Needles. It took in the tip of Nevada as far as Tatem and Searchlight where it turned to the west and came down on the California side to Nipton, Kelso to the west and Cadiz and Desert Center, but not as far to the west and south as Indio, cutting rather sharply south almost to Nyland, avoiding the Salton Sea, then curving around to Yuma so that it was an oblong area of approximately 10,130 square miles.

Area B was added soon. Bordered on its western boundary by the Colorado River, it was situated entirely in Arizona. It began at Yuma, went up to the east paralleling the Gila River to a point at about Gila Bend then turned sharply north skirting Prescott, staying well to the west of Prescott then back to the Colorado River. Area B

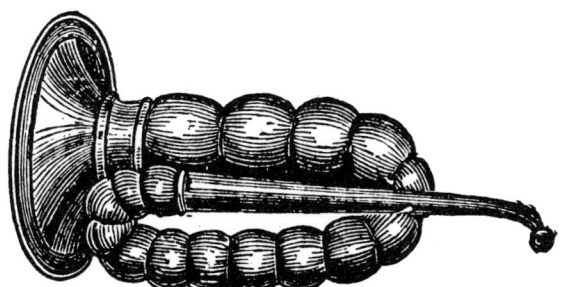

Japanned Ear Trumpet. Four Sizes.
Each $2 25 to $4 00.

Map of main areas of Desert Training Center from Study 15 Photo courtesy of U. S. Army Historical Section.

encompassed about 6,251 square miles. There was a smaller area designated Area C starting at Topock on the Colorado River, running east to Yucca on the Arizona side, skirting Kingman and Chloride then joining the Colorado River below Searchlight. Its western boundary was the Colorado River down as far as Topock. This area was approximately 1,500 square miles. The total maneuver area was roughly 100 by 200 miles in size. (1)

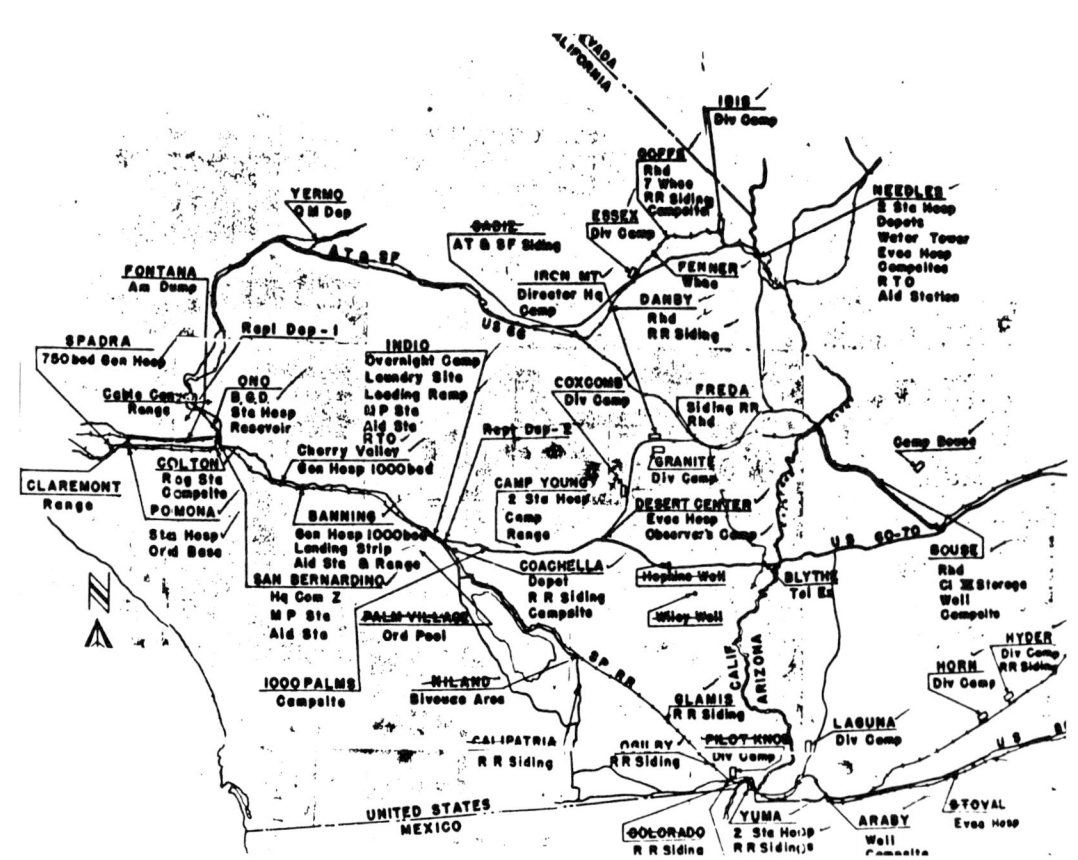

C-AMA Installations from Study 15 Photo Courtesy of U. S. Army Historical Section.

Assigned Strength of C-AMA

On April 30, 1942, at the time of the official opening of the camp, there were twenty officers present and these were the total strength at the site. From then on it built up fairly rapidly. On December 31, 1942, there were 4,115 officers 40 flight officers, 48 nurses and hospital dieticians, 70,331 enlisted men for a total of 74,784 present for duty. May 1943 through December 1943 appears to have been the time of greatest activity. For instance December 30, 1943, there were 10,615 officers, 469 flight officers, 617 nurses and hospital dieticians, 163,230 enlisted personnel for a total of 174,931 in the area. But in 1943 things began to wind down and at the time the camp closed on April 30, 1944, there were 490 officers, 21 flight officers, 68 nurses and hospital attendants, 9,161 enlisted personnel for a total of 9,740. The initial mass division of maneuvers was scheduled to begin August 31, 1942. But already there had begun the withdrawal of units from the center for deployment overseas, especially to the North African campaign and with General Patton, had already departed. Here it must be noted that as you read the official historical accounts and the experiences of the men who served in the area, General Patton may have been present for a short period of time, but his imprint on the training methods and the conduct of maneuvers remained throughout the existence of the training area. Those of you who have partaken of exercises in which you were forced to take evasive action because of an air strike will get a chuckle from this. During one of the early maneuvers an observer wrote, "At VII Corps headquarters, a complete officers mess for about 50 officers with the cookhouse, stood completely in the open about 50 yards from the commanding general's mobile office. The shining silver could have been seen for miles. The reporter was struck by the rather casual attitude of the senior officers in the matter." Well this raised some hackles back at the war department. Obviously Patton wasn't present when this sort of thing took place. A further note on these exercises stated, "Army Ground Forces had harped unceasingly upon passive air defense but the results were continually inadequate. After some two years of effort along this line, I am beginning to feel that it will take a red hot battle to do the trick, I trust the cost will not be too heavy." That is a quotation from General McNair and it may have been sort of premonition on his part.

You will recall that General McNair lost his life in Normandy because of a short air drop by the American Air Force bombing squadron. There was a rule in Normandy that went something like this: "When the RAF did a tactical ground close support bombing run, the Germans took cover, when the Luftwaffe made a run the British and Americans took cover, and when the American Air Force made a bomb run everybody took cover!"

Trials and tribulations

These are grouped under three main headings by the official historian. To begin with, the center was an innovation. Not only was it designed for desert maneuvers but also to provide pre- and post-maneuver training, for the testing of material tactics and techniques, and a promise from its inception to be more than a temporary expedient. (1) In the second place it was a war baby and instead of precise pre-planning it sort of grew like Topsy. There were always major shortages in certain types of service personnel and units, and this factor grew more critical as service units proceeded overseas, leaving no one behind to service incoming maneuver troops. (By service troops is meant quartermasters, ordinance, medical, all the other ancillary personnel who supply food, water, maintain vehicles, and all the other necessary housekeeping duties to keep a large body of troops in the field.) And third, the area itself was a thorn to the spirit with its desolation and abrasive dust and extreme shifts in temperature. Men had to become acclimated. The 5th Armored Division was warned to come ten days early before maneuvers, the 3rd Armored Division had suffered some heat prostration cases earlier. On occasion commanders did not properly inform themselves.

In July and August of 1942 some troops arrived wearing woolen uniforms. One participant who was stationed at the army air base at Blythe, California, (the site is now the local airport west of town) noted that when he arrived the army air corps had virtually no provisions for anything. They had no summer uniforms, so they went to town and bought coveralls for flying and working on the machines. He further noted, "Living conditions were bad, one six-week period of canned weiners, corned beef hash, bread and coffee. We sent home for underwear and shoes.

This was the summer of 1942." (2) At Camp Young some units set up containers with ice water and the result was the men were reported to have been attacked by cramps. (The physiologic explanation for this always eludes me, water intoxication and hyponatremia could do it.) One commander believed his men could not work in the heat so his men enjoyed a siesta after lunch until 3:00 p.m. This unit suffered a higher percentage of heat prostration than the neighboring unit which worked all day. (It doesn't say how fast they worked.) The maneuver surgeon under General George Patton warned the command that danger lurked in reaching for an object on the ground unless one was assured that a rattlesnake was not coiled in the immediate vicinity. He advised the men to drink liquids frequently and slowly, in small amounts, and to avoid overexposure to the sun. Salt loss in perspiration, (hyponatremia), was to be replenished by taking three ten grain salt tablets daily. He cautioned the men, when driving over desert plants in the open to be careful lest flying spines from these plants injure their eyes. This was not an infrequent occurrence. (1)

The Camp Sites

Little now remains of the camp sites which were widespread in the region of the Colorado River on both the California and Arizona sides in that World War II era. Little data is extant on the medical problems encountered with two notable exceptions. "Yellow jaundice" and San Joaquin Valley fever were soon demanding attention. Ask anyone who trained in this or other maneuver areas in Tennessee, Louisiana, Mississippi, the Carolinas or C-AMA, you may hear of the widespread intermittent diarrheas, or the "C" ration blues, and in season the flies, the flies, the flies. (Why is it that Mainland China is free of flies, what is it they know that we don't?) I recall one CO who berated the men of his command for the high incidence of diarrhea, propounding that it was due to the lack of care in cleaning and "caressing" mess gear in boiling soapy water and properly rinsing it. Two days later his driver reported the colonel made several unscheduled rest stops, roadside, on his way to maneuver headquarters. While the flies lacked the deadly B Typhosis latrinograms that were so prevalent in the Spanish American War, 1898, there was no shortage of the ubiquitous Shigella which loved to irritate the intestinal tract. The camp sites were temporary tent encampments. As you wander around these desert sites some forty years later, the street and road outlines are gradually returning to desert vegetation. Here and there a unit headquarters designated in a rock monument survives. The vast extent of a division camp site is best demonstrated from the air. Large storage buildings were used alongside railroad sidings but these have long since disappeared. Some Army Air Corps air bases survive such as the one at Ajo, Arizona, still an active air force base. Others are city airports such as Blythe, California. Still others can only be located by traces of runway such as at Rice, California. Time and the elements are great erasers of C-AMA.

From Camp Coxcomb, California, looking east toward Pallen Pass, 1982 Photo by author.

Administrative Foul—Ups

By January 6, 1943, there was a DTC (desert training center) general order dividing the maneuver area, C-AMA, into a combat zone, and if you can believe it, this combat zone was completely surrounded by a communications zone so if you ran through the combat zone you were bound, not to eventually come up in enemy held territory, but in another portion of the rear area of friendly troops, communication zone. This led to the usual squabble about who commanded what. The medical department didn't escape and the following is extracted from the official history: "Thus, during the maneuvers, the Surgeon of the Communication Zone unburdened himself to an umpire to the effect that many of his contemplated projects and recommendations were continually being disapproved by the Desert Training Surgeon." (1)

The DTC surgeon was the one with clout. The Medical Office of the Headquarters, Army Ground Forces, believed that both the DTC surgeon and the surgeon of the communication zone were trying to do their jobs in a conscientious manner; some of their differences arose from disagreement about the use of medical means available to the center such as the medical laboratory and medical regiment. Headquarters, Army Ground Forces, settled the immediate problem by ordering the surgeon of the communication zone to the AGF replacement depot at Fort George Mead. Soon after this, when they got around to it, there was a directive July 16, 1943 which corrected this anomaly of having the combat zone surrounded by the communication zone. (One wonders what happened to the beleaguered communication zone surgeon. What jungle in the South Pacific did he then grace?)

Auricles. $5 00.

Interruptions in Training

As might well be imagined there were a good many other non-medical interruptions in training, especially during the early phase when there was an urgent need for combat troops with some training for overseas duty. We have mentioned that General Patton had planned the first DTC maneuvers, but he departed the area before the time set for the mass maneuver August 28 through October 28, 1942. Besides the loss of officer personnel, three chiefs of staff were relieved and promoted to the rank of general officers, and were lost to the DTC when experienced and capable officers were at a premium, all during this hectic expansion in 1942. But now we come to the devastating delay, a serious epidemic of "yellow jaundice" in July which filled the hospitals.

Convalescents had to be tried out before they were capable of returning to duty. (1) This epidemic of "yellow jaundice" was so severe and widespread among the troops, not only in this area, but in some others, the surgeon general of the United States Army organized an investigative team conducted under the direction of Brig. Gen. G. S. Simmons, MC and Col. S. Bayne Jones, M.C. of the Division of Preventive Medicine of the Office of the Surgeon General with the assistance of many other medical officers and health installations. (3) Remember at this time the virus had not been isolated and the two or more types of infectious hepatitis were not differentiated. The study was exhaustive, it was done by field work in the area, together with questionnaires sent to what appears to be well over 100 army and navy installations of the western United States, running down the number of cases, the fatality rate and other factors which might have influenced the onset of "yellow jaundice." The investigators noted that there were no distinguishing symptoms which the cases in this epidemic could be differentiated from the so-called catarrhal jaundice, now more correctly designated as infectious hepatitis, commonly encountered in the civilian population either as scattered cases or in occasional epidemics. While no deaths occurred in the area under investigation up to the end of the preliminary field study, there were fatalities later. The case fatality rate for jaundice in army personnel in continental United States was approximately two per thousand and the pathological lesions were those of acute or subacute yellow or red atrophy of the liver, differing distinctly from that of yellow fever. As soon as the investigation disclosed a rather widespread incidence of jaundice among the troops in the west, the surgeon general was apprised in the following preliminary findings and recommendations: (3)

1. Since March 1, 1942 about 817 soldiers stationed at California army posts who were vaccinated against yellow fever at the end of September 1941 and first of January 1942 had developed a mild disease characterized by jaundice.

2. These troops were vaccinated against yellow fever principally but not exclusively with vaccine lots No. 331, 335, and 338 at Camp Davis, North Carolina, Jefferson Barracks, Missouri, Camp Callon, California, and Stockton and Moffet Field, California.

This, together with some other recommendations, resulted in the surgeon general taking action to stop "the use of all yellow fever vaccine manufactured by the International Health Division in New York for the time being and to use vaccine of the same type prepared by the United States Public Health Service in New York and at the Mountain Laboratory of the National Institute of Health." It was further stated: "As it seemed probable that an iatrogenic (physician related) agent had been introduced into certain lots of yellow fever vaccine manufactured in New York through the added normal human serum, both of these manufacturing laboratories found ways to modify their methods so that the human serum could be omitted entirely from the vaccine." (3) The cases elicited in this study totaled 10,284 jaundice cases with 31 deaths. It was further concluded that only nine batches of a total of 63 vaccine lots gave rise to cases of jaundice or deaths. Of these cases, and remember a lot of these case findings were from patient records, there were 1,655 cases in which they were not able to determine from which lot the patient had received yellow fever vaccine. There were 191 cases in which there were no vaccination records at all. In the former number there were two deaths and in the latter three. This did not mitigate against the firm findings and conclusions that the yellow fever vaccine was at fault and exactly which lots were contaminated. As previously stated, this was one of the factors which delayed the 1942 interdivision maneuvers that had been visualized by Patton as a final part of the training cycle for which the divisions were to be rotated into the desert. The entire evacuation chain was filled with these patients during the summer of 1942. (3)

References:

1. "The Desert Training Center and the California-Arizona Maneuver Area Army Ground Forces Historical Section Study No. 15," 1946.
2. Butler A F: *Personal Communication*, 1981. T/Sgt.USAAF trained with 46th Bomb Group (L) at Blythe Army Air Field.
3. Sawyer W A, et al: "Jaundice in Army Personnel in the Western Region of U. S. in Relation to Vaccination Against Yellow Fever." *American Journal of Hygiene* 1944; Vol. 40:35-107.

Part 2

As late as 1981 a textbook on *Pediatric Infectious Diseases* by Feingin and Cherry states, "The most famous epidemic of post-vaccine hepatitis occurred among U.S. military personnel in 1942. Anticipating that U.S. troops likely would be engaged in combat where yellow fever was endemic, a mass inoculation program was instituted early in World War II. Certain lots were stabilized with pooled human serum contaminated with hepatitis B. The contaminated lots gave rise to more than 28,000 recognized cases of icteric hepatitis, (yellow jaundice), two to six months later." Obviously there were comments in the lay press and also in the medical literature raising the question whether this sort of mass vaccination at the time, with the present state of knowledge of the disease, was justified. The threat of yellow fever was a definite threat, even in retrospect, but the mass vaccination is believed by most authorities to have been justified. You may be interested to know that there was published in *War Medicine* in 1944, a report concerning marijuana addiction in the army. It reported 35 confirmed marijuana addicts who came under observation during a period of seven months at an army air force regional station hospital at March Field, California. This may simply have been the early warning signal of the problem that the armed forces were to encounter years later.

Psychiatric and Neuropsychiatric Problems

There was a request from General McNair's headquarters in Washington concerning neuropsychiatric cases. General Haislip submitted a report covering the six divisions then in the desert, concerning their personnel and included those cases in hospitals and those carried as "absent sick." Those with psychoses, (definite signs of being insane); 139. Those with psychotic trends, 238; mentally deficient cases (below normal intelligence), 454; emotionally unstable (unable to adjust to field duty), 259. Total 1,130. The DTC surgeon stated that this total for six divisions appears to be about average and he did not feel that the desert was responsible for any unusual amount of mental trouble. (1) Deleting the mentally and physically unfit from a division had its own problems and following is information sent to us by Doctor Harold J. Halleck who served as division surgeon of the 80th Infantry Division and was on the desert maneuvers in the winter of 1943 near Yuma, Arizona. He quotes an annual report of the medical department in the 80th Division January 1 to December 31, 1944 and it reads in part: "While the division was on Tennessee maneuvers in 1943, 'limited service' as an entity was abolished. At the time, 200 enlisted 'limited service' men were members of the division. Action on clearing these men was deferred by higher headquarters until the division should reach a new station, but before action could be taken, the circular providing for such disposition was rescinded November 11, 1943." (5) In C-AMA every effort was made to clear the physically unfit from the Division under the provisions of memorandum No. 33, December 16, 1943, separating personnel under the provisions of War Department Circular No. 293, 1943. This action was continuous and positive. Four hundred forty-nine cases were studied by the division's Screening and Reassignment Board of which 383 cases were referred to C-AMA for action. Of the 383 cases, 213 were transferred to service units, 19 were remanded to the division for retention and 151 were pending action of any kind by C-AMA. Persistent requests by the division for action on these cases met with no success. (As one who served in a non-division medical installation for the duration, it seemed to me that all of the unfit from any other outfit of the army was reassigned to the medical units for retention.) You will note here that the report states, 213 were transferred to service units, such are the fortunes of war! Another experience related by Doctor Halleck is similar to that which was noted, not only in the official history but in the recollections of many of our correspondents who were on the desert.

It goes somewhat as follows: "On one maneuver, all installations were to dig in. The Division Clearing Station with one ward tent was set up in a wash to lower the silhouette and had a few casualties on cots when a torrent of water came rushing down from a mountain rainstorm suddenly inundating the facility. No loss of life ensued. This occurred on the desert north of Yuma." A similar devastating experience is related by the hospital personnel assigned to Camp Bouse, Arizona, which incidentally was a very secret installation. A station hospital with a complement of nurses and medical officers had been assigned to this camp. Here the nurses' pyramidal tents were set up in a wash, or close by a wash, by some unsuspecting tenderfoot who didn't understand the vagaries of the desert. Well they had a similar occurrence with a flash flood and it took a couple of days to reassemble the nurses and their gear to higher ground. No casualties were reported.

Dependent Medical Care

This must have presented a real problem—as we all were aware of in those times. Soldiers' families were bound to follow them, in spite of all directives to the contrary, if the troops remained in the states. On November 22, 1943, the headquarters of the communication zone of the California-Arizona Maneuver Area notified the commanding general of the army ground forces that, "It was recommended that personnel of all units entering the C-AMA be advised that military medical facilities are not available for treatment of dependents. Civilian sources for medical care are meager in large portions of the area—the limited service previously available to dependents at Torney General Hospital Palm Springs will be discontinued." It was further noted, "That several incidents have occurred recently which involved unusual hardship and tragic results for the families of service personnel due to inadequate medical service." But the hard hearted commanding general of the AGF, Army War College, Washington, D.C. disapproved this recommendation and a final letter states, "Facilities for limited medical service to dependents were resumed at Torney General Hospital, November, 1943."

The Dust-Hazard for Vehicles

On July 7, 1943, there is a report from a desert warfare board from the DTC at Camp Young, a report to the commanding general of the Desert Training Center, outlining a study of the dust conditions in the area. This survey was apparently stimulated because of the excessive wear and tear that had occurred on vehicles used in the area. The valley floor was described as being of three general types. One type was mixed sand and gravel which packs with traffic and yields very little dust. Another type, a loose, fine sand with more or less clay. This sediment varies from shifting dune sand which is pure and fine-grained to some stream deposit sand having a higher percent of loose clay. The third type, of boulder and clay beds, was known as desert pavement. It looks very firm but one vehicle will scatter it and plow deep tracks into the underlying clay. The gravel is not thick enough to provide traction in the clay. All 2 X 4 vehicles stick in the sand and 4 X 4 vehicles must use four-wheel drive, low range, to move through it. In dusty areas, vehicular wear and maintenance are excessive; servicing is impossible on windy days. (A map depicting these areas was not available in the printout which we received from the national archives.) There was a general recommendation that no permanent or semi-permanent installations be permitted in the heavily dusty areas. In certain areas only non-mechanized type units should be stationed and in such camps all roads should be graveled and vehicles should be rigidly restricted to the roads and these camps should be moved every three months.

There were other areas designated for semipermanent installations and these would be for armored and mechanized units. The tracked vehicles would be restricted to a minimum number of roads in order to give the sand on the other roads a chance to pack and sprinkling would help to facilitate this and should be tried wherever water supplies were adequate. They recommended that Camp Pilot Knob be moved to the vicinity of Ogilby and there should be some determination whether Camp Clipper should be moved to the southeast of the old Granite Mountain and Camp Ibis was to be moved north to the Nevada-California line. On the Arizona side, Camp Hyder and Camp Laguna were to be abandoned. None of this makes mention of the prevalence of coccidoidomycosis (Valley fever) among the troops in these areas, but as we shall presently see some of these areas were found to be heavily endowed with the fungus. The widespread habitat of the lowly spore was to remain a secret--no more.

Site of a mess kitchen at Camp Hyder, Arizona. Photographed long after the camp was abandoned. Photo courtesy Lt. Col. John Lynch.

*80th Division Medics "Digging In," Camp Laguna, Arizona, 1943.
Left to right: Major Charles E. Winston, D.C., Lt. Col. Harold J. Haleck, M.C., division surgeon, and unidentified digger.
Photo courtesy of Dr. H. J. Haleck.*

Maneuvers in the San Joaquin Valley

As early as 1941, a policy was established placing the San Joaquin Valley, California, out of bounds as a location for camps and maneuvers. The ground forces did experience one epidemic of Coccidioidomycosis as a price for violating the "no trespassing" warning for the valley. The 7th Motorized Division had maneuvered in the northwest corner of Kern County (Antelope Valley, an arm of the San Joaquin Valley) during June and July. An epidemic of severe respiratory illness ensued which was proved to be coccidioidal. Seventy-five cases of clinical Coccidioidomycosis were diagnosed; on the ratio of erythema nodosum (a type of inflammatory reaction of fat under the skin) to infection. Nodosum is a frequent allergic sign of cocci infection, it is estimated that there were between 300 and 400 infections. On August 18, 1942, army ground forces endorsed the July sanitary report of the 7th Motorized Division and approved the recommendation it contained, "That the western portion of the San Joaquin Valley, south of Fresno, California and especially the portion lying in Kern County not again be used for maneuver or training areas for army personnel." (1) (Page 293.) The lowly spore could be ignored—no more.

California-Arizona Maneuver Area

Doctor Charles Smith notes, "A serious problem developed in the California-Arizona Maneuver Area, the desert training center, which was located in the desert areas of southwestern California and western Arizona. Coccidioidomycosis constituted the chief health hazard peculiar to this area, although this fact was not recognized during the early months of the war." (7) Recognition of the problem began in 1943. Representatives of the desert training center discussed the possible hazard of Coccidioidomycosis with Doctor Smith. Sample skin testing surveys were advised, and it was suggested that medical officers be alerted to the danger of this infection, particularly in the spectacular and easily recognized form of erythema nodosum.

While this plan was under consideration the desert training center received the following information from the 54th Station Hospital near Yuma, Arizona. "We were out on grand maneuvers for three weeks returning to our base a week ago. Very suddenly we got a number of men with influenza like symptoms, and a bizarre lung finding, on physical and on x-ray. Today we have three positives out of five tests as well as an outbreak of 'Epidermothytid' (doubtless erythema multiforme, another frequent allergic skin sign of Valley fever, and erythema nodosum in the same patients). One of these is a man from the Royal Dutch Army, who has been in this country only one month, three weeks of which were on the desert, and one week in the hospital." (7) Subsequent serologic examination confirmed the epidemic as Coccidioidomycosis. The site of the infections was especially located in an area near Pallen Pass, 20 miles west of Blythe, California. This was in the maneuver area where personnel received final polishing. The information was sent at once to the surgeon general's office which immediately notified the surgeon, army ground forces, that a previously undetermined area was heavily infected with coccidioides. The medical officers initiated a Coccidioidomycosis control campaign and had a meeting at Stanford in the first week of May 1943. It was recommended (1) to educate the medical officers in the recognition of Coccidioidomycosis and provide them with diagnostic facilities, and (2) to delimit endemic areas by epidemiological investigations including selected skin testing surveys and a continuous search for erythema nodosum.

In August, the commanding officer of the 7th Medical Laboratory visited Stanford to institute the necessary diagnostic facilities. However, the work had only begun when the 7th Medical Laboratory was succeeded by the 9th (and this was the usual sad fate of the programs, about the time a unit or medical officers would become cognizant of the methods of detecting the disease and recognizing it, they would then be shipped out to another station and a new crowd would come in. Sometimes they took up the burden, sometimes they didn't.)

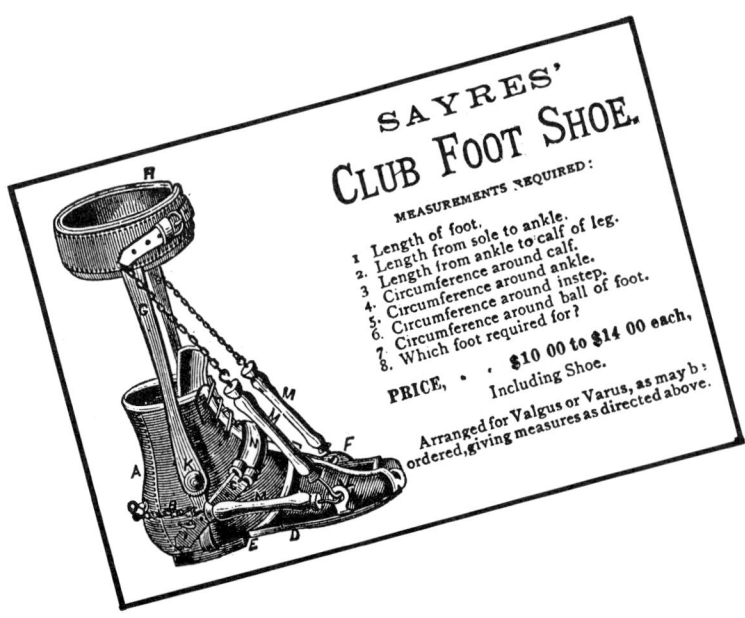

Some Medical and Non-Medical Notes about this Desert Training Center, 1942-1944

Part III

Coccidioidomycosis Among the Prisoners of War

There was a major camp for prisoners of war at Florence, Arizona. It was visited in September 1943 by Col. Verne R. Mason, M.C., medical consultant to the surgeon general of the army, Washington, D.C. He recognized that there were a number of probable coccidioidal infections and he alerted the medical officers and reported his findings to the surgeon general. The control commission detailed a reply and outlined a program for the control. Florence, the Arizona prisoner of war headquarters from which a number of side camps for field work radiated, was a known endemic area. Already, the Commission on Epidemiological Survey had supplied coccidioidin, serologic facilities, and consultive advice to the Japanese Relocation Center on the Gila River, not far away from Sacaton, because of outbreaks of cases there. From the experience and from the information garnered from Williams Field, Arizona, it was realized that the endemicity was high. There was no response apparently at Florence and it was not until December 1943 that the first serological specimens were sent for testing. The results of these tests, together with recognition of two deaths due to Coccidioidomycosis and a return visit by Col. Mason initiated action. Because of the reputation of the area for its salubrious climate, Florence Station Hospital was being used to hospitalize all tuberculous prisoners of war.

There had been recent German complaints that prisoners of war had been placed in unhealthful areas and so the surgeon general's office dispatched Dr. Charles Smith for his recommendations and inspection of the area. His studies substantiated the previous findings of the area at Florence and Williams Field.

"In that region, 50% of susceptibles were infected within six months' time. Indeed, ten tuberculous prisoners of war were found to be infected while they were hospitalized on the wards. One patient who had a tuberculous effusion on admission to the hospital, developed a coccidioidal effusion on the other side. The superimposed coccidioidal infections did not appear to affect the tuberculous infections adversely."

Doctor Smith, after carefully evaluating these cases, did not recommend that the tuberculous cases be transferred elsewhere but the surgeon general's office in Washington decided that to avoid any criticism of violation of policy governing hospitalization of prisoners of war, that the patients should be moved elsewhere. Florence was maintained as headquarters for Italian and later German prisoners of war working out of the various side agricultural camps.

Another outbreak of cocci among prisoners of war occurred the following year, 1945, in the San Joaquin Valley. (1)

Very often one could trace the location of medical officers aware of Coccidioidomycosis by the reporting of specimens from patients having recognized coccidoidal infections. This was evident in the assignments of Major Lewis T. Bullock, a pioneer worker on Coccidioidomycosis at Luke Field, Arizona, as he moved back and forth across the country.

Doctor Charles Smith summarized this great epidemiological study which was conducted by the armed forces in the continental United States under his direction somewhat as follows:

The leadership that was undertaken by the surgeon general of the army and his preventive medicine representatives in safeguarding the health of the United States troops was well portrayed in the experience of the armed forces with Coccidioidomycosis in World War II. The army air force demonstrated a kindred interest, thus there resulted a fine collaboration which developed a successful control program and performed extensive and rewarding research. The army

Adams' Splinter Forceps. 75c.

ground force was not as alert or responsive, its control programs and research were minimal, very largely dependent upon the unsupported enthusiasm and initiative of individual medical officers. Intrigued by this "new" infection, most medical officers contributed wholeheartedly to programs of control and research.

Headquarters POW Camp, Florence, Arizona
Photo courtesy of Florence, Arizona, Museum.

POWs arrive at Florence, Arizona, WW II
Photo courtesy of Florence, Arizona, Museum.

A Naval Experience

There is nothing quite like a case of acute Coccidioidomycosis among the medical staff to get their attention. The senior medical officer at the naval air station, Mohave, California developed the disease. After consultation with Doctor Smith a survey was done. (8)

Two skin test surveys of personnel were performed at 4-to-6 month intervals. Thirty percent of the original negatives became positive. Seven hospitalized patients with initial negative skin tests became positive. (The Chlamydospore was no respecter of army or naval service assignments.)

The Incidence of Coccidioidomycosis C-AMA

Doctor Charles Smith prefaces his portion of his report thus: "It is not possible to obtain accurate information as to the incidence of cocci in military and naval personnel in World War II." (7)

The reasons were multiple, this was a new and exotic disease for most of the physicians who reported for duty in the area. Rapidly, once the medical officers were indoctrinated, they were frequently transferred and except for the air bases, there was little continuity in the skin testing and reporting of recognized cases.

The data Doctor Smith was able to assemble for the years of 1942-1945 was 3,809 cases with 39 deaths. He continues, "The fact that 700 cases of Coccidioidomycosis or 18% of the army total were hospitalized in only five station hospitals in the San Joaquin Valley area indicates that 3,809 cases was a gross underestimate of the disease." (7)

Doctor Russel V. Lee commenting on the incidence of Coccidioidomycosis in the Western Flying Training Command states that: "The unprecedented opportunity for study of coccidioidal infection which the mobilization and training of troops in the southwestern United States provided, this was not neglected due to the foresight of Colonel Charles R. Glen and his successors." (9)

Anticipating the situation which actually arose, they enlisted the cooperation of Doctor Charles E. Smith, as a surgeon general's consultant representing the Army Epidemilogical Board even before mobilization began. He continues, "there was a hazard recognized in putting troops in this area. The decision that the climate advantages for flying outweighed the hazard of Coccidioidomycosis has been amply justified. The accident rate in flying a training mission in this command has been the lowest in the country and favorable flying weather has been the most important factor in achieving this record. Lives saved in this way far outnumber the lives lost from coccidioidomycocis."

He goes on to describe how carefully the flying command launched this campaign.

"All new personnel coming on air fields are tested when they arrive and the negative reactors are retested six months later or when they leave the field, if before this time has elapsed. All suspicious clinical cases in the dispensaries and hospitals are skin tested during the course of the disease and in addition specimens of blood are sent to Doctor Smith for confirmatory evidence when indicated. A campaign of medical education has been instituted due to the fact that Coccidioidomycosis was just news to most of the medical officers. As a result of this program, over a quarter million skin tests have been given, a thousand or more clinical cases recognized, nine complete autopsies done, and an enormous amount of statistical material has been collected."

From what we can gather from Doctor Smith's official account, and there is little other data available on the ground forces incidence, the medical department never inaugurated such a study among the ground troops or the medical personnel.

After World War II, when the reports of the Western Flying Training Command were evaluated by the Office of the Air Surgeon, Army Air Forces and later as a co-equal branch of the Surgeon General, United States Army, and when a separate USAF was established in 1947 and then a separate medical service by the USAF, when these training command reports were finally evaluated, a special study of the air force hospitals in the Southwest began.

Doctor Louis Kossuth, then assigned to the preventive medicine section of the surgeon general's office, USAF, monitored the study. (14) That cocci was not transmissible from patient to patient had been well established. But was it possible that in some of these old containment WW II type hospitals, that the cocci spore still resided in the crooks and crevices and baseboards of these hospitals of the Southwest, where the air force had learned to its sorrow that Coccidioidomycosis was not without a health hazard? (10)

So Major Harold V. Ellington was detailed to study and investigate these hospitals where cocci patients had been treated. It was decided to remove the baseboards, collect the dust and culture for fungus. Major Ellington succeeded against all expectations; he acquired the disease himself, and cavitated, lost a lung, but was finally rehabilitated and recovered and returned to active flight surgeon's status. Doctor Kossuth adds that his study did not destroy his friendship with Major Ellington, but he further adds that the investigation was never fully completed and, "He wonders about the rugs and baseboards of not only hospitals but all buildings where the flying Chlamydospores may be wafted by our intermittent dust storms." (14)

As a result of the first tests conducted in the Western Training Command in 1941 at Minter Army Air Force Base near Bakersfield, it was found that one-fifth of all susceptible personnel studied were infected during the summer and fall of 1941, in other words, a 20% incidence of the disease. Gardner Air Force Base at Taft, California, had dust ankle deep and cases were occurring with almost the same rapidity there. These studies and others quickly led the air force to inaugurate dust control measures which have been mentioned elsewhere.

"A death from coccidioidal meningitis at one of these fields served to emphasize the importance of careful diagnosis and medical surveillance of the disease." (7)

An excellent review of the air force experience in World War II was published in 1954 by Williams and Ellington and should be studied in the original for the excellent clinical and historical review. (10)

High Incidence Among Negro Soldiers—Another Cocci Surprise

"In April 1943, twelve colored soldiers were admitted with acute pulmonary cocci. All came from the same organization, engaged in construction work near Banning, California. Four cases disseminated and one died—all colored." (11)

From this and other experiences the authors concluded:

1. Colored persons are more susceptible than white and require twice as many hospital days as white to recover.
2. Despite the fact that California has long been known to harbor the fungus in the San Joaquin Valley and other limited areas, a new and larger area is suggested. It is roughly triangular, bounded by Banning and Needles, California, and pointing at Yuma, Arizona.

Recognition of Endemic Areas

Doctor Smith in the compilation of his prodigious efforts on behalf of the armed services has this to say about the status of cocciepidemiology prior to World War II.

"Knowledge of the endemic areas is of great importance in recognizing clinical coccidioidal infection and implementing its control. Prior to WW II, the endemic area in the United States was not clearly defined. It was believed to center in the San Joaquin Valley of California, while its northern limit was uncertain. On the basis of some cases reported from southern California, this area was also suspect. Just prior to the war, cases were reported in Tucson, by Doctor Orin J. Farness (1941), and Doctor Earle W. Phillips (1939) and from Phoenix.

"While the regions around El Paso and San Antonio, Texas had been established as other endemic areas by a few reported cases, northern Mexico was also suspect. The Chaco region of Argentina was the only other known area.

"The experiences of the army air forces, Western Flying Training Command, the army ground forces in California-Arizona proved that southern and central Arizona were the most highly infected of all of the areas in the United States." (7)

Dr. Keith Maddy later outlined the endemic area as corresponding to the Sonora life zone. Others noted, "Where the creosote bush grows there dwells the cocci spores." Maddy listed other mammals as victims of the ubiquitous spore: "Cattle, dog, horse, burro, sheep, swine, llama, monkey, gorilla, chinchilla, and various wild rodents." Great comfort; we are not alone!

Training Casualties

None of the critique reports on the various maneuvers were available to us for review. None of these reports encompass any real information about the effectiveness of training and the function of the medical units per se. Every maneuver this observer participated in had medical umpires all over the place as well as other line officials, and with long correction reports coming down at the close of the exercise listing what you did wrong. In any event, there is one report about casualties and it reads as follows:

"During maneuvers health was generally good. Sporadic cases of simple diarrhea occurred. In one month from August 17 to September 1942 there were seven deaths and 82 severe injuries resulting from the common causes. (1) Deaths and Causes: Accidental, crushed by boxcar rail head 1; skull fracture, motorcycle, 1; gunshot wound, 1; railroad versus tank 2. Suicide: Gunshot wound, 1; Disease: septicemia, (blood poisoning) 1; Total deaths 7. Injuries: Dislocations 11, burns 1, concussions 8, fractures 54, miscellaneous 2. Gunshot wounds, accidental 2, venomous snake bites 1, Venomous insect bites 2, internal injuries 1. Total injuries 82. The casualty figures represented a little over one-tenth of one percent of the average strength engaged in maneuvers which varied from 50,000 to 64,000 inclusive."

It was rather surprising with these thousands of troops in the field, for the most part living in the open, sleeping on the ground and certainly maneuvering through snake infested areas only one venomous snake bite was reported during this one month in the desert.

We have a few personal notes from physicians in the area and one of the most notable is of the late Doctor Ernest A. Born, a long-time physician and surgeon in Prescott, Arizona.

Doctor Born entered the service on June 10, 1942 and was assigned to a medical unit at the Desert Training Center, 7th Surgical Unit later designated the 92nd Evacuation Hospital, semi-mobile, and was located at Frieda, California. His surgical team developed a special technique for the care of ruptured livers—not a rare problem in the widespread tank maneuver area. The damaged, lacerated liver was packed and bound and the peritoneum (an abdominal membrane) closed, to be opened a few days later and the packing removed. Doctor Born reported that the survival rate was impressive. (12)

Another personal note was from Doctor Samuel I. Rothman of Phoenix, Arizona in commenting on the death of his friend Doctor Albert Bodanski.

"I first met Al at Camp Young, California in July 1942, a grand camp of army squad tents in the vast, forbidding desert between Blythe and Indio where mechanized divisions were being trained for the north African warfare. We were assigned to the 5th Field Hospital."

Doctor Rothman further recalls that he saw some army patients at the Community Hospital in Indio, California and among those were Mrs. George Patton, wife of the commanding general. (13)

Another observer noted that Mrs. Patton lived in Indio during the time that the general was in the desert, but that the general did not reside in Indio. One of his first moves when he came to the desert was to get his staff out of the Indio hotel and into tents at Camp Young where he also remained. Mrs. Patton was frequently seen in a command car with no top, but with an umbrella, in the field observing the action going on. This may well have been the area known as the King's Throne and must have been adjacent to the Desert Center. This was a rise in the terrain and was said from here, Patton could gaze out on a large portion of the flat maneuver area and see if his beloved tanks were performing up to his expectations.

Water, Weather and Rations

There are several accounts of individuals who believed their units were "first in the area," some of these gentlemen were misguided because the maneuver area encompassed such a wide geographic site that indeed his unit might be the first to have arrived in one of the great camps which spread across the desert for hundreds of miles.

Charles E. Keller, at the time a technical sergeant with the 773rd Tank Destroyer Battalion, writes:

"The Desert Training Center, also known as Camp Young, was our base and we helped construct it within the giant training area. The first

Camp Bouse, Arizona, today from the air
Photo Courtesy Lt. Col. John Lynch, U. S. Air Force retired.

150th Station Hospital, Camp Bouse, Arizona, 1943, Major C. F. Mueller, commanding
Photo courtesy U. S. Government.

training in the new center was known as "Little Libya" and was commanded by General George S. Patton, Jr. Our unit had come across the country driving their own vehicles from the Midwest."

Their truck convoy had stopped for a rest period at Indio, California and then resumed traveling toward Blythe and at about the 25th or the 29th milepost out of Indio, the convoy was stopped for what most of the members thought would be a routine rest stop.

"But this turned into a work stop at the beginning of Camp Young, Desert Training Center. Machete knives were issued and areas staked off which were to become company streets and battalion headquarters area. The first detail was cutting sagebrush and cactus in the areas, then it had to be gathered and piled up out of the area so it could be disposed of later. Next was the pitching of pup tents in company rows; supplies, motor vehicles and mess trucks were placed in cleared areas and within a week the camp started taking shape as the engineers moved in with bulldozers and other equipment. The battalion cleared more areas and pyramidal tents were set up in place of pup tents, also a mess hall was built consisting of an enclosed kitchen with a long overhanging open air dining area with just a roof overhead. There were tables and benches. These were not much good when sandstorms came and you didn't know if you were eating grits or sand. The intense heat of the day made the work on vehicles, layout, inspection of tools and equipment almost impossible at times. Tools once laid out could not be touched or picked up again during the day."

He adds, "During the summer months 130 degrees in the shade was common and there was very little shade. Even so, blankets were sometimes needed at night. More than 10,000 troops made up the first task force operating out of the new center." (15)

Patton didn't waste any time. It was here that Colonel Ray C. Hildreth, also a member of the same unit, recalled "General Patton's wife in a command car with an umbrella, following the maneuvers in over 100 degree heat. We had only one canteen of water for 24 hours during maneuvers." (17)

It was about this time that a submarine threat on the California coast put everyone on alert. One observer referring to this noted that "General Patton didn't know that he had no ammunition for most of the artillery that were on alert." Supply was meager and chaotic at times. But Williamson, this observer, a member of Patton's staff, felt that "General Patton would have run the tanks and other vehicles up and down the shore where the Japs were coming ashore and make such a racket and show, that they would scamper back to their boats." (16) No one came ashore and the alert

A rock monument around the cactus in beautiful downtown Butler Valley, Camp Bouse, Arizona, as it appeared May 21, 1981.
Photo by author.

subsided.

These camp sites on the California side were near the Colorado River or along the massive irrigation canals going to the Imperial Valley. These units could set up water points and have ready access to all the water they needed. There were some misguided generals who thought they could ration water and harden troops so that their water requirement became less as they stayed in the desert and this, as we shall see, led to some tragedies.

An observer of some of this was Captain Thomas A. Clark who served at the DTC headquarters through three successive maneuvers, beginning in July 1943.

He relates: "I visited engineer units which were stationed at Imperial Dam on the Colorado

River just north of Yuma. These were specialized engineer units and needed water for their functions. There was a pontoon bridge company and a water supply battalion. There may have been two of these because I remember one unit was commanded by Lt. Col. Pyle and his product was known as "Pyle's Bile" and the other water supply unit was commanded by an officer named Swatta and naturally his product was called Swatta's Watta." These jokes were bad enough that I have remembered them for thirty odd years." (18)

But many camps were not so fortunate, for instance at Camp Bouse, Camp Hyder and Camp Horn, Arizona, advance parties came in and drilled wells. At each of these wells a reservoir was constructed as a holding tank. Even so, water was scarce and a shower was a luxury. A few miles over the mountain from Camp Hyder is Aqua Caliente famous for its hot springs beginning in Indian and Spanish days, but now languishes with only some ranches in the area. During World War II the army constructed a cement swimming pool which was fed by the hot springs. The cement pool still squats there in the sun intact, but completely empty.

Early in the training cycle the order came down that there would be no ice in the company or division area and of course this meant that green vegetables and fresh meat were out. During August through September 1944 five different kinds of rations were used, "A," "B," "C," and "K," and a combination known as five in one. The latter consisted of a "B" ration made up into a lot from which five men were rationed and was issued to a vehicle crew. The quality of "A" and "B" rations was found satisfactory, but "B" ration lacked variety being evidently based on a three day cycle which resulted in constant repetition. The "C" ration was used in a number of instances but was furnished only in one menu. "K" ration was tried for a short period and it was found to be extremely satisfactory for longer periods, however, the amount of cheese was deemed excessive. (1)

As you can imagine, there was a shortage of transportation with all kinds of supplies coming into the area. The railroad facilities at Indio were woefully inadequate. "In early 1943 the daily ration train was put into operation from Colton to the desert center, it added to the problem of routing. Army hospital trains had the right-of-way and that held up traffic since there was but a single track between Colton and Yuma, the main line." Early on when General McNair sketched his training policies for the center and they were implemented by General Patton, "The hope for ice in the field was demolished." The main thrust of training was to be realism. They wanted all construction and equipment restricted to what would reasonably be expected in an active theater of war. At a conference it was decided, unless the ground surgeon could show cause for their retention, perishables would be dropped from the menu and ice boxes and screened kitchens would be eliminated. (Oh! the flies, the flies, the flies.)

The ground surgeon did not object to the use of "B" ration considering the vitamin content was adequate and the ration was fully utilized. He warned of the need to plan menus carefully in order to forestall monotony; Spam or sardines could not embrace every meal. The fly menace was variable and measurable in the center. Studies by the medical laboratory had afforded proof that flies were responsible for a near epidemic of dysentery. If the kitchens in the base camp were to be patronized only a few days out of the entire time the unit spent in the center, screening was not necessary. Many units, particularly service units had to remain in certain areas for long periods and for them screening was advised because of the great potential of fly borne disease. (1)

As so it was at 2400 hours on August 14, 1943, delivery of ice was stopped and the center went on "B" rations. Units were not permitted to become permanently attached to the base camp and this was considered commendable. But when the cat is away the mice will play. When General McNair visited C-AMA in December 1943 some six months later, he observed that the post exchange and the officers club at Camp Young were serving fresh milk and sandwiches. He ordered that stuff to be taken out without delay and to ensure that all troops in C-AMA subsided on field ration "B" with the exception being only for patients in the station and general hospitals, later broadened to include patients in the evacuation hospitals. This was soon modified so that in no case would any personnel be kept on "B" rations for periods in excess of two months without a break of several days in which "A" ration was fed. There were many complaints about the monotony of the food. (When the troops stop bitchin' watch out.)

Of course the army got a lot of criticism and advice from observant civilians. A Mr. James H. Gordon in charge of the weather bureau at Yuma, Arizona asserted that "Training has passed beyond a constructive into a destructive stage." And he further reported that heat prostrations were staggering. This probably was a newspaper report. At any rate a peppery surgeon, Doctor E. Payne Palmer, Sr., head of the Southwest Clinic in Phoenix, Arizona, wrote Senator Carl Hayden asking for an investigation. Well, of course, the senator wrote the surgeon general and stated in his

Chow line, field problem, 3rd Armored Division near Iron Mountain, California
Photo courtesy of M. McKee.

letter that Palmer "was characterized as one of the most noted physicians and surgeons in the Western and Southwestern United States and that he had called attention to an incident where three men had died and he hoped for an investigation of the training methods."

In that incident the errors in judgment by those in command were not of a nature to have brought a conviction even if the officers had been tried for negligence. The carrying out of a field problem caused a change in the route of an infantry platoon. No time being available for a detailed reconnaissance, the platoon was assigned a route not previously used. When the vehicles became stuck on a ledge, the platoon continued its march, inasmuch as the umpire had on a previous occasion instructed the platoon commander to continue the march and not concern himself with the vehicles, which carried water and rations, as these supplies were certain to be at the final destination.

The platoon arrived at a spot which they mistook for their destination and found no water or rations. The platoon commander returned on foot to secure water and rations for his men, but water was not available at the water point which compelled him to make a longer trip to secure it. The men were without food for about 24 hours and had about a half canteen of water per man for about 12 hours and during this time were exposed to extremely hot weather.

Private James H. Nash died. Sgt. Robert Powarn and Corp. Julius Oretga both of whom were in better physical condition than the other members of the platoon went for aid against the advice of Sgt. Joseph P. Morrison, acting platoon commander in the absence of a commissioned officer. The two lost their bearings and their bodies were later found by a search party. If they had remained with their platoon, their deaths would probably not have occurred. When remedial aid and vehicles were requested for the platoon, these were immediately dispatched. (1)

The late Senator Hayden's papers now repose at the Hayden Library at Arizona State University. We have searched through these but we are unable to find Dr. Palmer's letter or any of the other correspondence relating to this incident.

There were some commanders who tried to limit their troops to one canteen of water a day and they seem to have learned very slowly that water simply could not be strictly rationed and that troops could not be trained to exist on a constantly diminishing water supply. The official history does not mention fatalities resulting from this sort of deprivation, but there are rumors which persist

Medical Detachment 315 Engineers, 90th Division Desert, 1943
Photo Courtesy M. McKee.

to this day of such unfortunate events.

So water, weather and rations presented considerable problems to the maneuvering troops and it was anything but a tea party. But there were breaks. Men were allowed on weekend pass to go to the California side to Los Angeles. On the Arizona side they usually descended upon Yuma and Phoenix both relatively small towns, which could not accommodate the mass influx of troops,

The army set up a rest area at the old fairgrounds in Phoenix with tents, mess halls, soft drinks and beer so that when the facilities downtown were filled there was still plenty of space for troopers to relax. Many of the troopers looked forward to spending a weekend or a week at this rest area. There are several references to this from our various correspondents and they looked upon this as a welcome relief from the tedium of desert training.

We do not have access to a detailed list of hospitals and other medical units that supported the maneuver area or moved in and out at intervals. There is a list in the official history of the type of medical installations which were requested for the maneuver area and the accompanying tabulation shows that general and station hospitals together with medical laboratories, dental clinics and a medical depot were requested. Some were furnished, others were not. (See Table 4.)

As stated, we do not have an official listing of all the medical units involved, but the following hospital units have been gleaned from the scattered data available and from personal recollections of some of our correspondents: The 150th Station Hospital, Camp Bouse, Arizona; 41st Station Hospital; 21st Evacuation Hospital; 98th Evacuation Hospital; 36th Evacuation Hospital; 13th Field Hospital; 127th Station Hospital and the 13th General Hospital.

The company battalion regimental division corps and many other medical detachments came and departed with combat units they supported.

Temporary cantonment type hospitals on the periphery of the area, on the California side must have been numerous. At Yuma, Arizona and Needles, California station hospitals were given semipermanent quarters.

Cherry Valley General Hospital, near Beaumont; Banning General Hospital and Spodra General Hospital were among the supporting 1,000 bed general hospitals in the area, housed in semipermanent cantonment buildings. (19)

Table 4

Type of Unit	Requested	Furnished	Not Furnished
Medical			
Gen. Hosp. (100 bed)	3	3	0
Sta. Hosp. (250 bed)	5	5	0
Sta. Hosp. (150 bed)	1	1	0
Vet. Det. Sep.	5	3	2
Dental Clinic			
Cent. Dental Lab	1	0	1
Med. Lab (Army)	2	1	1
Co. Depot	2	0	2
Hospital Training	1	1	0
Hospital	0	0	0
Convalescence	1	0	1
Hospital, Field	1	0	1

Conclusion

Besides the problems of desert dust, supply, terrain and weather, at least two major medical problems plagued the maneuver area.

"Yellow jaundice," wholly unexpected following inoculation of troops with yellow fever vaccine. This delayed the initial mass maneuvers in the summer of 1942. The casualties plugged the entire medical evacuation system, and the slow recovery of patients and the need for physical retraining delayed their return to duty.

A more insidious cause of casualties was the widespread area of high coccidioides immitis infestation (the cause of Valley fever). It was known that the San Joaquin Valley was an endemic area, but an unknown threat or ignored threat existed in many other areas. The medical support of the Air Training Command took early action to control the disease at air training stations. The ground forces were less enthusiastic and effective.

The training standards were high, the climate and terrain tested the physical stamina of troops and the mechanical performance of all vehicles and weapons.

The austere training standards inaugurated by General Patton, with some lapses, were adhered to long after his departure. Patton knew that there is no "second chance" in combat and is said to have followed the old Roman axiom: "The legionnaires should fear their officers more than the enemy." (16)

Now the desert has for the most part reclaimed the area, a few rock monuments remain, and perhaps some ghosts of the long departed gallant men who trained there.

One ghost, Bullis fever, materialized in 1988 on the Letters pages of the *Journal of the American Medical Association*. (20)

The camp, near San Antonio, Texas during 1942-1945, was said to be the site of a tick (Amblyomma americanus)-borne infection that, according to a letter to the *Journal* by Jerome Goldfarb, Ph.D., affected about 1,000 of the camp's personnel. One death was reported.

Goldfarb, at the time, was associated with the United States Air Force School of Aerospace Medicine at Brooks Air Force Base, asked if another tick, Ehrlichia canis might have been mistaken for A americanus because both types of Rickettsia produce similar symptoms.

Not so, replied Thomas A. Eng, V.D.M., M.P.H., Joseph E. McCabe, Ph.D. and Daniel B. Fishbein, M.D., all of the Centers for Disease Control in Atlanta, Georgia.

While many symptomatic similarities do exist, they wrote, there are major differences that show them to be separate entities.

And, they add, only one case of Bullis fever occurred at the camp between 1942 and 1945, but 1,000 cases were reported elsewhere during that time.

Be all that as it may, Camp Bullis, Texas is the only World War II United States military installation to have a disease named for it!

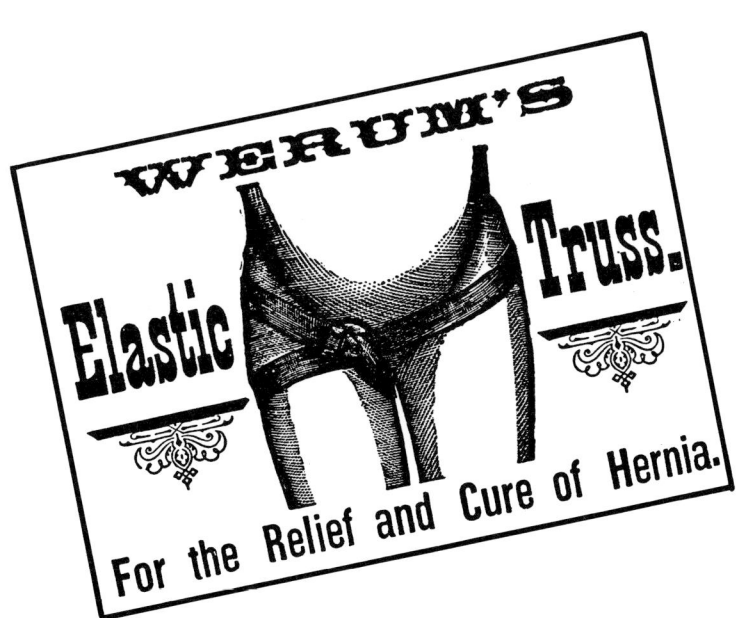

Acknowledgement

To John S. Lynch and Robert S. Wooley, stalwart pushers and pullers of the Council on American Military Past, I owe my interest in this World War II maneuver area. Their study of Patton's Desert Training Center in Camp Periodical, Volume XII, No. 2, December 1982 should be consulted for a detailed historical description of the area and exact locations of the major division camps.

Pope's Antrum Drill. $3.50.

References:

1. The Desert Training Center and the California-Arizona Maneuver Area Army Ground Forces Historical Section Study No. 15, 1946.
2. Butler, A. F.: *Personal Communications*, 1981. T/Sgt. USAAF trained with 46th Bomb Group (L) at Blythe Army Air Field.
3. Sawyer, W. A., et al: Jaundice in Army personnel in the Western Region of U.S. in relation to vaccination against Yellow Fever. *American Journal of Hygiene,* 1944; 40:35-107.
4. Marcovits, et al: Marihuana addicts in the Army. *War Medicine*, 1944; 6:383-391.
5. Malleck, H. J., *Personal Communication*, 1982. Division Surgeon, 80th Infantry Division, Laguna, Arizona, 1943.
6. Ltr. Com. Zone, C-AMA Subject: Discontinuance of Medical Service to C-AMA and endorsements. National Archives, November 22, 1943.
7. Smith, C. E., *Coccidioidomycosis*. Medical Department U. S. Army Preventive Medicine in WW II, Office of the Surgeon General, Department of the Army, Washington, D.C., pp 285-315, 1954.
8. Pfanner, E. F., *Coccidioidomycosis at the USMC Air Station, Mohave,* California. U. S. Naval Medical Bulletin, Vol. 46, pp 229-236, 1946.
9. Lee, R. V., *Coccidioidomycosis in Western Training Command California and Western Medicine.* Vol. 61, No. 1, pp 133-135, 1944.
10. Williams, J. J., Ellingson, H. V., *Studies on Coccidioidomycosis at the Air Force Bases in the Southwestern U. S. Unnumbered Report,* USAF School of Aviation Medicine, Randolph Field, Texas. pp 1-24, December 1954.
11. Willet, F. M., Weiss, A., *Coccidioidomycosis in Southern California. Report of a new endemic area with review of 100 cases.* Archives of Internal Medicine 1945, 23:319-385.
12. Yount, F., Memorial to Ernest A. Born, M.D., 1904-1980. *Arizona Medicine* 1981:37:582.
13. Rothman, S. I., Memorial to Albert Bodanski, M.D., 1904-1980. *Arizona Medicine* 1980:37:582.
14. Kossuth, L. Col., M.C. USAF, Retired: *Personal Communication*, 1982.
15. Keller, C. E., 773rd, Tank Destroyer BN: *Personal Communication*, 1980.
16. Williamson, P. B., *Patton's Principles MSC Inc.*, Tucson, Arizona, 1979.
17. Hildreth, R., Col.: *Personal Communication*, 1980.
18. Clark, T. A., *Personal Communication*, 1980.
19. Military Historical Section, National Archives.
20. Goldfarb, J., Eng, T. A., McCabe, J. E., Fishbein, D. B., *Journal of American Medical Association*, November 25, 1988, Vol. 260, No. 20, pp 3006-7.

XII.

Arizona Physicians

Introduction

The pioneering physicians whose untiring and almost singlehanded efforts to make Arizona a more healthful and better place in which to live, deserve more than the following descriptions of their achievements. Many of them, like Palmer Dysart, M.D., blazed the trails to modern medicine that did so much to raise the state to an eminent position medically. Others, like Clarence G. Salsbury, M.D., were mighty forces in breaking the stranglehold that political indifference and ineptness (traces of which, unfortunately, are still in evidence today) that were keeping Arizona in the Dark Age of medicine.

This cadre of determined physicians who struggled to give Arizona a medical reputation of which it could be proud, more often than not did so at considerable personal sacrifice and with no hope or expectation of recognition or reward.

Although these physicians and their often precedent-setting accomplishments are given, in these pages, the recognition long overdue them, there are others who will follow them.

Thus, it may not be amiss as an official tribute to these pioneer physicians as well as to those who now are carrying, and those to come who will carry on the selfless devotion to the betterment of medical care in Arizona, that a Medical Hall of Fame be established in their honor.

To borrow a phrase from Abraham Lincoln, "It is altogether fitting and proper that we should do this."

J. DeV.

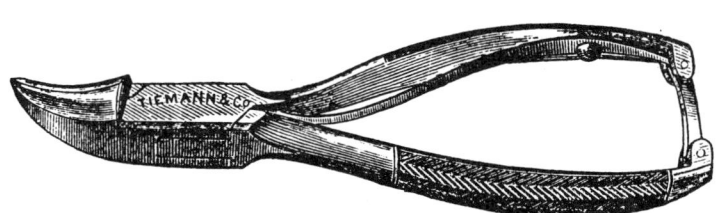

Fig. 531.—Nail and Bone Nipper. $2.50.

ORVILLE HARRY BROWN, M.D.
1875-1943

December 11, 1980, on advice of Doctor George McKhann we interviewed Doctor Paul Jarrett, a native Phoenician, and pathologist at Good Samaritan Hospital. Doctor Jarrett recalled Doctor Brown but not much else as he, Jarrett, was not practicing nor even through medical school when Doctor Brown was still active in medicine here in Phoenix.

Doctor Jarrett does remember that in the summer Doctor Sweek wore boots in the operating room filled with ice water because then there were no cooling systems to combat the high summer temperatures of Phoenix. No elective surgery was performed in the summer in Phoenix before WW II. After WW II, Jarrett came back to Phoenix to practice with Doctor Thomas Woodman, Doctor Hillary Ketcherside and Doctor Dwight Porter, general practitioner.

Doctor Jarrett suggested we contact Doctor Carl Holmes and it turns out that Doctor Brown was Carl's physician as he grew up, but have never been able to get any more information than that.

I contacted Doctor Carl Holmes' mother, the wife of the senior Holmes. She recalls Mrs. Brown and that they had a daughter but not much else.

From notes in *Southwestern Medicine Journal* in 1933, Doctor Brown of Phoenix headed, or was chairman of the Maricopa County Medical Society Welfare Committee and headed a fight against a constitutional amendment which would have permitted chiropractors to practice medicine and surgery. The amendment was defeated and the editor gave recognition to Doctor Brown for his work on behalf of organized medicine.

In November, 1980, Doctor Palmer Dysart through his wife, because of Doctor Dysart's failing health, was unable to be interviewed.

Doctor George McKhann doesn't recall anything special about Doctor Brown, although McKhann came in 1928-29, but with tuberculosis and didn't practice until the thirties.

As related before, Mrs. Fred Holmes, Sr. now in her eighties, knew Mrs. Brown well but no details about Doctor Brown. I talked to her by telephone.

Doctor McKhann, interviewed in November 1980, when asked about Brown, stated that he was a very high class physician but didn't know him well and didn't know of Brown's interest in medical history.

Doctor Carlos Craig, in November 1980, stated that he didn't know details or remember about Brown, except that Brown was well thought of and practiced good medicine.

Doctor L. D. Beck on the ninth of February 1981, interviewed by telephone, remembers Doctor Orville Harry Brown as a chubby, quiet sort of a physician but no particulars and he, Doctor Beck, did call on Doctor Brown during his terminal illness.

In *Southwestern Medicine, Vol. I*, 1917, there is a note, "Doctor Orville H. Brown, formerly Assistant Professor of Medicine of St. Louis University, located in Phoenix where he will confine his practice to internal medicine, being associated with Doctor W. O. Sweek."

There is a further note, "the only medical man in the third Arizona Legislature is Doctor Ray Ferguson of Patagonia, who is a member of the lower House from Santa Cruz County."

The following memorial to Dr. Brown appeared in *Southwest Medicine*, August 1943:

Dr. Orville Harry Brown, formerly of Phoenix, died July 25, 1943 in Arcadia, California, at the age of 68.

Doctor Brown retired from the active practice of medicine in Phoenix in 1940 and

Photo courtesy of Southwest Medicine.

moved to California to reside with a daughter, Mrs. Harold Roach. For the past several years Doctor Brown had bravely and cheerfully carried on in the face of an incurable and painful disease.

Born in Brown County, Kansas, Doctor Brown's education was received at the University of Kansas, University of Chicago and St. Louis University. He took his M.D. degree from the latter institution in 1905. The early years of his practice were spent in St. Louis, where he filled the position of assistant professor of medicine at St. Louis University. In 1916 Doctor Brown moved to Phoenix, where he entered the private practice of medicine, specializing in internal medicine.

Doctor Brown was a member of the American Medical Association and the Southwestern Medical Association. He was a diplomate of the American Board of Internal Medicine and a fellow of the American College of Physicians, besides belonging to the American Association of Biological Chemists and the Royal Society of Medicine (London).

Doctor Brown wrote many articles for the medical literature. He was the author of a textbook on asthma and another on laboratory physiology.

For several years he was editor-in-chief of *Southwestern Medicine Journal*. During his tenure he enlivened the pages of the *Journal* with numerous straight-hitting editorials. In these writings he displayed the characteristic of eternally hammering at what he conceived to be the truth, regardless of whether his attitudes and concepts might be popular or not. He was a man of gentleness, tolerance and high understanding. His opinion was respected and sought in the councils of organized medicine in the entire Southwest. He was a leader in medical and likewise civic endeavors. He often inspired younger physicians to emulate his habits of observation and deduction.

Doctor Brown occupied a high place in the affections of this writer. He will be missed by hundreds of us in the medical profession of the Southwest. God grant this good man his well deserved peace and rest.

TREVOR G. BROWNE, M.D.
1891-1977

Educator, physician and responsible citizen, Doctor Browne resided in the Valley for over forty years and was one of the earliest pediatricians to practice hereabout. He is known not only for his medical erudition but also for his forthright beliefs and ability to communicate them without equivocation or misunderstanding. A native of Canada, he was born in the province of Ontario near a town called Brockville on the St. Lawrence River, the youngest of seven children. By the time he was three years of age his father and mother had died. He was reared by his father's sister, a Miss Sarah J. Browne, and stayed with her only until he had finished high school, which was three years at that time. Now let's hear how Doctor Browne relates it. "I taught school at Adnac, Saskatchewan, a year, then I went to Regina and spent four years at the normal school.

"I then took a summer school, for no other vacancies were available at that time, at a place called Kilbach School. When I got there I discovered that no one could speak English, but I spoke fairly good high-school German, but they didn't understand me and I didn't understand them. I had quite a time before I devised a method of teaching these kids something and finally decided to devote the last hour of each day to learning their language, and it was surprising that in no time we were gabbing both in English and Suevi, their dialect was called, and the kids got along beautifully. When the inspector came he found the kids able to converse fluently in English with the teacher, and he wrote a magnificent tribute, the best of which I ever received."

He then acquired scarlet fever and "my doctor was a trustee of the Melville Schools, and he asked me to come and take the teaching job and be principal of a school at Melville, which was a big eight-room school. I said not unless I can have a permanent job. He said, 'Look how young you are, they ran the last guy out.' I said, they won't run me out because I have no place else to go. I will stay, they can go, but I won't.

"So, my first morning at the school, I was standing at the landing of the stairway, the janitor rang the bell and all hell broke loose. I never heard such a stampede, or such a roar in all of my life, as when they entered the school. I just stood out on the stairway and said absolutely nothing.

"After a while my silence got to them and everything quieted down. I said, 'Get out, when you can behave like human beings come back in.' I went down and locked the doors. It was 25 degrees below zero, so the weather was on my side.

"In a few minutes I went down and opened the doors and they came in like mice and went to their rooms. I stayed seven years in that place and never raised my voice to anyone in the system. During that time I decided for some crazy reason that I was going to become a doctor. I know I should have stayed in teaching because I made a damn sight better teacher than I ever made a doctor. But anyway I decided that I was going to study medicine so I applied for entrance to McGill and was accepted and sent my resignation in to the trustees of the school, they never said anything.

"At the end of the month of June three of them came to the school, the only time they had ever been in the school in the seven years I was there, and the chairman of the board was a lawyer. He said, 'What do you want?' I was taken sort of aback and said what do you mean, what do I want? I don't want anything. And then he replied, 'We will double your salary if you will stay, we will triple your salary.' That is where I made my mistake, I should have stayed another year, because it would have helped out considerably. I struggled through medical school.

*Trevor G. Browne, M.D.
Photo courtesy of Roundup.*

So I went down to McGill and took their combined course, it took six years. It was 1916 the year I went down and 1922 when I graduated."

On completion of medical school and while Doctor Browne was casting about for a place to go, he received an unexpected call from a Doctor Todd, who taught parasitology. Todd hadn't been in residence when Browne took his course so he was at a loss to know why all of this was taking place. At any rate, he went to see Todd, and Todd greeted him by saying, "How would you like to go down to Harvard in pathology?" Browne replied, "I have as much chance of going to Harvard in pathology as the proverbial snowball." He said, "No, I mean it."

He did manage for Browne to go down and take a position with Doctor Burt Wolbach, the professor of pathology at the Peter Bent Brigham Hospital. However, he secured time off before reporting in Boston to make a trip with a ship of the Hudson Bay Company across the North Sea to Norway to pick up 750 reindeer and plant them at Baffin Land, way up in the Hudson Bay country. When he was sent back a year later he could count only 175. The Eskimos must have had a wonderful year, not having to follow the caribou and eating reindeer instead.

To return to his experience with Doctor Todd, he went back to see his professor after he had landed the job in Boston and Todd volunteered, "You know why I sent you down there?" Browne replied he didn't have the foggiest idea. Well, Todd continued, "You were voted into some academic fraternity here and you got up and said that a certain gentleman from Jamaica who was black, had the same grades as you and you didn't see why he wasn't voted in, and that if he didn't go in you wouldn't go in."

Todd said he then decided that "if I ever have a chance to help that guy I will do so, because he is the first one here at McGill who could get up and express himself and leave nobody in the dark as to what he meant."

This same sort of single-minded respect for

his fellow man has been part of Doctor Browne's conduct all through life.

Doctor Browne remained two years as instructor in pathology in Boston but then he became enamored of pediatrics and went down to Hopkins to see if he could secure a position there.

A short time later he was called into Doctor S. Burt Wolbach's office, the little man with the enormous voice, boomed out: "What is this I hear about you wanting to go down to Baltimore?"

"Well," Doctor Browne explained, "I would like to go down there and get an internship in pediatrics." To which Wolbach rejoined, "I will arrange for you to have an internship at the Boston Children's, there is no finer place than the Boston Children's and you can go over there under Doctor K. B. Blackfan."

So he went over with Blackfan and did his internship. Later, he was sent to Ann Arbor as an assistant to Doctor Cowie. "I thought it was a rather nice compliment, so I went out to Ann Arbor and immediately began to work with Doctor Cowie, although he was ill for the two years I was in his department."

Now comes one of the experiences and forthright statements of plans of Doctor Browne. "Doctor Hugh Cabot was then dean of the medical school. He and Doctor Cowie were sworn enemies and he thought he had Cowie on the run when I went there. Of course, I gathered my forces together and nobody dared set foot in our department while we ran the show. We had 2,000 children a month come through the department, it was a wonderful experience.

One day I was summoned to the dean's office and Doctor Cabot exploded. "What are your plans?"

I said, "I do not think it is any of your business what my plans are."

"Well," the great Cabot rejoined, "this place isn't big enough for you and me, and I think you had better go."

Well, Browne turned the tables and said, "In that case I think you had better go, for I intend to stay here."

The dean very nearly had a stroke, and Browne continues, "The funny part of it was that Doctor Richard Cabot, a brother of Hugh Cabot, and I were very close friends and I stayed in Richard's house and visited many times back to Harvard Medical School, and I always attended his clinics, which were established at that time."

The upshot of this was that Doctor Hugh Cabot did leave Ann Arbor for some reason or other, not too long after that, but Doctor Browne stayed on two years in the pediatric department. But he found the weather there not to his liking.

He was always having respiratory infections so he took time off and traveled out to Death Valley to gather some ultra-violet. He stayed there a winter as hotel physician to one of the tourist hotels at Furnace Creek. It was a very fashionable hotel in those days and he got acquainted with a great many people in the west. Amongst them was Doctor Orville Harry Brown of Phoenix, who invited him down to join him, together with Doctor W. L. Reid from the Mayo Clinic. He wanted to start a group practice here in Phoenix.

So, he finally arrived in Phoenix on October 1, 1931. Browne continues, "I sort of tossed a coin to see whether I would stay here or whether I would go on to San Diego, as I had a license in California, also. So I said to myself this place will never grow up to amount to anything, with this horrible climate, I do not want a big town as I am sure San Diego will grow to be, so I will stay here. That was my reasoning at that time and

Dr. Browne with a Teddy Bear likeness of a polar bear cub, a souvenir of his two cruises in northern waters aboard the SS Nascopie. Photo courtesy of Roundup.

you can see how far off I was about it growing."

Doctor Reid, who was associated with them in the beginning, lost his life in an automobile accident, so he practiced with Doctor O. H. Brown for a good many years until Doctor Brown passed away.

Things were rather informal about getting a license to practice in Arizona in those days. Browne says that he came in 1931 but he didn't get his license until 1932. Nevertheless, he began to practice soon after arrival here. For the first fifteen years in Phoenix he practiced in the Professional Building and later moved his office to Seventh Street and McDowell, and still later to 2021 N. Central, where he shared offices with Doctor S. Caniglia.

Doctor Browne was long associated with St. Monica's Hospital, now Phoenix Memorial Hospital, and its founder, Emmett McLaughlin. As Browne recalls, he thinks it was probably about 1934 when Emmett McLaughlin came to St. Joseph's Hospital as a chaplain.

Browne's first venture into the medical assistance field was to establish a clinic for children in south Phoenix. In the meantime, he was appointed school physician for Phoenix Elementary School District #1, at the suggestion of Doctor Harry Carson, an early pediatrician in this city.

Browne goes on to say, "We had at that time in Phoenix, at Seventh Street and Monroe a building called Social Service Center, which had been donated to the city by Mrs. Dwight B. Heard. The city had for years allotted $40,000 to the running of the place in conjunction with Mrs. Heard's contribution. It had room for every type of clinic: internal medicine, orthopedics, surgery and pediatrics, and so on.

At the time that Ray Busey was mayor of Phoenix, the city attorney ruled that the city could no longer legally give money for curative medicine, it could only contribute money for preventive medicine. So they cut off this donation to social service and Mrs. Heard could not bear all of the financial burden herself and it closed."

This left Doctor Browne without a place to see his indigent school children. So, he went down to Memorial Hospital to see Emmett McLaughlin and "he gave me a room and permission to start a clinic there. We met every Wednesday and no child was allowed to come to that clinic unless he came with a note from the nurse or the nurse brought the child and guaranteed that the family was not able to pay a doctor, and that was the only way I could keep the doctors off my neck. That was the way our clinic got started and when I needed money I asked Emmett if I could form a women's auxiliary at the hospital. So I got my friend Mrs. Neil McCloud to get all of the fashionable ladies in town and start the Memorial auxiliary. They financed the clinic for 25 years.

In 1945, I ran for the school board. I do not believe anybody put pressure on me or asked me to run. I just decided I thought I had something to offer education, as education had always been kind of a hobby of mine. So, I ran for the school board and was elected. I ran five different times and spent 25 years on the school board and retired in 1970."

As he recalls, "One of the first things that staggered me when I got on the board was the insurance of the schools was held by 90 different companies. You can imagine dealing with that many—and the school district wasn't so large in those days. That had to be re-organized, and the idea was put out that no insurance would be sold or taken by a company which was engaged in any other business beside insurance. So many of the real estate offices had an insurance business on the side but this was whittled down by simply parceling out the insurance to only bonafide insurance carriers."

As a tribute to his contributions to education in the Phoenix area the Trevor Browne High School opened on the west side in 1972, on 75th Avenue at Catalina. With his usual foresight, Doctor Browne had guided the board in acquiring the land some 10 or 12 years previously, as he recalled it, there were 80 acres in all, 20 acres went to an elementary school, 60 acres to the high school, with a portion of that for a park.

In 1971 he was elected to the 50-year club in the Arizona Medical Association.

Along with Wade Hammond, Fred Wilson and Ray Busey, Doctor Browne was one of the original founders of the local Urban League. He was quite proud of this and attended the 25th anniversary celebration of its founding.

These then, are some of the career highlights of a physician who took his community obligations seriously and made many great contributions as a consequence.

He resided in retirement at The Beatitudes, but continued some of his board work at Memorial Hospital and served on some state and local education committees. While his loss of visual acuity deprived him of reading or television viewing, "It's like the '30s, he said." I listen to the radio for current events."

His wit and humor were as fresh and spring-like as ever. It was a pleasure to visit with this true physician and responsible citizen of the community.

LEWIS W. CLAYPOOL, M.D.
1916-1978

PHYSICIAN, PATRIOT AND FRIEND OF MAN

There was nothing equivocal about Lewis Claypool. He was positive, compassionate, and constructive in his private and professional life. Born in Iowa he was due to graduate from medical school at the University of Iowa in 1941, but he suffered an attack of pneumonia, which left him a severe asthmatic; he came to Arizona seeking relief (1939). In 1940 he returned to Iowa but his visit lasted only three days and he was forced again to return to Phoenix, where he again became employed as an orderly at the old St. Joseph's Hospital.

With the onset of WW II he was employed as a chemist in a chemical plant in California. He was refused enlistment by the armed forces, and later (as was frequently the case) was drafted and sent to the 4th Infantry. Now he was able to enter the ASTP program and finish medical school at Tulane. He again returned to St. Joseph's hospital in Phoenix as an intern in 1947. He was called up during the Korean conflict and served two years at Williams Air Force Base and returned to practice here in Phoenix. Thus began his long romance with the air force.

He joined the Air National Guard and thereafter gave it loyal service. The military "the world's largest fraternity" he served with relish. In the meantime he established a busy family practice with Doctors Carlos Craig and Robert Barfoot, first in the Professional Building and later at 1313 N. 2nd Street in Phoenix. In later years he was attracted to the professional suites at St. Luke's Hospital and established a solo office there. Lewis never limited his practice to one hospital. He was a staff member of the five Phoenix hospitals. He was never a drone, and at times served as chief of the medical staff at Memorial and St. Luke's hospitals and on numerous committees at these and other hospitals in the Valley. He was always a booster for organized medicine and served in various capacities in the county and state societies. Here indeed was the complete physician. Medicine was always a challenge, and he attended his patients with empathy and skill. Military pursuits were also a challenge and enjoyment. He retired with the rank of brigadier general. Most of all his wife, family and home were his greatest pride and enjoyment. Professional proficiency, military excellence and family pride, these were the unabashed motives in the life work of Lewis Claypool.

Photo courtesy of Arizona Medicine

PALMER DYSART, M.D.
1904-1984

Palmer Dysart, M.D. was born in Phoenix, Arizona Territory, in 1904, the son of a pioneer territorial physician, Louis Dysart, M.D. The father had graduated from Physicians and Surgeons School of Medicine in Chicago in the mid-90s. This school was later to become the University of Illinois Medical School.

Doctor Louis Dysart soon found himself in Mexico as an industrial surgeon, making house calls on horseback with a saddlebag of medications and instruments and a pistol on his belt. This was in one of the mining camps in northern Mexico. He then came to Bisbee, Arizona Territory, as a physician for one of the mining camps there and very soon after that came up to Phoenix to engage in medical practice. Palmer did his high school work in California, attended Phoenix Junior College for a couple of years in one of the first three classes and then returned to Stanford University to complete his pre-medical work and entered Northwestern University Medical School in 1925. He interned at the Cook County Hospital in Chicago and returned to Phoenix in 1931 to practice with his father.

In 1977, Doctor Dysart sat for an oral history recounting some of his early experiences in medical practice in Phoenix, later in the air force and, on his return to Phoenix, as a mover and booster for the State Vocational Rehabilitation Department.

In September 1928, he married a Long Island, New York girl, Miss Gertrude Jung. To this union was born one daughter, Dorothy. Mrs. Dysart was to remain his faithful helpmate and stabilizer through his subsequent long career and through what seemed to be an interminable terminal illness. Palmer Dysart had a long-standing love affair with physics, electricity and magnetism. Early on, he experimented with solar energy and built and perfected a parabolic metal trough mirror twelve feet across and eight feet long with a six-inch diameter boiler. It could be continuously directed at the sun and would generate solar power. He said about the only thing that came from that was "our steam whistle could be heard over much of the Agua Fria district, and it may have annoyed the jackrabbits." On his return to Phoenix, he perfected a transfusion apparatus, drew plans for an orthoscope (a device for the exercise of the eye muscles) and many other strange devices, none of which were patented. He related, "I built and ran a solid injection steam engine, similar in general principle to the diesel engine, except external heat was supplied to the small flash boiler." He applied for a patent for his blood transfusion apparatus with which he gave many blood transfusions in Phoenix, but he found that Baxter Company quickly put out the "vacoliter" and this made his apparatus for transfusions no longer necessary.

After his training at the Cook County Hospital in Chicago, he returned to practice with his father. This was the era of some of the early giants in medicine in Phoenix. Doctor Ancil Martin, Doctor Payne Palmer, Sr., Doctor Logan D. Dameron and many others whose names are hardly a memory now in this metropolis. His interest in flying was stimulated by Doctor Joseph Madison Greer, an early pilot in the Valley who owned a plane. "I was assisting him in surgery and as my assistant fee for surgery, I got flying time in an airplane that he owned that was being used by Karl Knier, an old time pilot and flight instructor here in the Valley." He continues, "I got my private pilot's license and several hundred hours of flying time and then, before the United States entered World War II, a group of us pilots decided to do something constructive for the impending war. The war was going on in Europe, so we organized and bought a training two-place

Photo courtesy of Roundup.

glider over in California, and all of us got checked out at Rosemand Dry Lake, which is just west of Edwards Air Force Base at the Rogers Lake in November 1941."

He was the only physician in this group. He continues, "We decided to train glider pilots for the war, but we had to train ourselves first. I designed a winch, and the Arizona Highway Department built it for us. At first we were using auto tow to pull the plane into the air. We would get the plane up a thousand feet before it would porpoise and would have to be released from the towing cable." The tow was Dysart's Packard automobile, and he states, "On my checkout flight on November 9, 1941, in California with four thousand feet of wire out (piano wire) by auto tow, I made an elevation twice of 2,200 feet before releasing. On the date of Pearl Harbor, December 7, 1941, we were flying this glider off Thunderbird Field, and it was here that they heard of the attack on Pearl Harbor." Various accidents and thrills were encountered by this group. One man was lost when he suddenly was caught in an updraft of such force that he was driven through the bottom of the glider and fell to his death. The glider was restored after each of these crashes and was finally sold to the Army Air Force and the last time Palmer saw it, it was being used for training at a glider field west of Wickenburg. All this time, he was engaged in a busy private practice of medicine, assisting Doctor Greer in his orthopedic work, and he related that it was here his "social conscience" became aroused and was later, after his World War II tour, to lead him into rehabilitation medicine.

His anticipation of our entry into the war, and in an attempt to prepare himself for it, met with little approbation by the air force when he endeavored to join. So, I'll let him relate it in his own words. "I went up to Salt Lake City in June of 1942 to volunteer. They sent me back to Luke Field; they wouldn't take my application in Salt

Lake City. I said to myself, 'To hell with that,' because I heard that those who went out to Luke Field might end up in the air corps, but many of them ended up in the army, navy, marine corps and even in the CBs. So, I went over to Williams Field and signed up there and was examined by two doctors whom I later met in New Guinea." He continued, "Time passed and I didn't hear anything, so I went to see Gen. Alexander Tuthill, who was chief of the Selective Service here. (Gen. Tuthill was chief of Selective Service in the state.) He suggested I write a letter to Senator Hayden. Hayden quickly replied that my previous application forms had been lost and I should reapply. This I did with a roving board, which was then in Phoenix, and they instructed me to apply for a majority because of my age and experience. In a week or so I received greetings from the President of United States addressed to 'Captain Palmer'."

He reported for duty September 1, 1942 at the Santa Ana Army Air Force Base. It was air force, not air corps by then. He continued his air force experiences thus: "I left Oakland by liberty freighter loaded with eight thousand tons of bombs and P-38s and trucks lashed to the deck on December 2, 1942. I landed in New Guinea on January 19 at my assigned base. Funny things happened along the way. We landed at Townsville, Australia. That is where the freighter docked. There was a group of a half dozen of us unassigned air force medical officers on this freighter, and we found that the headquarters of the air corps was in Brisbane. So, we went to the transportation office in Townsville, and with bold-faced lies, told the transportation officer in charge there that we had been ordered to report to the Air Force headquarters in Brisbane. That night we boarded a train after it was in motion. There were no accommodations. We slept on the floor and ate pineapples and bananas when the train would happen to stop at the crossroad where somebody had fruit. We arrived at Brisbane two days later with no knowledge as to where to go. We found the Army air force headquarters, and I walked into the commanding surgeon's office of the air force. Here, I met a white haired old time military doctor. I gave my snappy stateside salute and said, 'Capt. Dysart reporting.'

"He rared back to spit chewing tobacco into the spittoon clear across the room and said, 'What in the hell am I going to do with you?'

"Well, well," I said "You were sure in a hurry to get me down here. I'm fresh from the states and have only been in the service for three months."

"He said 'We'll find an assignment for you in Brisbane.'

"To which I replied, 'I don't like Australia and I want to get this damn war over with. How about sending me up to one of the islands?'

"Well," he replied to that, "Boy, we save that for the young fellers and the bad boys."

"Well," I said, "I'm not very old and believe me, if I get stuck down here in Australia I can get awful bad. So, you'll end up sending me to the islands anyway."

And the old colonel replied, "I guess you really mean it, by god I'll do it."

"So, he had orders for me to go north, and I landed in New Guinea the 19th of January 1943 after I had hitched a ride on a B17."

In January of 1944 he became ill, thought he was developing tuberculosis, but it was six months before he found out what the trouble really was. He had refused yellow fever shots because he had learned of the complications back in the states. And he continued, "I knew by that time that the military had over a hundred fatalities at least from the yellow fever shots. (All of this is now well documented by the army medical history series and an account of it in the California-Arizona maneuver area has been published in *Arizona Medicine* Vol. XL 1983.) So, his tour in the South Pacific ended in a station hospital in the spring of 1944 at Fort Moresby, New Guinea, and then he was transferred back to Australia, and at Townsville he met a physician who later practiced at St. Joseph's Hospital in Phoenix. He said he had a very dim view of the experience because he gave him a barium enema and then told him to go a quarter of a mile out to the latrine, which he didn't make and he didn't appreciate that very much. He was then transferred back to the states to the Letterman Army Hospital with a tentative diagnosis of carcinoma of the liver. At the Letterman General Hospital, as it was then known, "I got my first tub bath in many months and soaked in hot water and went to sleep under an open window. I hadn't slept for 90 hours or so crossing the Pacific by plane and was chilling much of the way, and when I went to sleep under an open window after a hot bath, I caught pneumonia. But I didn't mention it, and I was placed in charge of a troop train bound to Memphis, Tennessee.

"When I arrived at the Kennedy General Hospital in Memphis, I was really sick. When the train stopped at Ash Fork, Arizona, I paced up and down on the back end of the train wishing I had the ignorance, stupidity and guts to go AWOL and come down to Phoenix. But good judgment prevailed, and I landed in the Kennedy General Hospital and didn't see a doctor for a whole week." His experiences and the deficiency of the medical service at the Kennedy General Hospital

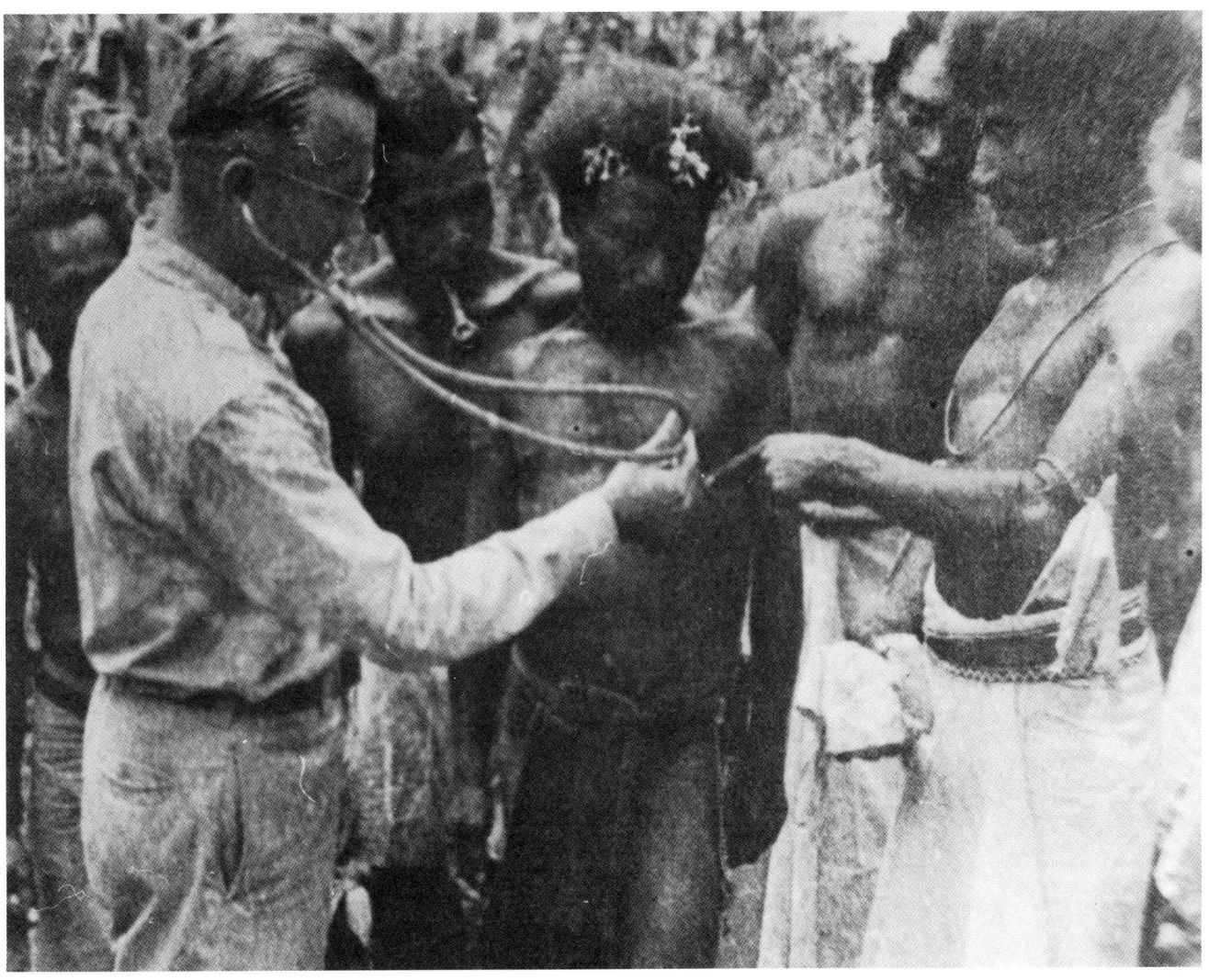

Palmer Dysart, M.D., U. S. Army Air Force, examines natives on New Guinea during WW II, 1944. Photo courtesy of Mrs. Palmer Dysart

would fill a book if you read his full account full of humor and tragedy! Eventually, he was transferred to the Lawson General Hospital in Atlanta, Georgia and given a medical discharge. When asked what the final diagnosis was, he replied, "When I didn't cooperate and die so they could get an autopsy, they settled for a diagnosis of hepatitis after I was examined by Doctor Arthur Patek at Goldwater Memorial Hospital in New York City in July 1944 while I was on sick leave. Doctor Patek concluded that I had hepatitis and gave me a copy of his report to take to Lawson General Hospital."

When he arrived in Phoenix in December 1944, his father was still practicing but was not well and soon retired in 1945 to his ranch on Willow Creek north of Prescott. He died in 1946. Here he related that Dysart School and Dysart Road of Phoenix were named after the Dysart Ranch out on the Agua Fria District, and his brother, that is the senior Doctor Dysart's brother, Nathaniel Martin Dysart, ran it. Doctor Louis

Dysart donated the land from the Dysart Ranch for a school. At the time it was the oldest ranch in continuous operation west of the Agua Fria and was surrounded by open range. It was one mile west of Peoria, west of the Agua Fria River a couple of miles, south of Grand Avenue, on the Wickenburg road on which is now Dysart Road. He father was an ardent pacifist and never quite forgave his son for going off to war. But now he was back in Phoenix and soon to resume his practice. But to go back or to retrack, so to speak, he stated that, "In the fall of 1931 I became a part-time surgical assistant to Doctor Joseph Madison Greer, who was interested in developing an orthopedic charity clinic at the Phoenix Social Service Center down on Adams and 7th Street and I joined him in that. We held a clinic there once a week." The building was built by Mrs. Heard, and she developed and maintained the clinic and did a wonderful job.

He continues, "We ran continually 10 to 15 major orthopedic cases in Good Samaritan and St. Joseph's Hospitals." This was before World War II and Memorial Hospital had not been built. The work went on until the war, and by this time Doctor James Lytton-Smith came to Phoenix. He was the first certified orthopedic surgeon in Arizona, followed later by Doctor Robert Hastings in Tucson. The Crippled Children's Society wanted Greer and Dysart to develop a crippled children's hospital in Phoenix, but they wanted a certified orthopedist at the head of it. "Neither of us wished to specialize to that extent. So, we suggested the name of Lytton-Smith to them and before World War II, we turned over our orthopedic clinic and all of this organized orthopedic work to him. Doctor Greer and I had even taken care of Indian orthopedics in Arizona, making annual trips to Ganado in northern Arizona." Doctor Palmer continues, "In the latter part of 1931, Harry Bene had organized a state vocational rehabilitation service and the only medical service that he could pay for were routine physical examinations. Since it was a medically oriented program, as all his clients had to have an impairment that was a substantial employment handicap, many required or needed medical services. Doctor Greer and I provided or obtained the services free for Harry Bene until the state legislature saw fit to provide them starting in July 1945. As a fundamental requirement, Doctor Bene needed a medical consultant in his office. By this time, we were across-the-street neighbors and Harry Bene was a patient of mine, so he asked me if I would accept the position of state medical consultant for his office." He continues, "The State Employment Service didn't seem to be effective in placing the handicapped in employment. This holds true today (1977). About the same figures are still present. I was working just part-time four hours a week for vocational rehabilitation and so the work got too much for one person on a part-time basis. The first associate I got for VR was Doctor William Wharton of Tucson." Then, he received the help of another doctor in Flagstaff whose name he didn't recall. He was succeeded by Doctor John Caskey and at the time of this interview (1977), Doctor Caskey was still in Flagstaff at the rehab office on a part-time basis. Doctor Palmer quit his state administrative job, and Doctor Samuel Hale became the state medical consultant.

He finally retired after 31 years with the VR system and was actually a pioneer and developed most of its services at that time. Doctor Palmer made it quite plain to me that vocational rehab is not a practice of medicine. "All examinations and treatments are obtained from outside sources. A vocational rehabilitation medical consultant does not see the clients; his function is to interpret medical reports to the counselors, advise them regarding medical matters and assure that the case is adequately documented medically and advise the agency regarding medical policy." Doctor Palmer described in some detail a method of evaluating the patients, and then he relates, "But in the last few years, much to my disapproval, we've taken on behavioral problems and so many of these cases are psychological. If they're not working just because they don't want to work, they may be provided services by vocational rehabilitation. Many cases are receiving VR services simply because they don't want to work. That proves there's nothing wrong with them because normally they would want to work."

Now, let's retrack a minute and recount some experience which now is practically unknown to the present generation. Doctor Palmer put it this way: "A tragic event occurred in 1933 when the Federal Emergency Relief Act was passed by Congress to assist the drouth and depression victims who were migrating westward and were being stopped first by the Pacific Ocean and then by the California Border Patrol who actually searched the person. If they didn't have money, they didn't get into California. And so they began backing up into Arizona. We saw the tragic occurrences in this group of people. In 1933 Doctor Leslie Kober set up a transient men's campgrounds for the single men who were caught in this problem. A clinic for the transient families was also started by this program. This was federally sponsored and this paid me $125.00 a month and I would hold a clinic twice a week at the fairgrounds for these transient families and hundreds of them would line up when I made house calls at motels and any other place they were living that the government could find space for them. Doctor Benjamin Herzberg and I got a great deal of satisfaction out of this work. It continued for over a year. One of the objects of my examinations at the clinics I held was to screen out those who didn't have any medical reason for being out here in this salubrious climate. And those who could be returned to their home states were sent back, being transferred by the Red Cross, who handled the transportation back to their homes." With the background of his work with Doctor Greer in children's orthopedic surgery prior to World War II and this experience with the migrant workers here in the Phoenix area prior to the war, Dysart continues, "With this background I became socially conscious and spent more time with charity work than with my own private practice. This continued after the war until 1945, when I organized the medical operation of Arizona Vocational Rehabilitation and was the only doctor in that service for seven years."

During this time, he traveled the state widely and we've already alluded to the fact that he got outposts in Tucson and Flagstaff early on. In July 1955, the State Vocational Rehabilitation Office took on the disability determination for Social Security and this was a tremendous job with a backlog of several thousand cases. He was very proud of the fact that he kept the state agency out of the practice of medicine, and all the time that Doctor Palmer was head of it, he flatly refused to extend treatment or physical examinations. This was to be done by the private sector. In 1957, Doctor Dysart retired from private practice and in 1976 retired completely from the vocational rehabilitation unit of the state. So this native son of a territorial Arizona physician contributed in no small measure to the medical development of his state. His wide and varied interests other than medicine, and his strong social conscience which led him to aid in the vocational rehabilitation organization of the state marks Palmer Dysart as a true physician who felt a great obligation to his patients and society.

STANFORD F. FARNSWORTH, M.D.
1906-1980

The son of a general surgeon, Doctor Farnsworth was born in Missoula, Montana, and obtained part of his secondary education there. In 1921, his father retired, the family moved to Berkley, California, where he finished high school and attended the university at Berkeley. He entered medical school at Loma Linda and after some misadventures, finally took his M.D. degree there and did a two year residency at the Alameda County Hospital in Oakland. He then entered the United States Public Health Service and was stationed at a hospital in Springfield, Missouri in charge of a ward of tuberculous patients. Soon he resigned and went back to California and obtained a position with the California State Health Department and stayed in public health and administrative medicine from then on. This was in 1936. For the next nine years, he was with the California Health Department, then to Johns Hopkins Medical School in Baltimore, Md. for a master's degree in public health. Then back to the U.S. Public Health Service, detailed to the rural public health program and more specially to the migratory medical care program.

It was at this time that he had his first visit to Phoenix and Arizona and to Eloy, where he was in charge of organizing a migratory health program for the 60 or 70 thousand seasonal workers. This was before the era of mechanical cotton pickers and most of these people were employed in the cotton industry.

He was appointed health officer of Oakland, California and was there until 1949. At that time, he was appointed a consultant to the World Health Organization and was first sent to Egypt to do a survey of the ministry of health and to help try to develop some local health programs. Then back to Oakland, and then in 1951, he went on a permanent basis with the Pan American Sanitary Bureau of the World Health Organization and on to Guatemala where he was assigned for 5 years in charge of all the Central American country programs. This encompassed the full range of medicine, developing schools of nursing, schools of medicine, helping countries to organize their own public health programs, medical education, preventive medicine, hygiene and nutrition. In 1956, he was sent back to Egypt by the World Health Organization to head its regional office in Egypt.

In 1958, he was back in the United States, and at this time the health department of Phoenix was seeking a new director. The local committee consisted of Ben Frissell, M.D., Milt Gan and Tom Sullivan, the latter on the board of supervisors of the county. Milt Gan was with the community council. Doctor Frissell was a representative of the county medical society. One of the first of his many successful missions locally was the amalgamation of the departments of health of the cities of Phoenix and Mesa and also the Maricopa County Health Department. This was in 1957-58. It was then, at least locally, that Stan's wonderful administrative attributes and abilities came to the fore. He never accepted a negative answer; he was very astute in his dealings with the political forces; and from his long range goals, he never wavered. He built up the administration of the department to improve all services, particularly communicable disease prevention and control, the control of tuberculosis, the well-baby clinics, the improvement of sanitation generally. He was instrumental in working with the various cities and their administrative departments to develop a sanitary sewer system for the entire Valley and to aid in the supervision of 96 separate water companies and the amalgamation of most of them into the various city water companies.

Then came the establishment of public health clinics because there were no physicians in Buckeye, Gila Bend and only two in Wickenburg, and so outlying clinics were established. (This

*Stanford F. Farnsworth, M.D.
Photo courtesy of Roundup.*

raised some eyebrows in the private sector, but the "void was filled!") It was a short jump then from preventive medicine to therapeutic medicine in the county hospital and the outlying clinics established under the leadership of the department of health. Farnsworth's amalgamation of the county hospital into the Maricopa County Health Department may not have been a first in the United States, but it certainly was one of the better models and is still functioning the same way. These are some of the highlights of the busy, exciting, and productive life of this great physician. With all of this, he never lost his concern and empathy for the individual patient and citizen. I met Stan Farnsworth relatively late in his career. To be specific, in 1968 when I was with the Center for Disease Control on assignment to the Arizona State Health Department. It was the general belief around the state health department that what Doctor Farnsworth wanted generally happened and what he didn't want rarely happened. Many readers will have known Doctor Farnsworth longer than I and recognize a certain truth in that belief. Doctor Farnsworth's career in public health began in 1935 when he joined the California State Department of Public Health, moving to Oakland as health officer in 1941.

Doctor Farnsworth left the Oakland Health Department to work with the World Health Organization first in Central America and then in the eastern Mediterranean. As coordinator for these activities, he was responsible for initiation of a program of early diagnosis and treatment of glaucoma; in the Central American countries he developed a program which produced a marked reduction of mosquitoes capable of transmitting malaria and yellow fever. He was committed to the prevention of disease, whether by mass immunization against yellow fever in Nicaragua or co-sponsoring with the Maricopa County Medical Society, the 1962 "Sabin Sunday" program in Maricopa County in which 75% percent of the county's population was immunized against polio. He believed that treatable diseases should be treated regardless of a person's income and he strengthened programs in tuberculosis and venereal disease. He believed that basic medical services should be available to all and obtained support for mobile medical and dental clinics to serve rural areas. He believed in regional environmental planning for sewage and solid wastes and was instrumental in implementing the systems now in place.

In the 1970s he strengthened programs in alcohol and drug abuse and combined the health department and hospital into a unified Department of Health Services with outlying clinics providing primary and preventive services while the hospital provided emergency, specialized outpatient, and inpatient services. With the support of the medical community he was responsible for spearheading the effort to upgrade or develop county health facilities and for improving the scope and quality of the training programs.

He retired in 1975 to pursue his many other interests. Those who worked with him appreciated his vision, his wisdom, his humor, and his political sense of timing. Those who opposed him frequently found themselves involved in committees to study or implement the programs they opposed. All respected him for his honesty and dedication. His standards were high and in gaining his approval, we also gained our own. The task was more rewarding by being more difficult. Doctor Farnsworth was a modest man—his walls were not adorned by his many plaques and honors; he was generous in giving credit to others; he even refused a retirement party. He would doubtless disapprove of this tribute but he may forgive me if I can assure him on behalf of all of us that we won't dwell too long on his memory and will get back to work doing what he believed in—living life to the fullest.

ROBERT S. FLINN, M.D.
1897-1984

A physician, philanthropist, soldier, sportsman and raconteur par excellence. "A man for all seasons." A saint he was not! Born in Nova Scotia, his parents moved to Kingman, Arizona Territory, in 1898. Soon, the family moved to Prescott where Bob grew up.

Now, a word about his father, John Flinn, M.D., who, himself suffered from tuberculosis. He established a sanatorium for the treatment of chest conditions in Prescott that became widely known, respected and attended. The elder Flinn was said to be abrupt and a positive leader in the community who, together with Doctors Looney and Yount, comprised what some of the old-timers termed the "Big Three in Arizona Medicine." Nothing took place in the state medical realm without their participation and their decisions.

After high school in Prescott, Bob was off to join the Royal Canadian Air Force in World War I. When he returned from France, he enrolled at Harvard College in Boston. With a wry smile, he related that he was not required to take entrance examinations because of his wartime service. Following this, he entered Harvard Medical School and graduated in 1925. He returned to Montreal for an internship in the same hospital where his father had trained earlier and was noted for one of its most famous medical exports. This was William Osler, M.D. who, after a sojourn in the United States at Philadelphia and Baltimore, took up residence as the Regius Professor of Medicine at Oxford University in England.

Doctor Flinn returned to Prescott and practiced with his father for a few years and a brother, Zeb, who also was a physician. They contributed some medical papers to *Southwest Medicine*, which was then the official publication of the Arizona Medical Association. These papers were well constructed, and Doctor Zeb Flinn was especially interested in the study of white blood cells and their response to tuberculous infections.

Doctor Robert then migrated to Phoenix in 1930 and practiced there the remainder of his career. As a rather late post-World War II newcomer to the Valley, my earliest recollection of Bob is a more or less extemporaneous historical sketch he delivered before the Maricopa County Medical Society at one of its meetings in the Good Samaritan Nurses' Auditorium. This was in 1950 when he was president of the Arizona Medical Association and at the peak of his medical career. He would disclaim any attributes of a medical historian, but he certainly had a wide collection and selection of anecdotes about prominent and not-so-prominent Arizona physicians of the early part of this century. One of these, which I vividly recall, he recounted with such clarity and wry humor that it sticks in my mind. It related to a Mrs. Brown. Next door was a Prescott physician of some renown, but they somehow did not agree on various topics. One day, while engaged in a conversation over the back fence with Mrs. Brown, the doctor allowed, "M'am, if you don't like my opinions you can go straight to hell." This seemed to incense her husband, Mr. Brown, who complained to the doctor that this was not appreciated by him and that he, the doctor, should apologize to Mrs. Brown. On reflection, the doctor decided that perhaps that was her due. So, in a few days, when they again encountered one another over the back fence, he made this sort of an apology: "Mrs. Brown, I am rather sorry about my directions to you, but you don't have to go to hell unless you really want to." This closed the incident. Others will recall many others of his anecdotes that he related at various times, and I'm sure many of them are more in the nature of real medical history than the foregoing.

Others will recall his sartorial splendor and that he always appeared professionally as if he'd been freshly turned out by Saville Row and with a boutonniere pinned to his lapel. He would appear

Photo courtesy of the Robert S. Flinn Library.

at the hospital very promptly soon after 5 o'clock or before in the morning, make his rounds, conduct his electrocardiographic laboratory readings and then off to his office where he would see patients. Then to tennis or the race track or both. It was in this era of the 1950s that he was also an enthusiastic follower of racing events, and he and his wife had a stable of race horses, and some of these, he stated, even won a race occasionally. Others will remember that during this era he was the perennial chief of staff at St. Monica's Hospital, (now Phoenix Memorial) developed and administered by Father Emmett McLoughlin.

Together with his wife, Irene, he established the Flinn Foundation and the largess and the accomplishments which flow from this foundation are better known and should be recounted by someone such as Donald Buffmire, M.D., longtime physician and confidant of Doctor Flinn and a moving force on the board of directors of the foundation. In the news account of Doctor Flinn's death, the following may be apropos: "Flinn, who founded the Flinn Foundation, a private philanthropic organization dedicated to improving health care in Arizona, was best known for his financial contributions to the medical field. In 1982, the Flinn Foundation gave $1 million to the University of Arizona College of Medicine to establish the Robert S. and Irene Flinn Chair of Medicine." Dean Louis Kettel stated: "Arizona and Arizona medicine have lost a truly remarkable supporter and colleague. Bob Flinn's impact on the state, its medical education system and the health of the citizens will be felt for decades to come."

In 1978, the Maricopa County Medical Society acknowledged this talented member with the following: "The Board of Directors of the Maricopa County Medical Society gratefully appreciates the outstanding contributions made by Doctor Robert S. Flinn to the field of medicine in this community. We proudly acknowledge the hundred years of medical care he and his father,

From left: Governor of Arizona Wesley Bolin, Robert S. Flinn, M.D., Max L. Wertz, M.D., and Arizona Congressman Eldon Rudd, at the dedication of the Robert S. Flinn Library at the Maricopa County Medical Society, January 18, 1978. Headquarters of the Society at that time were at 2025 N. Central Avenue, in Phoenix, Arizona.
Photo courtesy of Maricopa County Medical Society.

John W. Flinn, have given their patients. In recognition of his pursuit of professional excellence, his fostering ideals of private medical practice, his support of scientific progress and his deep respect for the historical perspective, be it resolved that the medical library of Maricopa County Medical Society be named 'Robert S. Flinn Medical Library'."

His remarks in response to the reception of this scroll are strictly a "Flinnism,": "I can't tell you how much I appreciate this demonstration. I try to be modest, but I can't be very modest today. I want to thank you all for what you've done." This was simply one of the many constructive contributions of the foundation. Perhaps the very latest one, the dedication of the Flinn Education Center at Yavapai Community Hospital on Saturday, July 21, 1984 in Prescott, was the closest to his heart and the accolades received there were warming. Since Bob and I shared a common avocation as "history buffs," I would simply remind you that at the turn of the century, when Bob made his appearance on this terrestrial platform, that Pasteur had established that bacteria could cause disease, that Koch had discovered the tubercle bacillus, Roentgen the x-ray and thereafter, modern scientific medicine flourished in a bed of scientific discoveries instead of empiric folklore. We shared two fascinating teachers in medical school in common (although he preceded me by several years), Harvey Cushing and John Homans at the Brigham. Cushing, who preferred to be remembered as a physician, is recalled by the present generation, if at all, for his pioneer work in neurological surgery.

But one of his prime interests and productive parts of his life was medical history, and this he imparted to his students. John Homans, who taught general surgery, in his textbook of surgery, now long out of print, preceded each chapter with a vignette of medical history of the subject to be treated. In the clinical demonstration to students, this medical lore was imparted and Bob and I frequently reminisced

From left: Doctors R. S. Flinn, E. A. Born, and D. W. Melick, early 1980s Photo by author.

about the tales that we heard from these fascinating teachers. One of the projects that the Flinn Foundation supported and is yet to come to fruition and was dear to the heart of Bob was a projected history of medicine in the state of Arizona to begin where a previous treatise, *Territorial Medicine*, left off. This was to encompass especially central and northern Arizona where he and his father had so long practiced. Bob contributed mightily to this effort.

We shall not see his likes again soon, for indeed he was a wise physician and dedicated to the needs of his patients and his profession. "A man for all seasons." The Flinn Foundation was established in 1965 by Robert S. Flinn, M.D., and

Airman Robert S. Flinn, Royal Canadian Air Force, WW I, 1916
Photo courtesy of Robert S. Flinn, M.D.

his wife, Irene. Its broad mission, simply stated, is to improve the quality of health care in Arizona. In the 1980s, the foundation had already made generous financial contributions toward its goals: to improve the functional capability of persons with chronic and disabling illness; to reduce self-imposed risks for principal causes of costly illness; to increase medical and dental care services to the underserved; and to increase the efficiency and effectiveness of the health care delivery system. In 1982, the foundation made 32 grants in support of projects totalling $1,186,165, and in 1983, 38 grants totalling $1,657,408. The average amount granted was $40,000.

R. LEE FOSTER, M.D.
1907-1979

Like many others, Lee came to Arizona for health reasons—arriving in 1926. His health had failed; tuberculosis struck while he was attending college in his native state of Illinois. After eighteen months in a sanatorium, he came west for the "climate cure." Fortunately his quest for health was successful. He worked variously as a radio repairman, the manager of an electrical supply house, he did a stint with radio station KFAD, now KTAR, attended Gradwohl Medical Technology School in St. Louis. Thence he moved to Los Angeles to complete his pre-medical studies and graduated from USC Medical School in 1941.

He returned to intern at St. Joseph's Hospital, Phoenix—and then did a preceptorship in radiology under W. Warner Watkins, M.D. at the pathological laboratory and became certified by the American Board of Radiology. Lee came into radiology near the close of an era. In many communities the pathology and radiology departments were directed by the same physician. Prior to WW II these specialties became separate in postgraduate training and practice. With the many subspecialty divisions of pathology and radiology at the present time, a super specialist in either of these fields of restricted proficiency, who can scarcely imagine a general radiologist or pathologist? And for one physician to function in both fields simultaneously? Ah, well, so it once was.

Lee spent his professional career as director of the pathologic laboratory and its successor, the Medical Center Laboratory at 1313 N. Second Street, Phoenix. Historically, the latter was among the first of the post WW II "medical centers" which proliferated ad infinitum in Phoenix and ended the supremacy of the Professional Building, 15 E. Monroe St., and the Grunow Clinic on East McDowell, at 10th St., which were then the principal centers of family practice and specialties in Phoenix. Lee was a doer and booster in professional and medical activities. A partial listing is imposing: He succeeded Frank Milloy, M.D. and served several years as the second editor of *Arizona Medicine*; he served as secretary of the medical staff of Good Samaritan Hospital; he was Arizona state councilor for the Radiological Society of North America; fellow of the American College of Radiology for the state; member of the American Radium Society, the American Roentgen Ray Society, member of the American College of Physicians, the county medical society, and the Arizona and American medical associations and was appointed to the first Arizona State Atomic Energy Commission. So well did he balance his time, and all the while devoted to his family, that it was difficult to tell his vocation, radiology, from his avocation, church duties, both local and national. He became a proficient pilot and served as staff radiologist to the Pinal General Hospital in Florence, the Hoemako Hospital in Case Grande and the Morenci Hospital in Morenci. The general radiologist is on the wane and with Lee we have lost one of those generalists.

To his devoted wife, Nelle, and his family we extend our sincere sympathy.

R. Lee Foster, M.D.

Photo courtesy of Roundup.

BEN "PAT" FRISSELL
1907-1984

Doctor Frissell, affectionately known as Ben Pat, came to Arizona almost 50 years ago and engaged in private practice most of that time. Like many other physicians of that era, he came to Arizona because of a health problem. In his case, it was rheumatic heart disease, and he was first associated the the Desert Sanatorium, Tucson. He was on the service under the direction of Doctor Louis Baldwin. Two years later or so, he moved with his family to Phoenix and was associated for a time with Doctor Baldwin in practice here and was later an independent practitioner. Doctor Frissell was born in Oakridge, Missouri. He graduated from George Washington Medical School in St. Louis with honors, A. O. A. (Alpha Omega Alpha—honorary medical fraternity). Ben was always known as a diligent, careful, caring physician whose obligation to his profession and to his patients was uppermost.

So far as I know he always refused any elective office in the county or state medical organizations, but he certainly labored in the trenches on many committees and boards of directors. He served 12 years on the county board of health and 12 years on the board of directors of the Maricopa County Medical Society before retiring in 1967. In 1961 he was honored by the Society, which presented him with its Doctor Joseph Bank Medal for community service—recognizing his work through the health board to upgrade medical care for migrant farm workers.

The Arizona Medical Association; presented him its A. H. Robins Community Service Award in 1968. How he found time to serve on all of these community projects is hard to visualize in view of the fact that he carried a very heavy load of private practice, but indeed from 1950-1959 he served on the board of directors of Arizona Blue Cross and was president in 1950.

In 1966 he was appointed a member of the Phoenix Board of Housing Appeals by then Mayor Sam Mardian, Jr. Doctor Frissell was licensed in Arizona in 1934 with No. 1463. He was always an ardent supporter of organized medicine and was a member of the Maricopa County Medical Society, the Arizona Medical Association and the American Medical Association. He was a devoted husband and father and leaves his wife, Harriett, a daughter, Charlotte, and a son, Nelson, a physician in Cody, Wyoming. Doctor Frissell was a straight-shooter, self-effacing; but everybody understood what he stood for and exactly what he would stand for.

*Ben Pat Frissell, M.D.
Photo courtesy of Roundup.*

FRANCIS HENRY GOODWIN, M.D.
1835-1892

This physician practiced in Tucson between 1867 and 1892. He was a graduate of Yale College and Heidelberg Medical School. He served in the Confederate Army as a major and was born in Cassville, Georgia. After the War between the States he settled in California and sold a controlling interest in Catalina Island for $5,000.00 and then moved to Tucson, 1 January 1867. He was a member of the fifth, sixth, seventh and ninth Territorial legislatures and was a sheriff of Yuma County from 1874 to 1876. He apparently spent a short time over on the river away from Tucson. In 1889 to 1891 he served as a regent of the University of Arizona..

Francis H. Goodwin, M.D.
He sold a controlling interest in Catalina Island, California for $5,000.
Photo courtesy of Territorial Medicine.

PETER HAYWARD-BUTT, M.D.
1911-1973

Doctor Hayward-Butt was born in South Africa, the son of a pioneer industrial mining physician in Johannesburg. He was educated at Cheltenham College, Cambridge University (1938) and completed his medical work at St. Bartholomew's Hospital (Old Bart) in London where he received his M.B.C.H.B. After the war he returned to Cambridge for postgraduate work and received his Master of Arts degree in 1945. Very soon after finishing his medical requirements WW II occupied his time from 1939 to 1945. He first served with the Royal Marine Commandos and later with the Royal navy on an aircraft carrier in the Pacific theater. Some may recall that these commandos were a special unit organized at the behest of Winston Churchill to undertake impossible missions.

Peter never dwelt much upon these experiences but over a period of some years some of the excitement of those days was recalled. There are still nurses and other attendants in the local hospitals in Phoenix who are aware of the rather bad experience they may have had if they tried to shake Doctor Hayward-Butt awake as he waited for another case. The instructions always were to pull his toe, in fact some of the doctors' lounges displayed notices to that effect. The background is that in their rigorous training, the commandos were warned that if they were ever shaken awake this meant an enemy and he was to be throttled immediately. So they always slept in groups of at least two men and one or the other was given the string attached to the other's toe, and that was the only way in which they were to be awakened peacefully. This conditioned reflex must have been well implanted in that special training because Peter reacted rather violently to those unsuspecting attendants who shook him and didn't pluck his toe. Some incidents and missions of the Royal Marine Commandos were discussed so dispassionately by Peter that one cannot be sure whether he was actually on the mission or not, but the following incident is in character. Intelligence reports indicated that a radio station in Iceland was giving accurate data on allied convoys using the North Atlantic run and Nazi submarine packs were playing havoc with convoys. Orders came down for the commandos to locate and destroy the radio transmitter in Iceland. It turned out to be in the German consul's dwelling. Landing from submarines the raiders avoided all guards, perhaps trussing up a few or giving them a period of anmesia. At any rate, the German consul was first aware of their presence when he looked around his bedroom and saw them standing quitely waiting for him and his frau to complete their intimacy. As you can imagine, the frau grabbed a sheet and retreated to the latrine. One raider suspected something was burning other than the lady's pride, as smoke oozed out over the transom of the bathroom door. Smashing down the door, he recovered the German secret code before it was destroyed.

After WW II Peter did postgraduate work at Cambridge and returned to Durbin, South Africa where he practiced and was a senior lecturer in anesthesia at Natal University Medical School. In 1947 Peter perfected a "Pocket Inhaler" to be used for short term anesthesia. It could even be administered by the patient himself. It was evolved for "the use of commandos, air, naval and tank crews, and ambulance personnel." In 1955 he announced a new combination of drugs using Pethidine-Daptoyal-poctotal,* in which he proposed that this combination produced an analgesia very helpful in various situations including childbirth. In fact there is a news item stating that the then Princess Elizabeth was to have this used for the birth of one of her children.

He removed his practice from South Africa to the University of Iowa in 1958 and two years later settled in Phoenix. In 1970 he accepted an

Peter Hayward-Butt, M.D.
Photo courtesy of Roundup Magazine

appointment as assistant professor of anesthesiology at the University of Chicago but this was cut short first by a mild coronary and then by a lung malignancy. Peter, to many of us, exemplified that pragmatic, peripatetic man of English origin and deportment, whose integrity and loyalty to friends stood as firm as "The Tower." He met "slings and arrows," which seemed often propelled against him, with surprised attention and a righteous outrage or with utter contempt. He bore accomplishment and adversity with equanimity.

To his dear wife, Diana, and three children, our sincere sympathy.

*Pethidene a trade name for Meperidine. Daptoyal-Poctotal—all this was in the literature describing the device—South Africa and not identifiable in current medical texts.

LOUIS KOSSUTH, M.D., M. P. H.
1913-1989

The footprints left by Louis Kossuth not only are deeply and firmly impressed upon the sands of time—they have left their indelible marks upon the sands of Arizona, the records of the nation's military establishment and in the annals of the world's medical progress.

His list of accomplishments in the health field, locally, nationally and internationally, is a long and distinguished one.

An indirect descendant and namesake of the Hungarian revolutionary statesman and lawyer who, in 1849, won brief but significant independence for his native land from Austria, Dr. Kossuth earned his M.D. degree in 1939 at Western Reserve University (now Case Western Reserve University) in Cleveland, Ohio. Seven years later, in 1946, he earned his M.P.H. degree from Harvard University's School of Public Health in Boston.

Shortly after his graduation from Reserve in 1939, Louis Kossuth and Velma Sorenson were married. She had received her Master's degree in nursing from Reserve's Frances Payne Bolton School of Nursing also in 1939.

Born August 13, 1913, in Wheeling, West Virginia, Doctor Kossuth's entire medical career was spent in public service. He never entered the private practice of medicine.

After completing his internship in 1941, despite some reluctance by the military to allow him to do so, Doctor. Kossuth entered the U. S. Air Force, retiring in 1969 with the rank of colonel.

During his military service, marked by many notable achievements, Doctor. Kossuth rose to become chief of preventive medicine at the Pentagon, deputy commander of the U. S. Air Force School of Aviation Medicine, commander of the USAF Medical Service School, and surgeon general of the USAF Air Defense Command and of NORAD (North American Air Defense Command.)

He served with distinction throughout World War II and Korea and was an important figure in the affairs of the World Health Organization and other international and national health groups.

Despite his many outstanding achievements, the honors of which Louis Kossuth was most proud were his successive terms (1956-1961) as Fellow, Regent and President of the American College of Preventive Medicine.

In Arizona, Doctor. Kossuth was the state's last health commissioner (1969-1974). Despite legislative opposition that faced him at almost every turn, he won significant victories in his battle to improve Arizona's public health status, particularly in the areas of air and water pollution.

Louis Kossuth was a giant in his field. His untimely passing leaves a void that not easily nor quickly can be filled and he will be missed more than can be comprehended now. Arizona is fortunate in having had him as one of its most distinguished and capable citizens.

In addition to his wife, Doctor. Kossuth is survived by four children: Dr. Karen Kossuth, professor of linguistics at Pomona College in California; George J. Kossuth, a computer software engineer in Boston, Dr. Sue Kossuth, chief plant physiologist with the U. S. Department of Agriculture in Gainesville, Florida, and Sally L. Kossuth, who was awarded her degree in medicine in 1989.

Farewell, my friend! Ended is the flight, And He whose hands upheld you in the air, Whose spirit guided you in darkness and in light, Has called you home. I bow my head in prayer. Adapted from a poem by Gunter Von Huenefeld (1893-1929).

Reprinted with permission from *Arizona Medicine*, June, 1989.

*Col. Louis Kossuth, M.C., U.S.A.F.
Photo courtesy of Mrs. Louis Kossuth.*

ROBERT N. LOONEY, M.D.
1870-1962

This physician, who incidentally never held a license to practice medicine in the State of Arizona, and was very proud of this fact, in a presidential address to the Arizona Medical Association delivered in Phoenix, April 20, 1910, and reported in the *Southern California Practitioner*, Volume XXV, No. 5, pages 218 to 220, May, 1910, had this to say about medical education: "The United States had as many medical schools as the rest of the world, 144 compared with 165 in the rest of the world, at that time. A large number of these medical schools conform to very low standards." He urged all physicians to lend support to the improvement of medical schools and advocated at least one year of college prior to the entrance to the medical school. This was the redoubtable R. N. Looney, M.D. of Prescott, who contributed so much to early Arizona organized medicine.

A contemplative Doctor Looney at his desk shortly after announcing his retirement, circa 1950. Photo courtesy of Dr. E. A. Born.

GEORGE G. McKHANN, M.D.
1895-1983

From tallow-tip to television to space shuttle, this marked the terrestrial stay of the complete physician. Medical discoveries were no less spectacular. From Rotentgen's discovery of the ray, Pasteur and bacteriology, Erlich and chemotherapy, Flemming and penicillin, to HMOs and national health planning—these were a few of the changes that ran swiftly by! Following the footsteps of his physician father, he entered medical school at Cincinnati University in 1916. WWI soon enrolled all medical students in the Army Reserve.

The war over and medical school finished, he went on to Creighton Hospital in Omaha, Nebraska to intern. After a time in Ames, Iowa, where he taught hygiene and worked at the student health department, he went to Lincoln, Nebraska and began clinical practice. There, he met his wife-to-be, Louise, married and went to Vienna, the post-graduate mecca of the time, for a year of study.

When he came back to the states, he located in Portland, Oregon to practice, but he, as did so many young physicians of the era, found his health impaired by the ubiquitous Koch's bacillus. He came to Phoenix for treatment of his pulmonary tuberculosis. During the three years of recovery, he spent a great deal of the time camping in the desert and acquired a devotion to the desert and a knowledge of mineralogy that made him a devoted "rock-hound," his lifelong avocation.

His medical interests were varied and always received his meticulous attention. He began to correlate blood cholesterol levels and coronary heart disease—before it became a fad—and proposed a dietary regimen for his fellow physicians to alter their cholesterol life-style. In the 1940s he began collecting photographic and other data on the smog menace. He foresaw some of the origins and the dangers—long before the environmentalists thought of the word.

A strong supporter of organized medicine, he served in many capacities of his county and state units. To use a trite phrase, "He was a physician of the old school." He treated his patients with meticulous care and his fellow physicians with meticulous courtesy. Each generation produces a few, sometimes it seems a very few, with such devotion to the art and science of medicine. He bore his terminal illness with detachment and courage. To use the vernacular—he was a straight arrow. He is survived by his wife, Louise, a son, George Jr., a brother, Charles F. McKhann, M.D., and three grandchildren.

GEORGE G. McKHANN, M.D.
1895 - 1983

Photo courtesy of Roundup.

ANCIL MARTIN, M.D.
1861-1921

This Arizona practitioner, Ancil Martin, M.D., had several firsts. He was the first ophthalmologist to locate and practice in Arizona. He reported cases of "rabbit septicemia," as early as 1907. This was not called tularemia because this term was not coined until 1911, when Doctor George McCoy worked out the true etiology of the disease in rabbits. Six cases were reported by this doctor at a meeting of the Arizona State Medical Association in Prescott in 1909 in a paper entitled "Infection of the Conjunctiva" and under the heading "Rabbit septicemia." In one of these case reports in *Southwestern Medicine*, where he reviewed it in 1926, the February number, he reports a case: "E. W., age 11, presented himself to me with the following history on August 5, 1907: 'Ten days ago, first noticed a small pimple on the upper lid of the left eye, accompanied by tearing, pain and swelling of the lips. The following day had four light chills.' He gave a history of having handled jack rabbits."

He recorded further that one of his patients he had seen in 1907 had blood drawn June 25, 1925 and this was reported to still have a positive agglutination "complete in one to ten dilution and partial in the one to twenty dilution." This was reported by Doctor Francis of the United States Public Health Service, the investigator who first established that the disease discovered by McCoy in the ground squirrels and rodents in Tulare County, California, that this indeed was transmissible to humans and that Doctor Ancil Martin had first recognized it. He termed Doctor Martin the "father of tularemia." Doctor Martin was the first to have an x-ray apparatus in the State of Arizona. He bought one in 1898 a few months after the announcement of the discovery by Roentgen, and he served as the first president of the Board of Medical Examiners of the state when it was organized. He practiced in Phoenix from 1895 to 1926.

Ancil E. Martin, M.D.
Photo courtesy of Territorial Medicine.

FRANK J. MILLOY, M.D.
1894-1958

Doctor Milloy was born March 1, 1894 near Omenee, N.D. Something of the coldness of that area made him reserved; this cloaked a warm, courageous interior.

In those early days he made many friends and one of them has written: "I have known Tommy (as we called him) since 1911, when he was in high school at Omenee, N.D. He was a good student and an outstanding basketball player in his high school days. We attended the University of North Dakota beginning in 1912, he was a very popular fellow at the university, he belonged to the Senigoy Fraternity, in which he was very active, was a member of the university band, and was considered an excellent student."

Another fellow Dakotan recalls that Doctor Milloy was a very conscientious student, and his college and medical school record was enviable. Here it should be noted that Doctor Milloy began at the University of North Dakota to study law. It so happened that his roommate was a medical student, and Doctor Milloy became so fascinated by the anatomy and physiology books that he neglected his law studies and later returned to the academic school and took some pre-medical work so that he was able to enter the medical school. After two years of medical study at North Dakota, he transferred to Northwestern University, where he graduated from the School of Medicine in 1920.

Doctor Milloy spent about two years at the Mercy Hospital in Chicago on the service of Doctor Bertram Welton Sippy. His training was received under this notable pioneer in gastroenterology; a treatment for peptic ulcers still carries Doctor Sippy's name. Milloy's was the first class at Northwestern Medical School required to have an internship before its members received the M.D. degree.

Among Doctor Milloy's papers was found a short note concerning Doctor Sippy. It might be interesting to those of us who were trained in a later generation of medicine. Doctor Milloy wrote, in part: "Doctor Sippy was a chemist and a keen research observer as well as a great clinician. The result was that his firm convictions on the subject of peptic ulcer were proved in the laboratories as well as in the living patient. In his heyday, Doctor Sippy had a hospital service averaging 200 patients, about 25 per cent of whom were peptic ulcer patients.

"There were those investigators in Sippy's time who believed that free hydrocholoric acid in the stomach had no connection with the development or presence of ulcer. Doctor Sippy's classical quotation: "Whatever the future may reveal as to the causes of ulcer and the influences that retard its healing. . .results. . .may be obtained by maintaining an efficient neutralization of free acid. . ." has withstood the test of time. Doctor Sippy demonstrated that the three chemical agents which produced this condition in the greatest number of patients were calcium carbonate, sodium bicarbonate, and magnesium oxide.

"Sippy recognized the beneficial influence of gastroenterostomy (establishing an artificial passage between the stomach and intestine) in bringing about a remission of gastric and duodenal ulcer symptoms and a reduction in acidity, and particularly through accelerated emptying of the stomach, thus reducing the duration of the corrosive action of the gastric juices. He demonstrated that the real cures, or the wonderful relief of symptoms was directly proportional to the amount of pyloric obstruction produced by scar tissue narrowing the pyloric ring. Doctor Will Mayo once remarked that if he had an ulcer of the stomach, he wanted to be treated nine times medically before he would submit to surgery."

During his second year on the service of

Frank J. Milloy, M.D.   *Photo courtesy of Arizona Medicine.*

Doctor Sippy, Doctor Moorehead, chief of staff of Mercy Hospital in Chicago, received a letter from Doctor E. Payne Palmer, Sr. of Phoenix, Arizona. Doctor Palmer was searching for a young man training in internal medicine and gastroenterology to serve with him on the staff of the Southwest Clinic which Doctor Palmer had organized in Phoenix.

In 1921 Doctor Milloy accepted this position with the Southwest Clinic and was associated with the clinic and with Doctor Palmer all during the time that this clinic was extant.

In 1922, Doctor Milloy married Ola Sue McCabe of Columbus, Nebraska. They met when Miss McCabe was a student nurse at Mercy Hospital. She graduated and received her degree in nursing from Northwestern Medical School. To the Milloy's were born three children: Frank Jr., a physician in Chicago, and, like his father a graduate of Northwestern; and two daughters, Mary Elizabeth Milloy of San Francisco, and Mrs. Kathleen Mulligan of San Diego.

Mrs. Milloy relates that there were some interesting experiences in Phoenix in that day, and some of the calls Doctor Milloy made in the country to visit patients.

On one occasion she accompanied him up Black Canyon way and they were forced to abandon the automobile and ride a horse across a swollen wash to reach the patient. They stayed all night before returning to Phoenix the next day. Mrs. Milloy suggested this was not altogether a proper experience to undergo while wearing a new spring suit.

On another occasion, while they were in church on Sunday morning, Doctor Milloy received an emergency call from over toward Buckeye. After making the drive of about 30 miles, they came to a camp of cotton pickers, and all from the fair state of Texas. It developed that a two-year-old boy had been bitten on the thigh by a rattlesnake. The Texans were parading the snake around to demonstrate to all hands what a magnificent five-footer he was, and not too much attention was being paid to the youngster. Doctor and Mrs. Milloy worked with the child until four o'clock in the afternoon. During this time they had put him in cold packs in order to keep the fever down and stop convulsions, and had given the child sips of strychnine and alcohol. The latter at least should have been pleasing to the Texans. Then it was decided, about four in the afternoon, they they should have something for Doctor and Mrs. Milloy to eat. She remembers that they came back from Laveen with a loaf of bread and some tomatoes. This, together with some so-called coffee, was the repast. While they sat at the table eating, closely scrutinized by the onlookers, Mrs. Milloy felt something nibble at her shoe. She felt that it was undignified to turn around and look under the table, so she managed to get through the meal. She was relieved to find that it was only chickens under the table pecking at some ornaments on her shoes.

The child was apparently improving, so they returned to Phoenix.

This medical adventure has an interesting finale. The Texan came in with his son the next morning and informed Doctor Milloy that he would now take his boy to his own doctor where he could get some good treatment. Such are the fortunes of practicing medicine.

In 1929, Doctor W. Warner Watkins organized a group of clinicians into what is now called the Clinical Club of Phoenix. Of the first six, Doctor Milloy was a member, this was later enlarged to 12 and from 1929 until the present, this group has met regularly to discuss Cabot* cases from the Massachusetts General Hospital. One of Doctor Milloy's associates related that Doctor Milloy attended these meeting faithfully during the last two years of his life, discussed these cases with great clarity, even though his health was failing rapidly.

In 1935, Doctor Milloy was certified by the American Board of Internal Medicine—further evidence of his professional proficiency.

At about this time he began investigating cases of amoebiasis. Little attention had been paid to this disease in this country prior to the outbreak in Chicago during the World's Fair. His enthusiasm in this direction may have been overactive. Nonetheless he awakened his fellow practitioners to the presence of the disease in Arizona.

Some of the senior practitioners will recall, before World War II, when theology and medical principals collided, he stood with his fellow physicians!

Another first of Doctor Milloy's is that he obtained and administered the first penicillin used in the Valley. This was during World War II when penicillin was restricted to use by the armed forces. The request went through all of the devious channels to the President and the penicillin was flown to Phoenix in an air force plane. (At least this was a desirable mission for an air force plane, some will recall that these planes, on occasion, flew Elliot Roosevelt's dogs.)

Doctor Milloy is given credit for introducing blood transfusion work into Arizona. This was the days of the direct transfusion methods. Those of you who can recall the Unger apparatus and the trials at keeping it clean and in working order will know that giving a blood transfusion differed slightly from the present method of simply placing the request on the patient's chart. One of his associates in the clinic in those early days has stated: "Frank went his way quietly and did his work in an expert fashion. He never got riled up and was always courteous to his associates and colleagues. He was always willing to give any service that was at his command for a patient and seemed always to 'get a kick out of his work.' His work was thorough and he was able to keep up with all medical advances."

Doctor Milloy was always very active in the Arizona Medical Association and was elected secretary in 1942. In 1944, he and Doctors J. D. Hamer and D. F. Harbridge, as editorial committee, began publication of *Arizona Medicine*, the *Journal* of The Arizona Medical Association. The editorials of the first volumes of this *Journal* range over a good many subjects and the first one concerns the birth of *Arizona Medicine* itself. Doctor Milloy wrote: "When the governors of *Southwestern Medicine* found it necessary to discontinue publication of *Southwestern Medicine* for the duration, the state society took the opportunity to publish a journal devoted entirely to the State of Arizona. While we regret deeply the loss of our many friends in New Mexico and El Paso, nevertheless the members of the state medical profession have long felt the need and necessity of its own journal. *Arizona Medicine* will be published bi-monthly."

After the war was over, an attempt was again made to re-establish the publication of *Southwest Medicine* to embody *Arizona Medicine;* this was strongly opposed by Doctor Milloy, and the continued publication of this journal was due, for the most part, to his efforts.

In this first issue, Doctor Louis B. Baldwin of Phoenix described the organization and origin of the Salt River Valley Blood Bank. There are some who have apparently forgotten the diligent work undertaken by Doctor Baldwin and his associates of the Maricopa County Medical Society in the organization of this institution.

The first two volumes carried letters from various members of the state association who were in the armed forces.

The U.S. Public Health Service, in cooperation with the Office of Civilian Defense, organized an affiliated base hospital unit in cooperation with St. Joseph's Hospital in Phoenix. Doctor Milloy was appointed director of the unit with the USPHS rank of senior surgeon. He continued to hold this reserve rank in the public health service until his death.

Doctor Milloy continued to publish and edit *Arizona Medicine* until 1952. he was so modest and such a quiet worker that few knew of his contributions to the organization of the state association and its Journal.

An editorial he wrote for the January 1947 number of this journal might well be considered the code by which he lived. It was entitled, "Professional Courtesy."

"No professional group is more entitled to hold heads high in praise of accomplishment than doctors of medicine. Probably no group is subject to more criticism by the laity, nor is the object of more sweeping legislative revolution. Only by unity of purpose, highly ethical conduct, and meticulous attention to the welfare of the patient, regardless of his economic status, can the profession hope to ride out the storm now raging.

"Unfortunately, a few individual physicians have extremely bad taste in criticizing the care contemporaries have given patients, openly to the patients and to their relatives. The prerogative of a patient to change to another physician is a sacred one. However, it is indeed unbecoming for the new physician to imply either by word or insinuation that the former physician was incompetent. Such conduct is unprofessional, unethical and reprehensible and serves no real purpose except to promote distrust of the medical profession as a whole. The old adage, 'If you can't say anything good about a person, say nothing,' still holds good. The Golden Rule will never become obsolete."

From the hills of North Dakota, to the Valley of the Sun, Frank J. Milloy set a high standard of personal and professional conduct.

*Cabot cases were dry clinics, a teaching method at which the patient's history and physical examination were discussed and a diagnosis proposed. Then the actual operative or autopsy findings were given.

JAMES R. MOORE, M.D.
1890-1983

AN APPRECIATION ON HIS 90th BIRTHDAY

Soldier WWI, mining physician and surgeon, hospital administrator, medical missionary, medical advisor to the Arizona Industrial Commission, consultant to Arizona Blue Cross and Blue Shield, physician par excellence. These are a few of the adventures and professional accomplishments of the beloved "Jimmy" Moore during his four score and ten years of productive living.

Doctor Moore was born in New Lisbon, Ohio, in 1890, his father was a Presbyterian minister. He attended secondary school in Virginia and graduated from Muskingum College in 1910. Then he spent a year teaching English at a mission college in Assiut, Egypt. He returned to attend Western Reserve Medical School but was forced, when a junior, to take some months off. All this time he had been working his way through college and medical school, and his last position had been that as more or less an extern and laboratory assistant in a tuberculous sanatorium. It was here that he apparently contracted tuberculous laryngitis and was forced to go to Ashville, North Carolina for some months to recover.

Following this he transferred to the University of Southern California Medical School and was graduated from there in 1916. He promptly traveled to San Francisco to take the state boards and spent a few months as an intern at the Los Angeles County Hospital but because of the death of his father and stringent economic needs, he took a position as assistant surgeon at the Cananea Consolidated Copper Company in Sonora, Mexico in June of 1916. He had several adventures there for this was the time when Pancho Villa was chasing people up and down the border; in fact one time they had to come back to the states because of revolutionary trouble. It was here that he met Doctor R. H. Thigpen, Arizona License #688, who was then the chief surgeon at the mine; who, along with another doctor, had been held captive by Pancho Villa for a period of time but escaped.

In 1917 since he was back out of Mexico, due to the revolutionary activities, he joined the American army. By now, "he kept us out of war," President Wilson had declared war on Germany. Doctor Moore was promptly transferred to France and spent time there with a front line unit. In the meantime he had received a letter from Doctor Thigpen asking him to join him in Jerome where Doctor Thigpen was now the chief surgeon of the United Verde Extension Mine. So after a time, he journeyed back to Arizona and was associated with the mining company from 1918 to 1925. Then his missionary spirit took over again and he and his wife spent two years, 1925-1927, in Egypt where he was a teacher and missionary physician. He returned to Jerome in 1927 and was there until 1933 when his progressive arthritis forced him to give up surgical practice.

In the meantime he had been president of the Yavapai County Medical Society and members of the society had carried on their own continuing medical education program by journeying to Prescott once a month where they met with the physicians there and with an assigned subject prepared papers which they debated one with another. He looked upon this as one of the early efforts in Arizona to form the Medical Education Club. When Doctor Moore came to Phoenix he was an early member of the Clinical Club which was organized by W. Warner Watkins, M.D.

Early after finishing medical school he married Grace Montgomery a childhood sweetheart from back east and he brought her immediately to the mining camp at Cananea and

JAMES RUSSELL MOORE, M.D
1890-1983

Photo courtesy of Roundup.

this led to some adventures. He came to Phoenix in 1933 appointed by Gov. Moeur as administrator of the state hospital and it was during his tenure that the famous Winnie Ruth Judd was confined initially. In 1937 he followed Doctor Ralph Palmer as an assistant medical advisor to the industrial commission and within a year or two became the medical advisor-in-chief and continued that for many years; probably until 1965. In the meantime he served as president of the Maricopa County Medical Society and was voted an honorary member of the Western Orthopedic Association.

Even before his retirement from the industrial commission, he became an advisor to the Arizona Blue Cross and Blue Shield and continued that work until 1975. Doctor Moore continued active in his church and in adult center activities. During all the years I have known Doctor Moore, I have never heard him mention or complain of the progressive and crippling arthritis which he has suffered. He always greeted you with a smile and was always interested in what is coming up next. So, with all of his other colleagues and friends we join in this salute to this young man of ninety plus summers.

IN MEMORIAM, 1890-1983: "I die adoring God, loving my friends, not hating my enemies, and detesting superstition."—Voltaire, 1778 Those of us who knew and admired "Jimmy" Moore are passing from the scene of active practice.

Doctor Moore died on June 7, 1983 and this is a short commentary on one of the most admired physicians of his era. On the occasion of his 90th birthday an appreciation appeared in *Arizona Medicine*. Its introductory paragraph said: "Soldier WWI, mining physician and surgeon, hospital administrator, medical missionary, medical adviser to the Arizona Industrial Commission, consultant to Arizona Blue Cross and Blue Shield, physician par excellence."

ADOLPHUS HENRY NOON, M.D.
1838-1931

This interesting physician was born in London in 1838, went to South Africa, served four years with the British Army; later he raised a company and was elected a lieutenant. He studied medicine with a Doctor John E. Seaman, an East Indian physician.

In 1864 he migrated to the United States and finished his education in San Francisco. In 1865 he founded the town of Eureka, Tintic District, Utah. Here he laid out the streets, built the first house, was appointed the first postmaster, and was elected the first justice of peace and served as a notary public. Later he moved back to San Francisco where he practiced until 1878, then he came to Arizona. Three of his long and interesting letters to the Chicago Tribune repose amongst the Orville Harry Brown papers and were extracted by Doctor W. V. Whitmore. The first, "A Visit to Tombstone City" dated January 5, 1879, gives a very interesting discourse on the early origin of this new mining community, a second letter dealt with his journey into Sonora, Mexico, and a third one deals with his Casa Grande to Tucson trip before the advent of the railroad. One quotation here is pertinent: "Doctor Handy is the oldest resident physician here. An able qualified man speaking Spanish like a Spaniard and he is probably well known throughout Mexico."

Doctor Handy as you will recall was the first chancellor of the University of Arizona. This physician of whom we speak was the first president of the Santa Cruz Medical Society and served many years as secretary later. He served as a county supervisor, as a representative to the state legislature, as a clerk of the district court, as court commissioner for one term, and in 1910 to 1911 served as mayor of the city of Nogales. He practiced in Arizona for fifty years in Pima County and lived to the youthful age of 92 summers.

Adolphus H. Noon, M.D.
Doctor Noon practiced medicine in Arizona for fifty years and served one term as mayor of Nogales, Arizona Territory.
Photo courtesy of Territorial Medicine.

ERROL PAYNE PALMER, M.D.
1876-1960

The son of George Alfred and Virginia (Payne) Palmer born in Church Hill, Mississippi, October 30, 1876, and died at his home in Phoenix, February 6, 1960. Doctor Palmer practiced medicine and surgery in Arizona well over fifty years and was considered by many of his fellow physicians as the "Dean of Arizona Surgeons." He had served as chief of the surgical service at St. Joseph's Hospital well over a decade and saw it grow from a twelve bed, "sawhorse surgery" to an expansive modern multi-storied general hospital with twelve exquisitely appointed operating suites accommodating 325 hospital patients.

Doctor Palmer stated that his earliest recollection was: "When I was four years of age, and I was living at Oak Grove, Church Hill, Mississippi, and at that time I began to ride horseback and a year later attended a country school several miles away. At six I learned to shoot and load a muzzle loading shotgun and we did a lot of hunting in those days." Doctor Palmer's early life was not all devoted to these pleasant pursuits for he stated that when he was eight years of age he began to make his first living picking cotton, he saved some of the money and "purchased a mustang pony that was brought with a drove of horses from Texas, and broke her for riding and driving. With her I made a cotton crop during my free time from school. I did all of the work in preparing the ground, seeding, cultivating and picking so that all of the profits were mine. As a result of my cotton crop, I made enough money to go to Chamberlain-Hunt Academy at Port Gibson, Mississippi."

Doctor Palmer has written in his direct, detailed manner, many of his experiences. With the permission of his widow, Mrs. Bertha Schantz Palmer, a good portion of this narrative is as he himself related it.

Upon the death of his father it became mandatory for young Palmer to be responsible for his mother and a younger sister; this quickly gave him a sense of responsibility. While he was in grade school during summer vacations, he worked on a plantation which belonged to an uncle and during this time he was in charge of the mail, purchasing supplies and paying off helpers. He hired the help and sold goods in the plantation store. He stated that he also learned to drive logging teams of mules and oxen and describes how, when a new land was to be cleared, that the Negro men of the community came to assist in the removing of logs and brush. "The good logs would be rolled and be pulled into position to be drawn to the sawmill, while the inferior logs would be piled into a big heap with the brush and burned. The Negroes were given a big feed and all the whiskey they cared for. It was dispensed by the barrel, free of charge, but with the heavy work they were performing rarely did anyone ever become intoxicated."

He, his mother and sister moved to Natchez in September 1888 and Doctor Palmer's first job "was a printer's devil at $2.00 a week, a promotion to delivery boy for the same firm at $3.00 a week was quite an advantage for a boy." It was here that he later became employed in a retail-wholesale drug and stationery house and "I was moved from one department to another, the main business office, assisting in various ways—and finally was placed in the retail drug store where I began to study pharmacy under the tutorship of Mr. F. A. Dix, the druggist in the store." Young Palmer continued to work and study in this drug store and took the Mississippi State Board of Pharmacy examination and passed receiving a license to practice pharmacy at the age of seventeen. It was at this time that Doctor Palmer became interested in the study of medicine

E. PAYNE PALMER, SR., M.D.   *Photo courtesy of Territorial Medicine.*

and he states that he bought his first *Gray's Anatomy* in 1894.

During all of this time he was supporting his mother and sister, and as noted, became a registered pharmacist. He moved his family to St. Louis and enrolled in Barnes Medical College. There were a few stumbling blocks to this. He found that he could not register directly in the medical school because he did not have the "proper certificate of education," so "I took and passed the teacher's examination and received a teacher's certificate for Missouri. This was accepted as satisfactory proof of my qualification to matriculate at the Barnes Medical College. I entered in October 1895, the term was for six months courses over a three year period."

In 1896 Palmer took the examination of the Missouri State Board of Pharmacy and secured a license to practice pharmacy in that state and all during the time he was in medical school he worked as a pharmacist in drug stores in St. Louis. One of his classmates in medical school was Doctor R. O. Raymond who came to Arizona a few years after Doctor Palmer and located in Williams and later in Flagstaff. They both practiced in Arizona over fifty years and were friends well nigh on to sixty years before the passing of Doctor Raymond in 1959. Their combined active medical practice careers was well over a hundred years—in Arizona. After graduation Doctor Palmer became an assistant to Doctor John Young Brown who was later the professor of surgery at St. Louis University Medical School.

During this time he, Doctor Palmer, opened an office and entered into the practice of general medicine and "soon became busy." He joined the St. Louis Medical Society and was a regular attendant at the meetings.

In the winter of 1900 Doctor Palmer had an attack of "influenza" and was advised by his senior physician, Doctor Brown, to go to Phoenix to recuperate. This he did and arrived in Phoenix on April 1, 1900. Since he was a Southerner by origin and disinclined to accept the foreboding winters of the Middle West, he located in Phoenix and began his practice of medicine here. Doctor Palmer related many times that "Phoenix was a typical Western town of 4,532 population, there were many saloons with women entertainers and wide open gambling of every known kind."

In June 1900 he took the Arizona Board of Medical Examiners test and was awarded license number 102 and opened an office at 108 North Center Street, now Central Avenue. His reputation was soon established as a skillful, well trained young surgeon and he became successful in his practice.

In the beginning of his practice here in Phoenix, Doctor Palmer liked to relate about making bicycle house calls in town but usually rented a horse and buggy from the livery stable for country calls. Apparently not too long after establishing here, he bought a beautiful bay mare which he states "was about six years old, she was part thoroughbred, had been raised in the mountains and trained to drive but was very high strung and easily frightened." Mrs. Palmer remembers well his horse, "Gypsy" and she agrees that the horse was "nervous and high strung." She many times went with the doctor to make house calls and states that the horse would seem to stand in the shade and sleep while the doctor was in the house but when he got in the cart or buggy the horse was "surely ready to go."

Mrs. Palmer first came to Phoenix in 1907 with her brother who had been advised to come to this area for his health, and met Doctor Palmer, her future husband, through Doctor Palmer's sister, Mrs. Lane. Mrs. Palmer's maiden name was Bertha Louise Schantz, her father was born in Germany, her mother in Indiana and she herself was a native of Dayton, Ohio and the eleventh of thirteen children. Doctor Palmer carried on a successful courtship of just three weeks before convincing the fair lady from Ohio that she should change her name to Palmer, which she promptly did August 1, 1907. After a delightful wedding trip they returned and made their home in Phoenix.

More about Gypsy. Doctor Warner Watkins used to relate how that when Doctor Palmer went to Europe to study in 1909 he sold this horse to Doctor Watkins who was going to look after Doctor Palmer's practice. Mrs. Watkins gives a vivid description about driving Gypsy one evening down to First Avenue and Adams Street, when the horse ran away, tipped over the buggy and frightened everyone considerably. Fortunately, Mrs. Watkins was not hurt. Well, this seemed to be enough for the Watkins' because Doctor Warner told me that he turned Gypsy "out to pasture" and continued making his calls on a motorcycle. A great many years later when the author heard these various stories, we asked Doctor Palmer if it was true that he had sold Warner Watkins a run-a-way horse some fifty years ago. In his careful, mellow, southern drawl, Doctor Palmer replied, "Young man that really isn't a good description of the horse, she wasn't a run-a-way horse but when you got in the buggy you had to be ready to go."

When Doctor Palmer returned from Europe, Gypsy was brought in from pasture and traded back to him. The financial transactions of this "horse trading" were never clearly understood by anyone but Palmer and Watkins!

When Doctor Palmer came to Phoenix, "St. Joseph's Hospital had twelve beds and no operating room, two carpenter saw horses were placed in the patient's room and boards were put across the two saw horses to make an operating table. The part to be operated upon was washed with warm water and soap, chloroform was the usual anesthetic and this was usually administered by some of the other surgeons."

In 1902 he "successfully removed a large brain tumor from a man who had received a head injury many years before," and during the same year he "performed a cesarean section," he believes that this may have been the "first of its kind or nearly so for each of these procedures in Arizona." Of the many calls which Doctor Palmer made into the surrounding area, Mrs. Palmer recalls an incident about which Doctor Palmer many times subsequently related, something as follows: This probably occurred about 1906 and Doctor Palmer was called to the Maricopa Indian Reservation to see the wife of the superintendent. She apparently was quite ill and it had been requested that Doctor Palmer bring a nurse with him. The Salt River "was at flood stage, and there was no bridge across the Salt River. We left Phoenix driving a double team and when we arrived at the river we were met by two Indians on horseback." Doctor Palmer has written this experience and we will quote it verbatim: "The Indians led the way across the river and as they crossed the river they divided further apart from us so I kept in a midway position in following them, when in the middle of the river one of our horses went down under the water in quick sand. This pulled the other horse down with him, and our buggy turned over dumping us into the swift current of the midstream of muddy water. The nurse was washed downstream and went under the water once. When she was up I swam to her and caught her by the hair as she was going down the second time. I brought her to the surface and swam ashore with her all of the time holding her by her long hair. Today with bobbed hair, she probably would have drowned. All of this time the Indian guides were on their way, never looking back to see if we were safe."

In 1906 Doctor Palmer went to Chicago and spent six weeks visiting the clinics of Doctor J. B. Murphy and Doctor Albert J. Ochsner, two of the leading surgical teachers of that era and city. This began Doctor Palmer's regular tour of visiting prominent clinics and surgeons, a habit which he continued all of his life. On this same trip he visited Rochester, Minnesota to see the work of Doctors William and Charles Mayo and both they and their families visited Doctor Palmer and his family in Phoenix on occasion. After practicing in Phoenix about ten years, Doctor Palmer decided to visit the Old World clinics. They left on July 1, 1909 making some visits on the way but eventually going to New York, Baltimore and Philadelphia where Doctor Palmer did special post-graduate work.

His practice in Phoenix was taken over by Doctor Warner W. Watkins, who had recently come to Phoenix. In New York Doctor Palmer enrolled as a special student in Cornell Medical College and studied pathology under Doctor James Ewing and attended the surgical clinics and lectures for the senior students. He also secured an externship in the New York Hospital where he worked with Doctors Hadley and Johnson in the out-patient department and assisted them on all patients who went to surgery. He also worked with Doctor Cooley of the Cooley Toxin fame at the Hospital for Ruptured and Crippled Children. They spent about one year or so in Europe dividing their time between Vienna, Berlin, Paris and London, all of this time Doctor Palmer spent acquiring more knowledge in the fields of pathology and surgery.

At completion of this period of post-graduate study, Doctor Palmer established himself in Los Angeles, California, but very soon removed back to Phoenix. He said, "There are too many earthquakes in California." It is entirely possible that his many real estate and mining interests which he had already acquired in Phoenix and Arizona had quite as much to do with his return to Phoenix as the "earthquakes."

Now began the long, fruitful period of his practice of medicine and surgery. During his professional life which continued well over fifty years, Doctor Palmer was the author and contributed over sixty-five formal papers to the literature. His range of subjects was legion. In the *New York Medical Journal*, November 17, 1906, he published, "Phoenix Arizona as a Health Resort for Tuberculous Patients." In 1904 he discussed "Normal saline solutions and their physiological uses." Then there follows a whole range of titles relating to cancer, its cause, individual case reports and the treatment of regional cancer. He was a pioneer in the use of lumbar spinal anesthesia and as early as 1910 on one of his visits to Baltimore he demonstrated the use of it to Doctor H. Young. In 1936 he was invited to address the Second International College of Scientific and Social Campaigns Against Cancer at Brussels, Belgium, in September of that year. This was his first extended trip back to the Continent following his earlier study abroad when he studied in Austria, Germany and England. *The Phoenix Gazette* which reported something about this trip in the March 21, 1936 issue also stated that "Doctor Palmer is Chairman of the Cancer Control Committee of the Arizona State Medical Association. Other members are Doctor R. N. Looney, Prescott, Doctor R. N. Kennedy of Globe, Doctor Charles S. Kibler of Tucson and Doctor Joseph M. Greer of Phoenix."

He was an active supporter of organized medicine and served as president of the Maricopa County Medical Society, the Southwestern Medical Association, and the Arizona State Medical Association. He was a charter member of the American College of Surgery and "Governor of the College for twenty-eight years from the State of Arizona." In 1958 he was awarded the distinguished service award by the American College of Surgeons. He "was honored as the originator of the College's Program of Hospital Standardization, first Fellow of the State of Arizona and a pioneer surgeon in that State, Governor of the College for twenty-eight years, and a devoted supporter of the ideals and activities for forty-five years."

One of the doctor's most lasting accomplishments, for which he is probably least known in the present generation of medicine, has to do with the establishment of highway first aid stations. In an article titled, "Airway and Highway First Aid Stations," published in *Surgery, Gynecology and Obstetrics,* Volume 62, pages 446 to 448 in 1935, he stated, "Since July 1931, I have laid my plans before many agencies for the establishment of First Aid Stations in the United States. In 1933, I interested the American Red Cross in setting up first aid stations on the highways. At that time they endeavored to sponsor the movement. Unfortunately, the general financial stringency at the time prevented them backing the movement to any extent. Today the American Red Cross is willing and anxious to establish first aid stations on both the highways and airways of our country. The officials at National Headquarters have just recently approved plans looking to the immediate establishment of stations along our main traveled roads and in emergency landing fields and airports. There are already seventeen First Aid and Life Saving Field Representatives of the Red Cross devoting their entire time to this work and there are 135 First Aid Stations operating now in the United States. Conservative estimates indicate that 1000 stations will be arranged before July 1, 1936." He recommended that each station might keep on hand a "sufficient quantity of First Aid supplies such as is contained in the Red Cross Kits; a blanket, wooden splints, a Thomas-Murray upper extremity splint, a Keller-Blake lower extremity splint and a stretcher. There should also be two or more trained persons at administering First Aid of the injured and a method of transportation available at all times at each station." He commented, "the approximate cost of equipping a station is about thirty dollars," now thirty years hence about all we can get for that amount of money is a roll of bandage and a box of band-aids, no stretcher, no splints, no blanket. This paper he presented at a symposium on fractures before the Clinical Congress of the American College of Surgeons meeting in San Francisco in October 1935.

As a point of interest, Mrs. Palmer states that many times on their Sunday afternoon rides through the country one of the children would point to one of the Aid Stations and exclaim, "there is one of Daddy's stations."

Now from this early work and foresight of this pioneer Arizona physician our entire country is dotted with Red Cross Aid Stations, an idea first germinated in the fabulous Valley of the Sun. In discussing "The Recent Advances in Surgery," in 1941, he was quick to perceive and recognize the value of the antibiotics but he was loath to discard some tried and true remedies. He stated: "Some of the old remedies seem to have quickly been forgotten by younger physicians, zinc peroxide has proved effectual in the control of fetor, infection and pain in necrosing canceral lesions. Drainage is markedly lessened."

In the early 1920s, Doctor Palmer organized the Southwest Clinic and during the next decade he was associated in this practice of medicine with several physicians. Doctor Frank Milloy, gastroenterology—the first specially trained specialist in this field in Arizona; Doctor Charles Vivian, urology; Doctor Spencer Whiting, chest disease; Doctor Elton R.Charvoz, obstetrics; Doctor Adams, gynecology; Doctor Dudley Fournier, obstetrics; Doctor Charles N. Ploussard, surgery. He is remembered by one of these physicians as: "He was always very kind and helpful to the young physicians and resented very much the fact that other older physicians did not give the younger men a helping hand."

Doctor Palmer was a stickler for precise, careful, surgical technique, he was also a stickler for promptness. Anyone who didn't appear promptly at the clinic for ten o'clock office hours was sure to hear of his tardiness before the day was over. Another physician who interned at St. Joseph's Hospital, remembers the prodigious work load which Doctor Palmer carried. He frequently did five to eight major surgical procedures a day. This intern made it his business to assist Doctor Palmer as frequently as possible—for Doctor Palmer was a meticulous, careful surgeon, and always striving to perfect his own technique and teach the younger men. Doctor Palmer took great pride in the fact that St. Joseph's Hospital was first in the state with an approved internship and a school of nursing.

Mrs. Palmer relates that while her husband attended many post-graduate meetings and traveled extensively visiting clinics, while he was in Phoenix on the job, his work was continuous seven days a week. He usually tried to have Sunday afternoons free to spend with his family but other than this he was devoted to his practice. He related how in his early years in Phoenix he slept in his office many times with his clothes on because this was the only way in which he could attend to all of his night calls and busy practice. Lo, how the years have changed the philosophy of young medical men! That's why we need a directory to search for a physician to do night calls.

The professional life was complimented by his church and community work. He was a member of the Knights of Columbus and a prime mover in the development of St. Joseph's Hospital, both its physical plant and surgical standards. In 1942 he was elected president of the Arizona State Medical Association and delivered his annual address in Prescott May 25, 1942. His topic was "Arizona Medicine in 1900 and Today" and this gives a good deal of his philosophy and not a little of the history of early Arizona medical times. The reader should consult it directly for its full impact. He stated: "We owe a deep debt of gratitude to the pioneer physicians of Arizona. They made possible the medical profession as we have it today. Prior to 1900, even in the best medical schools, training was insufficient; students memorized lectures from notes; there was little clinical instruction, no experimental training; even equipment was meager. Here in Arizona, physicians lacked hospital facilities and many pioneer physicians were located in remote places, they were unable to obtain assistance or consultants when needed. Those were the horse and buggy days, days with only paths, or at best poor roads to travel. In town many of the physicians made use of a bicycle for short distances and night calls, finding it less troublesome than hitching up a horse. The Arizona pioneer physician was a person of indomitable courage, striving to do his duty to his patients and to uplift the medical profession. This was the type I found upon my arrival April 1, 1900. They were friendly, but they were strong competitors. I was told that medical ethics prevailed in Arizona and must be observed. Forty-two years of practice, (1942), first in the Territory, and then within the State of Arizona, have taught me this if nothing more; life becomes worthwhile doing, not getting." E. Payne Palmer, he saw the tallow tip electrify to television; the saw horses traded for mechanical marvels in the surgical amphitheater; his cow town become a metropolis; some of the ranches acquire ribbons of concrete for screaming jets; his "aid stations" perched on the aprons of freeways and highways across the nation; and his program for hospital standardization adopted by the American College of Surgeons—now under different sponsorship—virtually the law of Hospital Land! Yes to Doctor Palmer, this pioneer physician of Arizona, we owe a deep debt of gratitude!

CLARENCE G. SALSBURY, M.D.
1886-1980

Doctor Salsbury's life work included that of a missionary, surgeon, hospital builder and administrator, founder of the first nurses' training program for American Indians, peerless administrator of the Arizona State Health Department, physician, and withal a friend of man. To describe this many-faceted physician would require a concerted effort by all organizations and medical activities he so valorously served. Salsbury was—if nothing else—an activist, in the true sense of the term. Born in Canada of New England Loyalist ancestry, he decided early on at high school to be a medical missionary. On completion of his high school work at the Union Missionary Institute in Brooklyn, New York, he entered the College of Physicians in Boston. After he acquired an M.D., he interned at the New York Lying-In Hospital, married Cora Burrows, a fellow student at the Missionary Institute, and accepted an assignment for missionary duties in Hinan, China. Next came twelve years as a medical missionary and builder of hospitals and a high school. He literally built a high school using a diesel powered saw mill and redwood timber he imported from the United States. The Communist takeover forced him and his fellow missionaries to leave China. Then it was back to the States where he served temporarily in an administrative position in New York with a central missionary board. This was not his cup of tea, so he finally agreed to serve temporarily at a mission hospital and school at Ganado, Arizona on the Navajo reservation. This was to be temporary; he still wanted to be assigned overseas. It turned out to be quite "temporary." He spent the next twenty five years of his life there with his wife, Cora, rebuilding, renewing, and establishing many innovative programs at this hospital and school. When he came, the hospital was without patients and was a 15 room adobe ramshackle building.

When he left they had a modern brick hospital building, the first nurses' school established for the training of Indian girls, a first-rate high school and secondary school. The hospital was the first of them accredited, in northern Arizona, by the American College of Surgeons. Some may not be aware that the accreditation program was inaugurated by the American College of Surgeons and that a Phoenix physician, E. Payne Palmer, Sr., was said to have introduced the resolution before a meeting of the college to inaugurate this program. Noteworthy is the fact that some Eskimo girls were also accepted to the nurse's school and during World War II, Japanese girls were accepted for nurses' training and they were not so accepted in any other place in the United States. The following statistics are from his records of 1948: "We produced 40 tons of alfalfa and 23 tons of oats. Three and 3/4 tons of vegetables were raised for campus consumption. The total of 285 chickens gave us 4,275 eggs; and we ate 420 pounds of chicken which had stopped laying. Our dairy cows produced 7,373 quarts of milk. We also consumed 8,051 pounds of pork which we raised ourselves and 2,370 pounds of beef. The number of patients admitted during the years was 2,252 and they spent 31,983 days in the hospital. We had 3,927 dispensary patients. The operations performed were 415; births 185." Doctor Salsbury had definite ideas about the inadequate Indian Bureau and perhaps one of the greatest chances for the improvement of that government bureaucracy was plowed under when Dewey failed to make it as president. Doctor Salsbury was slated to be director of Indian affairs.

On May 25th, 1950, he and his wife retired from their work at Ganado and he remarked, "our temporary assignment has come to 23 years. With our years in China before that we had a 36-year career as missionaries. Yet it didn't seem long. It was difficult to try to convince myself that I was

Clarence G. Salsbury, M.D
1886 - 1980

Photo courtesy of Arizona Medicine.

64 years old." Almost immediately he was offered a position with the State Health Department of Arizona as chief of the Bureau of Preventive Medical Services which had just been created. As he related it, nobody seemed to know exactly what his duties were but he soon outlined them and felt that he should do something to earn his income which was $7,400 a year, the biggest income of his life to that point.

He found that only about half of the physicians in the state were filing communicable disease reports so he offended them by asking them to do their paper work properly. He offended some other people by talking about syphilis and gonorrhea in public, and others were startled when he took out after open privies and venereal disease control in general. He learned by accident that a Mexican national had died of typhoid in a work camp in Casa Grande, so he took out after the primitive methods and unsanitary conditions amongst the agricultural work force and offended the ranchers.

A code was drawn up by the health department for labor camps and published and

In 1976, Dr. John Kennedy presented a special Maricopa County Medical Society plaque to Dr. Clarence G. Salsbury on his 90th birthday.
Photo courtesy of Roundup.

proclaimed the law of the State of Arizona. The health department sent out enforcers. There was a great difficulty around Marana where the ranchers claimed they couldn't afford this sort of accommodations for their workers, but as Doctor Salsbury noted, they quickly raised money when three of them were brought to court. They suddenly had an enormous amount of funds available for their defense. He was appointed health commissioner to succeed Doctor J. P. Ward and continued to jump from the frying pan into the fire with his campaign for better living conditions for farm workers, for better reporting of disease, for better case finding for venereal disease and tuberculosis. All of this bore fruit but gained him the enmity of the ranchers and many other segments of the population including the state legislature.

By now he was 75 and he had another retirement with many awards and accolades, but one he apparently appreciated as much or more as any was by Robert Price, M.D., then president of the Maricopa County Medical Society. Doctor Price said, "He was outspoken when he saw suffering humanity and was ready to publicize in every way possible the unhealthy conditions he found. His path was not a rosy one. He found opposition to many of his public health programs at times from the legislature, on occasion from influential lay groups, and even from members of the medical profession in a few instances." During this time the Maricopa County Medical Society had established a Clarence G. Salsbury Medal to be awarded for outstanding service. Salsbury himself was awarded the Thomas Dooley Medal for valor of service at the close of his public health career. "The ones who live are the ones who struggle, the ones whose soul and heart are filled with high purpose. Yes, these are the living ones." This description by Victor Hugo certainly personifies the life and work of Clarence G. Salsbury, M.D.

A symbol of admiration from the Navajo People is presented to Dr. Salsbury at his retirement from the Arizona Department of Health, 1961.
Photo courtesy of Roundup.

Clarence G. Salsbury, M.D. (left) and "Dry Gulch Jake" (John W. Kennedy, M.D.) in 1969.
Photo courtesy of Roundup.

W. O. SWEEK, M.D.

NEWS ITEM: May 3, 1940

"Discovery of an explosive one hundred times as powerful as nitroglycerin by the late Doctor W. O. Sweek of the Grunow Clinic, Phoenix, Arizona, was announced in Washington, yesterday by the Senate Naval Committee." Doctor Sweek must have had the great aptitude of causing explosions not only during his terrestrial stay but afterwards.

DR. GEORGE C. TRUMAN
1903-1983

After 40 years of busy medical and surgical practice this modest and highly skilled physician has laid aside his busy medical practice; his patients and his fellow practitioners wish him well in his new avocation. Born in Florence, Arizona Territory, he departed from his home state only long enough to acquire his medical education and has since continued to practice the art in Mesa, except for WW II. He was grievously wounded at Anzio, the effects of which he carries with fortitude to this day. His father, George E. Truman, served with Roosevelt's Rough Riders and gives this narrative of the "happening" at San Juan Hill. This part of the incident is not related in the Roosevelt writings. Roosevelt was riding a white horse and drawing a lot of fire "the Spaniards were shooting at Roosevelt, but were such poor shots that they were hitting the troopers all around him" (the troopers were afoot because their horses hadn't arrived.)

Doctor Truman relates, "My dad ran down and shouted 'Get the hell off that horse, you are drawing fire.' Then a negro sergeant of the 8th Cavalry and my father were the first up San Juan Hill, they helped each other through the wire fence." The senior Truman acquired amoebic dysentery, malaria and a few other trophies from his service in Cuba, and subsequently suffered with dysentery the greater portion of his life. A year after George was born his family moved to Phoenix from Florence and his father was appointed a citizen member of the "Territorial Border Control." He had charge of the insane asylum, the territorial prison and the Arizona state fair. He was the original organizer and managed the first state fair. Later, the family moved back to Florence, where George's father entered politics, serving as assistant supervisor, assessor, and county treasurer. There was an interval here in which the family moved to Ray, Arizona, where the father was asked to come and restore order.

This was in 1912 and in the previous year they had had a killing in the area most every week and wanted someone to clean up the place in the frontier tradition. George related, "My father was an expert with a pistol, rifle and shotgun. While he was sheriff of Pinal County he spent two years hunting for the Apache Kid, but like many others, he never caught up with him. During the time we were in Ray they had only one killing and that was probably because they insisted that anyone coming into town leave their knives and their guns with the bartender; and when they were ready to leave town, if they were sober, the bartender would return their weapons and knives. By doing this simple thing he managed to eliminate a lot of trouble that they previously had in the area before."

If you have ever wondered about the Greenway statue in the Hall of Statues in the capital at Washington, D.C., George can tell you. Greenway and George's father served together in the Rough Riders and of course Greenway was the famous developer engineer of the mining properties at Ajo. In 1919 he suggested that George take a scholarship at Massachusetts Institute of Technology and then he, George, could go down to South America where Greenway was planning to set up a plant like the one in Ajo, Arizona. George thought he had better taste the mining duties over in Ajo during summer out of school, but he acquired such a severe case of food poisoning that he had to return home to recuperate. That ended his mining career.

He then decided to take a pre-medical course at Santa Clara College in California with an additional year at Notre Dame University, then ended up at St. Louis University Medical School in 1926. He spent an additional year specializing in gynecology and followed this with a two-year preceptorship under Doctor Ralph Palmer in Mesa. In 1927, after he arrived back in Florence, he took

*George C. Truman, M.D.
Photo courtesy of Roundup.*

the job as physician to the state prison. But this he terminated rather quickly and, as he relates it, "The trouble was that Warden Scott White was supposed to hang five Chinamen for a killing that took place up in Globe. Right away he went to bed and called me over to his house and told me that his blood pressure was way up and he was going to have to go to bed and stay in bed and that we were going to have to hang those five Chinamen without his help. Well, that sure didn't appeal to me and the next day after I had gotten a report from Bob Jones, who was later governor, who dropped by my house and he told me that Doctor Ralph Palmer was looking for somebody to go into practice as his assistant in Mesa. So I went over to see Doctor Palmer. We arrived at an agreement and he asked me how soon I could come over. I told him I would have to give the government two weeks notice before I left. That was agreeable, I gave the two weeks notice and got out of Florence before I had to help officiate at the hanging."

One of his early experiences when associated with Doctor Palmer was the acquisition of brucellosis acquired apparently from an infected woman. Doctor Palmer had taken off for a few days rest to the coast and he had placed a woman in the hospital "with a high fever and a mucopurulent vaginal discharge. I was called down to deliver her and she had a breech and the baby was successfully delivered but lived only a few hours as it was premature. But that evening when I was washing up for supper I found a streak of blood on my left forearm which had apparently soaked through my gown and I had missed it so I ended up by getting acute undulant fever which laid me up for quite a while."

Doctor Truman in a few years embarked on his own private practice and continued thus until 1933 when Doctor B. B. Moeur was elected governor and appointed Doctor Truman to the post of secretary of the department of health. One of the first things he noticed was that there was a sad lack of good records of birth and death certificates.

So he corresponded with all of the recorders and health officers in the various counties and cities and asked them to send him their records so that they could make copies of them here in Phoenix. This took a little doing. Doctor Truman relates "we had to be very careful to work fast and make copies and get them back to their origin.

"During the time I was checking this out I found out that my brother Bill and I had never had a birth certificate recorded. Doctor George Brockway was in with the Doctor Wynn Wiley here in Phoenix and had delivered both of us. So I had two birth certificates made out and took them down and got Doctor Brockway to sign them and have them recorded."

In 1935 four cases of acute brucellosis were observed amongst residents of the Westward Ho hotel. "We checked them out and found out that these people had a habit of having a sandwich and a glass of milk or malted milk in a drug store close by. When we checked the milk we found that it was put out by a dairy in which all of the cows in the dairy were positive reactors to brucellosis. I had moved up from chairman of the Legislative Committee and Public Health Committee of the County Medical Society to the Legislative Committee and Public Health Committee of the state society and Doctor Fred Holmes was serving at the county level, so I called him and told him what had happened and indicated that we were in a pretty sad fix. We didn't want to start any big scandal but we had four patients out of the Westward Ho hotel with acute brucellosis and I had written the various dairies and they refused to pasteurize their milk." He continues, "So what I did was to have a card printed and it said, 'We serve only pasteurized milk here as recommended by the Public Health Legislative Committee of the Maricopa County Medical Society.' Doctor Holmes thought this was a wonderful idea and so we had the cards made up and went around to every place in Phoenix and we were able to get folks to cooperate, and we finally ended up by getting pasteurized milk within three weeks in the City of Phoenix and that was the first pasteurized milk in the state. Tucson followed suit and then the idea spread that raw milk was not a good thing to drink." So by this subtle method pasteurization of milk came to Phoenix, when it seemed that legislation could not be enacted to control the problem immediately.

Just as now, there were some unusual individuals practicing medicine in the Valley back in the 20s and 30s. "First of all there was Doctor William Sweek a very, very rambunctious type of person," says Doctor Truman. "One evening at the Maricopa County Society meeting in the old St. Joseph's Hospital, Doctor E. Payne Palmer reported on four cases of appendectomies, cases in which the Davis incision was used and he got them back to work in a hurry. Well, Bill Sweek popped up and said, 'When I examine a patient," he says, "I can tell the size of the doctor's intellect by the size of the incision he makes.' And they started to run towards each other and we all had to run and separate them. We finally got them calmed down and this always livened up our meetings."

Doctor Truman, always an astute clinical observer, made the following observations in 1928. "I was called in consultation by Doctor B. B. Mouer of Tempe to see a child about six years old whom he had admitted to the Southside Hospital. This little girl suffered a scorpion sting. She was drooling and running around and every once in a while she would have a convulsion. She finally died from exhaustion. I reviewed the medications that had been ordered for these cases in the hospital, and I noted that we had all been using paragoric or other opiates to control the convulsions. Actually, the experience of seeing that child reminded me very much of a case of rabies I had observed long before. So I decided that probably the best thing to do was to use phenobarbital and luminal to control the convulsions and with the permission of the superintendent of the hospital, Mrs. J. R. Hanson, I wrote a note that no persons stung by a poisonous scorpion were to be given any opiates. After that, to the best of my knowledge, we had only one death at Southside Hospital from scorpion stings. Apparently, this was the right method." Indeed this is still a standard method of treating scorpion stings in infants and children where the portion of toxin to body weight may lead to a fatality. The sting seldom does any more than irritate an adult.

Another clinical observation: "In June of 1969, in a week's time, I saw two 18-year old girls, they had been stung in the deltoid region by a so-called brown recluse spider. I examined the girls and the diagnosis was confirmed, that is the species of spider was confirmed by the Arizona State University Department of Zoology. In these instances there is intense local destruction of tissue. I gave each of them 2 ccs. of 2% plain Xylocaine underneath the area of the bite and I followed this by 100 milligrams of Solucortef. I kept them in the hospital for an hour and released them to be seen in my office the next day. The next day in my office there was no induration or any evidence that they had ever been bitten and I checked them a week later and the same result.

"This was a different method than we had used before to treat these conditions and apparently it is specific if the patient is soon seen after the bite. I estimated they had been bitten between three and five hours before I saw them in the hospital, and I feel that any person who is seen in that period and treated properly should have a good recovery." (A recent number of the rejuvenated *Saturday Evening Post* gives a fair description of both the black widow and the brown recluse spider and how to recognize them. Like all of the popular magazines it also gives the method of treatment and they further state that two children have died from grave blood disturbances following bites from the brown recluse spider. Steroids, antihistamines and antibiotics are given for the more severe reactions. Well, there you have it from the *Saturday Evening Post* but I will still rely on Doctor George Truman's observations.)

It must be evident, even from this short review, that dwelling in our midst is a man who has had a fabulous medical career and has gained the admiration and respect of both his fellow practitioners and his patients, for his masterful practice of the art.

(Editor's. Note: A list of Doctor Truman's appointments, accolades and memberships is indeed very long and very impressive. Selections from the many are these: Appointment by Arizona Governor Benjamin B. Moeur, to the office of Superintendent of Public Health, 1933-1937. Appointment by the governor of Arizona, Sidney Osborn, to the post of vice chairman of the Arizona State Civilian Defense Coordinating Council, in the Division of Health, Welfare and Consumer Interest, 1941. Fellow of the Royal Society of Health of London. Fellow of the American Society of Abdominal Surgeons. Member of the American Public Health Association. Active member of the New York Academy of Sciences. Member of the Pan American Medical Association. Member Maricopa County and Arizona State medical societies. Member American Medical Association.)

WARNER W. WATKINS, M.D.
1883-1956

This fabulous pioneer Arizona radiologist will be remembered not only for his medical activities and keen scientific interest but also for his ability as a raconteur of medical anecdotes during his time. One of them relates to himself when he was at Metcalf as contract surgeon for a copper company. There was a long incline from the living quarters of the mine on top of the hill down to the bottom where the ore was carried or ran down in cars. He liked to ride these ore cars up and down but the superintendent of the mines told him that he could either stop that or stop working. The young physician elected to stop riding the ore cars since these went at a terrific speed up and down the mountain and not infrequently people were killed riding them.

On the trail up to his living quarters from the canyon lived a miner by the name of Ford. He was rough and ready, had been a cow puncher and horse wrangler in time gone by. Our young physician said at the time he wore a plug hat, and this was similar to the one which later was characteristic of Sir Winston Churchill. In addition, the physician smoked cigars, and those of us who knew him in later days when he was a total abstainer from tobacco and spirits can hardly feature this activity. At any rate, he was told he shouldn't wear this plug hat out in the country as it was too much of the dude type of apparel. He persisted and on this particular evening while he was walking back up the trail to his quarters, Ford was sitting on his front step with a 22-caliber rifle. He shot the hat off of our young physician's head and then when asked what the next move was, our physician said he went over and became acquainted with Mr. Ford and after that they became fast friends.

In the summer of 1907, his mother and a sister came to visit our young surgeon at his living quarters on the top of this mountain, where more or less a barracks type of project was situated and these living quarters had a long hallway down the center. When the whistle blew everybody was supposed to take cover for this meant that a blast would be set off in the pit. This particular time the whistle blew, the blast went off and a boulder, weighing fifty or seventy-five pounds, came bowling down through the center alley of this house, through one door and out the other and struck a clothes basket and demolished it in the rear yard. This young mining physician soon forsook the thrills of riding the ore cars down into the pit, moved to Phoenix, practiced in a general practice for about four years, specializing later in tuberculosis and at St. Luke's Home established the first clinical laboratory in the Valley. From this later grew the pathological laboratory where he and his associates practiced pathology and radiology for many years.

W. Warner Watkins, M.D.
He was a founding, four-year member of the American College of Radiology and of the Roentgen Ray Society.
Photo courtesy of Territorial Medicine.

St. Luke's Home at Phoenix in 1907. At that time, it was a tuberculosis treatment sanatorium where W. Warner Watkins, M.D. established the first clinical laboratory in the Phoenix area.
Photo courtesy of Territorial Medicine.

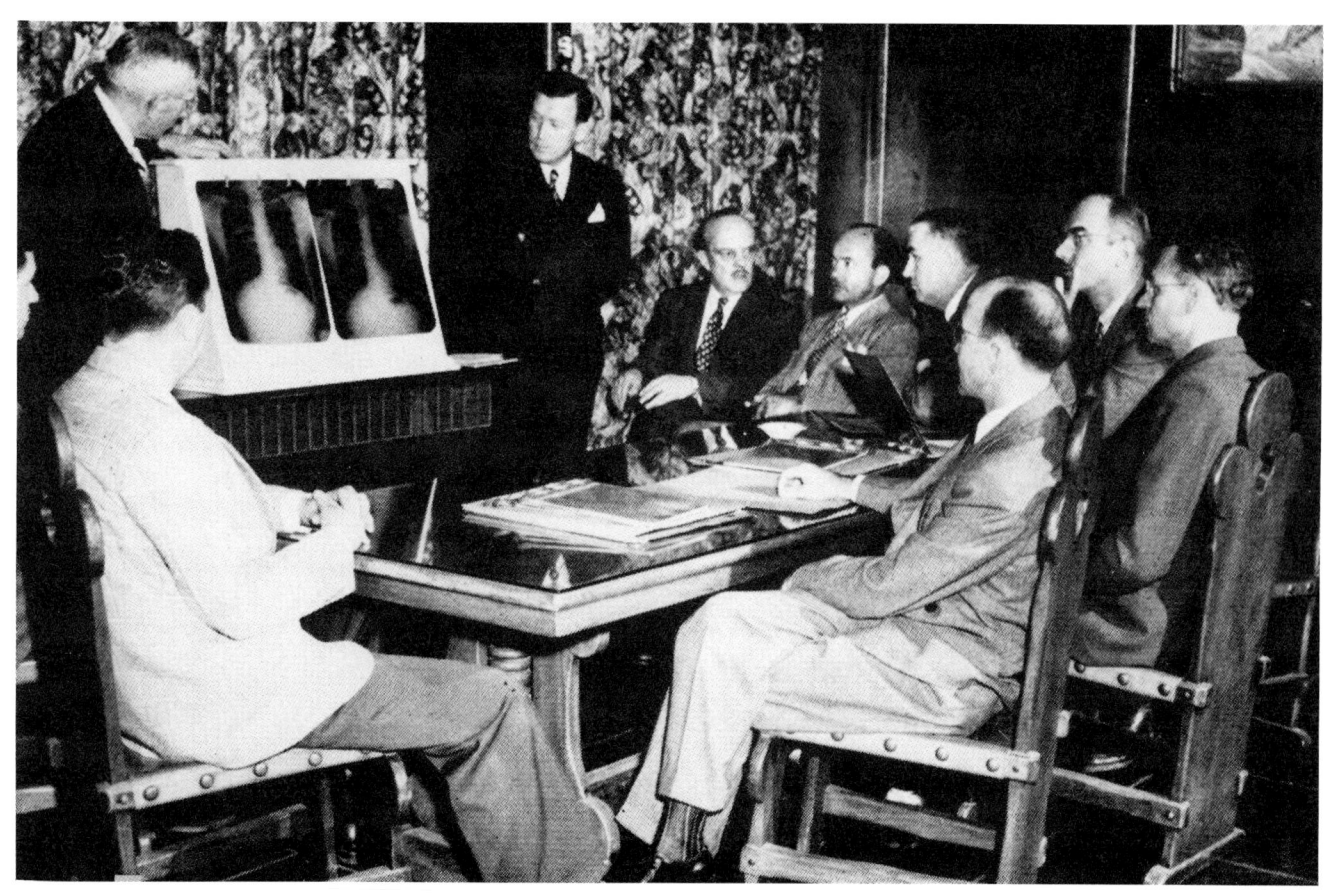

St. Luke's Chest Conference
Counter clockwise are Doctors Fred Holmes, Sr.; Hugh Hull; Dermont Melick; Leslie Smith; Kent Thayer; Bertram Snyder; Howell Randolph; Robert Flinn; Lloyd Swasey and Hilton McKeown, circa 1940.
Photo courtesy of Bertram Snyder, M.D.

W. V. WHITMORE, M.D.
1862-1940

Early Medical Conditions in Arizona

Read before the Pima County Medical Society, January, 1926

Editorial Note:

At the time Doctor Whitmore delivered this address (it was published subsequently in *Southwestern Medicine*, April 1927) it marked the first thirty years which he had spent in practice in Tucson. Doctor Whitmore wrote frequently on Arizona history, with clarity and entertainment, as he lived it. Later in his career, he was troubled by a charge of narcotics violation, was convicted, many felt unjustly, and was later fully pardoned by then U. S. President, Herbert Hoover.

An editorial in the *Tucson Daily Citizen*, October 26, 1930, is a glowing tribute to Doctor Whitmore. It was by way of welcoming him home after his incarceration and it reads, in part:

"After a long and distinguished career of usefulness both as a physician and a citizen, he was convicted of violations of the federal narcotic act. This he has expiated, and he has recently returned to Tucson after having been pardoned.

"We recite the fact not to further publicize his misfortune, but to predicate a suggestion. It is a delicate subject but it is a family affair of Tucson's and we hope it violates no canon of good taste. It is that Tucsonans now give complete substance to the pardon which has restored their old neighbor to his home and fellows.

"As to the conviction itself, we may dismiss it as a thing accomplished and irrevocable, after saying that few if any of us believe that Doctor Whitmore was consciously criminal in any of the acts on which the charge was based. Despite this, he submitted himself to authority in good faith and an unembittered spirit, and in that mood he has returned to the town which he loves.

"He has been a resident of Tucson for 38 years; he has been one of the most consistent friends which our university has had. He is a former chancellor of the institution; his only son is a graduate of it. Against this there is nothing to mark up but an unconscious, profitless violation of the law, and we think Tucson is big enough to wipe that out and remember it no more forever, giving this patriarchal healer a whole-hearted and unreserved welcome home."

Doctor Whitmore lived out his time in Tucson and died in 1940. There was never any question about the esteem of his fellow citizens.

"In making a survey of a third of a century, I can hope to hit only the high places. My coming to Tucson was one of the results of the murder of Doctor J. C. Handy in this city in September, 1881. Bad feelings had engendered between the doctor and Francis J. Heney—then a young lawyer here—because the latter had taken the case of Mrs. Handy for divorce against the doctor, after every other lawyer in the city had declined. The report is that for a year, whenever Heney happened to be within the sound of Doctor Handy's voice, loud threats were made against the lawyer. I suppose Mr. Heney is the only person who knows just what happened that September forenoon, when the two met at the southeast corner of the Court House lawn. The result of the meeting was that Doctor Handy was shot. He was taken to his home. Doctor Goodfellow at Tombstone was telegraphed for. A special engine brought him from Fairbanks. Some twenty perforations were found in four or five feet of the small intestine and Doctor Handy died upon the table.

"The Southern Pacific officials persuaded Doctor Goodfellow to move to Tucson, where he at once became division surgeon. My former

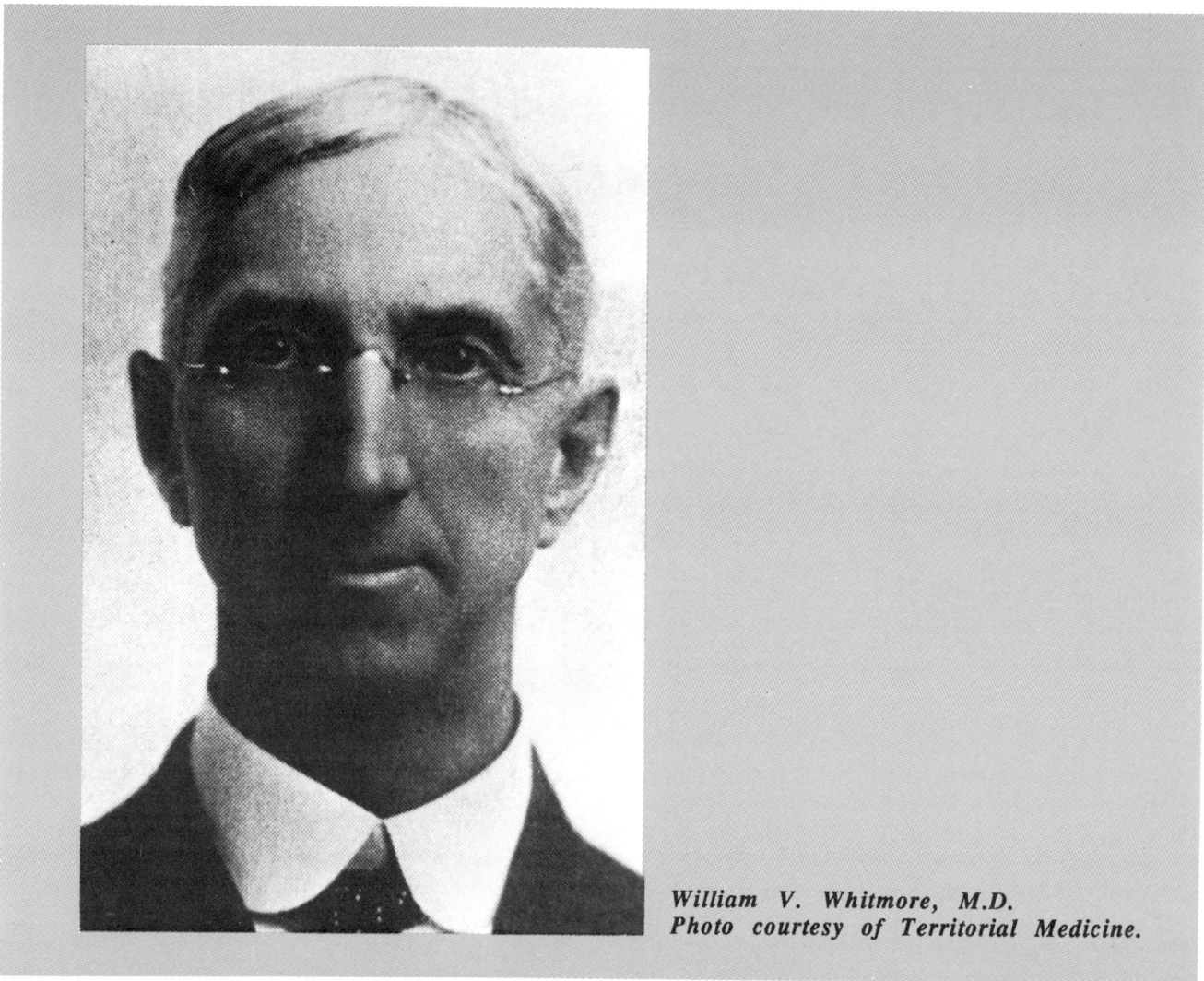

*William V. Whitmore, M.D.
Photo courtesy of Territorial Medicine.*

demonstrator of anatomy, Doctor I. B. Hamilton, of Los Angeles, took Doctor Goodfellow's place in Tombstone. The following March, Hamilton wrote me that he expected to join Goodfellow here in Tucson and wished me to go to Tombstone. After some two weeks of correspondence, he decided to remain in Tombstone and I came here.

"A word as to local conditions at that time. I made the sixth physician in Tucson. Doctor Goodfellow had been here seven months; Doctor Fenner, some ten years; Doctor H. N. Matas, the father of Rudolph, had practiced here eight years; Doctor Michael Spencer had been here several years—after twenty years in mercantile life in California; and Doctor J. T. Green, a young man (who was) tuberculous, died during my first year here.

"St. Mary's Hospital, opened twelve years before, was, at the time of my arrival—like the University of Arizona—an institution of one building, the central stone building. The sisters lived in an adobe house on the north side of St. Mary's Road, just outside the hospital grounds proper. In this building the nursery or orphanage was maintained for years. My understanding is that there was no operating room at St. Mary's until Doctor Goodfellow's arrival, for I distinctly recall the surgical nurse telling me that Doctor J. C. Handy attended to dislocations, fractures and amputations on the bed in the room or ward.

"I think we may conclude, then, that there was very little surgery, as we understand the word today, attempted in this vicinity in those earlier days. Until Doctor Goodfellow's removal to San Francisco in 1896, Doctor Fenner did no surgery, preferring family practice. But when he succeeded Doctor Goodfellow as division surgeon here, he began to do considerable surgery.

"Not for years—I would not attempt to say how many—after my arrival, was there a graduate nurse to be had in private work here. My recollection is that male nurses were occasionally leaving their cards with us.

"Dr. Goodfellow had practiced medicine in

Tombstone ten years. In order to have some conception of the results of such a residence upon a man of Doctor Goodfellow's ability, one must have some idea of the conditions of that time. Of course, you all know that Tombstone was not always the one-horse county seat that is is today. Discovered in 1878 by Ed. Schiefflin, it became in the early eighties a hustling camp.

"It boasted the largest number of inhabitants of any city, town or camp in Arizona. It then claimed 10,000, Tucson having only 5,000 and Phoenix a little over 3,000. At its height Tombstone was the greatest silver mining camp in the world.

"From all I have been able to learn, it was also the toughest. Nearly all the gunmen of the West gravitated to Tombstone. There eventually developed two rival factions. The four Earp brothers, who had all been professional gamblers, and Doc. Holliday, a tubercular dentist, constituted one faction. In the early eighties one of the Earps was Marshal of Tombstone and another was a Deputy U. S. Marshall. A gang of cowboy outlaws, who refused to acknowledge the local supremacy of the Earps, consisted of two Clanton brothers, two McLowery brothers and one or two gangs. The Earps certainly showed no great courage at the final meeting which led to almost the annihilation of the Clanton gang, attacking the latter when they were peaceably leaving Tombstone for their ranch, shooting them down practically from ambush and at a time when they knew that two of the Clantons were unarmed, as the Marshal himself had relieved them of their firearms the evening before. But as two of the Earps were so-called "peace officers," their action had some semblance of law and order, and it was so decided.

"A word of testimony from a man who was on the ground. In the late seventies the Episcopal Church of the country appointed bishop after bishop from the east, south, and middle states to take charge of their work in New Mexico and Arizona. Not one of them ever showed up; every one resigned. Finally they tacked this work on to Bishop Hall, who was in charge of California. In 1880 he visited the territory. He reported: 'Phoenix is a pleasing place; Tucson is an important town, and Tombstone is the condensation of wickedness.'

"With this little sketch of conditions in Tombstone, I think you will accept the truthfulness of Doctor Goodfellow's statement to me that he had presumably had greater practice in gun-shot wounds of the abdomen than any other man in civil life in the country. And I think we may conclude that this extensive practice laid the proper foundation, both in experience and courage, for him later to attempt operations—new both to himself and to everyone else.

"I had stated that there were no nurses here. The result was that, as far as Doctor Goodfellow's work was concerned, the nurse's work fell upon me. During the six months I served as his assistant, the greater part of his surgical operations were at the patient's home. At 8 o'clock on the morning of the operation I left the office with a carryall filled with impedimenta, viz.: an old-fashioned, small, wooden operating table and five large satchels filled with instruments, dressings, anesthetics, etc. Instruments and dressings were arranged for use upon antiseptic towels.

"About the end of my first week here came our first operation. The wife of a railroad man had been confined by Doctor Spencer six weeks before. Infection followed and Doctor Goodfellow removed ovary, tube and a part of uterus. My outstanding recollection of this case is that for about a week Doctor Goodfellow and I went to the house four times a day to irrigate that abdomen 6 o'clock in the morning, at noon, 6 o'clock in the evening and at midnight. In self defense, the patient finally recovered.

"My fourth week here was devoted to surgical operations. Doctor Goodfellow had been saving up cases. He and his friend—who was also my friend—Doctor Francis L. Haynes, of Los Angeles, came here and there were one or two operations a day for at least five days. The first case had rather interesting features. It was the divorced wife of Doctor Handy—a vaginal hysterectomy for cancer of the cervix. Neither of these surgeons had ever performed this operation. That was the day when large clamps were used to control hemorrhage. The surgeons had finished, just how many pounds of steel stood out into the world I could not say. The patient was put to bed, instruments were cleaned and we partook of luncheon, There was a persistent oozing of blood that worried the Doctors Goodfellow and Haynes. About 2 o'clock the patient was put on the table, anesthetic given and clamps readjusted. Before dinner I sneaked out and made some calls, but at 8 p. m. the procedure was repeated. At 11 p. m. the surgeons went home, leaving me in charge.

The next day I learned from Doctor Goodfellow that he had driven to the house at 5 o'clock in the morning expected that I would have all arrangements made for a first-class funeral, but he found the patient sitting up in bed and I was in another part of the house getting some sleep. The malignancy returned in some four months but, Mrs. Handy lived something over a year after the operation.

"The following day the same operation was

performed at St. Mary's upon a middle aged Irish woman from Bisbee. Everything went along nicely with this case. She soon returned to her home and I know nothing about the ultimate results.

"A very few weeks after the surgical week an interesting case came into St. Mary's from Florence—a Mrs. Trimble with a six month's pregnancy complicated with a uterine fibroid about half the size of one's head. There were seven doctors in the operating room; Doctor Goodfellow had invited Doctor Scott Helm of Phoenix. I assume that he was the leading surgeon there. But very soon thereafter—I think it was later the same summer—Doctor Helm was thrown from his horse and killed, in Los Angeles. Doctor M. F. Price of Colton, who was at that time stationed at Yuma, because of some contagion on the border, was present. Doctor Spencer gave the anesthetic. I have forgotten who the other two doctors were. A rather pathetic feature occurred. When the patient had been returned to her room, the nurses discovered, pinned to her undervest, a note which was to be given to her husband in case she did not survive the operation. She remained at the hospital, only a little time and after a short convalescence in Tucson returned to her home.

"Those of you who were present at the Chamber of Commerce luncheon, at the time this society last entertained the state association, some six years ago, will recall that when I introduced Doctor Cecil, urologist of Los Angeles, his first words were an expression of pleasure at being in Tucson, the home of Goodfellow, the father of prostatectomy. You will also recall that I was able to throw a little light upon Goodfellow's first two operations, as I had given the anesthetic. This was in the winter of '93. I was no longer assistant to Goodfellow but continued to give his anesthetics. Consequently I lacked the intimacy with these cases that I had had with the former ones.

"The first patient for this operation was E. B. Gage, a prominent mining man from Tombstone. Doctor Goodfellow used the scalpel only to get through the skin and perineal muscle. All further dissection up to the gland and its enucleation was done by the index finger. In a remarkably short time the gland was delivered intact. It was just about the size of a chestnut and of normal pink color. Some time after the operation I met Mr. Gage on the corridor of the hospital. He was as pleased as a child, stating that he could urinate like a school boy.

"Gage had a friend, a prominent attorney in Chicago, named Eames. He was at St. Mary's a few weeks getting ready for the operation. Conditions were quite different from the first case. Gland was at least two and half times larger, dark red color and quite friable, about one-eighth or one-tenth coming away piece-meal. After the operation—I think it was during the first night—there was quite an extravasation of blood into perineum and inner aspect of each thigh. This had Goodfellow worried for a while, but it all cleared up.

"I gave anesthetic for a few other removals of the prostate. But it is my understanding that it was after Goodfellow's removal to San Francisco, in '96, that he paid special attention to his operation and became one of the leading authorities, as he had been while here, the pioneer."

XIII.

Vignettes of Prescott Physicians
By Dry Gulch Jake

*John B. McNally, M.D.
Photo courtesy Arizona Historical Foundation and Territorial Medicine.*

John B. McNally, M.D.
1866-1928

*John W. Flinn, M.D. The father of Robert S. Flinn, M.D., he established in Prescott, Arizona Territory, a tuberculosis sanatorium.
Photo courtesy of Territorial Medicine.*

John W. Flinn, M.D.
1871-1944

John B. McNally, M.D. practiced in Prescott from 1896 to 1928. He was in some ways a "loner." Although he was never associated in practice with any of the other physicians in Prescott at that time, he had a great following of extremely loyal patients. One story is that when the Pope was quite ill in Rome his patients thought that if they sent Doctor McNally to attend him he would certainly recover. But the hierarchy never called Doctor McNally and the Pope didn't make it. Another loyal patient of his was the wife of Senator Henry Ashurst—one of the first senators from Arizona when Arizona was admitted as a state—who was known for his sonorous and sibilant oratory. Ashurst's wife was such a loyal patient of Doctor McNally that her wish was to be buried in the same cemetery as Doctor McNally.

Sure enough it came to pass. Doctor McNally founded a dynasty of physicians in Prescott with first his son, the late Doctor Joe McNally, and later with two of his grandsons, Doctor Gerald F. McNally and Doctor Joseph B. McNally.

Many of the physicians coming to early Arizona came because of their own health or to improve the health of a member of their family. Doctor John W. Flinn, a graduate of McGill Medical College in 1895, came to Kingman in 1898 from Nova Scotia, arriving in Prescott in 1902 where he resided and practiced until his death. He suffered from tuberculosis himself and on one occasion, when he had an acute relapse, was advised to come down to the Salt River Valley, Phoenix, and spend some time. This he did. On his way home he traveled by way of the Castle Hot Springs Resort (alas, it burned in December of 1976). Here, camping on his way back to Prescott, he met a physician from New York. This physician had acquired tuberculosis as medical students, physicians, nurses, and everybody associated with the health profession at that time was prone to acquire the disease because of close association with tuberculous patients. At any rate, this professor from Columbia had been forced to come to Arizona because he could not be admitted to Sanarac Lake Sanatorium upstate New

York. He discussed this with Doctor Flinn and suggested that there should be provision somehow for people of moderate means to be under medical supervision when they came to Arizona seeking therapy principally from the salubrious climate. He thought that it should be under medical supervision. This inspired Doctor Flinn, when he returned back to Prescott, to start his own sanatorium which was operated for a good many years by him. He pioneered the "fresh air" therapy for tuberculosis.

At the meeting of the Arizona Medical Association in 1901, in Phoenix, many papers were read concerning the beneficial effects of Arizona's climate in the cure of kidney diseases and on the treatment of tuberculosis. One prominent physician, Doctor Henry A. Hughes, stated that he hoped that not one more person with the disease would come to Arizona until there was some proper accommodation for their care and some measures adopted that would prevent the spread of the disease. Several doctors argued that if tuberculosis cases had been kept out of Arizona, they, themselves, would not have been able to receive the benefit of the climate.

There was no unanimity of opinion in regard to the treatment of tuberculosis. Bed rest with minimal exercise and a good food regimen, advocated by Doctor John W. Flinn and practiced in his sanatorium at Prescott, was not condemned but was thought by some to be insufficient. Doctor Flinn never retreated from his opinion that not only he but a great many other physicians of that era had come to Arizona to recover their health and that better conditions for new arrivals should be undertaken.

The Flinn Sanatorium laboratory in Prescott, now converted to a dwelling Photo by author, 1987.

The Flinn residence at Willow and Guerney Streets in Prescott. Photo by author, 1987.

This physician's son, Doctor Robert S. Flinn, related that at one public gathering, his father even went so far as to suggest that the Buckey O'Neill statue on the courthouse lawn at Prescott be replaced by a statue to the tubercle bacillus. Now this must had indeed been blasphemy to the ears of Prescott, for the statue is in honor of the Rough Riders. To be sure, Buckey lost his life in Cuba and was a member of the Rough Riders, but this author has been unable to find anything on the monument plaque to indicate that it was intended to be a likeness of Buckey O'Neill. Nonetheless, folklore has it so, and for Doctor Flinn to suggest that the tubercle bacillus should supplant Buckey O'Neill must have raised a few eyebrows. The reason Doctor Flinn suggested this was that the tubercle bacillus had brought to Arizona a great many people who became leaders in communities all over the state, and except for the ubiquitous growing of the tubercle bacillus in their pulmonary tissue, they would have remained elsewhere and not have contributed to the growth and progress of the Territory.

Charles Robert Niberg, M.D.

This physician, holding Arizona License No. 447, was the subject of the following report in 1913, "This physician of Maricopa County, a young man of talent and promise, died last night of a pulmonary hemorrhage, following a kick from a gun while hunting." They must have had powerful guns in those days, and poor record keeping. Files of the Arizona Board of Medical Examiners for that era do not contain the names of Dr. Niberg or of Dr. Purcell, (below.)

Walter B. Purcell, M.D.

This physician was reported to have been the first automobile casualty in Arizona. He was a well known physician of Tucson, Arizona and was killed by the overturning of his automobile a few miles north of Tucson on February 27, 1910. It was stated that he was an "expert automobilist" and he was supposed to have been the first to cross the desert from Los Angeles to Arizona in a machine in 1907. He was one of the four who started the trip and the only one to finish. This was reported in the *Southern California Practitioner*, Volume XXV, No. 4, April 1910, page 199.

XIV.

The First University Chancellor—John C. Handy, M.D.
1844-1891

With the establishment of a medical school at the University of Arizona in Tucson, the following notes concerning an eminent Tucson physician, who met his untimely death on the streets of that city, hold some interest. This is based upon newspaper accounts. I am indebted to Mr. Joseph Miller, of the Library and Archives, Capitol Building, Phoenix, for the material.

One of the earliest news items from the *Weekly Arizona Miner* (Prescott), March 20th, 1869, states: "January 20th, Lt. Guthrie, sixty-two soldiers, three guides with an interpreter, accompanied by Acting Assistant Surgeon Handy and his wife, Mrs. Handy, all under the command of Major Perry, started from here with strong spirits and a coyotero Indian called Phillippi, who said he would take them into Cachie's (Cochise's) camp.

"After fourteen days hard tramp they reached the Dragoon mountains, at which place the lady got unwell at night. In the fuss to get some mustard, the pickets became alarmed and commenced firing one on another, but no harm was done and the mustard was found. The guide said the Indians were near at hand, but the snow was deep and the night dark and they concluded to make camp." This account further relates that later they did contact Cochise and some of the conversation is recorded. Cochise: "You mean you came to kill me or any member of my tribe and that is all your visits mean to me. I tried the American's way once and they broke the treaty first, the offers I mean; this was at the Pass (Apache) I will go with you into Goodwin to talk with you, after I hear how you treat Indians there. I will send in two of my Indians who will let me know (he did send in two squaws). I lost nearly one hundred of my people within the last year principally from sickness. The Americans killed a good many. I have not a hundred Indians now, ten years ago I had over a thousand."

John C. Handy, M.D.
Photo courtesy of Territorial Medicine.

Cochise is described in this newspaper account as "about 6 foot, 3 inches tall, strongly muscled and with mild prominent features, hooked nose and looks to be the man that means what he says, age is beginning to tell on him. He is now about 50 years old."

There follow two accounts of the beginning of Doctor Handy's violence. "Word was received at Ft. Whipple last week, that Doctor J. C. Handy, contract surgeon at Camp Thomas in the Eastern part of the country, had shot and killed Mr. Hughey, a sutler at the post. A woman, we are told, was at the bottom of the affair." This was related by the *Weekly Arizona Miner* (Prescott), December 10, 1870. Another account states, "Doctor Handy who had difficulty which has resulted in the death of a man at Camp Thomas has returned as far as possible with Lt. Cushing. The doctor came here to give himself up but found that the courts had no jurisdiction so he goes on to Yavapai County. His actions are considered commendable." *Arizona Citizen* (Tucson) December 10, 1870. Nothing more in these newspaper accounts about the activities of Doctor Handy until a note in the *Arizona Citizen* (Tucson), August 12, 1871, stated that Doctor J. C. Handy had opened an office on the Church Plaza and his professional card appeared in the *Citizen*, the same issue.

In 1871, in the *Arizona Citizen*, various notes are found concerning Doctor Handy. "Saturday last, Governor Safford, Doctor Handy and a few others left for a trip in the mountains toward the San Pedro river. They returned Monday evening and reported finding some large veins of quartz in a field for prospecting." Another note from the board of supervisors, Pima County proceedings: "Doctor J. C. Handy's report as the county physician was received whereby it appears that six patients in the county jail and several other persons outside have received attention. Troy and O'Neil, hospital patients, were treated; the former was cured and the latter died October 23 from the effects of an abscess of the liver."

Then on March 23, 1872, *The Arizona Citizen* (Tucson) records an incident which could well be the first suspicion of malpractice in the territory. "Early this week Manuela Bosel became ill. She had called Doctor Jacinto Gierdo who did his work so thoroughly that the woman died on Wednesday. Suspicions of false treatment led to a post mortem examination of the body under the direction of coroner Thayer and a jury assisted Doctor Handy, and the verdict was that the death was caused by a probable malpractice. Upon this a warrant was issued, the doctor brought before Justice Myers who examined the case and found cause to commit him to jail in the default of $2,000 bail. Unless something hereafter appears to discredit the testimony given, Doctor Gierdo is surely a dangerous man as a physician and nothing but the charitable plea of insanity ought to shield him from severe punishment. In such event, he should be deprived of his liberty to prevent others falling victims to his practice. The country is too full of quacks and thousands of people suffer from their criminal work."

In October, 1873, Doctor Handy was reported as among "a group of substantial citizens listed as engaged in the actual work of prospecting, developing or procuring patents to mine along the Gila." Further notes about his interest in prospecting and mining are recorded in the *Arizona Citizen* (Tucson) in 1874 and 1875. To backtrack, the following note occurred in the *Arizona Citizen* (Tucson), July 19, 1873: "In the matter of the care of the indigent sick, proposals were received and read from Doctors C. H. Lord, J. A. Calendar and J. C. Handy, and it was decided to accept the latter, his bid being the lowest. For instance, attendance upon the indigent sick of the county and upon the sick in the county jail, $45.00 per month and for each additional one $50.00 per month. The contract with Doctor Handy is to commence August 1, 1873, and to continue for one year. A bond with penalty of $1,000 is to be given to insure the faithful performance of the contract as stated."—board of supervisors proceedings, Pima County.

Doctor Handy apparently became a substantial and respected citizen of the community and according to a communication from J. Byron McCormick, advisor to the board of regents of the University of Arizona, the following is quoted: "The records of the Board of Regents show that a John C. Handy "presumably Doctor J. C. Handy" was a member of the board from the latter part of 1886 until 1888. In fact he served during the period as Chancellor of the University of Arizona, and as such was ex-officio President of the Board of Regents. The Arizona Territorial Assembly, in 1885, established the University of Arizona and prescribed that the Board of Regents should consist of six members appointed by the governor of the territory and two ex-officio members, a superintendent of public instruction and the secretary of the Territory. The Act further prescribed that the Board of Regents should elect a chancellor of the University who should be the ex-officio President of the Board of Regents. It was to this office that John C. Handy was elected on November 27, 1886, according to the minutes of the meeting of the Board of Regents of that date. The last mention of his attendance at a Board of Regents meeting was at a meeting of January 31, 1888. Perhaps I should say that this was during the planning stage of the University before the institution was in actual operation. It was not until 1891 that the University was open to students."

Now Doctor Handy did indeed meet a violent end and the following is based on excerpts of newspaper accounts which were written at the same time and are quoted more or less verbatim from the *Arizona Daily Star*, Tucson, September and October 1891: "At 12 o'clock noon yesterday a shot rang out at the corner of Church and Pennington. A representative of the *Star* hastened to the spot and found that Doctor J. C. Handy and Francis J. Heney were engaged in a deadly struggle at a point near the intersection of these streets. Both parties were on the ground, both had hold of the same pistol and were trying to take it from the other. A crowd soon gathered and after some difficulty the officers secured the pistol in controversy. When the parties were separated, it was discovered that Doctor Handy was shot in the left side. He was taken to his office where examination was made. His shirt was powder burned which showed the pistol was held close to the body when it was fired. The ball entered right below the ribs and passed down to the base of the back bone. A herdick (a kind of litter) was secured and he was taken to his rooms on Main Street where all the physicians in the city tendered their services and Doctor George Goodfellow of Tombstone was telegraphed for. The Southern Pacific sent a special engine to this place. Doctor Goodfellow arrived last night at 9:00 p.m. and was directly driven to Doctor Handy's rooms.

"Soon after the unfortunate affair, Mr. Heney surrendered himself to the authorities and was released on $6,000 bail. Last night Doctor Goodfellow of Tombstone, Doctors Phenner, Spencer and Green of this city, held a consultation with reference to the doctor's condition and agreed that there was no doubt but what the intestines were perforated by the bullet and there was hardly a ray of hope for his recovery. They recommended a surgical procedure and this was done. Accordingly the patient was placed under chloroform anesthesia and the operation begun at 10:20 p.m. An incision was made in the left side about seven inches long, the entrails taken out, which proved to be perforated in more than a dozen places. There was also a large amount of blood in the cavity of the stomach caused by the internal hemorrhage, which was removed. Just as the operation was completed and last stitch being taken, Doctor Handy expired without a struggle at 1:00 o'clock in the morning." (The operation was a success even in those days but the patient died anyway.)

At the inquest, Doctor Goodfellow testified as follows: "I am a physician, knew Doctor Handy, was summoned to see him, found him suffering from a gunshot wound in the abdomen. The ball in its course had cut many intestines, an operation was decided upon and I performed it. I opened his belly, sewed up the intestines and washed out the blood. He died from hemorrhage caused by gunshot wound."

Later Doctor Goodfellow is further quoted not at the coroner's inquest but apparently by a reporter who interviewed him: "There were 19 perforations of the intestines, but not withstanding this fact, had the operation been performed within two hours of the shooting, he believes he could have saved Doctor Handy's life. Doctor Goodfellow states he has performed five similar operations on shooting victims and two out of the five recovered. As a matter of fact, he states that Doctor Handy was dying when he commenced the operation."

At the court hearing, a Mr. Wright testified in some detail about some of the circumstances that led to this affray. He stated that Doctor Handy called him into his office some days previously and asked him if he was a friend of Francis J. Heney and Mr. Wright allowed as how he was. And then the doctor had said, "Tell Francis J. Heney not to take Mrs. Handy's case," and the doctor insisted that he tell Mr. Heney not to do this and "tell Frank Heney that if he takes the case I will kill him, tell him not to take it." Mr. Wright remonstrated with the doctor but the doctor stated, "My wife is a morphine fiend, she does not deserve any. No lawyer can talk to her fifteen minutes without knowing that when any lawyer discovers that it is his duty to surrender the case. I will kill any lawyer who takes the case and stands between me and my children." Wright remonstrated with the doctor telling him that if he wanted to be a renegade he should turn outlaw and go into the mountains. This conversation apparently occurred not very long before the final meeting between Mr. Heney and Doctor Handy.

After the hearing, the judge gave the following verdict, "I have listened very carefully to the testimony which has been given, this is a case where much excitement and feeling has been engendered and is an important case. Two of the leading citizens of this place had an encounter and one is killed. As far as the standing of these parties goes, as far as their influence extends and the circumstances surrounding them, we have nothing to do. I concluded from the statements of threats made by the deceased that this was made in accordance with statements made by witnesses as how an attack should be made, how it should be conducted, taking into consideration the character of the deceased, who in his kindlier moments was one of the most just, one of the most kindest hearted men in the community, but in his enmity I may say that I have never known a man who would go farther to avenge a fancied or real slight or injury than Doctor Handy." And the judge goes on to state, "taking all this into consideration, that he decided that the defendant in this case acted in necessary self defense and committed a justifiable homicide."

Doctor Goodfellow later moved to Tucson, succeeded Doctor Handy as surgeon to the Southern Pacific Railroad. Gossip had it that he was not too solicitous for Handy's recovery. This certainly was an unjust criticism for he was probably the most skilled surgeon of the Territory. His experience with gunshot wounds, in Tombstone, was ample. 'Twas in Tucson he performed the first successful perineal prostatectomy—but that is another incision. (This was removal of the prostate gland in men, going directly through the skin just in front of the rectum, and not into the urinary bladder.) Thus closed the case of the famous Doctor Handy, who in one of the earliest accounts, after his arrival in Arizona Territory, it was related that he had committed homicide and he died in the same manner not too many years later. Be that as it may, a physician was the first chancellor of the University of Arizona at Tucson.

Photo courtesy of Territorial Medicine.

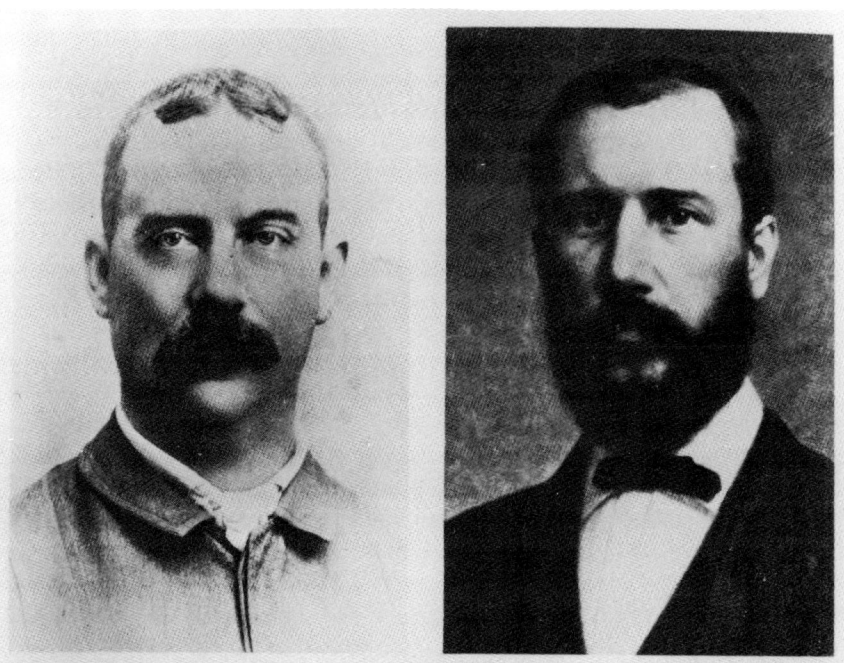

DR. GEORGE E. GOODFELLOW
(1855-1910)

DR. JOHN C. HANDY
1844-1891)

Arizona's two outstanding surgeons were principals in a tragic drama in 1891. Doctor Handy was shot on a Tucson street in an argument with his wife's attorney, apparently related to Mrs. Handy's announced intention to divorce the handsome doctor. Doctor Goodfellow hurried to Tucson from Tombstone on a special locomotive, himself taking the throttle in a vain race to save his friend and colleague. He was the principal surgeon in a three-hour emergency operation, but Doctor Handy died "as the last stitch" was being taken.

XV.

Origin and Organization of the Arizona Medical Association

Early in May 1892 the following letter was addressed to the Maricopa County Medical Association.

To The Physicians of Arizona:
Phoenix, Arizona, May 7, 1892

Dear Doctor:

At a meeting of the Maricopa County Medical Association held in Phoenix on the first Tuesday of this month the following preamble and resolution were unanimously adopted: Whereas it is evident that there are many earnest and zealous physicians in Arizona who are willing to contribute of their time and talent toward the general interest of the medical profession, and Whereas the greatest good to the profession can be accomplished through organization therefore be it Resolved First That we call a meeting of the physicians of the Territory for the purpose of organizing a Territorial Medical Society. And that said meeting be held in Phoenix on May 25th, Wednesday, in order that we may elect delegates to the American Medical Association which meets in Detroit, Michigan, June 7, 1892. Resolved Second that a committee of three be appointed to invite all regular physicians residing in the Territory to attend said meeting. In compliance with said resolution you are most cordially invited to be present and participate in the organization of the Territorial Association. We deem it unnecessary to enumerate the many reasons why we should organize as we take it for granted that they are evident to all thinking physicians.

Fraternally yours,
J. Miller, President
L. D. Dameron, Secretary
W. H. Ward, A. E. Martin, H. A. Hughes, Committee

There is the following note which indicates that these men were sincere and ready to proceed with an organization. The minutes of a later meeting then read as follows: Recognizing the call of the Maricopa County Medical Association, the following physicians of Arizona assembled in the parlors of the Commercial Hotel at Phoenix on the afternoon of May 26, 1892. Doctors M. M. Gilbert of Mesa city, Mauck of Tempe, J. W. Green of Tucson, Brack of Tempe, T. B. Hamilton of Tombstone, Thomas H. Sabine of Gila Bend, W. H. Ward, Rawlings, Hughes, Keifer, and L. D. Dameron, McIntire, Whorton and Ancil Martin of Phoenix.

The meeting was called to order by Doctor J. Miller as chairman. A temporary organization was then formed with Doctor J. Miller as chairman, Doctor A. E. Martin as secretary and after an eloquent and carefully prepared address by Doctor Miller upon the objects and future of the association, committees were appointed as follows: On the constitution, Doctors Hughes, Green and Gilbert. On nominations for organization: Doctors Dameron, Hamilton and Ward. Then the meeting adjourned for certain considerations by these committees and they assembled again at 8 p. m. in the evening. On assembly at 8:30 Doctor Miller was elected president by ballot and the other nominations, there being no opposition, were elected on acclamation. Adjournment until 10:00 a.m. May 26th.

The physicians gathered and then enjoyed a banquet at the Commercial Hotel put on by the members of the local Maricopa County Medical Society. Then the association was called to order at 10:30 a. m. May 26th by President Miller. As far as possible, the judicial council consisting of one member from each county was appointed. There were members then from Pima, Yavapai, Yuma, Cochise, Gila, Pinal, Coconino and

Maricopa counties represented on this committee. After some more routine business there was an adjournment and it was determined that the association was to meet again in Phoenix, June 2, 1892 and these minutes were signed by Doctor Green, secretary.

So there you have it, a bold beginning in Phoenix of what is now the Arizona Medical Association. There follows a copy of the constitution which was adopted. Of that, Article III on membership states: The membership of the association shall consist of members and honorary members. The members shall be alumni of regular and respectable schools of medicine provided they shall have fully complied with the laws of Arizona in existence at the time of their initiation and shall have been certified to by two members of the association and by the judicial council. There followed articles relating to the officers, the duties of the officers and how vacancies in the offices should be filled during the interval between meetings. There follows the by-laws which were adopted consisting of eleven articles, perhaps the most interesting of these is Article 10, Section 1: "A committee of one member from each county represented shall constitute a committee for nominations in place of meeting. Said committee shall report action in a day prior to adjournment." Further down it says "all questions of a personal character, including complaints and protests and all questions on credentials shall be referred at once" after the report of the committee of arrangements to the judicial council with a quorum of at least four members and without discussion.

The next meeting was held in Phoenix, February 28, 1893. Here are some extracts about what they had to say about that. After the preliminaries "it was moved by Doctor Hughes and seconded by Doctor Ward that the by-laws referring to admission of members be suspended and that those desiring to become members become such on signing the constitution. Motion carried." The names of 10 new members were added to the rolls.

The committee on medical legislation read a report of a bill providing for the establishment and maintaining of a board of health. Report received and accepted for discussion. On motion the two bills relating to creating and maintaining of a board of health were ordered read section by section. At a meeting in Phoenix dated March 1, 1893 there was again discussion of this resolution for the formation of a board of health and after it was reviewed and revised it was moved by Doctor Martin that after the bill was rearranged by the committee, it be placed in the hands of an attorney for further revision and that the president be ordered to fund the treasury for the necessary monies to pay the expense of the same. "Motion carried."

At a meeting March 1, 1893 a proposal for "an act to regulate the practice of medicine" was read by Doctor Dryden and it was adopted by the association. Now, there was a discussion of abortion. And if we think the wrangling today is out of bounds, listen to this. "Doctor Hughes presented to the association the following resolution: "Whereas the members of this association view with regret the wholesale murder of unborn babies and whereas the chief justice of the Territory has decided that there is no law against murdering an unborn fetus until after the 'period of quickening' therefore be it Resolved that we as the Territorial Medical Association urge upon our Legislature to enact a law that will put a stop to such 'wholesale crime'." This was passed and it was directed to be brought to the attention of the legislature. The third annual session of the association was held May 2 and 3 of 1894 at the offices of Doctors Hughes and Dameron, 44 South Center Street, Phoenix, Arizona. May 2, 1894.

Doctor William T. Berry, treasurer of the Arizona Medical Association made his report. A total of $95.00 had passed through his hands in these first three years of the membership and he gave a detailed report as to how some of the funds had been spent. At this meeting the names of Doctors D. M. Purman, Alice M. Givens and E. A. Ingalls were favorably reported on and duly elected to membership (this is the first mention of a woman physician in these proceedings that we have noted.) Nowhere is mention of scientific papers presented by members and the first one that we note is by a Doctor Ingallson on "The Use of Instruments in Labor." Doctor William T. Berry read a paper on "Menstruation" and Doctor D. M. Purman read a paper on "Aseptic and Antiseptic Midwifery." In the afternoon session, Doctor Berry read the annual essay entitled "Medical Ethics." This is the first mention of an essay read at an annual meeting and this custom continued for some time. Apparently it was considered an honor to be selected as an essayist at these early meetings. The relationship with the local newspaper editor was apparently quite happy. The following statement is entered in the minutes, "Mr. T. J. Wolfley, editor of the *Republican*, being called upon, responded in a hardy manner saying that he and his paper would be found at all times in accord with the medical profession and was ever willing to do what was in his power for the advancement of the association and medical science." (Those were the days.)

Now for the first time, Prescott was designated as the place of the next annual meeting to be held May 28, 1896. They were still trying to get the legislature to do something about a board of health and Doctor Miller moved that the legislative committee be instructed to confer with the Territorial legislature and arrange for a meeting with said body at such a time as would be convenient. Such meeting to be in the interest of "A Board of Health Bill" then pending in the assembly. (Things moved slowly through the legislature then as indeed they seem to now.) Doctor Charles W. Jones read the annual essay entitled, "The Duty of the Physician to the Patient." This meeting continued for two days. At various times various businesses were conducted and, of course, in the final day the annual banquet, which apparently was quite festive in those days from the description noted.

Unfortunately, these minutes do not enumerate the names of all the physicians who attended or, indeed, those physicians who were members of the association. At this meeting in Prescott the following men were recommended and approved for membership in the association: W. R. Hall, M.D., Prescott; T. B. Davis, M.D., Prescott; D. A. Sewall, M.D., Prescott; E. N. Gerard, M.D., Phoenix and J. N. McCandless, M.D., Prescott (they must have made a good haul when they moved the meeting to Prescott, probably most of the physicians in that area were now members of the association.) "Doctor E. N. Gerard read a paper on 'Calimo' which was very thoroughly discussed and all agreeing that it is one of our most useful drugs, yet of its modus operandi little is definitely known." Sic transit gloria, I wager that no active practitioner of today knows the modus operandi or even any use of the drug Calimo. Other papers read at the meeting were one on "Child Murder." Another one on "Nasal Catarrh" and they were referred to the committee on publication.

The sixth annual meeting was held in Phoenix, January 26 and 27, 1897. They convened in the "parlors of the Presbyterian Church in the city of Phoenix." The following doctors were admitted to membership: H. S. Gordon of Tombstone, Joseph B. Bullock of Sacaton, Otto E. Plath of Phoenix, Louise L. Graham of Phoenix, Winfred Wilie of Phoenix, W.V. Whitmore of Tucson, William Duffield of Phoenix, J. V. Jaff of Tucson, Ella Summer of Phoenix, J. E. Drain of Mesa and, Lindley C. Wright of Glendale. Please note that two more women physicians were admitted as members, more than most of us ever dreamed were practicing in the Territory at that time. So, at this time they made a change in the constitution and by-laws and amended it so that "the words gentlemen in the profession, occurring in Section 3 of the by-laws be changed to 'ladies and gentlemen'." (There is no mention that the women's lib existed or that the macho performance of the men was resented.)

The secretary "begs leave to make the following report." There has been collected as dues $57.25 which has been turned over to the treasurer. A note is made further that the proceedings of the last session were duly published and a copy forwarded to each regular practitioner of the Territory whose name and address could be secured. L. T. Dameron signed the report as secretary. Subjects of interest of the day were papers read by Doctor L. C. Toney on gonorrhea, Doctor J. Miller read a paper on opthalmia neonatorium. As usual, the discussions were getting a little bit out of hand so that a motion was made to limit all discussion of papers and subjects to three minutes! The legislative committee was still working on a medical bill, the contents of it are not given. The next day W. V. Whitmore of Tucson read a "most excellent paper on Chloralamid." (There is no further explanation of what this wonderful substance was or what it was used for.) The papers apparently were getting longer and the members more literary for there were six papers by different physicians that were read by title only. The minutes and business of the association were getting a little bit onerous and it was moved and approved that a secretary be employed for $20.00 or less.

The seventh annual meeting was held in Tucson May 17, 1898. The meeting place was the first M. E. church in the city and the meeting was called to order by the president, Doctor Charles W. Jones. The following doctors were approved for membership: B. B. Mouer, Tempe; A. W. Noon, Nogales; J. Dennet, Congress Junction; J. W. Watkins, Benson; W. F. Chenowith, Nogales; W. B. Purcell, Tucson; H. F. Walter, Wilcox; H. H. Pease, Tucson; N. H. Matas, Tucson; A. W. Olcot, Tucson; A. J. Gould, Tucson; M. A. Rodgers, Tucson. (It is later reported in one of the publications of the association some years later, I am not sure just when, that Doctor Purcell was killed in an automobile accident and that he was the first physician to meet this sort of an accidental death in the state of Arizona.) The presidential address was presented by Doctor C. H. Jones of Tucson and his subject was "Information Particularly Upon the Vegetable Resources of Arizona for Therapeutic Properties" and recommended that a research committee of five members be appointed to investigate the properties of our indigenous plants. Just what active plant origin material was used at that time is not delineated in these notes.

There was a presentation by Doctor Miller of the following ethical questions: 1. Is consultation permissible with with a practitioner who holds a diploma from a homeopathic college only and has not publicly denounced the dogma of homeopathy? 2. Is medical consultation with practitioners of the above standing permissible in part or in whole? 3. Is consultation permissible with regular physicians who consult with or assist the practitioners above? There follows a whole list of other things that he thought was VERY unethical. Lo and behold, this was duly considered by the proper committee and finally the following resolution was adopted: "Resolved, that it is a sense of the Association that it is a breach of the code of medical ethics of the American Medical Association for members of this Association to consult with homeopaths under any circumstances whereby the said homeopaths are recognized as physicians." (You will recall at about at this time there were some deviates from so-called regular or allopathic medicine. The eclectics and the homeopaths being the principal other subdivisions and tempers sometimes ran short amongst the contenders who practiced each of these theories of medicine.)

Now, in 1989, I suspect that very few of the present day graduates could differentiate these very sects of medicine in that ancient time. The eighth annual session of the Territorial Medical association met in Phoenix, January 31, 1899. Four new members were admitted to the association at this time. The transactions were still being published and forwarded to all physicians in the Territory for whom they had the name and address. The budget of the society was an even $100.00. The annual essay, which was considered quite an honor to be asked to give, was read by Doctor Ancil Martin and it was on "The Physiological Pupil." (Remember, Doctor Martin was probably the first specialist in EENT to arrive in the Territory.) The minutes dwell upon some possible revision of the medical legislation, but they do not give particulars as to what legislation they wish to have changed or to have amended. After due consideration it was thought the better part of wisdom not to tamper with the present medical legislation for fear that the whole thing would be thrown out.

The ninth meeting of the association was held in Prescott, May 29-30, 1900. They had trouble getting a quorum together to consider necessary committee reports. At this meeting thirteen new physicians from around the state were admitted to membership. There was not much mention of what business really took place at that meeting. The notes that were recorded consist mostly of mentioning who read papers and appointment of committees and election of officers.

The president who opened the meeting was Doctor T. B. Davis. After some preliminaries and reading an address, there follows a somewhat interesting report by the then secretary, Thomas H. Jones. It reads in part as follows: "Arizona Medical Association Gentlemen: Your Secretary takes pleasure in reporting progress that our organization is convalescing. A few words of historical statistics, if permissible, will be both instructive and invigorating to all. Nine years ago our association was formed with nine members. Today we have fifty six members and I hold twenty eight applications for membership awaiting the action of the judicial council, making a total of eighty four. There are in Arizona about two hundred regular physicians, very many of whom are not practicing at all; others doing some practice in conjunction with mining, farming and stock raising. The number who are practicing medicine exclusively will not far exceed one hundred, possibly one hundred and ten. We have then seventy five percent of all active practitioners in the Association, which I believe is a larger percentage than that of any other state or territory in the Union. Still more have signified their intention of joining and will in the coming year."

He further continues: "When we consider that these men are scattered over more than 200,000 square miles of territory, it would be impossible to convene at a point within three hundred miles of every member. But the spirit is good and the meetings are improving. After one or two more gatherings like the recent one when every member knows that there will really be a good meeting, the attendance will be much greater."

He further continues, "*Our Transactions*, the official publication, this year will make a neat volume which we can have printed and bound for about $1.00 or $1.25 each. I recommend that only such a number be ordered as is necessary to supply members in good standing and to exchange with such other state societies as will send us one in return." With some other notes this was signed by Charles H. Jones, secretary.

It is about the only note of historical importance at the tenth annual meeting of the association. One of the papers read at that meeting was by a Doctor Hughes on "Bubonic Plague." There is no mention as to how prevalent the disease may have been at that time. At this meeting is a paper on pulmonary tuberculosis by Doctor H. E. Stroud of Phoenix and as far as I can make out it was the first one directed to this subject, and as you can well imagine, as time went on, tuberculosis occupied more and more of their time.

A resolution passed at this time was: "Resolved: that the city council of every incorporated town in Arizona be requested to pass ordinances to better protect our citizens from the infection of tuberculosis. First by placing receptacles containing antiseptic solutions to be approved by the health officer at convenient stations approved by the health officers throughout the city and particularly in the public places. Second, to provide for the disinfection of rooms at boarding houses, hotels and rooming houses and wherever consumptive patients lodge and that the remuneration for the room disinfecting shall be through a fee deposited by the roomer with the proprietor of the house where he lodges, not to exceed $2.00 per room. That immediately upon the vacation of the room by the roomer that the health officer shall be notified within twelve hours and it shall be the duty of the health officer to see that this disinfecting is carried out properly. That any failure upon the part of the householder, lodging housekeeper, or hotel keeper to notify the health officer shall carry with it a penalty to be established by the city council sufficient to enforce the law." The resolution was adopted. The red bacillus had made itself an enemy in the Territory.

The next annual meeting was May 28, 1902 in Tucson and Doctor Palmer of Phoenix read a paper on asthma. Doctor Burton of Tucson read a paper entitled "Surgical tuberculosis." The secretary and treasurer combined their reports and stated that "we have seventy eight members and have twenty eight new applications, making a total of one hundred five, which is over eighty five percent of the available physicians in the state." It further continues, "we cannot expect all or even one half of our members at any one meeting because of the great distance they would have to travel and the many days loss of time, but the spirit is good and many of the absent members are as earnest as those present." The total expenditure of money by the treasurer during that year was $152.00.

The meeting in 1903 was May 27th at the Hotel Adams in Phoenix and was presided over by the president, Doctor William Duffield. (He had a reputation as quite a talker and also as a doer.) A paper was read by Doctor E. Payne Palmer of Phoenix on "Intravenous Injections of Saline Solution." We might here note that the committee on necrology always reported at these meetings and it is of some interest. For instance, Frederick Arnold Sweet, M.D. died in his forty first year. He was graduated as a doctor of medicine by the New York University Medical College in 1889. Harlow J. Phelps, M.D., he was only twenty eight years old. It doesn't give the cause of death in the case of either of these physicians.

The thirteenth annual meeting took place in Tucson on April 27, 1904. They made a note that they met on the "roof garden of the Santa Rita Hotel in Tucson." Among the other papers was one by Doctor Ancil Martin titled "A Satisfactory Tracheostomy Method." Then there was an exotic paper, at least by present standards. It was by a Doctor Burton and entitled "The Use of Paraffin to Replace Destroyed Bone and with Reports of Cases." He also showed the patient whom he had treated by this method. Doctor Martin said he had used paraffin in a large number of cases for correcting deformities of the eye and so forth. The objection to paraffin when used below the temperature of the blood is that embolism is liable to occur. It is essential to have the temperature above the body heat, say 109 or 110 degrees. Sperm oil, vaseline or olive oil were used to make it work easily. No benefit from the use of bone chips was reported. Bone grafting by vascular attachment had been very successful. There were case presentations on epilepsy and pernicious anemia and another one on "intestinal obstruction."

The fourteenth annual session of the association met in Prescott in the parlor of the Hotel Burke June 1, 1905. There was quite a lengthy discussion at this session about visual defects and pupils in the public schools. There was a discussion of a treatise by a Doctor Frank Allport of Chicago relative to the eyes and ears of school children and some of the points were: 1. Does the pupil habitually suffer from inflamed lids or eyes? 2. Does the pupil fail to read a majority of letters in the number twenty lines of the Snellen's test types with either eye? And it goes on and on with some other questions and it ends by saying if an affirmative answer is found to any of these questions, the pupil should be given a printed card of warning to be handed to the parent which should read something like this . . . "After due consideration it is believed that your child has some eye or ear disease for which your family physician or some specialist should at once be consulted. It is earnestly requested that this matter be not neglected." Respectfully, signed by the teacher. A resolution was adopted by the members to try to get schools to comply with this.

There was the usual plea by the secretary to get more members interested and by the treasurer to get more people to pay their dues. Doctor J. W. Flinn of Prescott read a paper on "The Best Treatment of the Pre-tubercular and Those in the Early Stages of Tuberculosis, a Homily." (Doctor Flinn, you will recall, was a tuberculosis patient himself and had come to Arizona from Nova Scotia for that reason. He established what was to become a well-known sanatorium for the treatment of tuberculosis is in Prescott.) Papers were read on "Acute Yellow Atrophy of the Liver" by Doctor C. T. Sturgeon, "A Plea for More Rational

Therapy in the Treatment of Tuberculosis" by Doctor F. M. Pottenger. (Can anybody describe the Pottenger sign which he elucidated?) Doctor C. E.Yount of Prescott discoursed on "Human Myiasis from the Screw Worm." Yount was a forerunner in discussion of new disease findings in Arizona.

Doctors R. N. Looney and C. E. Yount presented a case of "Ruptured Popliteal Aneurysm, Clinical Report of a Case with Specimen." Mary Neff discoursed on the medical inspection of schools. She was to later become one of the first trained psychiatrists in the state. Tuberculosis cases were increasing in number because of the influx of sufferers from this disease and the association was continually exhorting the cities to do something about it.

One resolution at this time stated in part: "Resolved: That we recommend all municipal councils to enforce the reporting of tuberculosis patients to the Health Board, who should cause all rooms having been occupied by tuberculosis patients together with bedding, clothes and so forth to be thoroughly fumigated by the health officer at the expense of the said municipality." And they further resolved that a copy of this be sent to all the municipalities of the state.

Doctor J. W. Foss, in his report of the secretary, made a plea for more active participation by the various county organizations and they were most earnestly urged to take cognizance of the affairs that had to do with the public health in their community and to pass on the resolutions regarding the same which have been transmitted to the territorial secretary and will be forwarded to the proper parties for publication. "I cannot impress too strongly upon the county societies the importance of their earnest attention to this matter. I also would call the attention of the county secretaries to the importance of reporting each month upon the cards furnished for that purpose any changes which may occur in the membership of their society, that is, new members added or removals. It is necessary that this be done, that the membership be known by the territorial secretary, as well as the secretary of the American Medical Association to whom your territorial secretary reports monthly." Well, he had troubles.

The sixteenth annual meeting of the Arizona Medical Association was held in Bisbee, Arizona May 28-29, 1907. It would appear that the most important piece of business to come before the astute society at that time was a resolution presented by Doctor Mark A. Rodgers of Tucson and to be directed to the Department of Agriculture of the University of Arizona and it was as follows, in part . . . "Resolved: that the Society request the Agricultural Department of the University of Arizona to make an exhaustive and scientific investigation of cow milk as supplied to the various communities in this Territory, and to report from the specific localities the constituents there in contained with reference to sugar and protein and with reference to pathogenic elements and especially with reference to tuberculosis." It was unanimously adopted.

At this meeting the new president was to be Doctor A. R. Hickman of Douglas to serve the ensuing year. The treasurer reported that the total disbursements for the year were $203.30 with cash on hand of $71.95. This was signed by Doctor A. R. H. Palmer of Mesa.

The seventeenth annual meeting of the Association was held in the Elk's Hall at Tucson, April 27-28, 1908. The annual essay was read by Doctor John W. Flinn of Prescott (subject not stated.) A paper, "Scarlet Fever Epidemic at Jerome," was read by Doctor L. P. Kaull. Doctor Granville McGown read a paper on "Some Unusual Phases of Tuberculosis of the Urinary Bladder." This doctor was from Los Angeles, California. Doctor E. B. Ketcherside of Yuma read a paper on "Doctors of the Past." This indeed would be of some great historical interest at the present time, but we have no note of its contents.

The annual banquet was held at the Hotel Rossi and a surgical clinic was held at the Whitewell Hospital conducted by Doctor Mark Rogers of Los Angeles, California. We mention these two sites as they may be of some historical interest in Tucson. There were two more papers on tuberculosis and the society moved "that this Association elect a delegate from each county to the International Congress on Tuberculosis to be held in Washington, D.C. in September." The following note will have limited interest, but if any of you ever served in the United States Public Health Service when it really was a health service, you may be interested in the following note: A Doctor Granville MacGown addressed the Association on the matter of placing the control of contagious diseases in all parts of the United States in the hands of the Marine Hospital Service."

The Marine Hospital Service was a forerunner of what we now know as the United States Public Health Service, which has been largely emasculated. At this time the president-elect was Doctor A. W. Alcutt of Prescott. The eighteenth annual session was held in the Yavapai Club in Prescott May 19-20, 1919. Mr. Morris Goldwater, mayor of Prescott, delivered a very cordial address of welcome. Part of it was recorded, "If I was a doctor I would be an iconoclast. One of the false ideas I would try to destroy is the belief that the mayor should always make the address of welcome at public gatherings." And he went on to belabor this a little and said he thought the whole thing was a mistake and that they should have been welcomed "by one of your own kind, say for instance, the mayor's medical advisor, the city health officer."

He continued: "Taken singly and professionally I do not like doctors and I think most of our people will agree with me in this dislike. But taken collectively, personally and on behalf of the city of Prescott, I am pleased to welcome you. We are glad to have you with us because we think your gathering here will be a good advertisement to our city." He went on to say he hoped this meeting would not be altogether in vain and that when "your brethren of the medical profession read in the medical annals the report of your doings, we hope they will look us up and learn of our splendid climate, our ideal situation, our resources and advantages and be so impressed with our health giving or health restoring facilities that there will be an influx of home and health seekers to this City of the Pines."

He went on to say, "you are in a land filled with copper, gold and silver, but unfortunately for both you and me, my jurisdiction does not extend over the precious metals; but such as I have, I give unto thee. You are welcome to our air, our climate and our pure water and we welcome you to our homes." All in all, as you read his entire welcoming address you are struck by the humor and chamber of commerce theme, and as most of you know, Barry Goldwater, a generation or so later, would respond in the same manner.

Then the Honorable Richard E. Sloan, the governor of the Territory, made some remarks. A Doctor A. J. Rosenberry of Jerome read a paper on "Anterior Poliomyelitis." There followed other lively papers and discussion on different methods of treatment by the use of surgery, different conditions, surgery in infancy, the open method of anesthesiology with ether, and abscess of the liver.

There followed several papers on control of infection, infectious diseases and what might be done, so that of course this all ended up with a resolution: "Resolved that the Arizona Medical Association recommends the formation of an Arizona Public Health Association whose object shall be a study of the public health problems, the education of the public and cooperation with the various boards of health of Arizona. Second, Resolved: that the Arizona Medical Association recommends a compulsory registration of all contagious and infectious diseases including tuberculosis and compulsory vaccination of school children and systematic revaccination." A third resolve was that it was recommend "that such legal steps be taken as will ensure thorough inspection and regulation of the milk supply, and fourth, that the association appoint a committee of five to report, through its official organ, to the practitioners and the secretaries of the various county societies such information as they can obtain regarding public health legislation and organization."

The members of the subcommittee were Harry L. Southworth, William D. Culter and Willard Smith. There were many other papers read of clinical importance that day and this seems, at least by the minutes which we have, to have been one of the most interesting and informative meetings of clinical medicine of any of the meetings to date. This, of course, is a tribute to the Prescott physicians who were responsible for the program. Remember, Prescott at that time was probably the center of medical leadership for the Territory.

The nineteenth annual session of the association was held at the Knights of Pythias Hall in Phoenix, April 20-21, 1910. It was called to order by Doctor R. N. Looney of Prescott. As a matter of curiosity, W. Warner Watkins of Phoenix read the annual essay. The title was "Similia Similibus Curantur." The thoroughness and consistency with which the subject was dealt were especially commented upon by Doctor J. Wilson Shields of San Francisco. (Maybe Warner and Shields were the only ones who knew what the hell the title meant.)

"A very exhaustive and thorough paper entitled "Ankylostomiasis" was read by Captain L. L. Cole of Whipple Barracks. He had a microscopic demonstration of both the ovum and the worms. Ancil Martin read a paper on "A Year's Work at the Eye Hospital of the Phoenix Indian School." In this paper was clearly shown the gradual elimination of trichoma from the Indians. Apparently they always had a "visiting nabob" from Los Angeles and this time it was Doctor W. W. Beckett who gave an oration on "Thoracic Surgery." Doctor C. E. Yount of Prescott delivered a paper on "Acute Edema of the Lungs with Report of Cases."

Among the other papers presented was one on "Autogenous Vaccines" by Doctor John Foss of Phoenix. During this session the Reverend Atwood of Phoenix extended an invitation to all to visit St. Luke's Hospital for tuberculosis. There was a paper by Doctor Hughes of Phoenix on "Revocation of a Physician's License for Neglect to Report Cases of Infectious Diseases, Births and Deaths." This was discussed at length concerning the justification and the injustice of such an action. Doctor Francis Redewill of Phoenix read a paper on pellagra. (Modern physicians probably know this disease only by its historical prominence, if at all.) There is a note for the first time that an editor was appointed. Doctor John W. Flinn of Prescott was appointed editor for the association in the ensuing year.

Now we come to the twentieth meeting and it was held in the parlors of the Hotel Van Nuys in Los Angeles, California on June 26, 1911. Apparently this was the first time they had considered electing a delegate from the Arizona association to the American Medical Association. Doctor Moeur of Tempe suggested that the delegate be elected for a two year term and this apparently was accomplished.

Already some problems with transfer of doctors from one territory or state of practice to another on the basis of the fact that they were members of a county society, could they transfer to another? Southern California said nothing doing because a doctor had just left Arizona and desired to transfer to the Los Angeles County Society and he was refused on the basis of transferring membership from one place to another. This was soon to be difficult not only for the transfer of a society membership, but for state license permission also.

Doctor Flinn of Prescott opposed the idea of publishing a medical journal and strongly advocated continuing our present relationship with the *Southern California Practitioner*. He went on to the history of publication of the proceedings of the association in the past and at considerable length. He pointed out that the present arrangement with *The Practitioner* had proven the most satisfactory both as regards the general results obtained and the money saved; but, as stated, that the secretary had received practically no assistance whatever in the past in obtaining and preparation of material for *The Practitioner* and deprecated the idea that we are yet in a position to publish a journal of our own. Watkins of Phoenix thought the fact that the secretary received no assistance from *The Practitioner* was an argument in favor of our own issuing a publication. There was more discussion and the superintendent of public health, who favored the state publication said that his office would contribute $240.00 a year toward the expenses of such a publication and in return for publishing the reports of his office.

After further discussion they decided to continue their present arrangement with *The Practitioner of Southern California* for publication of some of their material, but they would investigate very thoroughly to see the prospects for the next year, the next regular session, to decide whether or not to do a publication of their own. This was strongly supported by Doctor Warner Watkins of Phoenix, who in later years was to be a strong advocate of not only the publication but making it amount to something.

It was at this meeting that Watkins of Phoenix introduced a resolution, part of which is as follows: "Whereas the present custom of serving alcoholic liquor at banquets or dinners given to or by the medical organization is injurious to public morals and reflects upon the consistency of the medical professional disciples of health, Be it resolved that the Arizona Medical Association disapprove of this custom and request its county organizations to discontinue this particular phase of hospitality at their annual entertainment of the Association."

The minutes continue, "After quite a spirited debate in which Watkins and Roy Thomas of Phoenix and Doctor Hilary Ketcherside of Yuma favored the resolution and Moeur of Tempe and Flinn and Rooney of Prescott opposed, it was moved by Bacon and seconded by Simpson that the question be submitted to a general reference of the membership of the Association." This motion was carried. (When I came to Phoenix in 1949 some of the old time members of the association still joked about this proposal by Watkins.) Later at this meeting Doctor Bacon of Miami gave a short address on "Expert Medical Testimony" advising the association to take definite steps to remedy the present disgraceful condition. (I wonder what they would think about the blatant advertisements now undertaken by all segments of the profession?)

XVI.

Odds and Ends

Introduction

The following pages, with one small exception, have nothing to do with the history of medicine in Arizona. They are included in the present volume for whatever interest the student of medical history may find in them. The sketches taken from the life of Florence Nightingale should be an inspiration to nurses and nursing students everywhere. Many of her modern day counterparts may have only the vaguest idea of who she was and what she did, but were it not for her, their profession may not have become a profession at all. The "Lady with the Lamp" did indeed accomplish the "Mission Impossible." In the brief account on "Medicine and the American Revolution," we are again reminded that the real enemy in that conflict as well as in all other wars, was not "the other side," but disease, infection and political bungling. They claimed more lives than did the firepower of both sides combined. That sorry picture did not begin to change for the better until near the end of the first World War and improved immeasurably during the second global conflict when the antibiotics and highly advanced surgical procedures made their debut.

The only one of the following three accounts that remotely touches upon Arizona (even though the story makes no mention of it) is that dealing with Hansen's disease or leprosy. The disease never was a major problem in Arizona but sometime during late Territorial or early statehood days, a Chinese waiter in Phoenix was found to have leprosy. So great was the fear of the disease (a fear which probably still exists, albeit needlessly) that the poor fellow was chained to a tree that then grew at the intersection of Washington St. and Central Ave. for some three days until a federal agent from the leprosarium at Carville, La. arrived to take him away. The fear of leprosy stems from Biblical accounts in which any unhealed sore, a common sight in those days, was deemed to be leprous. The disease was falsely branded as being highly contagious, which it isn't. It has an incubation period of from one to 30 years.

Two other items of historical interest medically but which have no bearing on Arizona are found in Doctor Kennedy's notes, included no doubt because of his interest in radiology. They are included here because they do not appear elsewhere in his chronicles. One is the fact that the first military use of x-rays by Americans occurred during the Spanish-American War in 1898. The other details the little known fact that two-time Nobel Prize winner (1903 and 1911) Marie Sklodowska Curie of radium fame, drove an ambulance in France during World War I.

J. DeV.

The Winslow Incident

Editor's note: The following account appeared in the April, 1972 issue of *Arizona Medicine*.

With the coming of a new legislative session, likened by some cantankerous taxpayers, to the second coming of the locusts, now that they are sitting again, a bill has been introduced abolishing the coroner's jury and placing the responsibility with the medical examiner. Would that it should come to pass! One coroner's jury, 8th of April 1905, came up with the following verdict in the Territory of Arizona: "Gunshot in the hands of C. I. Houchs, sheriff of Navajo County, Arizona, in his official duty and we exonerate him."

This was rendered at Canyon Diablo then a dying town thirty-five miles or so east of Flagstaff about halfway between Flagstaff and Winslow on the Santa Fe Railroad. The deceased was said to have been John Shaw and he had run out his string in a gunfight in which he, Shaw, was killed and his comrade in adventure, one Bill Smythe, was wounded twice. The sheriff, C. I. Houchs, and his deputy, J. C. N. Pemberton, emerged unscathed.

"Twenty-one bullets were fired in seconds, and only one man violated the customary practice

Old grave sites are now almost totally effaced by desert growths.
Photo by author.

A sun-seared wall is all that is left of the original trading post that faced the railroad right-of-way.

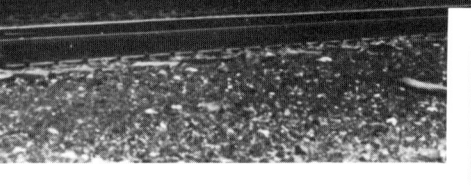

*Site of the Canyon Diablo Station on the Santa Fe railroad.
Photo by author.*

*Looking south from the trading post ruins across the Santa Fe railroad tracks toward the remains of the cemetery in foreground.
Photo by author.*

of loading only five cartridges by filling the sixth chamber of his gun. (1) That odd bullet saved the life of the sheriff and killed Shaw. How such a fusillade of bullets, at point blank range, garnered so few casualties was the talk of the Territory for months.

To retrack, the drama began something like this: Shaw and Smythe held up a saloon in Winslow the night before, but before doing so, had ordered drinks for the house. Then they robbed their fellow drinkers and gamblers and escaped by train to the West and the next day in the evening they were run down by the sheriff and his deputy. The gun play ensued, Shaw was buried across the tracks in the small Boot Hill Cemetery and his wounded buddy was taken to a hospital in Flagstaff. Well, the cowboys in Winslow soon heard of Shaw's demise, recalled that he and his partner set up drinks for the house, but didn't drink their own drink. With a snoot full of booze and a bottle full of the same material, fifteen of the cowpunchers boarded the train headed West to take a drink to their departed "friend."

So they arrived at Canyon Diablo Station, awakened the trading post owner and proprietor, borrowed a shovel, which he loaned to them if they promised to take some pictures of the exhumed. A trifle forgotten by the sheriff the day before, since the true identity of the dead robber was still in doubt. The pictures they secured should be ample proof that these cowpokes exhumed their erstwhile friend, gave him a drink and recorded it for all posterity. The pictures exemplify the smiling face of rigor mortis and the grave to which they returned their friend. There is no surviving record as to what the coroner's jury thought of these strange actions. Perhaps they all repaired to the saloon for solace.

References:

1. "A Drink for the Dead," by Gladwell Richardson, *Arizona Highways*, June, 1963, page 36.

Not So Ancient History, Oxygen— Tucson 1932

If you were a medical student or lowly house officer in the early 30s you may have had the additional duty—check the oxygen tents. Often as not the oxygen content in the tent fell far below the 40-50% desired to room ambient air level. So you sought out the harried nurse—bedside nursing was known and practiced by the RNs at the time, and together you remade the bed, adjusted rubber sheeting on the bed and tucked in the tent properly under the mattress. Some thought this "oxygen therapy" lowered the mortality from pneumococcus pneumonia, but true believers who had to type the sputum and give the specific rabbit anti serum, doubted such heresy.

The January 25, 1932 issue of *Time*, speaks well for the "new rapid Postal System" and describes an oxygen tent crisis in the Old Pueblo, (Tucson) 1932 style. St. Mary's Hospital needed another oxygen tent for a child in extremis following a mastoid operation. A canvass of the ten other institutions in Tucson revealed all tents in use. But one was released by a patient recuperating. Another chamber, (super tent) was ordered from New York, and departed by special plane from Curtis-Wright air field. This 'super tent' was a "Doctor Alvan Le Roy Barach Collapsible Oxygen Chamber." Bad weather and strong head winds forced the pilot to take three days to reach Tucson. The mastoid patient died. Those of you not around at that time may be amused at the importance attached to oxygen therapy at the time. For as we see each modern hospital room with its TV and oxygen wall jet, it is evident the oxygen habit is well established.

P. S.—Both the patient who died and the patient who released her tent were dependents of out of town newspaper bigwigs. I wonder what fate the non-newsworthy patients met—probably the same—with or without oxygen.

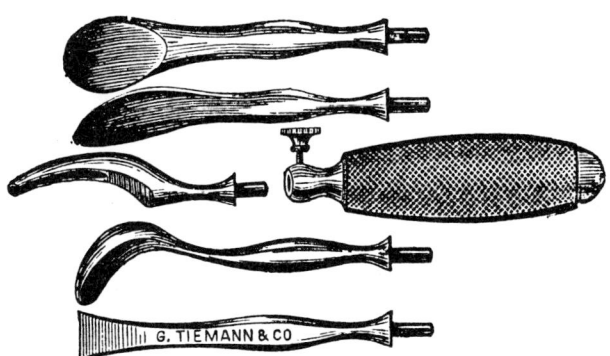

Fig. 533.—Darby's Gouges, Levators and Chisels. $7.00.

Case of the Century

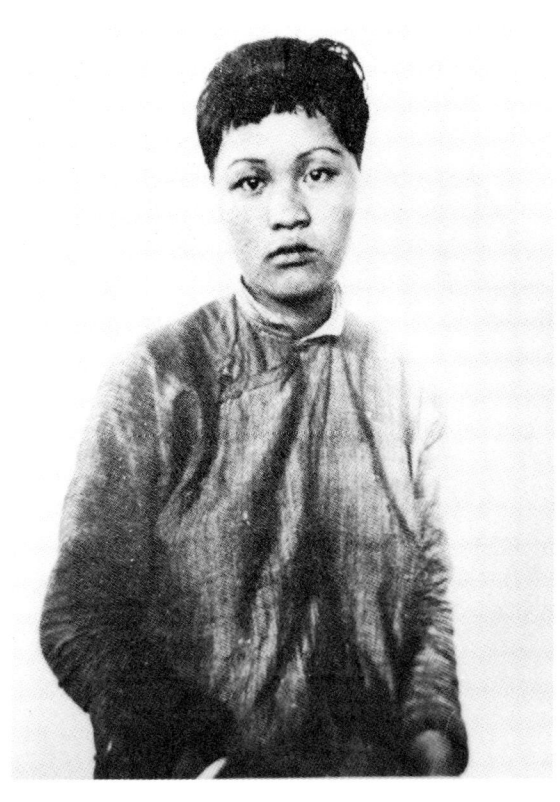

Sans pinnae
(without ears)
Photo courtesy of Clarence Salsbury, M.D.

This syndrome, thought to be no longer endemic, was noticed in a patient of Doctor Clarence Salsbury. He encountered this bizarre case while serving as a medical missionary on the Island of Hainan off the South China coast, (1915-1925). All the clinical objective signs of this syndrome are demonstrated in the photograph. (Sorry, no credit for continuing education fans). Doctor Salsbury supplied us with this photograph, clinical history and a liberal translation of the Chinese appellation of this condition, "Sans Pinna" (without ears). At that time it was still a custom to sever the ears from a wife who engaged in extramarital amorous adventures. This patient was brought to Doctor Salsbury to have the ears repinned, but alas this was not possible.

The Return of the Wapiti to Arizona: A Salute to Robert N. Looney, Pioneer Arizona Physician

This is an interesting sidelight for hunters and doctors. This unusual work of Doctor Looney confirms the wide interest that the early pioneer physician had—not only in his patients, but also in state wildlife conservation. It is a strong encouragement to all of us to take a more active part in our community. Many moons past, the Spaniards began the transplant of Caucasian homo sapiens, biped, to Arizona. About 150 years ago elk roamed most of the United States, foothills, woods and plains, from sea level to mountain tops. Since the elk were native inhabitants, why, you inquire, did they disappear from Arizona? Well, the answer is, they disappeared in the same fashion as many of our other natural fauna. The greedy, thoughtless, rapacious slaughter by man decimated the Wapiti. Authorities differ in opinion as to when the native elk finally disappeared from the Territory of Arizona.

Robert N. Looney, M.D.
Arizona Commissioner of Health, 1912.
Photo courtesy of Territorial Medicine.

An elegant elk—a descendent of the Looney transplant program, 1914
Photo courtesy of Dave Broughton, Arizona Game and Fish Department.

In the 1870s they began to become scarce, but even during this time elk meat sold in the general stores in the high country for seven cents a pound. (1) The last native elk was recorded as killed near Mount Ord in 1898. (1) By then about all that remained of the native species, Merriam elk, were a few skeletons which were found in the Mogollon Rim country. Doctor Looney, at the time health commissioner, but in active practice in Prescott, made the return of the Wapiti possible. Doctor Robert Nelson Looney was the pithy pioneer Prescott physician who authored and consummated the transplant of elk from the Yellowstone National Park to northern Arizona. It may come as a surprise to some that objects other than arteries, nerves and skin were subject to transplant, lo those many years ago.

Another physician, Doctor Shore, from the state of Washington (2) reported in August 1912 on "Trapping and Shipping Elk," to Washington and Oregon. Doctor Looney studied this article and quickly began to make arrangements for a similar transplant to Arizona. Doctor Looney was appointed state health commissioner in 1912 and served until 1917. Copies of his letters during the negotiations for these elk are extremely interesting and they start August 14, 1912. A letter to Governor Hunt, outlines his plan. (3) He had already begun to negotiate with people in Montana and with the Department of the Interior for permission to ship the elk. He noted, in his letter to Governor Hunt, that the cost would be about five dollars a head for the service of capturing them in Gardner, Montana. Doctor Looney corresponded with Mr. E. W. Nelson, head of the U. S. Biological Survey (now Fish and Wild Life Commission) and with the Boone and Crockett Club of New York (Teddy Roosevelt, first president). These people gave valuable assistance in suggesting how a game conservation law should be written, that a game refuge should be established, and they even offered to supply funds to help transplant the elk. Mr. H. Anderson, of Gardner, Montana, contracted to capture the elk. With the assistance of Arizona's Senator, Henry Fountain Ashurst, Doctor Looney made a trip to Washington with a petition to the U. S. Department of the Interior and obtained a permit.

It was about this time that Mr. Mulford Windsor, Doctor Looney and Governor Hunt established themselves as a committee to supervise this undertaking. Governor Hunt and Doctor Looney each put up five hundred dollars, and, as we will see, this was not enough to complete the

A political campaign photograph of George Wiley Paul Hunt, longtime governor of Arizona.
Photo courtesy of Arizona State Department of Library and Archives.

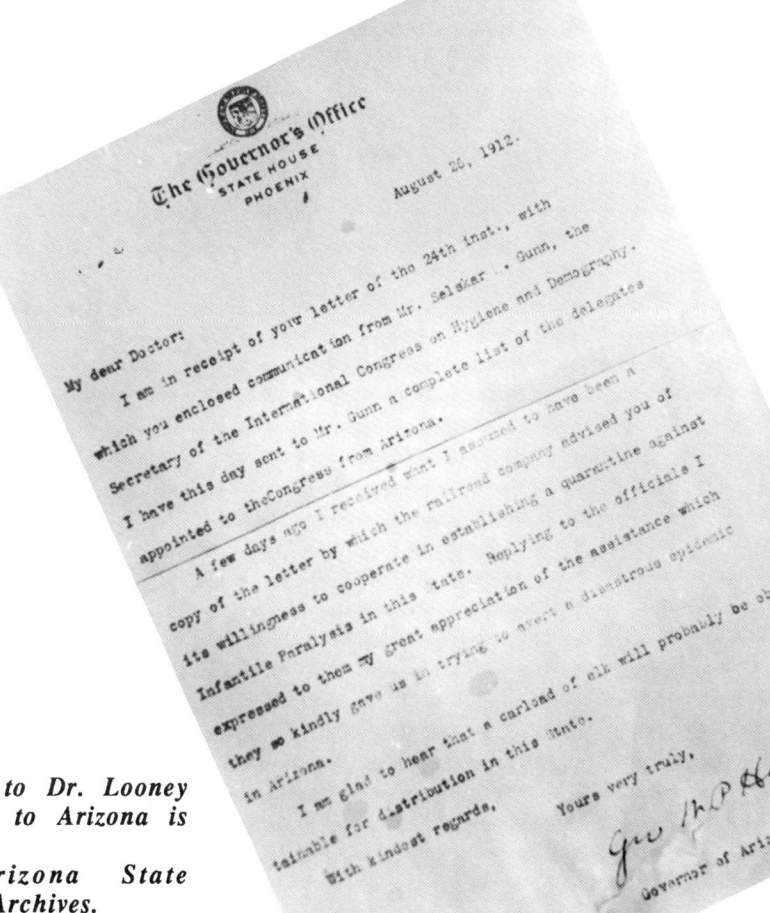

Letter from Governor Hunt to Dr. Looney in which return of the elk to Arizona is mentioned.
Photo courtesy of Arizona State Department of Library and Archives.

undertaking. The Elks Lodge of Arizona made this one of their projects and raised a considerable amount of money. The elk were corraled near Gardner, Montana, by Mr. Anderson, and shipped by stock cars, arriving in Winslow, February 16, 1913. The actual number loaded was 86 head, although the Department of the Interior authorized only 80 head. Anderson put in a few extra. According to Eldridge, (5) "they were shipped, double first class, traveling 24 hours and resting the same period, accompanied by a competent keeper the entire distance to Winslow, Arizona."

The 86 head of elk were 4 grown cows, 14 bulls, and 68 yearling heifers. Of the entire head, four were lost, one enroute and three on the way to the corral at the R. C. Cresswell summer camp at Cabin Draw. This is about 45 miles south of Winslow, Arizona, in the Sitgreaves National Forest. The elk were allowed to stay in the pens at the stockyards 12 days. They were then loaded into 12 wagons which were under the supervision of 11 men using 24 horses and 1 saddle horse. On their way to the corral, in the Sitgreaves Forest, they encountered a blizzard on March 13, 1913.

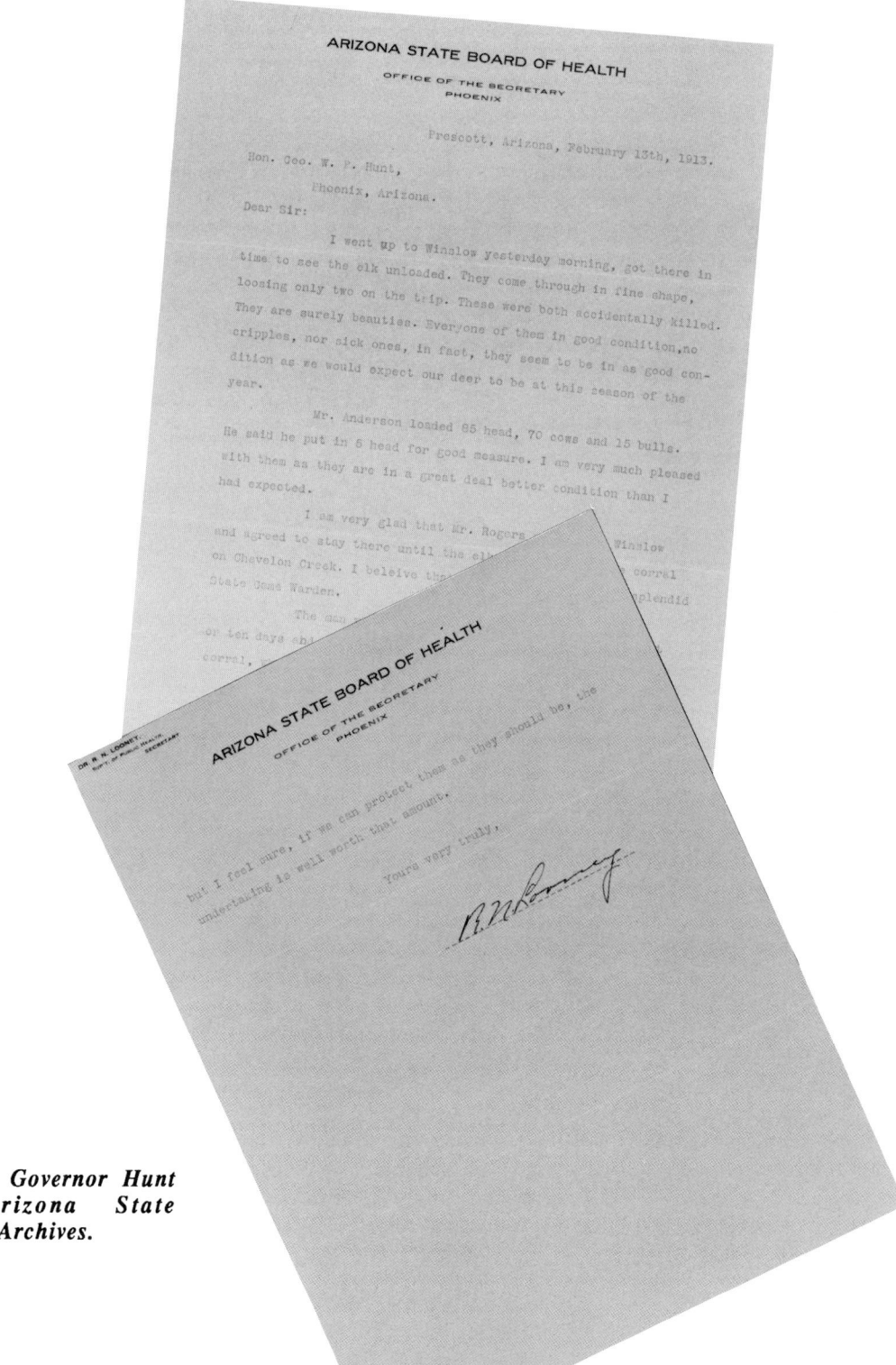

A letter from Dr. Looney to Governor Hunt Photo courtesy of Arizona State Department of Library and Archives.

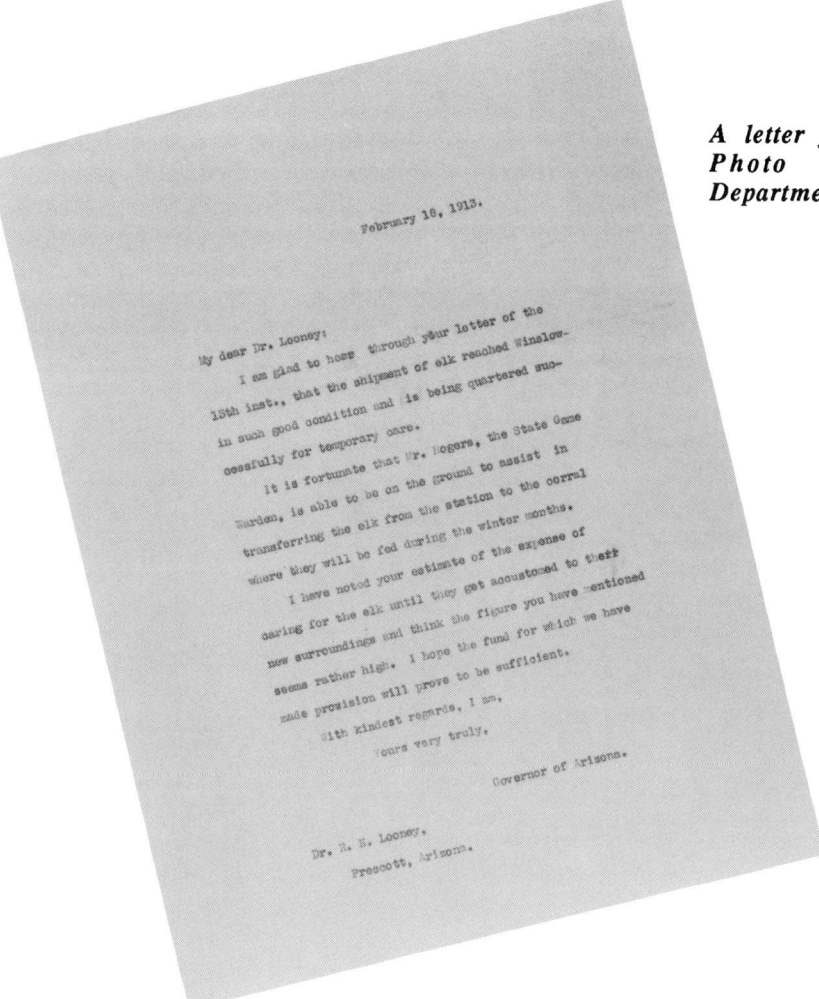

A letter from Governor Hunt to Dr. Looney Photo courtesy of Arizona State Department of Library and Archives.

They camped the first night 25 miles south of Winslow. One of the men who made the trip stated that it began sleeting abut 2:00 a.m., and by the time they started at five o'clock the next morning, the snow was a couple of inches deep. It continued to snow all during that day and it was with great difficulty that they got the wagons to the Creswell Ranch. (5)

Doctor Looney wrote, April 23, 1913, "On arrival in Winslow, the elk were in fine condition. They were held at Winslow about one week and then hauled in crates, built on wagons, 50 miles distance and placed in a corral where they were fed and cared for until April first. In moving them from the corral at Winslow to the enclosure on the range, three head were lost by being trampled to death. The last I heard, two weeks ago, they were staying together and seemed to be doing well on the open range." (3) In September 1914, the state game warden, G. M. Willard, gave the condition of the new herd as follows: "According to reports, the herd must have scattered badly during the summer and fall of 1913; but nevertheless, 53 head of them got back and wintered about 15 miles further in the mountains than where they were originally liberated."

An old trapper who had considerable experience with elk in the northern states, and who

Fig. 535.—Vaccinating Lancet. $1.00.

saw these 53 head during the months of March and April of 1914, was very emphatic in the declaration that they were by long odds the finest herd of elk he had ever looked upon. Reports indicate that at least four calves were born to the herd for the year 1913. "Not a bad showing, since there were only 6 or 8 head old enough to calve." The final fund account by Windsor stated that the cost of capturing, transporting to Winslow, hay and supplies, crates and wagons to Cabin Draw, came to $2,125.57. H. Anderson for capturing and loading elk, $400; and A.T.& S.F. RR Company, freight and feed, $802.20; all together about $265 per head (3).

There were "small additional shipments of elk in the late 1920s from Yellowstone and these were released in the San Francisco mountains near Flagstaff, Bill Williams Mountain near Williams, Captain Mountain on the San Carlos Indian Reservation, and the Graham mountains in Graham County. On February 12, 1927, 22 head were released at Campbell Blue, south of Alpine, on the Coronado Trail, and an additional 30 head were released about this time in the Hualapai mountains, southeast of Kingman." (1) This comprised the total elk transplants back to Arizona, probably less than one hundred and forty animals. The first authorized elk hunt was in 1930, at which time 249 permits were sold. There were 249 hunters afield and 85 elk were harvested or a 34.1% hunter success. (6) It is further reported that about 12,400 elk have been harvested between 1936 and 1960, from these original transplants, the first and most important engineered by Doctor Looney. The Game and Fish Department states that mountain lions and poachers have not submitted a return, so that the total number of elk harvested is not exactly known.

References:

1. Kartchner, K.C., *Elk Transplanting in Arizona*, Proceedings of the 20th Annual Conference of the Western Association of State Game and Fish Commission, pp. 145-149, 1950.
2. Shore, W. B., *Trapping and Shipping Elk*, Outdoor Life, XXX No. 2, pp. 96-104, August 1912.
3. Looney, Robert N., Historical Archives, Arizona, Department of Health, Phoenix, 1912-13.
4. Swank, Wendell G., *Bull versus Hunters Choice, the History of Elk Management in Arizona*, Arizona Game and Fish Department, 1954.
5. Eldridge, O. C., *How the First Elk Herd Was Brought to Arizona*, BPOE Elks No. 256, Meteor Winslow, Arizona, October, 1955. (The most complete and factual description of this event.)
6. Bulletin, Game Management Division, Arizona Game and Fish Department, Recommendations on 1961-1962 Hunting Seasons.

Remnants of a wagon used to haul elk from Winslow to the Chevron Creek area in 1912. Photo courtesy of O. C. Eldridge.

Florence Nightingale-Mission Impossible

Born in 1820 to parents of wealth and station, in England, she was to spend her early life in England and traveling on the Continent, but all the while dissatisfied with her inability to follow the usual tenor of her place in society or to marry. By 1845 she had made a partial break with her family and was determined to somehow study nursing. But this the Nightingales viewed with great horror. "In 1845 hospitals were places of wretchedness, degradation, and squalor. Hospital smell; the result of dirt and poor sanitation was accepted as unavoidable and was commonly so overpowering that persons entering the wards for the first time were seized with nausea. Wards were usually large, bare, and gloomy. Fifty or sixty beds were crammed in, less than two feet apart. Even decency was impossible."

This is how Cecil Woodham-Smith described conditions in his biography of Miss Nightingale, published in 1951. And it is from this delightful and searching narrative of her life that most of this material is extracted. Perhaps if every member of the nursing profession today perused this lively biography they would have better insight into the conditions of hospitals when Miss Nightingale embarked upon her career, which was to change nursing from one of the lowest levels of human employment to what is today a delightful and respected profession. Miss Nightingale wrote: "It was preferred, that nurses should be women who had lost their character, i.e. should have had one child. The level of decency among the patients was almost unbelievably low." She stressed bedside nursing. This seems to have lost its appeal to present day leaders.

The test of Miss Nightingale occurred when she had established a nursing home at One Harley Street in London but was drawn to the Crimea because of the tales of suffering of the British wounded. It was finally on November 3, 1854, in vicious weather that her little party sailed up the Bosphorus and gazed at the Asiatic shore where the enormous Barrack Hospital was located and was to be the scene of her travail. This enormous Turkish barracks still stands in what is called the Asiatic Scutari section and it is quite an imposing structure as you sail along the Bosphorus or gaze at it from the European side across to this enormous building which still sits like a hovering fortification. It is said that Miss Nightingale's office is still preserved in this barrack as a museum, but on a recent visit there, thanks to the present political climate, we were politely informed that this was now the headquarters of the First Turkish Army and that no visitors could be allowed. "The form of the

Florence Nightingale
Photo courtesy of the National Library of Medicine, Bethesda, Md.

St. Thomas' Hospital, built in London in 1868-71. It became the name for Nurses' Training School founded in appreciation of Florence Nightingale's work. The foundation stone was laid by Queen Victoria on May 13, 1868.
Photo courtesy of Arizona Medicine.

building was a hollow square with towers at each corner. One side had been gutted in a fire and could not be used. The courtyard in the center was a sea of mud littered with refuse. Within the vast ramifications of the barracks was a depot for troops, canteen where spirits were sold, and a stable for cavalry horses. Deep in the cellars were dark and noisome dens where more than two hundred women, who had been allowed by an oversight to accompany the army, drank, starved, gave birth to infants, carried on their trade as prostitutes, and died of cholera. The vast building hid a more fatal secret than met the eye. Sanitary defects made it a pest house, and the majority of the men who died there, died not of the wounds or sickness with which they arrived, but disease they contracted as a result of being in the hospital. When the war was over, it was found that the mortality in each regiment depended on the number of men which that regiment had been able to send to Scutari."

Remember that the main battle at Sebastopol was a day and a night at least, by ship, away from the Bosphorus and Scutari! "British army hospitals were a joint project of the commissariat, the Purveyors Department and the Medical Department and officials were trained not to spend money and never to risk responsibility." (Now our bureaucrats have no compunction whatever about spending money but the risk of responsibility stills fills them with horror.) When she reported to the hospital with her forty nurses she was immediately "stonewalled." The medical staff, in spite of the appalling conditions, made it plain that she was not welcome, and refused to give her more than the most depressing quarters, so that in the beginning all that she could do with the nurses was to cook some food. Then the real crunch came because that winter the hospital was absolutely without food, blankets, supplies or the vaguest type of any equipment or medicine whatever.

They soon learned that Miss Nightingale did control an abundance of supplies which was pouring in under her charge, and she had money, thirty thousand pounds credit with the authority to spend it. By the end of December she was "purveying the whole hospital, supplies, food, service." By this time reports had begun to filter back to England of the deplorable conditions and the government sent out a sanitary commission. Their report was devastating and they further reported that except for Miss Nightingale the hospital would have collapsed completely during the winter of 1854-55. Now she was recognized and had the co-operation of the medical authorities but as soon as the emergency abated the old jealousy reawakened and until her return to England in the summer of 1856, except for the gratitude of the troops, she was the continual target of bickering, jealousy and all of the other great attributes with which one human being can torture another.

Finally when she was ordered back to England, "she felt that her mission there had been more or less a failure but in England she was already a national heroine, and would remain so as long as she lived." By 1856 she had cleaned up the hospital, for now it was finally in the charge of a great personal friend, General Storks, a library had been established for the soldiers, food of a nutritious and wholesome character was provided, sanitation had been inaugurated, a method had been worked out for soldiers to send their pay home instead of spending it in the canteen on liquor; this apparently had never been accomplished before in the whole history of the British army. More than that, "during the winter of 1855-56, the picture of the British soldier as a drunken, intractable brute disappeared never to return." She taught, said one eyewitness, "officers and officials to treat the soldiers as Christian gentlemen."

Finally a general order officially recognized her position, "placed all nurses under her orders, none to be transferred without her consent, she was the general superintendent of the female nursing establishment for the Military Hospitals of the British Army." On July 16, 1856 the last patient left the Barracks Hospital. This is how her biographer summarizes her accomplishments in the Crimea. "Miss Nightingale had stamped the profession of nursing with her own image. Jane Evans and her buffalo calf, Mother Bridgeman and her proselytizing, Mary Stanley's ladies and their gentility, the hired nurses and their gin have faded from history. The nurse who emerged from the Crimea, strong and pitiful*, controlled the fate of suffering, unselfseeking, superior to consideration of class or sex was Miss Nightingale herself. She ended the Crimean War obsessed by a sense of failure. In fact, in the midst of the muddle and filth, the agony and the defects, she had brought about a revolution." The British navy wanted to send a special ship for her return to England but she evaded all of her well wishers, landed in London and went to her home unbeknownst to all even her close family. "In the succeeding years she never made a public appearance, attended a public function, or made a public statement."

She met Queen Victoria and became her confidant. Through unremitting personal pressure she forced a royal commission to investigate the entire British medical service and to inaugurate many changes which she personally recommended. She spent her life working behind the scenes always to improve the lot of the nursing profession and most of all, the patient. By the time of her death August 13, 1910, over two thousand nurses' training schools had been founded all over the world, the majority of them in the United States. Not one nursing school of this type existed when she spent that harrowing winter in Scutari at the Barracks in 1855-56. Indeed she did accomplish the impossible mission to which she assigned herself.

*Obviously, the biographer meant "compassionate."

Reference:

Woodham-Smith, Cecil, *Florence Nightingale, 1820-1910*, McGraw-Hill Co., New York, London, 1951.

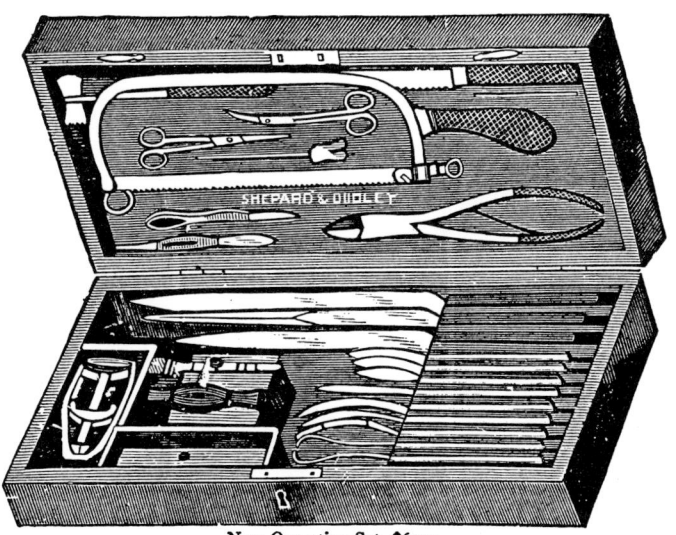

New Operating Set, $60.00.

Florence Nightingale—The Revolting Revisionist Historian Perspective.

It was bound to happen, but nonetheless it is exasperating. Quite innocently one of us asked a recent RN graduate, university type, what had been said of Florence Nightingale. "Oh," she cheerfully rejoined, "Flo had syphilis." Since we were sure that this was simply an aberrant sampling, other recent graduates of the nursing profession were asked the same question and about two out of three came up with the same "syphilis vomit." Pressed as to what else Miss Nightingale may have contributed to the women's lib or nursing education there seemed to be little if any knowledge. Something about "she carried a lamp in a war and was thought to have been a nurse." So with this great new generation, the permissive crowd, which has reintroduced syphilis and gonorrhea in epidemic proportions, we have the revisionists, historians who feel that they must be mean and belittle anyone of historic fame. Why they should direct their venom to this brilliant woman who brought their profession, nursing, literally from the gutter to that of respect and knowledge, just why they should wish to do it to Miss Nightingale, is beyond the ken of "us squares."

When Miss Nightingale died at the turn of the century (1910) there were over a thousand approved schools of nursing flourishing here in these United States alone. When she went to the Crimea in 1853, not a one existed. Just as President Lincoln, when told of General Grant's alcoholic propensities allowed, well if he could find generals to win battles like Grant, he would gladly supply the nectar. So if the present revisionists could discover a pristine leader, an innovative someone to bring nursing care away from the ill equipped nurses' aides and place it back into the hands of qualified trained nurses, they are welcome to all of the tickling from the treponema pallidum which their cerebral cortex can harbor. Perhaps such a leader could re-discover and re-splendorize bedside nursing which, except for those jewels in special care units, and an occasional ward nurse who has not yet been surrounded by glass and turned into a pencil pusher, some of us would welcome such a saint on the scene. And while the present faculties of nursing contemplate the blood gasses, chemotherapy, physicians' assistants, and all those other exotic goodies of present day hospitals, they might pay passing attention to the fields of medicine which Miss Nightingale enlightened and originated such as: Bedside nursing; hospital construction to make the rooms light and airy and cheerful; proper diet care and preparation; record keeping, record the observations on signs and symptoms of the patient and the nursing procedures given.

Florence Nightingale forced the re-organization of the medical department of the

British army against the bureaucratic odds of gigantic proportions. "The mortality of the Crimean disaster, 73% in six months from disease alone was the ghastly fruit, not of war, but of the system which controlled the health administration of the British army." (And we might add also it was the product of the unenlightened physicians who were in charge of it.) "After Miss Nightingale's return from the Crimea she never made a public appearance, never attended a public function, never issued a public statement. All that she accomplished thereafter was done by goading and friends and government functionaries." She became a confidante of Queen Victoria and gained leverage over the dilatory government bureaucracy.

She had many setbacks and failures and this not infrequently drove her into long periods of melancholy and depression. None of the records of her health or her work make any mention of a leuetic infection and just where this myth arose, except in the pea-brains who now teach non-bedside nursing, has yet to be disclosed. And if any of these great revisionists think she was a prude and not knowledgeable about the facts of life you might consider what she wrote in 1862 about the causes of vice in the army believing they were "moral but not physical. They are," she wrote, "1. Filthy, crowded dwellings. 2. Drunkenness. 3. Ignorance and want of occupation." The way to improve the soldiers' morale was to improve his living conditions. "In civil life you don't expect that every workman who does not marry before he is thirty will become diseased," she wrote in 1861. "In military life you do. Why? Because a workman may have occupation and amusement and consort with honest women. People always say a woman can't know anything about it. It is because I know more about the actual working of the thing than most men, that I cannot hold my tongue."

She advanced views with such force that in 1862 she was officially invited to submit a paper, giving her first hand experience in barracks and hospitals. Her study of the administration of the army in India and her recommendations for sanitary change in conditions there made her position "in Indian affairs" even more extraordinary than her position at the war office. "She had never been to India, she never did to go India, yet she was considered an expert on India and consulted on the affairs by men who lived there all of their working lives. She possessed prodigious powers of absorbing, retaining and marshalling masses of facts, and when she completed her task, a whole vast, teeming country lay before her mind's eye like a map."

Three years after she returned from the Crimea, at constant urging, she had worked out the plans for a nursing school. One of her biographers describes the selection of the matron. "Mrs. Wardroper, matron of St. Thomas's Hospital, a gentle woman by birth, had been left a widow at the age of 42 and had taken up nursing," Miss Nightingale wrote, "Her force of character was extraordinary, and she learned from intuition." She was appointed matron of St. Thomas in 1853 and held the post of superintendent of the Nightingale Training School for 27 years and the greatest part of the success of the school was due to "her energy and determination." In May 1910 and the Jubilee year of the founding of the Nightingale Training School, there were over one thousand training schools for nurses in the United States alone. Syphilis, indeed!

References:

1. Nutting, M. Adelaide, R.N., and Dock, Lavinial, R.N., *History of Nursing,* Vol. II, G.P. Putnam's Son, London, 1907.
2. Woodham-Smith, Cecil, *Florence Nightingale 1820-1910* , McGraw-Hill, New York, 1951.
3. Kinglake, R. , *The Invasion of the Crimea,* Vol. VI, London, 1880, p. 409.

Blood Banking History in Arizona

The Salt River Valley Blood Bank was finally opened for operation on October 4, 1943, so writes one of the founders of this institution in Volume 1, No.1, *Arizona Medicine*, 1944. This original name can hardly be recognized from the present organizational name, "Blood Services of Arizona."

Doctor Louis Baldwin, commenting upon the early trials and tribulations in the organization of the blood bank proceeded further to state, "About two years ago, the Maricopa County Medical Association felt that because of the size of the community, because of the difficulty of obtaining blood in adequate amounts at a moment's notice, and because of the need for plasma, not only for civilian use, but for military hospitals in this area, a blood bank should be established."

At a meeting it was therefore voted by the members that the Maricopa Medical Society would sponsor a blood bank and that it would elect three of its members to sit on the executive committee of the blood bank and that these members in turn would elect a member of the medical auxiliary and a lawyer to make up the five members of the executive committee, the function of this body being to direct all the policies and attend to all the work necessary for the establishment of this organization.

Over a period of several months, the necessary money was raised by private contribution, from individuals, from business concerns and as well from the United War Fund. Money was also advanced by the county as a deposit against a withdrawal of blood and plasma in the treatment of the county poor. With this capital, the necessary architectural changes were made in the east wing of the Social Service Center, generously donated to house the bank, the actual labor and cost of the materials having been donated.

After a certain number of priority difficulties, the Salt River Valley Blood Bank was finally opened for operation on October 4, 1943. Doctor Baldwin further comments upon the policies of the blood bank and mentioned some areas of research and study that would be followed in the future by the bank. Today, Blood Services has blood banks in 22 cities covering 12 states. This system serves 827 hospitals and is the largest medically sponsored not-for-profit blood bank system in the nation. Last year alone Blood Services furnished 204,965 transfusions, traveling almost one million miles to get the blood to the hospitals it serves.

Blood Services also maintains a Reference Laboratory Service to assist hospitals with immunohematology problems. In addition, over $100,000 has been spent in research projects dealing with testing for hepatitis and antibodies in plasma. No doubt the present organization will have a suitable commemoration of their twenty-fourth anniversary this fall, but they should not forget that the founders were members of the Maricopa County Medical Society, and it is due to their efforts and theirs alone that the early organization was put together and made to work.

Cupping Apparatus, Scarificator.

XVII.

Arizona Medical History Quiz

Almost every journal now has a section devoted to continuing medical education. Indeed, membership in our own state association is predicated upon assiduously applying ourselves for hours to these great and laudable endeavors. So, with the spirit of the times, the following short review of some territorial and early state medical happenings is presented. Sorry, this is a no credit course.

Question 1.

Name this fabulous, but now little known Nogales physician who had the following exciting travels. Born in London 1838, died in Nogales, Arizona 1931. Entered the British army and served in South Africa, and after twelve years service left to study medicine. He entered medical practice in 1865 in the State of Nebraska and later the Wyoming area. Then on to Eureka, Utah to practice, when this was a booming mining camp. The camp folded, and in 1873 he pushed on to California and practiced in San Francisco three years. He was then enticed to come to Arizona and settled in Oro Blanco, eight miles south of Arivaca, and here he established the only medical practice between Tucson A.T. and Hermosillo, Sonora, Mexico. A post office there was named after his family name and, of course, the postmistress was the doctor's wife. Another depression halted mining operations and he then moved to Nogales in 1893. Here he practiced for many years. He served in many city, county and state positions of trust.

Question 2.

What Phoenix physician and his wife spearheaded the drive to establish a blood bank in Arizona in WW II times? When did the Maricopa County Medical Society take affirmative action to sponsor the undertaking?

Question 3.

This "beloved practitioner of the art," for so he was regarded by many patients and fellow practitioners alike, practiced in Tucson some 38 years. He wrote some delightful recollections of his early practice in Tucson and especially those experiences when he assisted Doctor George Goodfellow in early perineal prostatectomies. He served on the Board of Regents of the University of Arizona and for one term was the Chancellor. Along with Orville Harry Brown, M.D. of Phoenix, this Tucson physician began a collection of Arizona medical histories.

Question 4.

What Arizona physician and surgeon served over 40 years with the U. S. Army and National Guard as a line officer, but never as a military surgeon, starting service on the border before WW I?

Question 5.

What Phoenix physician was first to diagnose a case of "rabbit fever," a disease later recognized as tularemia? He was also the first ophthalmologist to practice in the state as a specialist, brought the first x-ray tube to the state, and also the first magnet designed to remove foreign metallic bodies from the eye.

Question 6.

Who is credited with being the first to perform perineal prostatectomies?

Question 7.

This pioneer Phoenix surgeon first proposed inspection on the accreditation of hospitals to the American College of Surgeons and proposed that aid stations be set up on a national scale to give first aid in traffic accidents. The latter was adopted in a modified form by the American Red Cross.

Question 8.

What Prescott physician recognized that "hydrophobia skunks" were not a special species as indeed the Department of Agriculture promulgated, but simply rabid skunks?

Question 9.

What U. S. Army surgeon serving in Arizona at the time, won a Congressional Medal of Honor for his action in one of the last campaigns against the Apaches, when Geronimo was finally captured? This medical officer later commanded the Rough Riders, Roosevelt was the executive officer. He went on to become governor general of Cuba, chief of staff of the United States Army, and later governor general of the Philippines.

Question 10.

At what Arizona territorial army fort did Walter Reed serve as an army surgeon long before his yellow fever research made him famous?

Question 11.

This fabulous early Prescott physician reintroduced elk into northern Arizona after they had become extinct. As a matter of fact, they had all been murdered by hunters. He also served as a state health officer, and on one occasion cleaned up a smallpox epidemic in the Benson-Douglas area by carrying in his pocket an authority to declare martial law, granted by the governor, if the residents down there didn't turn to and implement the quarantine which the local health officer had tried to enforce.

Question 12.

This physician came to Arizona about 1869 as an acting assistant surgeon in the army. He had a proclivity for trouble. In 1870 he shot and killed Mr. Hughey, a settler at Camp Thomas. But, apparently nothing ever came of it. By 1871 he had left the army and announced the opening of his office in Church Plaza opposite the convent in Tucson, A.T. In 1873 he was selected by the Pima board of supervisors to care for the indigent since his bid for this service was lowest. It included attendance upon the indigent sick of the county, sick in the county jail for $45 per month, for hospital accommodations to include board, lodging, washing, fuel, water etc., for the first patient at $55 per month and each additional one for $50 a month. He served on the board of regents of the University of Arizona and was the first chancellor. On September 25,1891 he engaged in a street fight with an attorney, Francis J. Heney, and during the altercation the doctor was shot. In fact, his belly was perforated several times. This occurred at Church and Pennington streets in Tucson. Doctor Goodfellow, then famous for his treatment of gunshot wounds in Tombstone, was summoned. Goodfellow operated and repaired the intestinal wounds, but the wounded doctor died of shock and hemorrhage. It turned out that the attorney, Mr. Heney, represented the doctor's wife in her suit for divorce, this led to the ill feeling. At the conclusion of the hearing the attorney was released by the judge who stated, "The conclusion I arrive at in this, is that the defendant in this instance, acted in necessary self-defense and committed a justifiable homicide."

ANSWERS

1. Doctor Adolphus H. Noon, 1838-1931.

2. Doctor and Mrs. Louis Baldwin. They made a presentation before the Maricopa Medical Society at its regular meeting on February 7, 1944. Now this organization is known to us as Blood Services with headquarters in Scottsdale and with processing and service centers in over twenty major cities scattered through the Midwest, southern and western states. It has long since become an independent service and no longer affiliated with its parent, the Maricopa County Medical Society.

3. Doctor W. W. Whitmore, 1862-1940.

4. Doctor Alexander McKenzie Tuthill, M.D., Captain, Second Troop Cavalry, National Guard 1905, Colonel, 158th Infantry, National Guard, 1910; Brigadier General, 79th Brigade, 40th Division, U. S. Army 1917; Major General, commanding 45th Infantry Division National Guard 1928; Lt. General, Arizona National Guard, 1952.

5. Doctor Ancil Martin, 1861-1926. He described the first case of "jack rabbit fever" in 1907, one possibly as early as 1902, but not until 1911 was the true etiology recognized by Frances of the United States Public Health Service, who credits Doctor Martin as the "the father of a disease."

6. If you don't know this one you haven't been reading very closely the last few paragraphs, Doctor George Goodfellow, then practicing in Tucson, Arizona.

7. E. Payne Palmer, M.D., 1876-1960.

8. C. E. Yount, Sr. M.D, 1874-1954.

9. Doctor Leonard Wood, first stationed at Fort Huachuca, Arizona.

10. Fort Apache, A.T., where his eldest son was born.

11. Doctor Robert N. Looney, 1871-1962.

12. Thus ended the career of the early Arizona physician, Doctor J. C. Handy.

XVIII.

Willa (Billie) Kennedy
1910-1984

This is to thank all who were friends and associates of Willa. I thought a few notes on her terrestrial tour might be apropos. As many of you know—late in life—she seemed to gather strength for world forays. Postwar Europe twice, Africa, Russia, Afghanistan, Nepal, India, Australia, New Zealand, Malaysia, Thailand, Tahiti, Chinese Peoples' Republic, twice, and Hong Kong, many times, Philippines, Japan, Korea—she looked upon these trips as high adventure!

Born in Holcomb—a farming community in southeast Missouri—she never lost her love for the land and rural values. Born 27 December 1910—died 29 January 1984. The youngest of a family of seven children, her father died when she was eight. The family fell into dire straits and quickly disintegrated. She clung to her mother. She was determined to finish grade and high school, usual now but perilous at her place and time. Meantime the family had dribbled to Flint, Michigan, where for a time she did factory work. The depression, strikes and union disorders made this living precarious. So with her usual foresight and fortitude, she enrolled in nurse's training at Hurley Hospital in Flint, Michigan. After graduation she was to become office manager, nurse assistant, surgical nurse—a one woman factotum to Doctor W. W. Stevenson, a busy eye, ear, nose and throat specialist. She later observed that when she entered the Army Nurse Corps in 1942 that three girls were hired to do her work!

First station, Lawton General Hospital Atlanta, Georgia Stateside duty was not for her—on to the 300th General Hospital training at Camp Forest, Tennessee. This was a Vanderbilt Unit—with, as was usual in those affiliated units,—a closed society to outsiders for promotion. Thence to the 39th Evacuation Hospital staging at Camp Forrest for shipment overseas. She became the room-and-tent-mate of Byrle (Danny) Waters and a friendship formed steadfast to the last.

Her talents were finally recognized when the unit entered combat in Normandy just prior to the Avranches breakthrough. The shock ward, which now carries the name of "intensive care" and other "hifalutin" terms in present day civilian hospitals, the shock ward at our first set-up in France—became itself—a disaster area. The C. O. to his credit—little else was credible—directed First Lieut. Willa Hinkle to take charge and clean it up! He promised supplies and personnel to do it and kept his promise. This nurse—First Lieut. Hinkle—didn't suffer stupid nurses, corpsmen or medical officers lightly!

Billie had total recall and some years later began writing her WW II experiences. For some years laid it aside and in the last few months she had resumed but got no further than Morhange, France when the Third Army swung north to relieve Bastogne. Her decorations include: The Legion of Merit, ETO Ribbon with 5 battle stars, American Defense, etc. Billie resigned from the Army in 1949.

We were married in Denver, Colorado at the Fort Logan Chapel. The chapel subsequently burned, the state took over most of the post and populated it with psychotics! That says something, not sure what. For a few months we lived in Denver—where I was employed by the VA—a first class disaster area! Thence to Phoenix, where we lived since January 1950. All this time, until we both retired from the army reserve, we were assigned to a local general hospital reserve unit. She as chief nurse and was the first army reserve nurse in the state to attain the rank of lieutenant colonel.

She had a major break in health in 1952—but took up life and duties full blast—in spite of a limited physical capacity—which she concealed from the army and many friends. Her subsequent surgical and medical history was dismal. Nonetheless she went all out in the army reserve,

First Lieutenant Willa R. Hinkle, ANC
U. S. Army Nurse Corps, 1944.
Author's collection of photos.

figure skating, civil defense lectures, (her stance was unpopular with the local defense slotfillers) the Women's Overseas League and was founder and charter member of Scottsdale Sweet Adelines. Although inactive of late—she took great pride in the accomplishments of the Scottsdale chapter. But it was the Army Nurse Corps that held her most cherished and lasting memories. Despite her diminished physical stamina she became an accomplished gourmet cook—Chinese and Japanese cuisine especially.

In 1966 she stood a retirement retreat ceremony at Fort Huachuca—a place where we both enjoyed some reserve active duty summer training. In late years she was affectionately known as The Little Colonel or Squaw Peak Billie—a nom de plume she sometimes used in writing. So to all of us she has said her last farewell.

XIX.

Billie
Squaw Peak Notes

The following pages, while not containing material relevant to the medical history of Arizona, have been included as a supplement to this volume because they, too, are historical, albeit anecdotal, in content, and, as such, of interest to the medical historian. They were written by Mrs. John W. Kennedy, wife of the principal author of this volume, and entail her often amusing experiences as an army nurse during World War II, both in the United States and in Europe. The experiences of that war created many strange and often grim circumstances which Mrs. Kennedy, in these pages, reports with a sanity-saving sense of humor that makes her accounts delightful reading. Medicine, both military and civilian, has made remarkable progress during the 20th century, with most of the advances stemming from the desperate needs that accompany the ravages of war. But too often, science and administration fail to keep pace or even contact with each other. The results are the snafus and frustrations that have given rise to a bit of doggerel that was popular during World War II. It goes: "Guys who want to be a hero are practically zero. But guys who want to be civilians can be counted in the millions." The episodes described herein by Mrs. Kennedy give ample support to that observation. Readers of Mrs. Kennedy's adventures and misadventures as an army nurse will find a distinct aura of similarity between the experiences she describes and those so well and humorously portrayed in the late, long-running television series, M*A*S*H. However, we are assured by Doctor Kennedy that there is not the slightest actual connection between the two. Like so many important scientific discoveries, each were developed independently of the other.

"Billie," (Mrs. Kennedy) "never submitted any ideas or wrote anything for M*A*S*H," Doctor Kennedy said. But, in the opinion of this writer, she could have. In fact, she could have written the entire series!

J. DeV.

First Lieutenant Willa R. Hinkle, Army Nurse Corps, draws her water ration from a Lister bag, used in the field to purify water for human use.
Author's collection of photos.

SQUAW PEAK NOTES I
MY INDOCTRINATION

Jake reports that he is "un-cerebrated" and has asked (forced) me to write the article for this issue.

Thirty years ago, June 6, 1944, we were jolted out of a deep sleep by the roar of planes. To find out if they were the usual "Bed Check Charlies," Nazi pilots, we went outside where we could see distinctive white crosses on the sides of the planes. It was the beginning of "D" day in Europe.

We were in a general hospital six miles out of Cirencester, England, where we had been sent for further military training. Actually, the idea was to get us off the streets of Manchester, England, where we were billeted in British private homes. We had been there for six months undergoing more military training and drawing equipment for our hospital unit, prior to joining Gen. Patton's 3rd Army in the assault on France.

The way I happened to be there is quite a saga of army intrigue. I entered the army on the 1st of April, 1942, commissioned as a second lieutenant. My ignorance of the army was phenomenal. I knew that there were men in it and that they were fighting a war. Yep, I was single at the time. Being curious, (not yellow) was my reason for volunteering.

My indoctrination began with a few basic instructions. I would not be permitted to socialize with anyone lower than a second lieutenant. Having written my mother of this fact she wanted to know, "What is lower than a second lieutenant?" Nurses at that time had only "relative" rank and a very poor relative at that. We had all the privileges of officers but not the pay. We received the total sum of $60 a month plus subsistence and uniforms.

Outfitted in my new army white uniform, bars and caduceus in the proper places, I ventured on duty. I didn't know a private from a general and was ready to try and salute anything that wore a uniform. (I really had no idea of how to salute and did a lot of out-of-the-way walking in order not to come face to face with someone else in uniform.)

When I signed up for duty, I was given a list of installations and was told I could choose whichever I wanted to join. I didn't know the difference between a general hospital and an evacuation or field unit. All I was anxious for was to be shipped overseas.

So, I chose the Lawson General Hospital in Atlanta. The nurses here were not very encouraging. They told me I would be stuck there for the duration. It was a "fixed" hospital and wouldn't go anywhere, they said. If one did go, it was a numbered general hospital and it went to one place and spent the duration there. I was shattered. Going through channels, (mostly sewers) I got a list of hospitals that were ready for overseas service and signed up with six of them.

The first unit that got me was the 300th General from Vanderbilt University. There was a cadre of personnel from Vanderbilt and the rest of the unit was made up of casual personnel like myself. I joined the unit at Camp Forrest, Tenn. From the beginning it was obvious that an outsider wouldn't have a chance for promotion. The alumni got first choice. The chief nurse was promoted to captain within exactly one month of service.

We began our basic military training with close-order drill, formal retreat parades and the whole smear. We began at reveille, and it was a mess, because none of us had any idea of what to do or how to do it! But that was quickly remedied. We were lined up on the parade ground in four platoons of 30 women each. We had a captain (Mac) whom we called a male WAC who indoctrinated us into the close-order drill routine. After the first day of commands and lousy executions, each platoon was assigned a platoon leader. Naturally, due to my big mouth, I was chosen to be one of them.

It was our duty as platoon leaders to give the commands for our respective platoons. The old barracks hall rang out with commands and executions as the four of us (in deep shock) marched back and forth trying to recall what each command was, which foot to execute it with and how to communicate it to the rest of the platoon. It was a disaster for the first couple of weeks, but then we began to shape up.

Our days began at 0600 with fall out for reveille, breakfast and then the day's activities. We had classes in every phase of military training, close-order drill and field marches.

Eventually we became proficient in all the marches and drills. So much so that we were ordered to march in a retreat parade before all the "brass" of Vanderbilt University.

The day of the parade was "ungood," rain and a light drizzle with no sun visible. The nurses' uniforms were starched white cotton with cap, white shoes and stockings, navy blue wool capes and black overshoes over white shoes. I was the first platoon leader and first to begin the parade, out front barking out commands with the platoon sharply executing them. Bellowing out cadence between commands.

We had executed the first turn when I happened to glance at the grass ahead of us and saw a wriggling mass of gray fur. My voice was clearly audible for all to hear, but it wasn't cadence, it was a scream and the platoon spread like an accordion. It turned out to be a nest of rabbits! When they were removed the parade began again, with my eyes glued out front from then on. The drizzle continued throughout the parade and we finished with our white caps flat on our heads like big, wet rags, and our white uniforms and stockings spattered with mud. We were anything but sex kittens. Wonder why I was passed over for promotion?

Author's collection of photos.

Lt. Hinkle in England, WW II
Author's collection of photos.

After six months of training, orders came for us to depart for the port of embarkation. At the same time, I got orders from the other six hospital units I had signed up with. But I ended up staying with the unit because our commanding officer assured me we were going overseas.

Author's collection of photos.

Lt. Hinkle in England, WW II
Author's collection of photos.

So, we stencilled our names on all of our gear and were ready for the big moment. But, it never came and our orders were cancelled. Instead, we were assigned to duty at the station hospital at Camp Forrest. It looked as if my future had ended as far as overseas duty was concerned.

U. S. Army nurses of the 39th Evacuation Hospital take a brief respite in England during WW II. Lt. Hinkle is at the far right.
Author's collection of photos.

SQUAW PEAK NOTES II
THOSE WERE THE DAYS—ARMY LIFE

Tic-toc, tramp, tramp. Time marched and training continued, with close-order drills, formal retreat parades, lectures, training films on everything from VD to sex education, military discipline and ad infinitum.

On one of our 25-mile hikes with all 120 females, the drill instructor made me the commanding officer for the whole thing. This was ego-inflating for me to be able to yell out commands to that many women and not have them retaliate with a few thousand words.

We departed early in the morning and were returning to the camp parade grounds late in the afternoon, and marching at "route step," meaning they could talk and keep in formation but not in step.

Our approach to the grounds was through a wooded area along a dirt road used by heavy vehicles. In front of us on the parade ground a corporal and a squad of new recruits were going through the rudiments of close-order drill. To show how sharp we were, I called the company to attention and began counting cadence, really strutting out in front. The corporal halted the recruits so they could watch and my ego just about reached the popping point.

Suddenly, directly in front of me, crawled a big, fat snake, in the process of crossing the road. When it got in the middle of the road it stopped and raised its head to get a good look at me, I thought. Well, I kept my cool but gave one of the fastest commands of my career. American soldiers never retreat, as everyone knows. I gave a "to the rear march" and we reversed on the double--while the enlisted men got their "enjoys" and my ego got deflated again.

Our next toughening-up event was the obstacle course used by the combat units, men only so far, but we changed that.

The course consisted of a large area, with three-foot trenches filled with water on either side. Crisscrossed over the top was barbed wire just high enough to crawl underneath. The object was to jump into the first trench of water then crawl underneath the wire while live shells exploded overhead. It meant you not only kept your head down but the rear end, as well. After completing the crawl across the course, you had to again fall into the trench filled with water, crawl out of that and then run 25 feet back to the safety zone. All of this was supervised by a combat unit which shot off the shells and watched from a high observation tower.

We did not have fatigues to wear and we didn't want to soil our civilian slacks either, so each of us borrowed a pair of fatigues from the men. Mine were much too large. So I ripped out the front belt, took a few tucks in the front and haphazardly sewed them up again. They fit better and I felt quite neat. We also wore leggings, the old fashioned type that laced up to just beneath the knees and into which the bottoms of the fatigues were tucked in to blouse over as the men wore them. To complete the outfit, we wore "Lil Abner" field shoes and the good old iron pot helmet and liner.

The day of the big event began with a cloudburst but then the sun came out and it got hot and sultry. We arrived on the scene in GI ambulances and then lined up to wait for the signal to crawl in. I took one look at that dirty water in the trench and the mud covered course under the barbed wire and hesitated jumping in. But someone gave me a gentle push and in I went. It was like crawling through thick grease, slippery and sticky. Half way across we had to turn over and finish the course on our backs. No one was curious enough to raise their heads for those machine gun bullets were coming over fast and loud.

I was the last one to get across, and after crawling out of the water in the other trench, I found it hard to run in the soaked pants. But I was so intent on getting out of that spot that I didn't know anything was amiss until I heard a loud guffawing and the public address system playing "Ain't She Sweet." When I finally got to the safety zone and looked at myself I discovered my stitches hadn't withstood the crawling and the weight of the water. They had parted in the middle and the middle was down to my knees. I looked for a place to hide but nothing larger than a blade of grass was available to get behind. Who says neatness pays?

Needless to say, we were enjoying ourselves and nothing we were doing had any relation to nursing whatever. We all gained weight but our clothes were smaller. We were about as solid as stone with not a sign of a bulge or flab. But we were never too tired after a day's activities to go out dancing at night. That was the only time we could dress in formal civilian clothes, to attend about three formal dances each week at either the officer's club or a division's smaller private club.

Our salary had risen to a fabulous $90 a month, all went for formal attire. Boyfriends were so numerous that each of us had about eight or more.

We were billeted two girls to a room in the men's barracks—wooden cantonment buildings with two floors, one latrine with only two showers for 120 women, male urinals plus four toilets, which were situated in the middle of the building. By the entrance was a recreation room with chairs and a desk, where one girl acted as hostess every night to call the girls for their dates.

My roommate and I had the top room over the recreation room. It had a tiny balcony over the front entrance and wooden ladder for a fire escape by the side of a small lower porch. Rather than go all the way back to the middle of the building to the staircase, when our dates arrived, we descended via the ladder, plopping down on the porch with a billowing formal, usually to the amazement of our dates.

We traveled to dances by motorcycle, tank, armored car, jeep, 6 x 6 army truck or else walked across the golf course, which had greens made of cotton seeds. After a rain you had to remove your shoes and wash them and your feet before proceeding to the night's activities. And if anyone enroute via the golf course sat down for any reason, it was easy to tell where they had been.

Our living quarters were something worth describing. We had two small army cots, with mattresses at least 2 inches thick with good old wire springs that let down in the middle and up on the sides. There was one window and a three-sided wooden closet for clothes with no front cover we called an "air raid shelter."

We ate at the station hospital mess hall, where we really got gourmet food. The mess sergeant had been a former meat inspector for the State of Michigan. Breakfast was ala carte, anything you wanted cooked to order. We had steaks that were unreal, lobster, shrimp, prime beef, hot rolls and pastry the Danes would envy. Army life was never so good and at the time we took it for granted. We thought we were roughing it. Ignorance is bliss and we were ecstatic.

The post field house provided us with bicycles which we used almost every day to ride out 9 miles to Cumberland Springs Lake where we would swim until dark and then ride back.

It was at this time that General Benny Lear got into a controversy over soldiers making "wolf calls" at some girls on the golf course. He was visiting Camp Forrest the day I took a ride on the bike, wearing a pair of shorts, and because it was chilly I had on boxing gloves to keep my hands warm. I was riding along the road with a second lieutenant from the armored division when Benny came along in an open jeep and saw us. The lieutenant saluted but I pretended to be a civilian and avoided getting the reprimand he got. Seems I never missed an opportunity to "goof."

The weeks dragged into months but no order came for us to depart for foreign shores. The orders we finally got were shattering. It cancelled the overseas orders, and assigned us to duty in the station hospital at Camp Forrest.

SQUAW PEAK NOTES III
CAMP FORREST

After a few weeks, orders arrived cancelling our overseas duty. We were then assigned to the station hospital at Camp Forrest, a wooden cantonment-type structure with approximately 2,500 beds, and a large prisoner of war installation with its own individual hospital.

We were made quite welcome by the nurses who had envied us our training activities while they had been pounding the ramps and taking care of patients. My first assignment was night duty. Twelve hours a night, seven days a week for one month, that was one of those 31-day months—the others didn't count even if it was February.

I was assigned to 13 wards, all connected by one enclosed ramp. (We were known then as "ramp tramps" for tramp we did, all night long.) I had the EENT (eye, ear, nose and throat) wards and one pneumonia ward for good measure, with from 25 to 30 patients in each ward and only one enlisted man in each ward to assist me. To say that I was busy was an understatement. I ran most of the night because the pneumonia ward was at one end and asthmatics on the other with the rest of the EENT patients scattered in between.

All medication had to be administered by a nurse but the enlisted men did help with back rubs and bed changing. At 11:00 p.m. bed checks had to be made and then at midnight we had to do the good old army morning reports. These had to be accurate, although they were sometimes a bit confusing, especially if some GI decided he was having too much fun to get in by my (not the army's) bed time. But I would cover for them. When the officer of the day came around with a flashlight to re-check my bed check, I would just make up the beds with pillows. They never caught my un-GI maneuver.

At the end of one month's night duty we were given two days off: one for sleeping and the other for recreation. The sleeping one was ignored and we took off instead for Atlanta, Chattanooga or other cities in the area, to take care of the recreation bit.

I requested duty in the EENT clinic after the night stint, because I was qualified for that job. I had been in charge of the one at Lawson General, and, in civilian nursing, I had worked for an EENT man as an assistant in surgery at the hospitals. In the office I was the anesthetist for tonsillectomies as well as the surgical assistant. And I also did all the bookkeeping, dictation, typing, billing and all the duties not done by the doctor himself.

So, they put me in the EENT clinic at Camp Forrest where all of the surgery treatment, physicals, refractions (eye examinations) and all things pertaining to that specialty were performed.

There were seven doctors in the clinic and about ten enlisted men. It was a busy service and some of the treatments I saw there were undreamed of. One of our sadistic majors, for example, liked to do punch operations on antrums (a type of nasal surgery) without any anesthetic. When I reported it to the chief of the service he wouldn't let him touch another sinus infection. Instead he was given the menial (to him) job of removing sebaceous cysts (wens). There were several to be done each day, but he was so lazy he made me do them. This was nothing new to me as I had been taught how under close supervision by my former employer. I really poured in the anesthetic and never got an infection from doing one. Afterward I would have the doctor check to be sure I had all the sac, then he would sit with a magazine propped up in front of him while I sutured it up and took on the next one.

Most of the surgery was submucous resections, (nose jobs) a few polyps, Caldwell—Lucs (a type of sinus surgery) and sometimes a frontal sinus, plus some minor eye surgery, such as chalazions (eyelid lumps) and sometimes an enucleation (removal of an eye) from accidents that happened during training, mostly on obstacle courses.

The Rangers had an obstacle course that made the one we went through look like a child's sand pit. One was crossing a rope bridge over a stream, while live dynamite exploded in the water below. Sometimes a man would fall into the water, and others were injured with machine gun backfire and other "fun" things the army used to toughen them up.

You may think this old girl didn't make too many mistakes in this situation. Tain't true at all. One of the many things we had to do, which I trained the enlisted men for, was to wash out impacted cerumen (ear wax) with a big metal syringe, the type with the top that had to be screwed back on after use so it would be ready for the next case.

One day we had a brigadier general come in for a physical so he could get his promotion. He had impacted cerumen. Rather than run the risk of having the enlisted men do this one I felt it better that I do it. I carefully explained to the general what had to be done and that I would be as gentle as possible. Then I had an enlisted man hold the emesis basin (a small, curved receptacle) under his ear while I inserted the tip of the syringe, giving it a push to expel the water into his ear. All a once there was a loud "pop" like a canon exploding. What it must have sounded like in the general's ear! He put his hand up to his ear, bent over double and yelled "Gee-sus-Keerist!" I was positive I had punctured the tympanic membrane as I dashed out in search of the chief of service. When I got back with him the general was smiling and "apologized" to me for his outburst. I was speechless and just stood there like an idiot with my mouth open. The chief explained to the general what had happened. The last enlisted man that had used the syringe had neglected to screw the top back on, and when I put the pressure on the thing popped.

It was then that I decided that generals were the nicest officers in the army, and this was later confirmed by another incident a few days later.

I was in the operating room picking up a tray of instruments covered with alcohol. I looked up and all I saw were stars, four of them, two on each shoulder. It was the commanding general of the 79th Infantry Division and he had just come in for treatment of a sinus infection. I started to stammer an apology, envisioning a firing squad, at least. But then, unbelievably, the general began to apologize to me! He said he had no right to come barging in where he didn't belong, and that he should have waited in the waiting room as the other patients did. Well, I was so relieved I could have kissed him. We were great friends after that and when he came in he would stick his head in the door and say, "Is it safe today?"

By this time many of the mavericks, like myself, had become disillusioned with the 300th General Hospital unit and had gotten transferred out. One of my dearest friends went to Ft. Devins in Massachusetts and others scattered throughout the states. I was beginning to get the same idea and was keeping a close lookout for just such an opportunity, when I heard of a new unit being formed by the air force composed of nurse paratroopers.

This was a latrine-o-gram, from the third seat down. I loved the idea of being a paratrooper, as I had been dating one part-time, myself. But to see if I really would like it, I decided to take part in a jump his division was having then at Camp Forrest. He got me the complete jump suit and boots so I was there ready to go aboard the C-47 with the troops. Then the commanding officer saw me and that ended that.

The next big event with the 300th General Hospital came up on a Saturday. It was the nurses' day off. But that was not what was in store for us.

It seemed that F.D.R. was to make an inspection of the camp and we were to be the only women represented along the parade route. You guessed it, I was made the officer of the day with the duty to march the whole four platoons out to the line of parade and wait for the big moment. We had to wear our steel pot helmets, our "lovely" two-toned wool uniforms, with skirts hanging down a few inches lower in the back than the front and with a belt that hit us about the rib cage, along with white shirts, black ties, grandmother black oxfords and the usual olive drab stockings.

In addition to ourselves, there were about 20,000 troops lined up on either side of the route waiting for the big arrival. It was hot and sticky but finally, after standing there for about 3 hours, we heard the 21-gun salute. None of us had passed out, yet, but we began having doubts. At long last there came an assemblage of motorcycles, cars by the numbers and somewhere in between, the touring car, top down, with F.D.R., Eleanor with her arms piled high with roses and a big top hat and that two buck teeth smile, and Ma Perkins, secretary of labor. When they came near our formation I ordered "eyes right" so all the others had to do was turn their heads and look, but me, I had to salute and hold it until they passed. It was big temptation not to let my thumb slide down to my nose, but again the vision of a firing squad changed my mind. F.D.R. threw us a big kiss and on they went, much to our relief.

That was when I decided enough was enough and asked for a transfer to the air force. But just then they received orders to leave within a week and Washington issued orders that no one was to be transferred out of the army into the air force.

What did I want to do? The chief nurse asked. I said I wanted to be sent with an evacuation hospital ready for a port of embarkation.

SQUAW PEAK NOTES IV
THE CAMP FORREST BLUES

One week prior to the departure of the 300th General Hospital for overseas, the commanding officer issued an order: "No one will be allowed to transfer out of this unit." He meant me, but the day the order was issued my orders arrived assigning me to the station hospital at Camp Forrest. It was a real challenge to get those orders, relieving me from the 300th, but going through the usual channels, sewers included, it was accomplished.

When the paratrooper unit didn't materialize, that's when the chief nurse at Camp Forrest asked me what I would like to try for next. My reply was that I wanted to go with an evacuation hospital that was ready for the P.O.E. (port of embarkation.) She said she would see what she could do about it. That was September, 1943. In November, night duty came around again for me, the usual 12 hours a night for 31 nights. In addition to 13 wards of various types of patients including Rocky Mountain spotted fever and other oddments such as heat prostration, it also included the prisoner's ward in the back of one building and the emergency room and admitting office. My duties began at 7 p.m. sharp, with obtaining the reports for the 13 wards from the off-going duty nurses then on the emergency, admitting and prisoner's wards.

First the prisoners' ward. Most of them were in the hospital "goldbricking," to keep from staying in the stockade and going on work details. So they worked up some imaginary illness, instead, and got into the hospital. Here they had nothing to do but sleep, eat three meals a day (marched to the mess hall by the military police), play cards and gripe.

Seldom did anything surprise me in the army; but that prisoners' ward was something else. To say it was filthy was putting it mildly, and that went for the men, as well. Their beds, which were three-tiered bunks, were littered with dirty linen and cigarette butts, ashes, candy wrappers and a few unmentionables were strewn all over the floor. The latrine and showers were so bad you needed a gas mask to inspect them.

The first night I entered the ward everyone was yelling for "blue heavens" or "yellow jackets," cough mixtures containing codeine that would give them a "high" or let them sleep a little more. This continued for three nights—my tolerance limit.

The hospital itself was inspected each day, but it was obvious someone was avoiding the prisoner area. So, ignoring channels, I went directly to the CO of the hospital and asked if he would mind coming over to the ward that evening when I was on duty.

At 1930 hours there he was—perplexed, but he must have figured it to be something serious. I took him back to the prisoner ward and let him see for himself.

He said nothing until we were back outside. Then he asked, "Well, lieutenant, what do you want me to do about it?"

"Sir," I replied, "I would like to try some psychology on this matter."

"Anything you do will be alright with me," he said after a few moments, and left.

After making my rounds on all the wards and giving medications, rubbing backs and seeing that every patient was comfortable, it was about 2200 hours when I got back to the office and prisoners' ward. Meanwhile, the sergeant in the admitting office had assigned all his men, at my request, to scour the hospital for all the cleaning equipment they could borrow: scrub brushes, brooms, buckets, scouring powders and good old GI soap. He had all this assembled for me when I returned to the cat calls, dirty language and the requests for medications.

I had a clip board and as each one requested a pill or whatever, his name was recorded until I had the whole roster completed. Only one patient's name wasn't included and he had appendicitis. After this, I left the ward and in came my personnel from the emergency room and admitting office. As each name was called, they were each given cleaning equipment and instructions as to what to do with them.

There was utter amazement on their faces at first, but we stood there and the cleaning began. They first cleaned the bunks, washing them thoroughly, then making them up with clean linen. The floors, windows, furniture and anything that didn't move also was thoroughly cleaned. Then they were given clean pajamas and told to shower. It was about 4 a.m. when they finally got to bed. There was complete silence the rest of that night.

The next night when I returned for medication requests no one wanted a thing. But that didn't stop my psychological warfare. Each one was called out again, given the same equipment and not only did they do their ward but the rest of the building as well. In less than a week, we had one lone patient left. The others had requested duty back at the stockade. Even the one patient with appendicitis made a rapid recovery and left. After that very few prisoners came in for treatment of any kind.

These men were not bad. Some had done various things against army regulations, while others were awaiting a hearing and had been sent to the stockade for a short period. Today, they would be listed as the nicest young men in the country. They were only trying to beat the brass, and who wasn't? Including me.

Each night after completing my other ward duties, I would work in the emergency room and help admitting patients. None of the clerk typists here could type so it was fun for me to help them out with all the copies of papers that had to be completed. (In those days my typing was faultless!)

One night everything seemed to happen at once. There were ambulances lined up for a couple of blocks, some containing at least four litter cases and others with six or more ambulatory patients. We couldn't understand what had happened until we discovered the the 39th Evacuation Hospital, which had been on maneuvers supporting the field troops, got orders to close and get ready for overseas duty. As a result, they emptied out the whole hospital and we got them all at one time!

After an hour or so of working like mad (the line was endless!) it was time for me to make rounds on my other 13 wards. And what a surprise awaited me there!

About 20 of these new admissions had been sent to my ward; and it was now my duty to do all the paper work there, too, in addition to getting the officer of the day to examine them, prescribe treatment and, finally for me to carry out the orders.

That was my last stint of duty at Camp Forrest's station hospital, before the chief nurse called me into her office (she was suffering from high blood pressure and Vat 69) and gave me orders assigning me to the 39th Evacuation Hospital.

After what the 39th had done to me, it was quite a shock. But after having my orders for overseas duty from seven other hospitals cancelled, the last being the 300th, it occurred to me not to try to do anything about it. Instead it was with reservations that I took my orders in hand and proceeded to the 39th hospital headquarters.

SQUAW PEAK NOTES V
ESCAPE FROM CAMP FORREST

At long last it looked as if my escape from Camp Forrest was coming to fruition. The 39th Evacuation Hospital, to which I had been assigned, had finished with maneuvers in the fields of Tennessee and were ready for some real action.

Uniforms were issued: 6 pairs of nurses' fatigues, 2 pairs of olive drab leggings, 2 pairs of Lil' Abner boots, long, olive drab, wool ribbed stockings, 3 pairs each, 1 army olive drab overcoat with woolen liner, musette bags, 1 pistol belt with canteen and first aid kit attached plus a duffel bag and a bedding roll. That took a few minutes on one day to get together.

The next morning at reveille, the chief nurse decided to take me aside to explain that they did close order drill, formal retreat and all the other things the army has to offer. She didn't ask me if I knew any of those things, instead she proceeded to show me all the commands and executions. I just kept my mouth shut and listened. But when we fell in for marching and she gave the commands on the wrong foot (messing up the platoon) I found I couldn't remain humble any longer and I blurted out: "As you were," to cancel her command. Guess who became the platoon leader from then on? I never learned to keep my big mouth shut.

Our chief nurse, by the way, was a captain (the commanding officer was a lieutenant-colonel in the regular army) and just normally obnoxious. She would have been about 5' 2" if she had straightened up, but she was always stooped over, reminding me now of the cartoon character "Hazel" but at that time Hazel wasn't born yet. She also had terrible front teeth which should have fallen out long before, a beard that required she shave every day, and always a cigarette dangling from the corner of her mouth. She and the CO had mutual respect for each other. Hate! On the other hand, our assistant chief nurse was a skinny, old maidish type who never learned to march or execute an about-face using only one foot, but she was a "yes" gal to the chief, so she got along pretty well.

Well, here I was ready to get into "this man's war" and see what it was all about, but the army had other things in mind: more basic training, for one. This was required before we could hope to get out of that lousy place.

Having had this stuff for 13 months already there wasn't anything new they could show me. So, when training films were shown it was siesta time; lectures meant book reading time. This routine broke down only once.

One day while sitting in the back of the lecture hall, I had a very funny book concealed and was just beginning to thoroughly enjoy it when someone announced the speaker of the day would be a Capt. John Kennedy who would discuss how to abandon ship.

It was his dry wit that caught my attention. I even laid down my book to listen. Later my roommate said he was their radiologist and "the best in the army."

After that, I saw him every day, saluted and said "Good morning, captain," and went on about my business. It had been my policy not to date doctors, after doing so a few times and learning they were more intent on continuing their anatomical studies by the braille system! So they were a no-no in my book. The infantry, armored division, paratroopers and just any of the field officers were the standbys for my dating social life.

About this time people started pouring in to camp from all over the U.S. to fill the vacancies that existed in the unit, and soon we had our full complement of nurses, enlisted men and officers.

Orders for our departure came soon after, in January, 1943. And, in a short time, were were boarding a train (we knew not where) and saying "adieu" to good old Camp Forrest, Tennessee. We nurses were assigned to a Pullman car that was so old it must have been used during the Civil War, but they salvaged it for just this last trip.

After hooking up to a modern diesel engine we took off and were literally airborne for the rest of the trip because the car was too old to stay on the tracks. And we stayed that way until the next night at midnight when we pulled into Washington, D.C. We were so excited all 40 of us wanted to get off and see the Capitol. But that was halted abruptly by the military police who were on hand just to see that didn't happen. So there we sat for about four hours looking out the window, until we hooked up to another diesel and began our flight again.

Hours later and fast asleep our raucous-voiced chief nurse woke us up with: "Get out of those sacks, get dressed and get off this train in 10 minutes!" Then she began counting each of us again and again for the whole time she was with us. If one of us dared to bend over to tie a shoe lace she would count us still one more time, because she was sure one of us had gone AWOL.

We had officially arrived at Camp Kilmer, New Jersey. And after being herded like cattle into 6 x 6 army trucks we were hauled to our barracks.

The next morning we were up and ready to explore the new area, just in case we might be stuck there a while. It was a flourishing army post with a station hospital, even though it was also a port of embarkation as well. I couldn't help thinking about Camp Forrest and seeing us being put on duty in this hospital for the duration. But that wasn't to be.

In the meantime, we were informed not to write, telephone or let anyone know of our whereabouts. In letters, we were particularly not to mention anything about Joyce Kilmer's poem, "Trees"—a dead giveaway. I adhered to the rule, but I did write my sister about how happy I was that I had brought along my new jersey formal gown which she had made for me. She got the letter and the message. The gown arrived, in violation of the standing order that we were not to have any type of civilian clothing with us, only army equipment and uniforms. But I wasn't the only felon in the group. It was amazing how many of us had formals when we got invitations to the officers' club dance.

At this point we still did not have specific orders for our overseas shipment, so we used those few days to loaf around camp, after finishing

Author's collection of photos.

with a bit of close order drill, orders of the day, etc. And then we got lucky. Six of us got into New York City at a total expense (including round trip cab fare) of $6.00.

Everywhere we went in the city we were treated like heroines, and our admirers even paid for all the food and drink, each of them trying to outdo the other. And we accepted gratefully; and indulged extravagantly. Every night thereafter we had dates to go to the officers' club for dinner and dancing. It seemed like the fun would never end. But it did. One afternoon an old boy friend from Camp Forrest showed up and was going to take me to one of the club dances. That afternoon our plans were shattered by an announcement from our headquarters that we were shipping out next day, and, consequently, no one could go anywhere except to the unit party (our unit only) at the nurses' recreation barracks.

That was about the most appalling party for me to contemplate, but there was no escape. I went determined that it was going to be a lousy evening.

SQUAW PEAK NOTES VI
ANCHORS AWEIGH—AT LAST

(In my last verbal ballistic missile, it states that the chief nurse of the 39th resembled Hazel of the cartoon. The analogy was meant to be Hazel (an ape at the zoo.)

We attended the unit party at Camp Kilmer, which was ghastly, but after a few potions of scotch it didn't seem too bad. Our plastered (plastic) surgeon had anchored himself by the record player and insisted on playing nothing but congas. Finally I started a conga line and behind me was John. After the consumption of more scotch until the supply was depleted, he asked me if he could walk me back to the barracks. He did and bid me a curt "goodnight" and went on his way. All the nurses were aghast at his behavior. He had been so reserved they didn't think he ever looked at a girl.

We knew we were going aboard a ship but the destination was secret. The chief nurse and commanding officer got a sadistic delight in knowing something they would not divulge to the rest of the unit. About 4 p.m. we got into the nurses' limousines, (6 x 6 trucks) and departed for the Jersey ferry. John came aboard and sat next to me and pointed out his office in West New York, New Jersey, across from 42nd Street in New York. That didn't impress me at all. I had no intention of living either in New Jersey or New York.

We were unloaded on the New York Port side and there waiting for us was this big white British luxury liner, converted into His Majesty's Troopship "Andes." It was built for the South Pacific and had a flat bottom for that purpose. It certainly was not intended for the Atlantic, as we later discovered.

Dinner was served at 6 p.m. and consisted of fish, a vegetable and delicious hard rolls with butter. We didn't know it at that time, but that was to be the staple for the rest of the trip, alternating with mutton.

Our rooms, which once had been a spacious luxury suite, had been made into one big room to accommodate seven persons, with bunk beds going up to the ceiling, and one bathroom. Fresh water was available for one hour in the morning and a half-hour in the evening. Bathing with fresh water was verboten, as was hair washing.

We sailed sometime during the night without benefit of convoy and so missed saying goodbye to Ma Liberty. Breakfast was served at 6:30 a.m. and that was the best meal of the day: bacon and eggs with hard rolls, coffee or tea.

We had only two meals a day, no lunch. The ship's sales store opened at lunch and we could purchase kippered herring or sardines, but no crackers or biscuits. We were always hungry! I wrote my family that if I ever took another trip like that I would throw all my clothes away and take nothing but food and drink.

Other than lifeboat drills at 10 each morning we had nothing to do but play cards, sing and gripe. Mostly the latter.

After being at sea for a couple of days, we not only hit a violent Atlantic storm, but the ship had to zigzag off course due to the German submarines that spotted us. We were not in a convoy, but alone as this was a very fast ship.

Mal de mer became epidemic and one of the first to fall was our chief nurse. She refused to go to the sick bay, she didn't trust us to take care of her. She stayed in her room and the assistant chief took care of her. I think she just turned her over three times a day to prevent bed sores.

The sick bay filled up with casualties and most of them required IV fluids, as they were so dehydrated. That took a couple of nurses each day to care for them and this was done on a rotation basis. Several of our officers also were sick, but they were too ashamed to go to the sick bay. They never ate a meal.

I saw John on deck one time. He sort of had a chartreuse color to his face, which was all that was visible, as he was wrapped in a long overcoat and a scarf up around his chin. He went to the dining room but ate very little. He spent most of his time in his bunk reading. (So he said.)

Dinner was served early and we did not have to go to bed until 10 p.m. We had so much energy that we gathered in the corridors of the ship and raised so much fuss that the captain finally let us use the officer's dining room to amuse ourselves and get us out of the way.

We had some marvelous talent aboard and put on impromptu shows. This gave my "Gleesome Threesome" a chance to sing. This consisted of my roommate, Danny Johnson (who later worked in the operating room at the J. C. Lincoln Hospital in Phoenix) and another nurse. We received so many accolades we never stopped singing all through combat and afterwards.

The ship's decks were boarded up and all doors were tied open in case they might jam. When you were walking you were horizontal but in a perpendicular position.

The no bathing rule was a bit too much. Another girl and I decided we would fill the bathtub with salt water and take a bath. We were both in the bathroom and the tub was full of water. The ship lurched forward and quickly rolled to one side. Both of us were caught and fell head first into the tub of water, clothes and all. My hair was a gooey mess so the next morning I went without breakfast and took advantage of the fresh water to wash my hair. I asked one of the girls to bring me a hard roll and butter, which she did, wrapped in a linen napkin. I had cranked up my hair on Kleenex for curlers and was sitting in a chair in front of the heater drying it, roll in hand when the ship rolled to one side and my chair—with me in it—took off for the open door.

When it reached the door I put out one foot to stop my journey. The chair leg caught and held fast, but not me. I went sailing out in the corridor in front of the purser's office where all the men and officers had gathered to get their orders for the day. I landed flat on my back and all I could see were shoes and pant legs. But I still clutched the hard roll. The men were alarmed and concerned that I was injured, which I was not. It was such a funny predicament that the thought of how ludicrous I looked made me laugh.

They helped me up and I retreated back to my room, fearing that someone would report me to the ailing chief. But my luck was good for a change.

The storm did not abate until the morning of the eighth day at sea. Suddenly it became very calm, the decks were opened and we saw the sun for the first time. Finally, I decided I wouldn't drown this time but soon would land on that unknown shore. Where would it be, I wondered, Italy, France or Germany?

SQUAW PEAK NOTES VII
AN AUSPICIOUS ARRIVAL

16 February 1944. Eight days of our pleasure cruise had terminated. In the early afternoon the ship docked in Liverpool, England. (We called it "Liverpuddle" but not to the British.)

The mal de mer casualties suddenly made a remarkable recovery, much to our dismay, including our chief nurse. She was counting all of us every few minutes, issuing orders we mostly ignored. We thought we would disembark immediately, but obviously all the other passengers went first and it was very dark when our turn arrived. Chiefy was a busy gal dashing from one room to the other, each time counting us and checking our equipment. It seemed as if she suspected that some of us had abandoned ship. Perhaps we should have.

We had adequate time to get into our equipment and off the ship. The whole sum of three minutes. That meant getting into the heavy wool lining of the overcoat, plus the coat, gas mask, pistol belt with canteen, musette bags crammed full of toiletries, etc. and get off. We didn't even have time to consider a last trip to the bathroom which was a tragic mistake.

The first thing that hit us was the intense, penetrating cold—then the complete blackout. We tried to form into a platoon formation which was accomplished entirely by touch and then the chief gave orders to march. We stumbled over the rough cobblestones, bumping into each other, while she was somewhere out in front. Without a preparatory command she would yell, "Halt," and everyone did—by bumping into the person in front of them. When this happened a few times, my overstuffed musette bag would hit me in the lower abdomen, putting an extra pressure on a vital organ. The proper medical terminology would be, "retention with overflow" and that is precisely what was happening with each thud against the person in front of me.

The climate here is the worst in the world. It is a damp, very penetrating cold and this, too, added to our discomfort. By the time we had arrived at the railroad station we were all cyanotic (blue.)

Here was light and a train waiting for us. We were assigned six to a compartment, which had two parallel seats with three on either side and a door on either side. The lovely British Gray Ladies were there with hot coffee and donuts for us. We had nothing but our canteen cups to drink from and each one held at least a pint. They filled them to the brim. The coffee was horrible! We had to drink it as they stayed with us chatting and there was no way we could dump it. So down it went, which further insulted our condition.

We were confident as soon as the train left the station we would be able to find a latrine. We could scarcely wait to get going. Imagine our horror when we inspected every inch of that compartment and found nothing resembling a W.C., and those initials didn't represent Winston Churchill. The train had all the curtains down, as it was in complete blackout too, although we had light inside. (Later we were to learn that a train with a corridor was the only kind with bathroom facilities and this one definitely did not possess such a luxury.) Our discomfort became critical.

One girl suggested we open the door a crack and try that. They let me go first. The girls held onto my coat so I wouldn't catapult out the door and my endeavor was successful to some extent. But the wind coming through the open door blew the contents of that emission back into the car onto the floor. They released their hold and trying to close the door, I sat down in it. (Dry apparel was available in my musette bag.)

After that fiasco, the other five decided to use the outside cover of their K ration boxes that were heavily coated with wax. This they did, with the intention of opening the door and throwing them out. But the door stuck, and the contents of those boxes leaked on the floor as well. One of the girls, though, happened to have a "pressing cloth" in her musette bag which she and I used on our hands and knees to mop up the mess, when the train suddenly stopped and both doors were flung open. We were inside a well lighted railroad station in Sale, a borough of Manchester, where we left the train. We made the quickest exit in our career at this time.

SQUAW PEAK NOTES VIII
'HALE, HALE, THE GANG'S ALL HERE'

The 6x6's were waiting for us in the blackest spot they could find. To climb into these instruments of torture you used built-in iron footsteps mounted on either side. They were intended for statures of six feet or taller, not for overloaded, short-legged nurses. Not one of us could reach this inaccessible footing without the driver pushing from behind and his assistant inside pulling the other end. Loaded down with all the army equipment made it even more difficult.

On the inside were two slatted wooden benches that folded up when not in use. These we sat on. The truck was covered with a heavy olive drab tarpaulin so one could see a bit of scenery (but not this night) out of the back. The shock absorbers were in the middle of one's backside. The drivers were never known to have missed a hole or rock. We were well "shook" before the word entered today's slang.

When we were all aboard, we departed for a short ride to Hale. (Our name for it was another four letter word with different letters.) The trucks came to a sudden stop and we did a replay in reverse to get unloaded. We could reach the foothold on the way down, from which point, you either dropped with a thud or someone gave you an assist, usually ending with both of you plummeting to the cement together.

We were ushered into an enormous brick house. The living room was immense and the only thing in it was a minuscle fireplace. The house was a tomb except it was colder. But it was getting late and we were too miserable to tell and cared less at this point. Our only concern was finding the WC.

The house yielded only one, so a queue was formed by most of us, while two of the nurses tried to build a fire in the fireplace, which was impossible to do. When the queue finally came to an end we had to go back out into the cold night to the limousines which whisked us away to a huge building being used as a mess hall. Here was some heat but not enough to permit us to take off our gloves. We had coffee and donuts and sat on the wooden benches for hours. Our male officers had arrived at the same place, having undergone the same circuitous route we had. We were a sad, frigid lot at this point.

After hours of waiting, our "chicken" colonel (not by rank but morality) arrived and announced we would all depart for our barracks. Nurses left first and we were taken to another huge house.

The living room was not empty but filled with double-decker beds with the bottoms covered with nothing but fence wire. These we were to sleep on that night. The fireplace was a little mirage, cold also. It looked anything but merry to us in "Merrie Olde England" at that point. Suddenly, we all had the same impulse, we wanted to go home.

After the queue for the one WC, Danny and I decided we were too cold to try and sleep, so we took a reconnaissance of the building before we would park our torsos on those gurus' beds. To our utter delight and amazement, we found a kitchen which had an enormous coal-burning range with two 50-gallon garbage cans of hot water setting on top, bubbling away. There was a dining table, the GI type used in England, beside the stove. It was about 30 inches wide but we piled up on it and made our bed on it comfortable and warm.

Eventually, we got thawed out and fell asleep, only to be rudely awakened by the raucous voice of the chief nurse yelling: "Where the hell are Waters and Hinkle?" She never called us by our first names. We kept still but she found us anyway, and was so angry she almost had apoplexy. Why didn't we tell the others we had found a warm place, etc., she complained, referring to our ancestors as being derivatives of the canine family. (Boy, that woman could swear!)

She hadn't slept and neither had the other 40. (There were 42 of us, including two Red Cross workers.) But she was grateful for the hot water as were all the others. Then it was daylight and we were collected again and hauled to Altrincham to our own unit headquarters and mess hall.

Our headquarters was an abandoned house, brick, with numerous rooms and a huge kitchen. We had our first meal in the United Kingdom and soon realized that things in Britain were austere.

We had powdered milk, cereal and coffee. Mess kits and canteen cups had to be used. (What a sensation to drink scalding coffee from an aluminum canteen cup!) The mess kits and canteen cups had to undergo the GI washing in the backyard, in 50-gallon garbage cans that had individual oil burning stoves to heat the water. One hung everything on the handle of the canteen and immersed it into the boiling, soapy water, scrubbing with a long handled brush. After this it was doused into two cans of clear, boiling water and swung into the air to dry. Failing to adhere to this army regulation could result in what was termed "The GIs" or the "Latrine Lope."

Our headquarters building was large enough for all the administrative offices, mess hall, etc. We had wooden tables with metal supports and long wooden benches, with the same type of support, to sit on. The benches were treacherous in that the supports were placed so that the ends were unsupported. When anyone sat on the ends, with no one to balance in the middle, they were dumped on to the floor in a very undignified manner.

Thus my first night on foreign soil had ended. It found me with a 10 per cent increase in pay, tired, cold and miserable, and wondering what other goodies the army had in store for me.

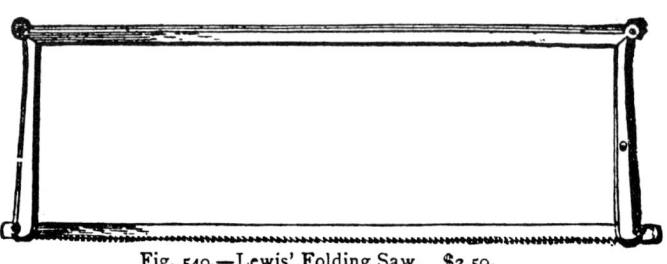

Fig. 540.—Lewis' Folding Saw. $2.50.

SQUAW PEAK NOTES IX
GETTING KNOCKED UP EVERY MORNING IN ALTRINCHAM

The response to my former articles has been zilch! Nada! Until the other day, all at once this postcard came pouring in. In spite of it, I will not be discouraged. It proves that at least one doctor in Maricopa County takes *Roundup* home so his wife can read it, if she so desires. And I sort of whish this one hadn't. But I can take it.....

There we were, bedraggled, tired, apprehensive and miserably cold, waiting for the next maneuver. This was the assignment to billets for all of the officers. A few were taken at a time, given names and addresses of families in whose homes they were to live. This arrangement was accomplished by the local government who called townsmen and informed them that they would billet a certain number of U.S. officers. They received the large sum of $3.50 per day per officer. All they had to furnish was the room, ablution facilities and nothing else.

It took several hours for this to be accomplished and it was about 10:00 a.m. before they came to the six of us and gave us the name and address of the family who furnished our billets. It was a couple of blocks from our headquarters, but trying to walk on an incline up to the house gave us all dyspnea, (shortness of breath) which remained with us for our entire stay. It was that lousy weather!

The only visible part of the houses on this street was the top two floors. Each house had a stone fence with a high hedge on top. There were no numbers on the residences, names only. We were assigned to "Elmhurst," Bentynck Road, the residence of Mr. and Mrs. Herbert Pearce. It took us a half hour, at least to reach this establishment. We arrived at the door, huffing and puffing and shivering with the cold.

We looked like a bunch of old haversacks left over from WW1, when I rang the door bell and Mr. and Mrs. Herbert Pearce emerged. They had such a strange, dismayed, perplexed look on their faces that we thought we had goofed and gone to the wrong place. Mrs. Pearce was the first to resume her composure and assured us we were at the correct place but they had assumed that we would be males. They said all they had been told was that they would billet six U.S. Army lieutenants and they had never seen any female U.S. officers.

We were ushered into the foyer of that gorgeous house and Mrs. Pearce immediately padded off to show us our quarters. First to go were Danny and me and we had a lovely big room all to ourselves. The other four had to share one big room. There were only nine bedrooms in the house and those rooms were enormous in size. Our room had three huge picture windows, very high ceilings and a little mirage for a fireplace, just about 12" x 12," no fire, of course There was a bed, dresser, closet and the usual accoutrements for a bedroom.

Mrs. Pearce returned to our room to chat. She told us of their austerity, about the blackouts, queues for everything and about her family. She had always wanted a daughter but had three sons instead. The two older ones were in India in the army, but the younger one, Freddie, was home.

They were strictly rationed on everything. They got only dried milk, fresh was only for older people and children, three ounces of meat for the three of them per week, and she had to queue up even to get fish.

Mr. Pearce was an electrical engineer and commuted by train each day to Manchester where he worked. Freddie, who went to school in Manchester, had to ride his bicycle nine miles over and back each day. He had little for lunch, if anything, and was so thin with a pasty white color. He had to serve three nights a week as a warden to check on houses and buildings for blackout infractions. She told us that the coal we had to burn in the fireplace would be furnished by the army, as they were rationed on that too. There was no central heating in any of the houses at that time. Mr. Pearce would say to us, "All one needs do is take a brisk walk if one feels cold." Bathing was permitted but only 5" of water in the tub was allowed.

We had begun to unpack our belongings, and she knew how tired we were so she suggested we go to bed. That was exactly what we had in mind, but what a shock to get into bed and find real linens on the bed, colder than the army muslin we had been used to. We heard the padding of feet on the stairway and here was Mrs. Pearce with a hot water bottle for our feet. We had never seen one like it. It was ceramic and in the shape of a rolling pin, but we were so grateful to get it. We put on as many clothes as we had taken off and got into bed where we fell asleep as soon as we got warm. About 4:30 in the afternoon we were awakened by Mrs. Pearce so we wouldn't miss the evening meal. We had already skipped lunch!

She showed us the house and it was, and still is, beyond description. Three floors and a basement. We were on the second floor where there were five big bedrooms, four more upstairs on the 3rd floor. Down about five steps from our room was the WC in a closet type room, very small but it didn't need a lot of space. That was all that was in there. Down another eight steps was the bath with only a tub and wash basin. No heat whatever, not even a fireplace.

On the 1st floor were the kitchen, dining room, living room, den, enormous library, etc. It was all beautifully furnished with priceless pieces of all types of antiques as well as some contemporary.

The lawn was terraced with the most gorgeous flowers I had ever seen. Grass remains green all the time and how it does was beyond my imagination, as it was bitterly cold. Trees were gnarled into lovely shapes as the wind blows 365 days a year there. Holly is so lovely that they use it for hedges as well as trees. It grows profusely everywhere.

After our refreshing sleep, we tried to build a fire in that fireplace. It was impossible so again we were in the same state of frigidity that had been with us since the ship debarkation.

We heard the gentle padding of feet on the stairway and the gentle knock on our door and here was our lovely little mother to show us how to build a fire. Very simple when done correctly as she showed us. She seemed to have adopted us and we felt as if she had always been our mother. She had gray hair, the most beautiful sparkling blue eyes and with her clipped cockney accent she was a delight.

We knew we had to take a bath regardless of the cold, so we decided what our strategy would be. One would go down and turn on the hot water and let it steam up the room. As soon as this was done both of us tore down and popped into the tub scrubbing each others' backs. Never have I had such fast but cleansing baths! Then we rushed back to the little fireplace and rubbed like mad with the towels and got into our clothes, faster than a striptease artist when the police raid the joint. The room never got warm and one side of your anatomy would burn until you turned, but one could never get the whole torso warm at one time.

After our ablutions, we went down to headquarters for chow and to find out what was to happen next. We were informed that we would report at headquarters at 0700 hours.

After eating the food, which was filling but horrible, we had nothing to do until time to go home. John, Danny and I went to inspect the tea houses. Little old ladies wearing gloves, Irish wool tweeds, cotton stockings and hats were the only occupants. We had the tea and then explored the pubs. That was called "pub crawling," which we later found out was actually that.

You went to so many and drank so much that there was not other way for mobility. We met more of the gang at the pubs and being the Americans that we are, we were laughing, and making all sorts of noise and singing.

We asked Mrs. Pearce if Mr. Pearce would get us up in the morning, as we had no alarm clock and had to be at our headquarters at 0700 hours. He got up at 0600 hours in order to commute to work. She replied, "Oh yes, Mr. Pearce would be happy to knock you up in the morning." So, every morning we were knocked up by Mr. Pearce with a gentle tap on the door and the message, "Time, ladies, it is 6 a.m."

Aren't you a bit ashamed for all the dirty thoughts you had from the beginning?

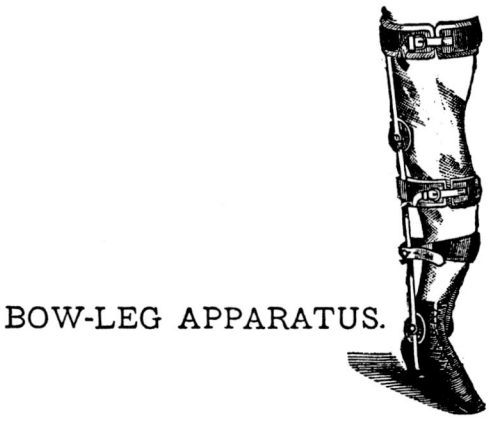

BOW-LEG APPARATUS.

SQUAW PEAK NOTES X
WE GET BOMBED WITH CALVADOS AND YELLOW JACKETS!

First Lieutenant Willa R. Hinkle, R.N., being awarded the Legion of Merit by the Surgeon of the United States Third Army in Hershfeld, Germany in 1945. Author's collection of photos.

We departed the wheat field early in the morning from St. Lanellin for our luxurious tour of the French countryside. Ten nurses were in each truck, along with all of our personal gear, packed together like sardines sans the oil. It was a long trek, over a hundred miles, pit stops few and no comfort stations, usually an open field where concealment was impossible. A blanket latrine was improvised. Two girls held up the blanket in front of us. We always faced the blanket. In the event the whole third army might be watching from the rear, we were not aware of it and could relax and let nature handle the procedure. Unfortunately no one was blessed with anuria (inability to urinate) or constipation on these safaris.

We arrived at the cow pasture in the afternoon, outside the farming village of Vitre. We hauled ourselves out of the truck and had time to go to our segregated area where our tent billets were located, deposited our gear and rushed back to the hospital to unpack and set up the equipment. I was permitted to remain on day duty as I had only been on that shift three days prior to moving.

The men had the ward tents and O.R. (operating room) set up and after hauling out the cow calling cards, we got down to the business at hand. The area was surrounded by trees which were inhabited by yellow jackets. In setting up the tents, the men must have disturbed the insects. They dived into us with a ravenous appetite for revenge. Any exposed portion of the anatomy was a target and their aim was perfect. The stings were extremely painful and most everyone had swollen eyes, lips, faces arms or any portion of anatomy

Dieffenbach's Artery Forceps. $1 00.

that was exposed.

The weather was hot, this was July, and all the tent sides were rolled up to permit as much cooling as possible. This permitted the yellow monsters to enter ad lib. They swarmed over everyone and everything. It was not easy to set up equipment and cots, constantly swatting these yellow devils. Only after dark did these bombing attacks subside.

Casualties began arriving before we were set up, most of them for my ward. We were busier than a neat cat with diarrhea in a cement sand box. Every type of injury had been inflicted on these men. Head, chest, facial, belly, crushed bones, amputees, (some quadruple), burns of all degrees and intensities, blast, etc. Each one was in profound shock. It was superfluous to use a stethoscope and sphygmomanometer (blood pressure measuring device) to ascertain that fact.

The doctors were the only ones who used the two we had. No one went around with a stethoscope draped around his neck as is done today. We were not out to impress anyone with our medical skills and knowledge. The main object was to save the lives of these men. I got over my reticence of starting whole blood after the first incident and the order was S.O.P. (standard operating procedure.) Every patient needed it and got it. In all the other procedures, it was the task of the nurses to train the enlisted men, not only to give blood, plasma and nursing care, but to recognize symptoms before diagnosis, and understand the diagnosis of each patient. Sorry to admit, that after instructing the men in the procedure of giving IVs (intravenous injections) they surpassed me and the doctors as far as getting into those collapsed veins, particularly those of infants and children, of which we had many. We never had to cut down on a vein. We just used smaller needles until we succeeded. Another of my brazen acts was to correct doctors who tried to get into veins by inserting the sharp end of the needle first which would go through the vessel, ruining it. First I would loudly instruct the enlisted men of the importance of inserting the bevel edge of the needle down, but when the doctors didn't heed the advice I would tactfully suggest to them that I had been taught by an expert. If that didn't work, I did not hesitate to tell the CO. Somehow they got the message.

Every patient was in shock. Some were comatose and the ones who were not were usually in intense pain, although the majority of them had received 1/2 grain of morphine tartrate given by an aid man at the time of injury. Due to impaired circulation, they would not be able to absorb it. It was a tenuous situation for us. If we gave them morphine sulfate after too short an interval, and after their having received enough whole blood to improve the circulation, they would get the full effects of both medications. We had some very close calls.

Officers and enlisted patients were side by side. We had no screens to provide privacy. Sheets were hung on ropes along one side of the tent to conceal the POWs. This I named "Kraut Haven." These POWs received the same care as the GIs, but priority was given to our men. The Wehrmacht were not bad patients, but the SS were mean, belligerent and uncooperative. Every meal time they would all yell for the urinal. Never at any other time. We only had 10 of these and it would require two men to meet their requirement. After a few times of this my little Rumanian corporal would give the one on the end one urinal and have him pass it along. That cured the demand.

We had a refrigerator on the shock ward and it was kept well stocked with whole blood. If we had a shortage it would be that some of the units were marked "give to type A or B only." These we would use on the POWs. We had only type "O" for everyone. When moving, the blood was stored in the kerosene refrigerator in the pharmacy.

We were always short of personnel. Due to the the large number of captured prisoners the ones with medical training were assigned to work on the wards, taking care of the Germans only. Others were given jobs around the hospital. They were good workers and a big asset.

Seems I digress a bit too much. By seven we had a ward full of casualties, all under treatment. Surgery had a big backlog and casualties still arriving. The night crew came on duty and then we could go get out our cots and sleeping bags and unroll those lumpy bedding rolls for our army bed of roses. Bathing was done from the helmet as the shower tent was the last thing to be set up. Laundry was also done in the helmet in cold water. Those heavy cotton twill fatigues were as rough as No. 10 sandpaper, but we managed to remove most of the gunk. In clean clothes we were ready to explore the area. John, Danny, Sigie and some other officers set up our club for the evening. One of the men had a bottle of Calvados (we were now in that area.) I had never tasted it and just as I took a swig, I also sat down on a yellow jacket. I don't know which was the more painful. Bed Check Charlie came zooming over and that was the signal to get to bed and ready for the next day.

Daylight came very early and with it the yellow jackets came buzzing into our tents like P38 bombers. Any odor attracted them, soap, lipstick or whatever. They were in our clothes so that in order to get dressed we had to shake everything constantly trying to evict them. Poor Danny got into the operating room and discovered one in her fatigue blouse. Without hesitating she ripped it off before all patients and personnel. Anyone would have done the same. The mess tent was even worse as these demons were having a convention with the food. One had to continuously blow on each bit to get it into one's mouth and this was not always successful.

On duty before seven, the day began. All cots were filled. Other patients were in X-ray or the O.R. After serving the breakfast and taking temperatures, nursing care began. Soap, razors, combs, toothbrushes, shaving creams, toothpaste, all of the essentials needed were furnished by the quartermaster. The CO had assigned these supplies to the two Red Cross workers assigned to us. They did not open up their tent until noon. They spent the evening in the admitting tent greeting the patients as they came in on the litters. They would give them coffee and cigarettes. They felt it was so nice for these battle casualties to see an American girl. They didn't know if they were giving coffee to a chest, belly or whatever type of wound and when we got the patients to the ward, we got the vomitus in our face and found the cigarettes soaked in blood on the bottom of the litters. I went to the CO and took the supplies and had one of the enlisted men take over the distribution. That was also true of the cigarettes. They were not furnished by the Red Cross but by the QM (quartermaster).

Shortage of equipment was alleviated as the Americans overran some of the German medical facilities. We received enough stainless steel wash basins so that each patient had one of his own. We also received emesis (vomit) basins, instruments and linens which we always needed. We used plasma by the gallons and we fashioned drinking tubes from the tubing. By filling the bottles with water, setting them on the ground, putting the glass connectors on as a tip and pinning it on the pillow, a patient could get a drink if he were able to move his head. The glass Baxter bottles were used for Wangensteens, (gastric drainage procedures) chest drainage, oxygen, etc. These were discarded in each area as we always had an adequate supply as soon as we began treatment in a new area..

The yellow jackets were tenacious. We were fighting them in our tent when I got the brilliant idea of smoking them out. We had been issued heavy ribbed wool stockings, just long enough to scarcely cover our knees, two pairs each, which made a total of 10 pairs in our billet. We got them in a pile and set them afire. It did nothing to the yellow jackets, but the smell drove out the occupants. Danny had a jar of jam that her mother had sent her which she had concealed in her sleeping bag. They found it, and her, when she lowered herself into the receptacle. She howled louder than a banshee! They had an affinity for her. To ease the pain of the stings she took off on the double for the shower tent without her leggings. The chief nurse saw her, caught up to her and really gave her the "ream job." She made Patton sound like a Sunday school teacher! All of us sort of got the message that we had to be in complete uniform when outside a tent. We adhered to this until we got out of the cow pasture, then the helmets were removed and carried by the strap as a purse to hold our bartering material that we would acquire, very chic, we thought. Another reason we wore or carried the helmets was because we always kept an adequate supply of TP (toilet paper) in the liner. A necessity in France even if it were not during war time!

We faced many crises in the shock ward and the challenges were gargantuan. It is difficult for one to believe that these combat wards were the forerunners of today's intensive care units. If only we had had a few of the conveniences! There were no bedside tables, no call lights, and no monitoring devices other than our own eyes and ears. It was not easy! How did we cope?

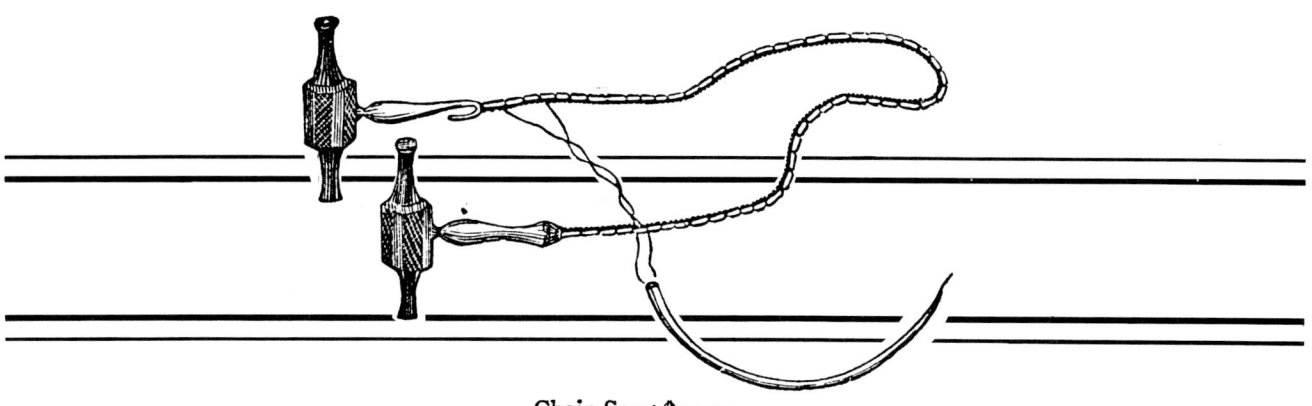

Chain Saw; $10.00.

XX.

POSTSCRIPT

And so ends our narrative. We hope you enjoyed reading it as much as we enjoyed making it possible for you to do so. As you have gathered, it is not a complete history of medicine in Arizona, nor is it a scholarly work. We leave the pursuit of those goals to hardier souls who someday may choose to broaden the path we have trod. What we hope we have accomplished in following that path, however, is the gathering together between the covers of one book an array of facts, anecdotes, incidences and recollections about, and in many instances, by Arizona's medical pioneers. Some of them blazed medical trails that have had worldwide impact. Doctor George Goodfellow's surgery for prostatism in 1891 is an example. Another is the role played by early Arizona physicians in tracking down the cause of Valley fever. To borrow a phrase from Lincoln's Gettysburg Address: "The world will little note, nor long remember, what we say here, but it can never forget what they did here."

Who can forget the redoubtable and inimitable Doctor Clarence Salsbury? History, medical or otherwise, is not a dry chronicle of dates and events. It is, instead, if properly recorded, a fascinating account of human endeavor, some bad, some good, over the years. And, as Irish, Nobel Prize winning poet and playwright William Butler Yeats wrote in his verse drama, The Countess Cathleen, in 1892: "The years like great black oxen tread the world. And God, the herdsman, goads them on behind." It is the historian's task to follow those oxen and to preserve for posterity the hoof prints they leave upon the face of the earth.

The Editors

Finis
Author's collection of photos.

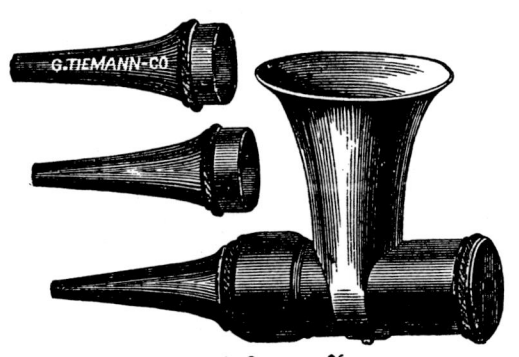

Brunton's Otoscope, $6.00.

INDEX

A. H. Robins Community Service Award, 148
A.T.& S.F. RR Company, 212
abortion, 86, 87, 197
Adams, John C., 1
Adams, Sam, 2
Adelaide, Nutting M., R.N., 217
agglutination, 87, 158
Ainsworth, F. K., M.D., 26, 27, 52
Alcutt, A. W., M.D., 198, 201
Alfred, George, 168
Allen, K. D. K., M.D., 20
allergic asthma, 81
allergy, 79
Allport, Frank, M.D., 200
Alsap, John, 41
Alvan Le Roy Barach Collapsible
    Oxygen Chamber, 207
American Ranch, 48
Anderson, H., 209, 212
Angelicus, Gilbertus, 83
Antelope Station, 49
Anvil Rock, 48
Apache Kid, 178
Apache Pass, 9, 13, 192
Aqua Caliente, 118
Argentina, 77, 114
Arieti, Silvano, M.D., 24
Arizona Bulletin, 89
Arizona Citizen, 193
Arizona Copper Company, 60
Arizona Daily Star, 193
Arizona Gazette, 21
Arizona Highways, 206
Arizona Medical Association, 82, 129, 141, 148,
    155, 162, 190, 196, 197, 199, 201-203
Arizona Medical History Quiz, 219
Arizona Medical Society, 148
Arizona Republic, The 60
armadillo, 91
Aronson, Joseph D., M.D., 76
Arrow Wounds, 8
Ascheim, Elizabeth Fleischman, 18
Ashurst, Henry, 189
Atwood, Rev., 202
B melitensis, 86
B. abortus, 86
Baldwin, Louis, M.D., 81, 148, 162, 218, 221
Balmie Expedition, 64, 83
Bang, B., 86
Bangladesh, 84
Bank, Joe, M.D., 81
Banning General Hospital, 120
Barfoot, Robert, 130
Barrack Hospital, 213
Bartlett, Josiah, 1
Batchelder, Albert, 98
Beals Springs, 48
Beck, L. D., M.D., 124

Beckett, W. W., M.D., 202
Bed Check Charlies, 225
Bene, Harry, 136
Berry, William T., M.D., 197
Bicetre Hospital, 24
bilious remittent fever, 86
Billings, John S., 6
Birsner, J. W., 77
Bisbee, Arizona, 65, 66, 68, 71, 72, 75, 85, 95, 132,
    188, 201
Bishop Hall, 187
Black Smallpox, 85
Black Vomit, 98
black widow, 181
Blackfan, K. B., M.D., 128
Bledsoe, N. C., M.D., 85
Blood Services, 218, 221
Bloody Thirteenth, 27
Bodanski, Albert, 122
Boone and Crockett Club, 209
Boot Hill Cemetery, 206
Booth, Governor, 25
Borglum, Solon, 54
Bosel, Manuela, 193
Brachamonte, Col., 75
Brack, 196
Bramen, Dennis J., M.D., 70
Brandes, Ray, 43, 44, 46
Brazil, 84, 98
Bridgeman, Mother 215
Brigham Young University, 27
Brockway, George, M.D., 180
brown recluse spider, 180, 181
Brown, John Young, M.D., 55, 169
Brown, Orville Harry, M.D., 124, 128, 166, 219
Browne, Sarah J., 126
Browne, Trevor, M.D., 80, 126-129
Bruce, R., 86
Brucellosis, 87, 88, 179, 180
Buffmire, Donald, M.D., 142
bulbar paralysis, 96
Bullet Proof Hotel, 10, 60
Bullis fever, 121
Bullock, Joseph B., 198
Bullock, Major Lewis T., 111
Burrows, Cora, 174
Bury, James, M.D., 22
Busch, L. A., 87
Busey, Ray, 129
Butler, A F , 106
Butterfield Overland Mail Company, 13
Butterfield Stage Route, 11
C A M P, 49
Cabin Draw, 210, 212
Cabot, Arthur, M.D, 56, 128, 162, 163
Cabot, Hugh, M.D., 128
Calendar, J. A., M.D., 193
California State Medical Association, 35

California-Arizona Maneuver Area, 99-122
Calimo, 198
Callies, Col., 75
Camp Beale Springs, 5
Camp Bouse, 4
Camp Calhoun (later Camp Yna), 43
Camp Callon, 106
Camp Clipper, 108
Camp Colorado, 48
Camp Crittenden, 5
Camp Davis, 106
Camp Forrest, 222, 225, 227, 229, 230, 231, 233, 234
Camp Grant, 7
Camp Horn, 4, 118
Camp Hualapai, 5, 48
Camp Ibis, 108
Camp Kearney, 60
Camp Kilmer, New Jersey, 234, 235
Camp Lincoln, 5, 8
Camp Lowell, 6
Camp McDowell, 8, 43, 44
Camp Pilot Knob, 108
Camp Reno, 5
Camp Stephen D. Little, 5, 11
Camp Supply, 5
Camp Thomas, 5, 192, 221
Camp Verde, 5, 7, 48, 90
Camp Whipple, 7
Camp Young, 104, 108, 115-118
Canal Defense Light Project, 4
Caniglia, S., M.D., 129
Carell, P., 59
Carl, Crowly & Abernaty, 29
Carleton, Brigadier Gen. James H., 13
Carson, Harry, M.D., 129
Carter, R. A., 76
Caskey, John, M.D., 136
Catalina Island, 150
catarrhal jaundice, 105
Celaya, Teresa, 12
Chapin, Charles W., 82
Charvoz, Elton R., M.D., 172
Chenowith, W. F., 198
Cherry Valley General Hospital, 120
Children's Crusade, 84
Christian, Henry, 12
Christy, William, 28
Church, Benjamin, 2
Churchill, Winston, 151
Circular No. 3, 8
Circular No. 4, 6
Clanton brothers, 187
Clarence G. Salsbury Medal, 176
Clark, Capt. Thomas A., M.D., 26, 27, 117
Clinical Club, 162, 164
clofazimine, 91
coccidioides, 76, 77, 79, 82, 121
coccidioidomycosis, 4, 64, 65, 76, 77, 80, 82, 109-114, 122
Cochise, 13, 27, 68, 95, 192, 196
Cochran, J., 2
Coconino Sun, 89
Cole, Capt. L. L., 202
Colliers Encyclopedia, 89

Collings, Robert, M.D., 91
Columbia Encyclopedia, 24
Conquistadors, 83
Corliss, Captain, 49
Cota, Juan, 21
Council on America's Military Post, 3
cowpox vaccination, 1, 24
Craig, Carlos, M.D., 124, 130
Crecelius, Gilbert, 77
Cresswell summer camp, R. C., 210
Crimea, 213, 215-217
Crook's Trail, 49
Crook, General George, 5, 17, 22, 44, 55
Cuba, 5, 6, 54, 56, 93, 178, 191, 220
Culion, 93, 94
Culter, William D., 202
Curie, Madame Eve, 19, 20, 21
Curie, Marie Sklodowska, 204
Cushing, Harvey, 57
Dameron, L. D., 132, 196, 197
Davis, Edward, M.D., 21
Davis, T. B., M.D., 198, 199
De Witt, 43
Dennet, J., 198
Desert Fever, 79, 81
Desert Rheumatisium, 79
desert sore, 81
Detroit Copper Company, 60
Devine's, 49
Diana, 152
Dickson, E. C., 76
Digby, Anne, 24
diphtheria, 67
Ditch Fever, 79, 80
Dix, Dorothea, 25
Dix, F. A., 168
Dock, Lavinial, R.N., 217
Doctor on Horseback, 90
Douglas Daily Dispatch, 68
Drain, J. E., 198
Drance, V. E., 89
Drinker, Philip, 96
Drum, William, 8
Dryden, M.D., 197
Duffield, William, M.D., 70, 198, 200
Dugan, George, 8
Dutton, Thomas, 8
Dysart, Louis, M.D., 132
Dysart, Nathaniel Martin, 135
Dysart, Palmer, M.D., 124, 132-137
Earp brothers, 87
Ehrenberg, 47, 49
Eight Foot, 49
Eldridge, O. C., 210, 212
Elks Lodge of Arizona, 210
Ellington, Major Harold V., 114
Emmons, Chester, M. D., 76
Eng, Thomas A., V.D.M., 121
Epidermothytid, 110
erythema multiforme, 110
erythema nodosum, 76
Ethiopa, 84
Eureka, Tintic District, Utah, 166
Evans, Alice C., 87
Evans, Jane, 215

Faget, Guy, 91
Farness, Joe, 76
Faulk, O. B., 54, 59
Ferenbaugh, Thomas L., 86
Ferguson, Ray, M.D., 124
Finlay, Carlos, 98
First Aid Stations, 171, 172
Fishbein, Daniel B., M.D., 121, 122
Flinn Foundation, 142, 144
Flinn, Irene, 142
Flinn, John W., M.D., 189, 190, 20, 201, 203
Flinn, Robert S., M.D., 141-145, 191, 203
Flinn, Zeb, M.D., 141
Flying Chlamydospore, 64, 76, 77, 79, 114
formaldehyde, 66, 85
Fort Apache, 5, 47-49, 55, 95, 221
Fort Bowie, 4, 5, 13-15, 53
Fort Defiance, 5
Fort George Mead, 105
Fort Grant, 5
Fort Hayes, 88
Fort Huachucha, 5, 11
Fort Lowell, 5, 49
Fort McDowell, 4, 5, 8, 43-45, 49
Fort Mohave, 5, 47, 48
Fort Rock, 48
Fort Whipple, 5, 8, 48, 52
Fort Yuma, 5, 47, 48
Foss, J. W., 201
Foster, Mrs. Nelle, 22
Foster, R. Lee, M.D., 22, 146, 147
Four Peaks, 43, 44
Fournier, Dudley, 172
Francis, Edward, 82
Francis, Frances, 82
Franklin, B. J., 32
Freeze Wash, 48
freezum, 74
Fremont, John C., 26
Frissell, Ben "Pat", M.D., 79, 138, 148, 149
Fulton, J. F., 59
fumigating, 66
Gage, E. B., 2, 188
Gan, Milt, 138
Ganado Mission, 82
Ganado, Arizona, 174
Gardner Air Force Base, 114
Garrison, F. H., M.D., 24, 84
Gatewood, 54, 58
Gerard, E. N., M.D., 198
Geronimo, 4, 5, 9, 44, 54, 58, 59, 220
Gierdo, Jacinto, M.D., 193
Gifford, Myrnee, 76
Gila monster, 70
Gilbert, M. M., 196
Giltner, Lt., 77
Giomone, A., M.D., 84
Givens, Alice M., M.D., 197
glaucoma, 139
Glen, Col. Charles R., 113
goldbricking, 231
Goldfarb, Jerome, Ph.D., 121
Goldwater, Barry, 202
Goldwater, Morris, 201

Goodfellow, George Emory, M.D., 70, 186, 188, 194, 244
Goodwin, Francis Henry, M.D., 150
Gordon, Alan, M.D., 23
Gordon, H. S., 198
Gould, A. J., 198
Graham, Louise L., 156, 198
Grant, General, 216
Great Britain, 64
Green, J. T., M.D., 186
Green, J. W., 196
Greenway, 178
Greer, Joseph Madison, M.D., 42, 57
Gretzer, John, Jr., 16
Gustetter, Albert L., M.D., 71
Gypsy, 170
Hadley, M.D., 171
Hagerdorn, Hermann, 46, 59
Hale, Samuel, M.D., 136
Hall, Lyman, 1
Hall, W. R., M.D., 198
Halleck, Harold J., M.D., 107
Halsband, Robert, 84
Hamblin, Ira B., M.D., 31
Hamer, J. D., M.D., 162
Hamilton, I. B., M.D., 186
Hamilton, T. B., 196
Hammond, Wade, 129
Hancock, John, 2
Handy, John Charles, M.D., 6, 166, 185, 186, 192-195
Hansen's Disease, 64, 91-94, 204
Hansen, Gerhard Henrik Armauer, M.D., 91
Hanson, Mrs. J. R., 180
hara kiri by virus, 65
Harbridge, D. F., M. D., 42, 162
Harding, Warren G., 57
Hardyville, 48
Hastings, Robert, M.D., 136
Hatch, Frank C., 28, 29, 40
Hayden, Carl, 118
Haynes, Francis L., M.D., 187
Heard, Dwight B., 129
Helm, Scott, M.D., 188
Herzberg, Benjamin M.D., 137
Hickman, A. R., M.D., 201
Hildreth, Col. Ray C., 117
Hoagland, Paul, M.D., 79
Holliday, Doc., 187
Holme, J. G., 59
Holmes, Carl, M.D., 124
Holmes, Fred, M.D., 180
Homans, John, 143
Hoover, Herbert, 185
Hopkins, Johns, 57
Houchs, C. I., 205
Hughes, Griffin, 98
Hughes, Henry A., M.D., 31, 190
Hughes, Louis C., 31
Hughes-Wiley, 196
Hugo, Victor, 176
Hunt, George W. P., 67, 68, 209
Hunter, John, 83
Hyder, D. C., M.D., 4, 11
Hyder, Prentiss, M.D., 4, 11

hydrophobia skunk, 70, 88-90, 220
hyponatremia, 104
Iceland, 151
Index Medicus, 6
infectious hepatitis, 105
Ingalls, E. A., M.D., 197
Ingallson, M.D., 197
Inoculation, 1, 83, 89, 107
Insane Board (Poem), 40
intermittent, 8
Iron Lung, 96
Irwin, Bernard J. D., 9, 10
Jackson, W. T., 47
Jaff, J. V., 198
Jarrett, Paul, M.D., 124
Jefferson Barracks, 106
Jenner, Edward, 83
Jenner, William, 24
Jiggerville, 72
Johnson, Danny, 235
Jones, Bob, 179
Jones, Charles H., 198, 199
Jones, Charles W., M.D., 198
Jones, E. E., 77
Jones, Col. S. Bayne, 105
Jones, Thomas H., 199
Jones-Connally Act, 87
Jorgen Hospital, 91
Joseph Bank Medal, 148
Journal Miner, 89
Journal of the American Medical Association, 24, 121
Joy-House, 68
Judd, Winne Ruth, 165
Kartchner, K.C., 212
Kaull, L. P., M.D., 201
Keefer, C. S., 87
Keifer, 196
Keller, Charles E., 116
Kennedy, Willa (Billie) R. N., 171, 222-243
Kenya, 84
Kern County, 76
Ketcherside, E. B., M.D., 201
Ketcherside, Hillary, M.D., 124
Kettel, Louis, 142
KFAD, 146
Kibler, Charles, M.D., 171
Kilbach School, 126
Kilmer, Joyce, 234
King's Throne, 115
King, F. B., 66
Kinglake, R., 217
Kit Peak, 11
Knier, Karl, 132
Kober, Leslie, M.D., 136
Kossuth, George J., 153
Kossuth, Karen, M.D., 153
Kossuth, Louis C., M.D., 65, 95, 96, 113, 122, 153, 154
Kossuth, Sally L., 153
Kossuth, Sue, M.D., 153
KTAR, 146
Lane, J C., 59
Langford, Ned, 94
Lawson General Hospital, 225

Lawton, Capt. Henry W., 5, 9, 53-55, 58
Lear, General Benny, 229
Lee, Russel V., M.D., 113
Leonard Wood Memorial, 94
leprosarium, 93, 94, 204
leprosy, 91-94
Lincoln, Abraham, 216
Lincoln, Oscar, 28
Lone Star Ranch, 95
Looney, Robert N., M.D., 65, 66-68, 70, 71, 86, 87, 141, 155, 171, 201, 202, 208, 209, 211, 212, 221
Lord, C. H., M.D., 193
Lowden, Frank Orren, 57
Lowell Improvement Club, 72
Luke Field, Arizona, 111, 133
luminal, 180
Lyman Hall, 1
Lynch, Lt. Col. John S., 3, 122
Maddy, K. T., M.D., 77
malarial fever, 3, 6, 7
malnutrition, 3
malpractice, 193
Malta fever, 64, 65, 86-88
Manning, George Felix, M.D., 70
Mardian, Sam, Jr., 148
Maricopa County Medical Association, 148, 196, 218
marijuana addiction, 107
Marius, Bishop of Avenches, 83
Marquise de Ganay, 20
Marshall, George, 53
Martin, Ancil, M.D., 21, 82, 132, 158, 159, 196, 199, 200, 202, 221
Mason, Col. Verne R., 111
Matas, Henry N., M.D., 70, 186
Matas, N. H., 198
Mauck, 196
Mavante, Rufino, 21
Mayer, Edgar, M.D., 81
Mayo, William and Charles, M.D., 171
McCabe, Joseph E., Ph.D., 121
McCabe, Ola Sue, 161
McCandless, J. N., 198
McCloud, Mrs. Neil, 129
McCormick, J. Byron, 193
McCormick, R. C., 25, 41
McCoy, George W., 82
McGinnis, W. A., 30
McGown, Granville, M.D., 201
McKenna, Thomas, 17
McKhann, Charles F., M.D., 156
McKhann, George, M.D., 124, 156, 157
McKinley, 5
McLaughlin, Emmett, 129
McLowery brothers, 187
McNair, General Wesley J., 99, 103, 107, 118
McNally, Gerlad F., M.D., 189
McNally, John B., M.D., 189
McNally, Joseph B., M.D., 189
measles, 98
Melick, D. W., M.D., 46, 77
Memorial Hospital, 129
meningioma, 57, 94
Mercer, Hugh, 1

Meserve, M.D., 70, 71
Mexico, 77
Middleton, P., 7
Miller, Joseph, M.D., 30, 40, 88, 89, 192, 196, 198
Milloy, Frank, M.D., 146, 160-163, 172
Milloy, Mary Elizabeth, 161
Miner, L. L., M.D., 65-67, 71
Minot, George Richards, M.D., 52
Minter Army Air Force Base, 114
Mission House, 66
Moeur, B. B., M.D., 179
Moffet Field, 106
Moffitt, H. C., 76
Mogollion Rim, 49
Montagu, Mary Wortley, 83
Montano, Romona, 12
Montezuma, Carlos (Wassaja), 43
Montgomery, Grace, 106
Morgan, John, 2
Morrison, Sgt. Joseph P., 119
Mouer, B. B., M.D., 179, 180, 198
Mulligan, Kathleen, 161
Murat, Princess, 20
Murphy, J. B., 171
Murphy, N. O., 31, 33
Murphy, William Parry, M.D., 52
Musterberg, Professor, 22
Myer, K. F., 76
Naco, 74
Nash, Private James H., 119
Neff, Mary, 201
Nelson, E. W., 209
Nelson, J. B., M.D., 70
New York Medical Journal, 171
Nightingale Training School, 217
Nightingale, Florence, 204, 213, 216, 217
Nix, Robert, 8
Noguchi, Hideyo, 98
Noon, A. W., M.D., 166, 167, 198
Novy, Frederick G., M.D., 82
O'Neal, M.D., 20
O'Neill, Bucky, 54
Ochsner, Albert J., M.D., 171
Ophuls, W., 76
Oretga, Corp. Julius, 119
Oriflamme, 98
Osler, William, M.D., 141
Oyers (olliers), 7
Packwood Ranch, 48
Pallen Pass, 110
Palmer, A. R. H., M.D., 201
Palmer, Bertha Schantz, 168
Palmer, E. Payne, Sr., M.D., 118, 168-174, 180
Palmer, Ralph F., M.D., 90, 165, 178
Palmer, Virginia (Payne), 168
Palo Cristi, 80
Palo Verde Foundation, 25
paragoric, 180
Paraguay, 77
Pare, Ambrose, 1
Parker, R. L., 87
Pasteur treatment, 88, 90
pasteurization, 180
Patek, Arthur, 135
Patton, General George S., Jr., 3, 4, 10, 99, 103-105, 117, 118, 122, 225
Pease, H. H., 198
pediatric infectious diseases, 107
Pemberton, J. C. N., 205
Pena Blanca, 11
penicillin, 156, 162
Perkins, Ma, 231
Pershing, General John Joseph "Black Jack", 3, 4, 10, 57, 93
Pest House, 85
Phelps Dodge Corporation, 60
Phelps, Harlow J., M.D., 200
phenobarbital, 180
Philippines, 56, 93
Phillips, Earle Wood, M.D., 79, 114
Phillips, R. W., M.D., 76, 81
Phoenix, 4, 21-23, 27, 29, 41, 49, 57, 64, 76, 79, 81, 82, 84, 89, 114, 118, 124, 125, 128, 135-138, 141, 146, 148, 151, 155, 161, 162, 164
Phoenix Gazette, The 171
Phoenix Stationery and News Co., 40
Phoenix Tent and Awning Company, 90
Picker Mobile Unit, 20
Pinel, Phillipe, 24
Pita, Maria, 83
Plath, Otto E., 198
Plousssard, Charles N., M.D., 172
pneumonia, 76, 130, 134, 207, 229
poliomyelitis, 96
pomme-de-terre, 61
Porter, Dwight, M.D., 124
potassium permanganate, 67
Pottenger, F. M., M.D., 201
Powarn, Sgt. Robert, 119
Prachal, C. J., M.D., 77
Price, M. F., M.D., 188
Price, Robert, M.D., 176
Priestly, J B., 64
professional courtesy, 163
promin, 91
prostatectomy, 188, 194
psammoma, 57
pulmonary tuberculosis, 199
Purcell, W. B., M.D., 191-198
Purman, D. M., M.D., 197
Pyle, Lt. Col., 118
Quaker Retreat, 24
quarantine, 67
quarreling and quarantine, 68
Quebbeman, F., 59
radiological car, 19
Rambaugh, Mildred
Randall, F. W., M.D., 70
rations, 118
Rawlings, 196
Raymond, R. O., M.D., 169
Reagles, 43
Redewill, Francis, M.D., 202
Reed, Walter, 5, 75, 220
Reid, W. L., M.D., 128
remittent fever, 8, 44
Richardson, Gladwell, 206
Rider, Jane, 70
rifampin, 91

Riggs, Harvey and Mary, 12
Riley, H. D., Jr., 84
Rixford, E., M.D., 76
Roach, Mrs. Harold, 125
Robert S. Flinn Medical Library, 143
Robertson, Edward, 95
Rocky Mountain spotted fever, 231
Rodgers, Mark A., M.D., 198, 201
Roentgen, William Conrad 16
Roosevelt, Theodore, 5, 93
Rosenberg, C., 24
Rosenberry, A. J., M.D., 202
Rothman, Samuel I., M.D., 115
Rough Riders, 5, 54, 93
Round-Up, 94
Ruby mine, 11
Ruffner, Budge, 68, 69
Rush, Benjamin, 1, 2
Russo-Turkish War, 19
Sabine, D. S., 1, 2
Sabine, Thomas H., 196
Safford, A. P. K., 25
Salk and Sabin, 96
Salsbury, Clarence, M.D., 64, 65, 77, 82, 174-176, 207. 244
Salt River Valley Blood Bank, 218
Salvation Army, 66
Salveny, 83
San Joaquin Valley, 76
San Joaquin Valley Fever, 79
San Juan Hill, 178
Saturday Evening Post, 181
Sawyer, W. A., 106
Scantlin, J. W., 88
scarlet fever, 67
Schiefflin, Ed., 187
Scottsdale Sweet Adelines, 223
scurvy, 6
Scutari, 214
Seaman, John E., M.D., 166
Sells, Main and Gentry Circus Companies, 40
Sewall, D. A., 198
Sharfstein, Steven S., M.D., 24
Shaw, John, 205
Shaw, Louis A., 96
Shields, J. Wilson, M.D., 202
Shigella, 104
Shippen, William, 2
Shore, W. B., 212
Siamese fever, 98
Simmons, Gen. G. S., 105
Simmons, H. L., 88
Sippy, Bertram Welton, M.D., 160
Skinner, John O., 10
Sloan, Richard E., 202
smallpox, 1, 3, 65, 85
Smart, Charles, 7, 43
Smith, Charles, 110, 113
Smith, James Lytton, M.D., 136
Smith, Willard, 202
Smythe, Bill, 205, 206
Snellen's test types, 200
Snowden, Andrew, 8
solar power, 132
soldering, 21

Solucortef, 180
Sorenson, Velma, 153
Southern California Practitioner, 203
Southwestern Medicine, 124
Southworth, Harry L., 87, 202
Spanish-American War, 16
Spencer, Michael, M.D., 186-188, 194
spigole, 89
Spodra General Hospital, 120
Sprague, Marion, 65
St. Monica's Hospital, 129, 142
Stanley, Mary, 215
stegomyia aegypti, 98
stegomyia calopus, 98
Stevenson, W. W., M.D., 222
Stewart, Madison W., 28
Stiles, W. H., 84
Stinson, Byron, 98
Stirling, F. S., M.D., 7
Stockton, California, 25, 106
Storks, General, 215
streptomycin, 87
Stroud, H. E., M.D., 199
Sturgeon, C. T., M.D., 200
Suevi, 126
Sullivan, Tom, 138
summer flu, 81
Summer, Ella, 198
Summerhayes, Lt. Jack, 47
Summerhayes, Martha, 4, 44, 47-51
Swank, Wendell G., 212
Swatta's Watta, 118
Sweek, W. O., M.D., 124, 180
Sweet, Frederick Arnold, M.D., 200
Sweet, William M., M.D., 22
syphilis, 3, 66
Territorial Board of Health, 65
Territorial Medical Society, 196
tetracycline, 87
Thatcher, James, 2
Thieving Thirteenth, 27
Thigpen, R. H., M.D., 164
Thomas Dooley Medal, 176
Thomas, Roy, 203
Thornton, Matthew, 1
Thrapp, D L., 59
Tilton, Henry R., 10
Tilton, James, 1
Tin Town, 85
Titus, I. S., M.D., 29
Todd, M.D., 127
Tolone, Frank, M.D., 79
Tolone, Ingrid, 80
Tombstone, 187
Toney, L. C., M.D., 198
Torney General Hospital, 108
Tragesor, Conrad, 8
Tritle, F. A., 26, 28
Truman, George E., 178-181
tuberculosis (phthisis), 8, 34, 64, 77, 79, 81, 98, 121, 134, 138, 139, 141, 146, 156, 176, 182, 189, 190, 199, 200-202
Tucson Daily Citizen, 185
Tuke, William, 24
tularemia, 82

Tuthill, Alexander M., M.D., 3, 4, 10, 60-63, 74, 134, 221
typhoid fever, 44, 67
Unger apparatus, 162
United War Fund, 218
University of Arizona Press, 27
University of Pennsylvania, 93
Urban League, 129
vaccination, 83
vacoliter, 132
Valley Fever, 4, 79
variola, 83
venereal disease, 6
Venezuela, 77
Verdon, 61
Victoria, Queen 215
Villa, Pancho, 3, 10
viral hara kiri, 98
Vivian, Charles, M.D., 172
Wagoner, J. J., 27
Walker, Mary, 9
Walter Reed Army Hospital, 57
Walter, H. F., 198
Wapiti, 208
Ward, J. P., M.D., 176
Ward, W. H.
Wardroper, Mrs., 217
Warren, 75
Warren Ranch, 74
Warren, John, 1
Wassaja (see Montezuma, Carlos)
Waters, Byrle (Danny), 222
Watkins, J. W., 198
Watkins, W. Warner, M.D., 23, 81, 89, 146, 162, 164, 170, 171, 182-184, 202, 203
Webster, C., 24
Weekly Arizona Miner, 192
Westward Ho Hotel, 180
Wharton, William, M.D., 136, 196
White, Scott, 179
Whiteside, John R., 65
Whiting, Spencer, M.D., 172
Whitmore, William V., M.D., 70, 166, 185-188, 198
Whorton, 196
Wilie, Winfred, 198
Willard, G. M., 211
Williams Field, Arizona, 111, 130, 134
Williams, Francis, M.D., 22
Williams, Onie, M.D., 93
Willow Grove Springs, 48
Wilson, Fred, 129
Windsor, Mulford, 209
Wolbach, Burt, M.D., 127, 128
Wolfley, Louis, 30
Wolfley, T. J., 197
Wood, Leonard, M.D.
Wood, Leonard, Journal of, 54
Wood, MacDonald, M.D., 23
Woodham-Smith, Cecil, 213
Woodman, Thomas, M.D., 124
Wooley, Robert L., 3
Wright, Lindley C., 198
Wurtzburg Physico-Medical Society, 21
Wylie, Harriet Amesbury, 41
Wylie, Win, M.D., 41
x-ray, 16
Xylocaine, 180
Yeats, William Butler, 244
yellow fever, 56, 98
yellow jaundice, 105
Young, H., M.D., 171
Yount, Barrister Robert, 47
Yount, Clarence E., Jr., M.D., 47, 86-89, 90, 122, 141, 201, 202, 221
Zulick, C. Meyer, 28, 29